RESTORATION

THEOLOGY

⚜

Kevin J. Conner

Copyright © 1998
Kevin J. Conner
K.J.C. Publications

All rights reserved. No part of this publication may be reproduced, stored in a retrieval system or transmitted in any form or by any means, electronic, mechanical, photocopying, recording or otherwise without the prior written permission of the author.

ISBN 0-949829-44-7

DISTRIBUTORS

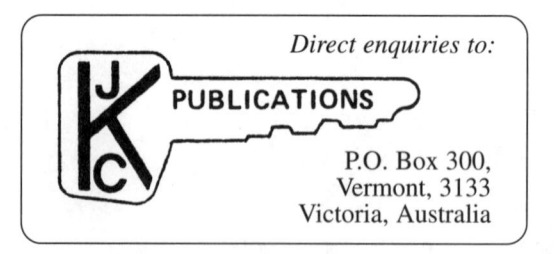

Direct enquiries to:

PUBLICATIONS

P.O. Box 300,
Vermont, 3133
Victoria, Australia

Printed in Australia at
Acacia Press Pty Ltd
Blackburn, Victoria

FOREWORD

The Church is living in frightening yet exciting times: frightening as to all that is going on in the unregenerate world, but exciting as to all that God is doing in the Church!

The Church is living in **"times of restoration"**, all of which will be expounded, clarified and amplified in the course of this text.

In brief, this course on **"Restoration Theology"** concerns God's dealings in the Church, (corporately), and with Mankind, (individually). Since the entrance of sin into the universe and the Fall of mankind in Adam, God has been seeking to restore mankind (whether Jew or Gentile) back to Himself, back to the image of God from which man fell. Since the birth of the early Church and its fall from early glory, God also has been seeking to restore the Church back to the glory from which it fell. These are the major areas of restoration with which this text deals.

The end of the age is upon us and God's work of restoration will be completed ultimately at the second coming of our Lord Jesus Christ. Men can either accept or reject God's restorative work, but none can stop it. It will proceed from "glory to glory", "grace to grace" and "victory to victory" and "faith to faith" unto the glorious consummation. Our God is indeed the God of restoration!

May this text give the greatest sense of direction to believers, leaders and ministers of the Church, the Body of Christ in the last of these last days as it did to the author when **"Restoration Theology"** became **"Present Truth"** many years ago!

(**Note:-** Woven throughout the text is some material adapted, as appropriate to this text, from several other textbooks which this writer has written).

Kevin J. Conner
P.O. Box 300
Vermont, Victoria 3133
AUSTRALIA

1998

RESTORATION THEOLOGY
TABLE OF CONTENTS

FOREWORD

PART ONE
THE PROPHETS

CHAPTER

1. The Prophets and The Restoration 2
   A. The Prophets 2
   B. Times of Restoration 3
2. The Law and The Prophets 5
   A. The Law and The Prophets 5
   B. Use of the Old Testament in Acts 6
3. The Laws of Restoration 8
   A. Definition of Restoration 8
   B. The Laws of Restitution 9
4. The God of Restoration and Redemption 12
   A. The God of Restoration 12
   B. The God of Redemption 12
   C. The Book of Redemption 12
5. Things Not To Be Restored 14
   A. The Devil and Hosts will not be restored 14
   B. Unrepentant Mankind will not be restored 15
   C. The Mosaic Covenant System will not be restored 15
   D. Jewish Nationalism will not be restored 16

PART TWO
THE CREATION

6. The Principles of Restoration in Creation 20
   A. The Original Creation 20
   B. The Ruined Creation 20
   C. The Frustrated Purpose 22
   D. The Need for Restoration 22
   E. The First Principle of Restoration 22
      1. The Spirit Moved 22
      2. The Word Spoken 23
      3. Let There Be Light 24
      4. Light and Darkness Divided 24
   F. Creation to Redemption 25

PART THREE
THE CREATION OF MAN

7. The Creation of Man 28
   A. The Original Man 28
   B. The Original Purpose 28
      1. Fellowship 28
      2. Character 28
      3. Dominion 29
      4. Fruitfulness 29
8. The Ruined Man 31
   A. The Creation of Man 31
   B. The Probation of Man 31
   C. The Temptation of Man 31
      1. Tempted in Body, Soul and Spirit 32
      2. Tempted to Lust, Pride and Self-Will 32
      3. Tempted in Relation to the Law 33
   D. The Fall of Man and Its Effects 34
      1. Immediate Effects of the Fall 34
      2. The Long-Range Effects of the Fall 35
      3. Divine Judgment Pronounced and Executed 36

		E.	The Ruined Man	37
9.	The Covenant of Restoration and Redemption			39
	A.	The Need of Restoration		39
	B.	The Covenant of Redemption		39
		1.	The Terms of the Covenant	39
		2.	The Sacrifice of the Covenant	40
		3.	The Mediator of the Covenant	40
		4.	The Sanctuary of the Covenant	41
	C.	The Redeemer and Restorer		42
	D.	The Restored and Redeemed Man		42
		1.	Restored Fellowship	42
		2.	Restored Character	42
		3.	Restored Dominion	43
		4.	Restored Fruitfulness	43

PART FOUR
THE NATION OF ISRAEL

10.	The Abrahamic Covenant and Israel			46
	A.	The Abrahamic Covenant		46
	B.	The Promises of the Covenant		46
		1.	The Personal Blessing	47
		2.	The Blessing of Others	47
		3.	The Blessing by Others	47
		4.	The Blessing of Messiah	47
		5.	The Blessing of a Great Name	48
		6.	The Blessing of Multiplicity of Seed	48
		7.	The Blessing of Land	49
		8.	The Blessing of Victory over Enemies	49
		9.	The Blessing of Kings	50
		10.	The Blessing of Divine Relationship	50
	C.	The Terms of the Covenant		50
	D.	The Oath of the Covenant		50
	E.	The Sacrifice of the Covenant		51
	F.	The Priesthood of the Covenant		51
	G.	The Sanctuary of the Covenant		52
	H.	The Seal of the Covenant		52
11.	The Divine Purposes in Israel's Election			54
	A.	Israel - The Chosen Nation		54
		1.	Not Chosen for Numbers	54
		2.	Not Chosen for Righteousness	54
		3.	Chosen Because of Divine Love	55
		4.	Chosen Because of Divine Covenant	55
		5.	Chosen to Bless All Nations	55
	B.	Israel - Chosen to Receive Divine Blessings		55
		1.	The Adoption	55
		2.	The Shekinah Glory of God	55
		3.	The Covenants	55
		4.	The Giving of the Law	55
		5.	The Service of God	56
		6.	The Promises	56
		7.	The Fathers	56
		8.	The Oracles of God	56
		9.	The Messiah	56
	C.	Israel - A Brief History		56
12.	Israel's Decline, Apostasy and Rejection			58
	A.	The Desolations and the Captivities Foretold		58
		1.	Desolation of the Cities	58
		2.	Desolation of the Sanctuaries	58

		3. Desolation of the Land	58
		4. Desolation of the People	59
	B.	Israel's Divorce	59
	C.	Judah's Rejection	60
		1. Desolation of Jerusalem	60
		2. Desolation of the Temple	60
		3. Desolation of the Land	60
		4. Desolation of the House of Judah	60
	D.	The Present State of Jewry	61
13.	Israel's New Covenant Restoration		62
	A.	The "No-Restoration" School	62
	B.	The "Mosaic Restoration" School	62
	C.	The New Covenant Restoration School	62
	D.	The New Covenant	63
		1. What Jeremiah Said	63
		2. What Jesus Said	63
		3. What Paul Said	64
		4. What Hebrews Said	64
	E.	The Old Covenant	64
		1. The Hebrews Epistle	64
		2. The Corinthian Epistle	65
		3. The Galatian Epistle	66
	F.	The Restoration of Israel	66

PART FIVE
RESTORATION OF THE CHURCH

14.	The Church, God's New Ethnic		70
	A.	The Gentile Nations	70
		1. Their Condition	70
		2. Their Salvation	71
	B.	The Church - The New Ethnic	71
		1. Definition of the Church	71
		2. The Calling of the Church	72
		3. The Composition of the Church	72
		4. Significance of the Church	73
15.	Christ's Vision of the Church		74
	A.	What the Church Is	74
		1. "Ekklesia" has a Greek Background	75
		2. "Ekklesia" has a Hebrew Background	75
	B.	What the Church Is Not	76
		1. The Church is not a Material Building	76
		2. The Church is not an Extension of Judaism	77
		3. The Church is not a Sect or Denomination	77
		4. The Church is not an Individual	77
		5. The Church is not a Para-Church Organization	77
	C.	What Jesus said about the Church	78
		1. It would be a Church He would Build	78
		2. It would be His Church	78
		3. It would be a Church Built on the Rock Foundation	79
		4. It would be a Church against which the Gates of Hades could not prevail	80
		5. It would be a Church having the Keys of the Kingdom of Heaven	81
		6. It would be a Church which would exercise a Binding Ministry	82
		7. It would be a Church having a Loosing Ministry	83
		8. It would be a Church having Heaven and Earth Connections	84
		9. It would be a Church exercising Disciplinary Ministry as necessary	84
		10. It would be a Church that Christ as Risen Head would be in the midst	85
16.	Symbols and Types of the Church		88
	A.	Pauline Revelation of the Church	88

		B.	Symbols and Types of the Church	89
			1. The Church is God's Household	89
			2. The Church is God's Temple	89
			3. The Church is God's Family	89
			4. The Church is the Body of Christ	90
			5. The Church is the Bride of Christ	90
			6. The Church is the Army of the Lord	90
			7. The Church is the Flock of God	90
			8. The Church is a Kingdom of Priests	90
			9. The Church is God's Spiritual Israel	90
			10. The Church is God's Vineyard	90
			11. The Church is God's Discipleship School	91
			12. The Church is God's Dwelling Place	91
			13. The Church is God's Lampstand	91
			14. The Church is God's Holy Nation	91
			15. The Church is God's Olive Tree	91
			16. The Church is God's Seed	91
			17. The Church is God's Peculiar Treasure	91
			18. The Church is God's Pearl of Great Price	91
			19. The Church is God's New Jerusalem	92
			20. The Church is the People of God	92
			21. The Church is the Bread of God	92
			22. The Church is a Mother in Earth	92
			23. The Church is the Revealed Mystery	92
			24. The Church is the Pillar and Ground of The Truth	92
			25. The Church is God's Tabernacle of David	93
17.	The Purpose of the Church's Existence			94
	A.	Ministry unto the Lord		94
	B.	Ministry to the Saints		94
	C.	Ministry to the Sinner		95
	D.	Ministry to Conquer Satan's Hosts		95
	E.	Ministry and Guardian of Truth		96
18.	The Church - The Guardian of The Truth			97
	A.	Christ - The Word of Truth		97
	B.	The Spirit of Truth		98
			1. The Gospels	99
			2. The Acts	99
			3. The Gentile Epistles	99
			4. The Hebrew Epistles	99
			5. The Pastoral-Personal Epistles	100
	C.	The Church - The Guardian of The Truth		100
			1. The Truth	101
			2. The Faith	101
	D.	"The Truths" in "The Faith" Once Delivered to the Saints		103
19.	Departure from Truth - Decline of the Church			105
	A.	The Early Glory		105
	B.	Opposition and Persecution		106
	C.	The Age of Syncretism		107
	D.	Departure from The Faith		107
	E.	Decline into the Dark Ages		108
20.	The Age of Corruption and Substitution			112
	A.	The Woman, The Leaven, The Meal		112
			1. The Woman	112
			2. The Three Measures of Meal	113
			3. The Leaven - Old Testament, New Testament	114
			4. Application of the Parable	115
	B.	The Leaven in the Meal		116

21. The Need and Promise of Restoration..119
    A. The Eight R's of Restoration 119
        1. Repentance - A Change of Mind...119
        2. Return - A Change of Direction..120
        3. Refreshing - A Change of Seasons 120
        4. Recovery - A Change of Climate 120
        5. Reviving - A Change of Condition 120
        6. Receive - A Change of Place...120
        7. Retain - A Change of Position...121
        8. Restoration - A Change of Ownership 121
    B. The Promises of Restoration..121
22. God's Method and Principle of Restoration 123
23. The Restoration of the Scriptures 125
    A. Five Great Movements 127
        1. The Albigenses..127
        2. The Waldensians 127
        3. John Wycliffe..127
        4. John Huss..128
        5. Jerome Savonarola 128
    B. Foundation for the Reformation 128
    C. Light and Truth 129
24. Restoration - Justification by Faith 130
    A. Repentance from Dead Works...132
    B. Faith towards God..133
25. Restoration - Water Baptism..135
26. Restoration - Sanctification 140
27. Restoration - Priesthood of all Believers 145
28. Restoration - Divine Healing 147
29. Restoration - The Baptism in the Holy Spirit..151
    A. Topeka, Kansas 151
    B. Azuza Street, Los Angeles...152
    C. Holy Spirit Catechism 157
30. Restoration - The Triune Name in Baptism...161
    A. Historical Data on 'The Name' in Baptism 162
        1. Baptism in the Gospels...162
        2. Baptism in the Acts...163
        3. Baptism in the Epistles 163
    B. Baptism in the Early Centuries of Church History 164
        1. A History of the Christian Church 165
        2. A Remarkable Biblical Discovery...165
        3. Dictionary of the Apostolic Church..166
        4. The Latin Vulgate 167
        5. Dr. A.C. Gaebelien..167
        6. F.B. Meyer 167
        7. Names and Titles of the Holy Spirit 167
        8. The Didache - The Teaching of the Twelve 167
        9. Christianity in the Apostolic Age..168
        10. Testimony from the Fathers 168
        11. Britannica Encyclopaedia 11th Ed. 168
        12. Hastings Dictionary of the Bible...168
31. Restoration of the Laying on of Hands 173
    A. Seven Main Visitation Truths 177
        1. Reverence..177
        2. Restoration..177
        3. Unity..177
        4. Laying on of Hands 177
        5. Not to Justify Ourselves 178

		6.	Whose Battle is it?	179
		7.	World-Wide Vision	179
	B.	The Doctrine of the Laying on of Hands		179
		1.	The Old Testament	180
		2.	The New Testament	180
32.	Seed to the Sower - Bread to the Eater			182
	A.	The Spirit and The Word		183
	B.	The Latter Rain Outpouring		184
	C.	Apostles and Prophets		185
	D.	The Gifts of the Holy Spirit		185
	E.	Local Church Government		186
	F.	The Prophetic Presbytery		187
	G.	Restoration of all Things		187
	H.	Prophecy, Tongues and Interpretation		188
	I.	First Principles of the Doctrine of Christ		190
	J.	The Heavenly Choir		191
	K.	The Unity of the Body of Christ		193
	L.	The Victorious and Glorious Church		194
	M.	The Feast of Tabernacles		194
	N.	The Communion Table		195
33.	The Sacrifice of Praise			201
34.	Covenant, Temple, Priesthood and Sacrifice			205
	A.	The Covenant		205
	B.	The Temple		205
	C.	The Priesthood		206
	D.	The Sacrifice		207
		1.	Old Testament Sacrifice	207
		2.	New Testament Sacrifice	208
	E.	The Sacrifices of the Church		209
		1.	The Sacrifice of Thanksgiving	209
		2.	The Sacrifice of Joy	210
		3.	The Sacrifice of Praise	210
		4.	The Sacrifice of Righteousness	210
		5.	The Sacrifice of Obedience	210
		6.	The Sacrifice of a Broken Spirit	210
		7.	The Sacrifice of Hospitality	210
		8.	The Sacrifice of Lifted Hands	210
		9.	The Sacrifice of Tithes and Offerings	211
		10.	The Sacrifice of Time	211
		11.	The Sacrifice of Giving	211
		12.	The Sacrifice of our Bodies	211
35.	The Tabernacle of David			212
	A.	The Tabernacle of Moses		213
	B.	The Tabernacle of David		213
	C.	The Theology of the Tabernacle of David		214
36.	Restoration of Davidic Worship			217
	A.	Worship in Spirit and in Truth		218
		1.	Worship in Spirit	219
		2.	Worship in Truth	219
	B.	Davidic Expressions of Worship and Praise		219
		1.	Ministry of Singers and Singing	220
		2.	Ministry of Musicians with Instruments	220
		3.	Ministry of Levites before the Ark of God	220
		4.	Ministry of Recording	221
		5.	Ministry of Thanking the Lord	221
		6.	Ministry of Praise	221
		7.	Ministry of Psalms	221

		8.	Ministry of Rejoicing and Joy	222
		9.	Ministry of Clapping Hands	222
		10.	Ministry of Shouting	222
		11.	Ministry of Dancing before the Lord	222
		12.	Ministry of Lifting Hands	223
		13.	Ministry of Worship	223
		14.	Ministry of Seeking the Lord	223
		15.	Ministry of Spiritual Sacrifices	223
		16.	Ministry of Standing before the Lord	224
		17.	Ministry of Kneeling before the Lord	224
		18.	Ministry of Saying 'Amen'	224
37.	A Catechism of "Worship and Praise"			227
	A.	Is Worship and Praise Important		227
	B.	How are we to Worship and Praise God		227
	C.	What does Worship and Praise Signify		228
	D.	How should we Worship and Praise God		228
	E.	Why should we Worship and Praise the Lord		228
	F.	Who is to Worship and Praise God		229
	G.	When are we to Worship and Praise the Lord		229
	H.	Where are we to Worship and Praise the Lord		229
	I.	In what ways are we to Worship and Praise the Lord		229
		1.	Old Testament - 'Praise/Worship'	230
		2.	New Testament - 'Praise/Worship'	230
38.	Restoration - Kingdom Truth			232
	A.	The Charismatic Movement		232
	B.	Kingdom Truth Emphasis		233
		1.	The Kingdom of God and Discipleship	234
		2.	The Kingdom of God and Demon Deliverance	235
		3.	The Kingdom of God and Shepherding	235
		4.	The Kingdom of God and Covenant	236
		5.	The Kingdom of God and the Church	237
	C.	The Parable of the Wine and the Wineskins		239
39.	Lost and Restored (Sermon by Aimee Semple McPherson)			242
40.	Restoration in the Prophet Joel			259
	A.	First the Natural		259
		1.	Joel Chapter One	259
		2.	Joel Chapter Two	260
		3.	Joel Chapter Three	261
	B.	Afterwards the Spiritual		261
		1.	The Church is God's field, His garden, His vineyard	261
		2.	The Church Failed in Obedience to God's Word	261
		3.	The Lost Years of Church History	262
		4.	The Church in Restoration	262
		5.	The Church in Harvest Time	262
41.	The Old Testament Restoration Books			263
	A.	The Former House of the Lord		263
	B.	The Latter House of the Lord		264
		1.	The Restoration Ministries	264
		2.	The Restoration Message	265
		3.	The Seven Things Restored	265
			(a) Restoration of the Temple, the house of the Lord	265
			(b) Restoration of Davidic Worship Order	265
			(c) Restoration of the City of God, Walls and Gates	266
			(d) Restoration of the People of Judah	266
			(e) Restoration of the Early and Latter Rains	266
			(f) Restoration of the Feasts of the Lord	267
			(g) Restoration of the Lost Years	267

		C.	The Early Church	267
		D.	The Last Day Church	267
42.	Prophetic Types of Restoration			270
	A.	The Restoration of Job		270
	B.	Restoration in the Life of Samson		271
		1.	Samson's Ministry and Decline	271
		2.	The Church's Ministry and Decline	272
		3.	Samson's Repentance and Restoration	272
		4.	The Church's Repentance and Restoration	272
	C.	Restoration of Davidic Worship		273
		1.	The Tabernacle of David Established	273
		2.	The Temple of Solomon	273
		3.	The Godly King Jehoshaphat	273
		4.	The Godly King Hezekiah	273
		5.	The Godly King Josiah	274
		6.	The Restoration of Judah from Babylon	274
		7.	The Prophecy of Amos	274
		8.	Application to Church History	274
	D.	The Restoration of the Wells		275
		1.	Abraham - the Father	275
		2.	The Philistines - the Enemies	275
		3.	Isaac - The Son and Restorer of Wells	275
		4.	The Wells Restored	276
	E.	Restoration in the Year of Jubilee		277
	F.	Shorter Pictures of Restoration		278
		1.	The Restored Axehead	278
		2.	The Restored Son	278
		3.	The Restored Inheritance	278
		4.	The Restoration of David's Army	279
		5.	The Restoration under Elijah	279
43.	Maintaining Balance, Avoiding Extremes			281
	A.	Maintaining Balance		281
	B.	Avoiding Extremes		283
44.	Learning Lessons from History			284
45.	Seventeenth Century Theological Gleanings			287
46.	The Future Church			292
		1.	Increased Outpouring of the Holy Spirit	292
		2.	Increased Illumination on the Word of Truth	292
		3.	The First Principles of the Doctrine of Christ	292
		4.	The Gospel of the Kingdom Harvest	294
		5.	The Feast of Tabernacles	294
		6.	The Ascension-Gift Ministries and the Body of Christ	295
		7.	The Prayer of Jesus	295
		8.	The Church Triumphant	296
		9.	The Double Portion of the Spirit	296
		10.	The Manifestation of Mature Sons	297
		11.	The Order of Melchisedek	297
		12.	The Glorious Bridal Church	297
		13.	The Redemption of the Body	298
		14.	The Kingdom of God in the Earth	299
47.	The Present Truth			301

SUPPLEMENTAL

Order of Worship Established – Two Tabernacles 304
Diagram – The Church: Departure, Decline and Restoration 305
The Decline as seen in Church History 305

BIBLIOGRAPHY 307

PART ONE

THE PROPHETS

CHAPTER ONE

THE PROPHETS AND THE RESTORATION

Without doubt, the greatest passage on the subject of "restoration" in the New Testament is the passage found in Acts 3:18-26, which is quoted in full here.

"But those things, which God before had shewed by the mouth of all His prophets, that Christ should suffer, He hath so fulfilled.

Repent ye therefore, and be converted, that your sins may be blotted out, when the times of refreshing shall come from the presence of the Lord:

And He shall send Jesus Christ, which before was preached unto you:

Whom the heaven must receive until the times of restitution of all things, which God hath spoken by the mouth of all His holy prophets since the world began.

For Moses truly said unto the fathers, A prophet shall the Lord your God raise up unto you of your brethren, like unto me; Him shall ye hear in all things whatsoever He shall say unto you.

And it shall come to pass, that every soul, which will not hear that prophet, shall be destroyed from among the people.

Yea, and all the prophets from Samuel and those that follow after, as many as have spoken, have likewise foretold of these days.

Ye are the children of the prophets, and of the covenant which God made with our fathers, saying unto Abraham, And in thy seed shall all the kindreds of the earth be blessed.

Unto you first God, having raised up His son Jesus, send Him to bless you, in turning away every one of you from his iniquities…"(Authorized Version). This is the apostle Peter's second "Pentecostal" message. During the course of his message, he tells his listeners that the heavens have received Jesus Christ until the times of restitution (restoration) of all things which God has spoken by the mouth of all His holy prophets since the world began (Verse 21).The hearers were basically Jews and understood, at least, in measure, what was meant by "the times of restoration". As Jews they had the highest respect for the "holy prophets" and their writings and utterances. These are the two important points of reference which need to be considered in this passage.

A. The Prophets

The key word in this passage has to do with the word "prophets", used about six times in all, as well as the mention of the names of Moses and Samuel.

1. God foretold by the prophets the sufferings of Christ-Verse 18.

2. God spoke by the mouth of His holy prophets of the times of restitution-Verse 21.

3. Moses was the greatest of prophets in that all other prophets who spoke were judged by what Moses had spoken - Verse 22

4. Moses foretold the coming of Christ THE Prophet (THE WORD made flesh) like unto himself. Anyone who did not hear and obey THE Prophet would be destroyed from among the people of God - Verses 22,23.

5. Samuel was also an important prophet in his time - Verse 24. The Scriptures links Moses and Samuel together (Acts 3:22,24 with Jeremiah 15:1). Both were great intercessors for the people of God. Moses represented the Law. Samuel represented the Prophets. Moses was the letter of the Law. Samuel was the spirit of the Law. Samuel seemed to be the one who originated the Schools of the Prophets. Here the letter of the Law that had been given to Moses was quickened under the ministry of Samuel by the Spirit. The Spirit, however, would never contradict the letter (John 6:63; 2Corinthians 3:2-6; Romans 7:6).

6. All the prophets from Samuel onwards foretold of the New Testament days - Verse 24.

7. The Jews listening to Peter were actually "the sons of the prophets", that is, in spiritual sense - Verse 25.

Christ had come as the fulfilment of the covenant given to Abraham, as "the seed to bless all nations", beginning with the chosen nation, Israel, first. Christ had also come in fulfilment of the prophetic writings. He is the fulfilment of both the Covenant and the Prophets!

B. Times of Restoration

The next important point of reference is that which pertains to the "times of restoration". In verse 21 Peter tells his audience that the heavens have received (Lit. retained) Jesus Christ until the times of restitution (or, restoration) of all things spoken by God through His holy prophets since the world began.

Israel, as God's chosen nation in Old Testament times, had their whole life, both social and spiritual, governed by the Lord's appointed "times and seasons" as the following Scriptures attest to.

1. The Festival occasions of Passover, Pentecost and Tabernacles were Divinely appointed times and seasons, held in the first, third and seventh months, respectively (Leviticus Chapter 23).

2. To everything there is a time and a season, to every purpose of God under heaven. God makes everything beautiful in His time. Note that the word "time" is used in this passage some thirty times (Ecclesiastes 3:1-8,11,17).

3. Jesus told His disciples that it was not for them to know the times and seasons which the Father has put in His own power when it comes to Israel as a nation (Acts 1:7).

4. Jesus also foretold the fact that Jerusalem would be trodden down and underfoot of the Gentiles until "the times of the Gentiles" would be fulfilled. In AD.70, the Christians took Christ's warning and fled from the city as from a sinking ship. The Jewish Historian, Josephus, tells us that not one Christian was known to have lost his life in the siege. They understood the times and seasons in God (Luke 21:24).

5. Paul was given revelation of the times and seasons as pertaining to events and the second coming of the Lord Jesus Christ (1 Thessalonians 5:1; 1 Timothy 4:1).

6. Paul also spoke of the dispensation of the fullness of times when all things in Christ, whether in heaven or earth, would be gathered together in one (Ephesians 1:10).

7. Jesus reproved the Pharisees because they could discern the weather signs, but could not discern "the signs of the times" (Matthew 16:1-4). The religious leaders missed Christ's coming because they failed to discern the signs of the times.

So in this message, Peter speaks of "the times or seasons of refreshing" that would come from the presence of the Lord. He also reminded his hearers of the "times of restoration" of which the prophets had spoken (Acts 3:19,21). The listening Jews understand in some measure what the "times of restoration" were all about!

For Israel and for simplicity sake, TIME was divided into basically three parts: Time past, Time present and Time future. For the Christian, the cross of Christ is the dividing of time

	Time Past Former Days Sundry Times	Time Present Last Days Hebrews 1:1-2	Time Future
Abraham	Moses (Letter) Samuel (Spirit) The Prophets		
		Times of Refreshing Times of Restitution	Ages to Come

as the following diagram illustrates.

The following Scriptures speak of "time past" and point to the "time present" (Hebrews 1:1-2; Galatians 1:13; Ephesians 2:2,11; 1Peter 2:10). The writer to the Hebrews speaks of the "time of reformation", the "time of the new order" (KJV/NIV) - Hebrews 9:9,10.

It should be remembered, therefore, by the reader that the early church had no New Testament as yet! The New Testament was being revealed to them but was as yet not written! Therefore, in order to understand what Peter was talking about, it is absolutely necessary to go back to the Old Testament writings - the Law and the Prophets!

CHAPTER TWO

THE LAW AND THE PROPHETS

As noted at the conclusion of the previous chapter, the early Church had no New Testament writings when Peter was speaking. In the Book of Acts, as also through the whole of the New Testament writings, the apostles continually appealed to the Old Testament writings for all that God was doing in their midst. In other words, they appealed to **"the law and the prophets"**.

If we, this side of the cross, and with the completed canon of Scriptures, both Old and New Testaments, want to understand what, in measure, the hearers understood, then it is imperative to consider "the law and the prophets". It is the **"law and the prophets"** which speak of **"times of restoration"**. The meaning and significance of these times, therefore, cannot be understood apart from the law and the prophets! Let us note a number of Scripture references which speak of these "two witnesses".

A. The Law and The Prophets

1. Jesus said, "Do not think I am come to destroy (abrogate, subvert, annul), the Law or the Prophets. I did not come to destroy but fulfill (satisfy, cause to expire, complete, abolish by fulfilment)" (Matthew 5:17).

2. Jesus said, "Whatever you want men to do to you, do also to them, for this is the Law and the Prophets" (Matthew 7:12).

3. Jesus said, "For all the Prophets and the Law prophesied until John" (Matthew 11:13). The Law and the Prophets were temporary. John closed off the Old Covenant and introduced Jesus of the New Covenant.

4. Jesus said, "On these two commandments (Love God and Love your neighbour) hang all the Law and the Prophets" (Matthew 22:36-40).

5. Jesus said, "The Law and the Prophets were until John. Since that time the Kingdom of God has been preached, and everyone is pressing into it" (Luke 16:16).

6. Jesus said, "... all things must be fulfilled which were written in the Law of Moses and in the Prophets and in the Psalms concerning Me" (Luke 24:44).

7. Philip told Nathanael, "We have found Him of whom Moses in the Law and also in the Prophets wrote - Jesus of Nazareth ..." (John 1:45).

8. The rulers of the synagogue read on the Sabbath days from "the Law and the Prophets" (Acts 13:15).

9. Paul worshipped God "believing all things which are written in the Law and the Prophets" even though he was charged with heresy (Acts 24:14).

10. Paul expounded and testified Jesus and the kingdom of God to the Jews in Rome out of "the Law of Moses and the Prophets" (Acts 28:33).

11. The righteousness of God by faith has been witnessed by "the Law and the Prophets". The Law and the Prophets are like "two witnesses" (Romans 3:21).

Restoration Theology

12. Moses represents the Law and Samuel represents the Prophets as seen in Peter's message to his hearers (Acts 3:18-26).

All of these references certainly show the importance and relevance of the Law and the Prophets both to Jews and the New Testament believers.

Undoubtedly the scene on the Mount of Transfiguration demonstrated the same truth and the significance of the Law and the Prophets.

Moses and Elijah appeared with Jesus on the holy mount. As Jesus was transfigured before His disciples, both these Old Testament saints appeared under the Father's command. Both spoke to Jesus about His decease (His crucifixion) that He should accomplish in Jerusalem. Moses represented the Law. Elijah represented the Prophets. The Father's voice to the three disciples - Peter, James and John - was to listen to His Son, for Moses and Elijah had pointed to Him in their earthly ministries (Matthew 17:1-13; Mark 9:1-13; Luke 9:27-36).

The simple diagram again illustrates the truth in this chapter.

The Law	The Prophets		The Kingdom
Moses	Elijah		Jesus

"The LAW and the PROPHETS were until JOHN, since that time, the KINGDOM of God is preached and everyone presses into it" (Luke 16:16).

Because the New Testament Scriptures had not as yet been written, the New Testament apostles, preachers, teachers and believers made much use of the Old Testament Scriptures. They saw the fulfilment of the Law, the Psalms and the Prophets, first in Christ, and then in His Church.

As seen already in Peter's sermon, the emphasis is on the Law and the Prophets. In Acts 3:22-24 Peter speaks of Moses. In verse 24 he speaks of Samuel. Then he speaks of all the prophets as many as have spoken, who foretold of these days - the last days! These days are the days we are living in. The "last days" began with the first coming of Christ and today the Church is living in "the last of these last days".

B. Use of the Old Testament in Acts

It is worthy to note briefly the use of the Old Testament as seen in the Book of Acts. These quotations from the Prophets, the Psalms and the Law show us clearly how the early Church and the apostles understood, interpreted and applied the utterances of the Old Testament writers to that which was being fulfilled in the Church. It has been said that "the New Testament writers are the infallible interpreters of the Old Testament Prophets".

Following is a brief list of the Prophets or other writers who were referred to or quoted by those in the Book of Acts. They are continually applied to the CHURCH, to spiritual Israel, and to that which takes place for those who are now "in Christ!"

MATTHIAS CHOSEN

"Let his dwelling place be desolate — and let no one live in it. Let another take his office"

1. Acts 1:15-20. The Psalms spoken by **David** spoke of Judas betrayal.
2. Acts 2:14-21. The Prophet **Joel** foretold the coming of the Holy Spirit. *PETER*
3. Acts 3:19-23. **Moses** as a Prophet foretold the coming of Christ.
4. Acts 3:22-5. **Samuel**, as all the other Prophets, also spoke to the future.
5. Acts 2:22-36. **David** in the Psalms spoke of Christ's sufferings and glory.
6. Acts 4:23-30. **David** was as a Prophet and a King and pointed to Christ.
7. Acts 8:28-37. The Prophet **Isaiah** foretold Christ's sufferings and glory.
8. Acts 10:43. **All** the Prophets pointed to the Messiah Jesus.
9. Acts 13:15,38-41. The Prophet **Habakkuk**, along with **David** and **Isaiah** also spoke of the coming of Christ (Acts 13:33-35; 13:47).
10. Acts 17:2-3. Paul opened to the Bereans the Old Testament Scriptures.
11. Acts 15:15-18. The Prophet **Amos** foretold the coming on the Gentiles into the Tabernacle of David.
12. Acts 28:23-31. Paul reasoned with the Jews out of the Law and the Prophets. **Moses** and **Isaiah** spoke of the hardness of the heart of their generations also.

The whole of the New Testament is the revelation of that which was in seed-form in the Old Testament; the Law, the Psalms and the Prophets.

The Gospels, the Book of Acts and the Epistles abound with quotations, allusions, references and interpretative revelation of that which was hidden in the Law, the Psalms and the Prophets!

In order, therefore, to understand what is meant by **"the times of restoration"**, and **"the Law and the Prophets"**, New Testament believers need to turn to what Moses (who represents the Law), and Elijah (or Samuel) representing the Prophets, said both to their generations and also to our generations.

The apostle Peter writes:

"The prophets who prophesied of the grace (Divine blessing) which was intended for you, searched and inquired earnestly about this salvation. They sought to find out to whom or when this was to come which the Spirit of Christ working within them indicated when He predicted the sufferings of Christ and the glories that should follow them.

It was disclosed to them that the services they were rendering were not meant for themselves and their period of time, but for you. It is these very things which have now already been made known plainly to you by those who preached the good new (the Gospel) to you by the same Holy Spirit sent from heaven. Into these things (the very) angels long to look! (1Peter 1:10-12, Amplified New Testament)."

Restoration Theology

CHAPTER THREE

THE LAWS OF RESTORATION

In this chapter, we turn to the Laws of Restoration as set forth by Moses in the Law and confirmed by the Prophets. However, the word "restoration" needs to be defined. The words "restoration" and "restitution" are used interchangeably as being synonymous. In this order then we consider (A) the definition of the word and then (B) the laws of restoration as given to Israel.

A. Definition of Restoration

Following are definitions of this word taken from various Dictionaries.

1. Strong's - Hebrew

The Old Testament word **"Shalam"** (SC 7999) means "to be safe (in mind, body or estate); fig. to be (caus.make) completed; by implic. to be friendly; by exten. to reciprocate (in various applications). It is translated: make amends, make an end, finish, full, give again, make good, repay (again), make, to be, at peace (-able), that is perfect, perform (make) prosper (-ous), recompense, render, requite, make restitution, restore, reward, surely.

2. Strong's - Greek

The New Testament word **"Apokatastasis"** (SC. 605, from SC 600) means "to reconstitute", or to reconstitute in health, home or organization. It is translated "restitution, or restore again".

3. Collins Dictionary

The word is defined as "the act of restoring or bringing back to a former place, station, or condition; revival; recovery, as of health or spirits; re-establishment, as of peace, concord, etc; renewal from a fallen or vicious state; theologically, the redemption of all created things from sin and its curse.

The word "restore" is defined as "to return, as property to the owner; to replace; to put a thing, or person, into its former or right place; to bring back, to recover; to recover from ruin or decay; to rebuild; to repair; to recover from evil; to renew; to regenerate; to recover from disease; to heal; to bring back to life; to resuscitate; to re-establish, as intercourse or friendship; to make restitution of, or satisfaction for; to give in place of; to recover from error or corruption, as the text of a book; to render or insert, as the true sense or words ..."

4. Webster's Dictionary

a. A restoring or being restored; reinstatement.

b. A putting or bringing back into a former, normal or unimpaired state or condition.

c. In theology, the doctrine of the final recovery of all men from sin and alienation from God to a state of happiness.

d. The word "restore" is to give or bring back; to return to a person, as a specific thing which he has lost, or which has been taken from him and unjustly detained; to make restitution of; as to restore lost or stolen goods to the owner.

It is to put a person back into a former position, place, rank or condition; to replace; to return to a former place. It is to bring back to health and strength. It is to recover, to renew, repair, rebuild.

As can be seen, the word has a rich and varied meaning. But basically, it is to bring a person or thing back to an original condition or state. Or, it is to restore to a person that which has been lost, stolen or taken by force. It is the putting back into existence or use that which has been lost, misplaced or stolen. Illustrations of this are seen in these several Scripture references.

The man with the withered hand was told by Jesus to stretch it out, and **"it was restored whole, like as the other"** (Matthew 12:10-13; Mark 3:5; Luke 6:10).

The man who was blind, after being touched the second time by Jesus **"was restored, and saw every man clearly"** (Mark 8:25).

The lame man, at the Gate Beautiful, after receiving from Peter and John, knew what it was to be **restored**, made whole, as he was healed. No wonder he went walking, and leaping and praising God into the temple of God (Acts 3:1-11). His limbs were brought back to their original condition and use. Whether he was born lame or not, health and vigour was restored. That which he had lost or had stolen by lameness was now given back to him. He was healed, brought back to normal life!

In Summary:-

Restoration is the causing, naturally speaking, to return to a former position or condition, by renewing or returning that which has been taken away, either stolen, lost, destroyed or forcibly removed.

Spiritually speaking, restoration is God causing fallen mankind to return to his former condition, by bringing man back to the glory which he lost in the Fall through the entrance of sin. With regards to the Church, it is the Lord recovering to the Church all that has been lost over the centuries of Church history. It is a full recovery and returning to the Church all that has been lost, stolen, or taken away by Satan and his evil hosts or by the fallen, sinful, humanness of man's nature. It is the bringing of the Church back to its early possessions and condition and its early and original glory - and more!

B. **The Laws of Restitution**

In the Old Testament Scriptures, God gave certain laws to the chosen nation of Israel. These laws governed possessions which were lost, stolen or destroyed, as the following Scriptures clearly show.

1. If an ox was lost, then five more oxen were restored for the loss of the one ox (Exodus 22:1).

2. If one sheep was lost, then four sheep were restored for the loss of one sheep (Exodus 22:1).

3. If an animal was stolen, then twice as much worth of the animal had to be restored (Exodus 22:2-4).

4. If a person caused a field or vineyard to be eaten by another man's beast, then of the best of his own field or vineyard he was to make restitution (Exodus 22:5).

5. If fire broke out in thorns, stacks of ears of corn, or standing corn in the field and such was destroyed, then the one who caused the fire was to make restitution (Exodus 22:6).

6. If theft took place, then twice as much money was to restored to the person who suffered the theft (Exodus 22:7-13).

7. If something was lost, then a fifth part more was to be added in restoration (Leviticus 6:1-5).

8. All things which were lost were to be fully restored to the individual who lost them (Deuteronomy 22:1-3).

9. At times, sevenfold restoration took place (Proverbs 6:30-31).

10. In the fiftieth year, the year of jubilee (Lit. "shouting"), all land was returned and restored to the rightful owner, all debts were cancelled, and all families were re-united. Jubilee year was a time of restoration for every person in Israel (Leviticus 25:8-14). What a glorious year in Israel!

These Scriptures certainly set forth the laws of restoration, of which Peter's Jewish hearers were knowledgeable. If anything was lost, stolen or destroyed, or damaged by fire, etc., whoever was responsible was to make restitution - and more - depending on the value.

As seen in these laws of restoration, an offender must make restoration for any loss incurred on another. In the restoration of material or natural things, the offender was responsible to make restitution. In spiritual and eternal things, it is God who is offended by man's sin and it is God who takes the initiative to make restoration of all that man has lost. Man himself in his fallen state cannot do it! Therefore God takes the initiative.

Again, as seen in these laws of restoration, restoration must be made for any loss of another. The restoration must be either in greater measure, or more of substance, or better in quality than the original loss incurred. In other words, more was to be restored than that which was possessed before the loss occurred!

When the hearers heard Peter's word, therefore, of **"the times of restitution"** of all things spoken by the Prophets, they understood the significance of these laws. Something had been stolen, something had been taken, something had been lost or destroyed. Someone has to make it good and better! Someone would have to restore all that was lost, stolen, taken by force or destroyed.

This restoration must be in greater measure, both quality and quantity than before the particular loss the person experienced!

It is by way of anticipation in the content of the following chapters, we see how GOD has obligated Himself to restore to mankind that which was lost, stolen and taken away by Satan in the Fall in Eden's garden! Man cannot restore himself or his lost inheritance. It is GOD who takes the initiative! But this brings us to our next chapter!

"THE TIMES OF RESTITUTION"

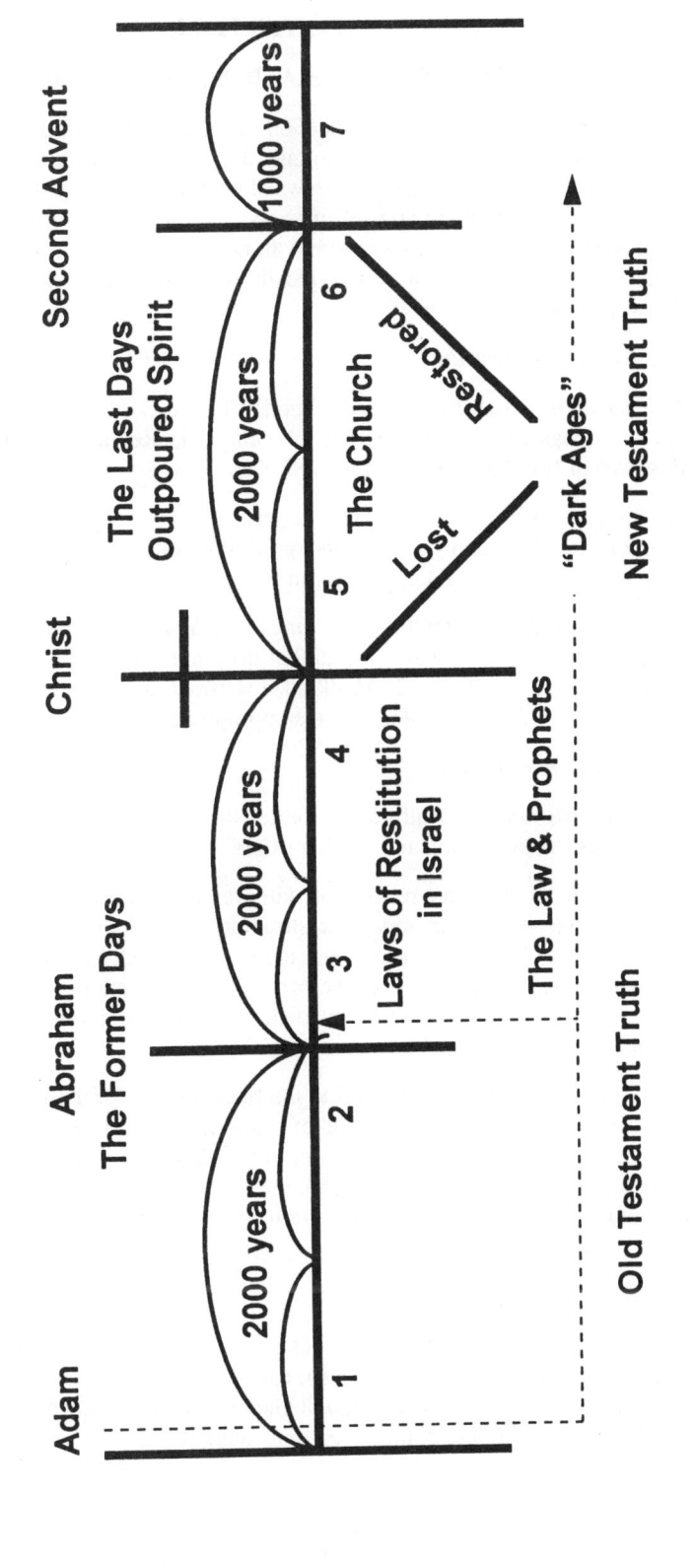

Adam	Abraham The Former Days	Christ		Second Advent
			The Last Days Outpoured Spirit	

2000 years — 2000 years — 2000 years — 1000 years

1 — 2 — 3 — 4 — 5 — 6 — 7

Laws of Restitution in Israel

The Church — Lost — Restored

The Law & Prophets

"Dark Ages"

Old Testament Truth — New Testament Truth

Restoration Theology   11

CHAPTER FOUR

THE GOD OF RESTORATION AND REDEMPTION

The Bible clearly reveals that God is the God of restoration. An important truth to keep in mind is that God never ever gives laws to man that He Himself cannot, does not or will not fulfill. He would not and did not give the laws of restitution to Israel without Divine purpose. He gave laws to Israel that He Himself was going to fulfill, but on a much higher plane, a much higher level and much more glorious. In other words, the principle is that God often asked men in the Old Testament to do typically what He Himself was going to do actually in the New Testament.

A. The God of Restoration

A designation which truly may be applied to the Lord is found in Isaiah 58:12-13. There it speaks: "... And you shall be called the **Repairer of the Breach and the Restorer of the Paths to dwell in**" (NKJV).

Sin brought about a breach, a gap, a great gulf, between God and man. Only God Himself can bridge that gap, span that gulf. Sin took man out of the paths that God had intended him to walk in. Only God can bring man back to these paths.

It may be asked: What then are the things that God the Repairer and God the Restorer has to restore? The Scriptures reveal that there are several areas which need restoring, these being (1) Creation, (2) Mankind, (3) Israel and (4) The Church, the Body of Christ. These will be considered in the appropriate chapters.

B. The God of Redemption

There are two words or truths in Scripture which cannot be separated from each other, these being "**restoration**" and "**redemption**".

The one and only way that restoration will ever take place is through redemption. There is no possible chance or hope of restoration apart from redemption. The God who restores is the God who redeems and the God who redeems is the God who restores. Restoration and redemption are like two sides of one and the same coin. They can be distinguished but they cannot be divided. It is redemption only that makes restoration possible.

From the Fall of man in Genesis 3 to the final chapters of the Book of Revelation, the God of the Bible is seen to be a God of restoration and a God of redemption. If there is no redemption, then there is no restoration. Man cannot restore himself back to the glory and image of God from which he fell, because man cannot redeem himself. The God of creation is the God of redemption. The covenant of creation pointed forward to the covenant of redemption.

C. The Book of Redemption

John saw in vision a seven sealed book in the hand of Him who sat on the throne. He wept much because no one in heaven, earth or under the earth was worthy to take the book and break the seals. The Lamb of God, the Kinsman-Redeemer, alone was worthy to take the book and break the seven seals thereof.

That book is the book of redemption, the book of a lost inheritance (Revelation Chapters 4-5).

The Bible is primarily the book of restoration because it is a book of redemption. Basically there are only two chapters given over to the account of creation, these being Genesis Chapters 1-2. Genesis 3 is the account of the entrance of sin into the world of mankind. The Fall of man into the kingdom of Satan, the kingdom of darkness is accounted for.

From Genesis 3 to the closing chapters of Revelation (Revelation 21-22), the rest of the Scriptures deal with restoration. As seen previously, this restoration is through redemption. The Bible is therefore a book of restoration because it is a book of redemption.

As the Bible is studied, it will be seen that God provides picture after picture, type after type, prophecy after prophecy about restoration through redemption. Restoration theology is seen in types and symbols, shadow and substance, prophecy and fulfilment, and this will be seen through the course of this study.

The Bible tells of a Fallen Creation, a Fallen Man, a Fallen Nation of Israel and a Fallen Church, but it also tells us of the restoring and redeeming God.

The Bible also shows God's principles of restoration. Man must obey these principles in order to know complete restoration to the glory of God from which he fell. Sufficient for this chapter is to know that the God of creation is the God of restoration and this He does as the God of redemption!

CHAPTER FIVE

THINGS NOT TO BE RESTORED

Every time a facet of truth is recovered to the Church, the Devil seeks to distort it and make it heretical. We may ask: Which came first - Truth or Error? The answer, of course is TRUTH! Error or heresy could not exist apart from truth. Counterfeit could not exist apart from the original. What then is heresy? Heresy is taking a portion or fragment of truth to its extreme, out of proportion with the whole body of truth. Many of the early Church Creeds were the result of hammering out heresies on the anvil of truth!

Heresy has been wrung out of the wonderful truth of Restoration. There are those who are called "Restorationists", or "Universalists", or "Ultimate Reconciliationists". These have taken the truth of restoration to its absolute extreme. They teach that "restoration is the ultimate salvation of all mankind, including the Devil and his angels and demonic hosts". They teach that eventually all will be saved and reconciled to God. Because of these things "restoration theology" has been rejected by many of God's people!

Peter speaks of those who handle the truth and (literally) "torture the truth on the rack" (Note 2 Peter 3:16; Strong's Concordance on the word "twist"). The apostle Paul also speaks of others who "handle the Word of God deceitfully", or literally "peddle the Scriptures" (2Corinthians 2:17 with 4:2, Amplified New Testament).

These kind of people have made heresy out of the truth of restoration. Hence, it is important to set out in this chapter what is **NOT** to be restored, and what is meant in this text by "**restoration!**"

A. The Devil And Hosts Will Not Be Restored

There are those, as noted above, that believe and teach that the Devil and all fallen angels and demonic spirits will be restored. They teach that the "restitution of **all** things" includes the redemption of Satan and his hosts. They abuse the Scriptures which speak of the fact that "Christ died for **all**" which includes Satan and his evil kingdom and hosts. They argument that, if God is all-powerful, then none can escape His mighty hand and power of redemption, that all will, in due time be reconciled to God and subdued unto His sovereign will.

The Bible, however, does in no way teach or intimate this in any verse or passage. This heresy is known as "Universalism" or "Ultimate Reconciliation". However, none of the Biblical writers know or speak of such a thing. There is no reconciliation for the unrepentant. Christ did not die to redeem Satan or fallen angels or demonic spirits. These spirit beings sinned in the blazing white light of God's holiness. For any to teach such a reconciliation is to distort, twist and pervert the Scriptures to their own deceived ends.

The Bible tells us that Gehenna (Hell fire, the Lake of Fire and Brimstone) was prepared for the Devil and his angels (Matthew 25:41). It also tells us that this is eternal judgment and the fires of Divine judgment will burn for ever. The final mention of the Devil is that of being cast into the lake of fire and brimstone to be tormented eternally along with his hosts (Revelation 20:11-15; 14:9-11).

B. Unrepentant Mankind Will Not Be Restored

Unrepentant mankind will not be restored. This heresy belongs to the previous, as already seen. It teaches that Christ died for "all" and "all" will eventually, either in Time or Eternity, be ultimately reconciled to God. They may be punished by judgment for some period of time, but eventually they will come to repentance and are therefore reconciled to God.

The Bible, however, shows that, although Christ died for all mankind, and provided salvation for all, this salvation can only be received on God's terms: Repentance and Faith! The God who provided salvation also lays down the terms by which this "so great salvation" can be received.

Scripture teaches that all unrepentant mankind, whether Jews or Gentiles, will be judged at the great white throne of God. Those whose names are not found written in the Book of Life will be cast into the Lake of Fire and Brimstone and will know eternal torments. These torments will be because they have rejected salvation provided by the Lamb of God. The apostle John, in Revelation 14:9-11 makes it clear. All those who receive the mark of the beast will be tormented in the lake of fire for eternity. They will be tormented in the presence of the Lamb of God they rejected and in the presence of the holy angels. That indeed will be hell! They will be cast into Gehenna along with the Devil and his hosts (Matthew 25:41; Revelation 20:11-15). The Bible teaches that mankind will live eternally with the one they served in time! Serve the Devil and sin in Time, and live with the Devil and sin in Eternity! Serve the Lord and righteousness in Time, serve the Lord and righteousness in Eternity!

C. The Mosaic Covenant System Will Not Be Restored

Ultra-Dispensationalists teach that, in the end of this age, or in a future Millennial Age, the Mosaic system will be restored. This group of teachers use Scriptures such as found in Ezekiel Chapters 40-48 with Zechariah 13-14 to substantiate this line of teaching. Along with other Scriptures these things are taught. They teach that there will be a restoration of:

1. A restored and rebuilt material temple in Mt Moriah
2. Restored animal sacrifices and oblations
3. Restored festival occasions, such as Passover, Pentecost and Tabernacles
4. Restored rite of circumcision
5. Restored Sabbath days and years
6. Restored Jerusalem as the holy city of God in the earth
7. Restored Aaronic and Levitical Priesthood services
8. Restored Mosaic Covenant ceremonies and all therein.

All of this kind of teaching arises out of, what may be called, Covenantal confusion. It is a confusion of the Old and the New Covenants especially.

When Jesus died on the cross and the veil of the temple was rent in two from top to bottom, and this by God Himself, it signified that the Mosaic Covenant economy was for ever abolished and fulfilled. It would never be reinstituted. It would never be restored, neither in this age or any age to come. Jesus instituted the New Covenant in His sacrificial death; in His own broken body and shed blood.

Animal sacrifices, Sabbath days, festival days, circumcision, the Aaronic and Levitical priesthood, material temples, and so forth – all were abolished at the cross. The rent veil signified the end of the Mosaic or Old Covenant, and the introduction of the New Covenant. The Old Covenant was temporary. The New Covenant is eternal. To restore anything of the Mosaic economy is to go back to the other side of the cross. The believer is under the New Covenant and lives this side of Calvary and this side of Pentecost. To restore the Mosaic economy in any part is to violate the whole teaching of the New Testament, especially the Book of Hebrews.

In Hebrews we have a better temple, a better tabernacle, a better sacrifice, a better priesthood, a better covenant! The old was good, but everything in the new is better. He takes away the first covenant, and all that pertains to it, to bring in the second, the better, the New Covenant.

To restore the Mosaic sacrifices, the Aaronic priesthood and the old system is the greatest insult to Calvary and the perfect, once-for-all sacrifice of Jesus Christ. The Mosaic Covenant will never be reinstituted. It will never be restored. The Law-Covenant made nothing perfect or complete. It could never deal with sin. Only the New Covenant can do that. The New Covenant is personified in the Lord Jesus Christ. God has taken away Moses to establish Jesus. "This is My beloved Son - hear Him!" (Matthew 17:1-13).

D. Jewish Nationalism Will Not Be Restored

Closely linked and actually a part of the teaching of the restoration of the Mosaic Covenant economy is the teaching of restored Jewish nationalism.

Ultra-Dispensationalism teaches that, in due time, either the end of this age or more particularly a future Millennial Age and Kingdom, the Jews will become the head of all nations. With a restored Mosaic economy, all nations will have to go to Jerusalem for the annual Feast of Tabernacles and the offering of the associated sacrifices. The Jews in this time will become the great "missionary nation" to the whole world. All nations will benefit by the ministry of the Jewish nation. The Old Testament prophecies concerning "Israel" and her national destiny will all find fulfilment in this time. Many, many Old Testament Scriptures are used to support this teaching.

The fact of the matter is, however, that absolutely nowhere is there any indication of this in the New Testament writings. The New Testament writers all show that the Jew and the Gentile can only come to God through Christ and the NEW Covenant. There is not one way for the Jew and another and different way for the Gentile. All have been concluded under sin. All need the mercy and grace of God in Christ.

The Epistle to the Romans shows that, once a Jew or Gentile accepts Christ, they are baptized into one and the same body; the mystery Body of Christ. Paul in Corinthians confirms this truth (Romans 12:1-6; Ephesians 2:19-22; 1Corinthians 12:13; Ephesians 3:1-12).

The great chapters dealing with the so-called "Jewish problem" are found in Romans Chapters 9-10-11. This will be considered in the appropriate chapter. In brief this can be said. The Jew was broken out of the faith-olive tree because of unbelief. The Gentile is grafted by faith into this faith-olive tree, in and through Christ. This faith-olive tree consists of believing Jews and believing Gentiles, and all stand by faith. It is unbelief that takes one out of this faith-olive tree, whether Jew or Gentile.

As God has and is visiting all nations by the outpouring of His Spirit, so the Jewish nation will receive an outpouring also in the end time. They will have their eyes opened to their long-rejected Messiah. They, if they abide not still in unbelief, will be grafted in again to the faith-olive tree. This is the teaching of the New Covenant writers. Nowhere do they speak of the Jewish nation being the head of all nations in this age or any age to come. The only hope of salvation for all nations is in Christ and in Him alone!

The Jew cannot be saved by the works or ceremonies of the Mosaic Covenant, nor will they be missionaries to Gentile nations by ministering the Mosaic economy sacrifices and Levitical priesthood. All can come to God through Christ's sacrifice and His Melchisedekian Priesthood, for He lives in the power of an endless life (Hebrews 7-8-9-10 with Psalm 110).

In Conclusion:-

It is important therefore, to understand, that, when the truth of restoration is spoken of, it is **NOT** a restoration of the Devil, fallen angels, unrepentant mankind, or the Mosaic Covenant economy or Jewish nationalism!

The "**restoration of ALL things**" is limited and confined within the framework of "**that which was spoken by the mouth of the holy prophets**" since the world began (Acts 3:18-26). The prophets nowhere speak of any restoration of these things dealt with in this chapter.

PART TWO

THE CREATION

CHAPTER SIX

THE PRINCIPLE OF RESTORATION IN CREATION

As seen in an earlier chapter, there are four major things that the Scriptures speak on when it comes to restoration. These are: Fallen Creation, Fallen Mankind, Fallen Israel and the Fallen Church. In this chapter we begin with the restoration of a fallen creation.

The first picture we have in Scripture of restoration is found in the first five verses of the Genesis Book.

Genesis 1:1-5 reads:

"In the beginning God created the heavens and the earth. And the earth was without form and void and darkness was upon the face of the deep. And the Spirit of God moved upon the face of the deep. And God said, Let there be light, and there was light. And God saw the light, that it was good, and God divided the light from the darkness. And God called the light day, and the darkness He called night. And the evening and the morning were the first day."

These are the first few verses of the first book of the Bible and this writer believes that they set forth a pattern of restoration for the rest of Scripture. This will be evident in the consideration of these verses. It must be recognized, of course, that different schools of interpretation understand these verses differently. But, there would be far more agreement on the important points than disagreement on other points.

We consider in some detail this first picture of restoration as seen in the original creation. The principle seen here extends to the whole plan of restoration through redemption.

A. The Original Creation

Verse one simply says, "In the beginning God created the heavens and the earth". Who can find "the beginning?" There is no "time element" given here. Simply, it is "in the beginning". No human being can find that beginning. In the beginning God created the heavens and the earth.

The Hebrew word for "God" is "Elohim". It is a Hebrew uni-plural word, denoting plurality of Divine Persons without stating the number. Subsequent Scripture shows the word to be significant of the Godhead, as Father, Son and Holy Spirit. Genesis 1:1-5 may be compared with John 1:1-3 and Job 26:13. In the Scriptures we find that the eternal Godhead, Father, Son and Holy Spirit, were each active in creation - the original creation of the heavens and the earth. God is the Creator of all things whether seen or unseen, visible or invisible.

B. The Ruined Creation

In verse two we are told: "And the earth was without form and void, and darkness was upon the face of the deep".

Concerning the interpretation of this verse, there are two major different schools of interpretation which seek to explain the condition as set out here.

One school says that the earth "without form and void" was like unformed clay in the potter's hands and awaited formation and order. This school says that the earth was created as a shapeless mass like a lump of clay. That is to say, it was created without form (shape) and void (a waste, a ruin and emptiness), and darkness was on the face of the deep. It was as if God was the great Potter, and after creating the earth as formless matter, He set about to shape it, and fashion it into the beautiful earth as seen in Genesis Chapters 1-2.

The other school of interpretation says that the earth **became** without form and void and in this chaotic condition through the fall of Satan (Lucifer). It is this theory that is pursued in this picture.

The prophet Isaiah provides some additional information and light on these verses in Genesis. He lends further weight to the theory followed here. In Isaiah 45:18 the prophet says,"Thus saith the Lord, who created the heavens, who is God who formed the earth and made it, who has established it, who did not create it in vain, who formed it to be inhabited. I am the Lord, there is none other". (NKJV)

The language certainly links up with Genesis. The Lord is the One who created the heavens and the earth. In the beginning God created the heavens and the earth. Then Isaiah says that the Lord God formed the earth and made it and established it. He did not create it "**in vain**". It is the same Hebrew thought as in Genesis. The earth was "**without form and void**", but God did not create it that way. It became that way. Something must have taken place. Something must have happened to bring about this condition.

There is, again, difference of opinion over the word "**was**". The first school says that the earth **was** created that way. The second school says that the earth **became** that way. So it is said: "In the beginning, God created the heavens and the earth. And the earth **became** without form and void, and darkness was upon the face of the deep".

If this theory is so then it would appear that something climatic took place and brought the original creation into a condition of formlessness, a waste, a ruin and emptiness - "without form and void".

To add to this picture, Genesis tells us that "**darkness** was upon the face of the deep". Scripture tells us that God is **light** and in Him is no darkness at all (John 1:5). It also says that God dwells in light and no man has seen God nor can see God as He dwells in unapproachable light (1Timothy 6:15-16). From where did this darkness come? How did the earth become without form and void, a waste, a ruin and emptiness?

The school that teaches this theory believes that the original creation was ruled over by Lucifer, the Day Star, and Son of the Morning. When he rose up against God and the Word in self-will, he was cast out to this earth and brought about the chaotic condition we have here in Genesis.

Jesus, in speaking to the Seventy on their return from mission, said, "I beheld Satan as lightning fall from heaven" (Luke 10:18). When lightning strikes the earth, it brings destruction so often, striking trees or animals, buildings or even mankind. Lighting is falling light. It is light gone chaotic. It is light that has become destructive. How much more so when this is applied to Lucifer, the falling Day Star, Son of the Morning, the

Light-bearer! He fell as lightning, striking the earth, and brought about the chaotic condition on earth, making it "without form and void" - a waste, a ruin and emptiness.

Satan also is the king of the kingdom of darkness (Colossians 1:13; Revelation 16:10). God did not create it that way. The Amplified Old Testament says that "He did not create it a **worthless waste**". The New American Standard says, "He did not create it a **waste place**". It is this theory that presents to us a ruined creation!

C. The Frustrated Purpose

The prophet Isaiah, in the passage under consideration, goes on to say: "He created it not in vain, **He formed it to be inhabited**". To be inhabited means to be lived in, to be dwelt in by people, to be occupied.

So God's original purpose for this earth was habitation. It was created, like a house, to be lived in, to be inhabited.

If the theory followed is right, then it can be said that **SIN** temporarily frustrated the purpose of God. Perhaps we have here a clue as to God's purpose in creating man - Adam and Eve -and why the serpent, Satan, envied them being given dominion over this earth. It helps to explain why he brought about their fall. He wanted to get this planet, earth, back under his domain. Satan saw Adam and his wife as "rivals" to his territory.

D. The Need For Restoration

Again, if the theory is so, it shows the need for restoration. The earth had to be restored back to its original glory, as when God first created it. The earth being without form and void, a waste, a ruin and emptiness, could not restore itself to its previous glory. GOD would have to take the initiative and this is what He did.

How then did God restore the fallen creation from its chaotic conditions, its worthless state, its depth of darkness?

E. The First Principle of Restoration

Regardless of which school of interpretation the reader follows, these first several verses in Genesis do set forth a pattern of restoration that is seen throughout the Word of God. It may rightly be called, "The First Principle of Restoration" This is seen in the following steps that God took in restoring the earth and making it a suitable place for the man and woman He was about to create. Let us consider these steps of restoration of the marred creation.

1. The Spirit Moved

Genesis 1:2 says, "And the Spirit of God moved upon the face of the waters". The Amplified Old Testament says, "The Spirit of God was moving (hovering, brooding) over the face of the waters".

The first thing here is **movement - movement of the Spirit**! Of the Divine Persons in the Godhood (Elohim), it is the third Person who is seen moving, hovering, brooding over the face of the waters. The Holy Spirit is likened to a dove throughout the Word of God. This is the thought that is conveyed here. The Spirit was moving, brooding, fluttering and hovering like a dove in the midst of the condition here. The Spirit of God takes the initiative here.

In the midst of the darkness on the face of the deep, and in spite of the formless, waste and empty condition, the Spirit of God **MOVED**! The Spirit of God is initiating what will be "**a week of restoration**" consummating with the creation of Adam and his bride! The Spirit moves to bring about a restored earth.

This is the first specific mention of the Spirit in the Bible. The Holy Spirit is mentioned only three times in the Book of Genesis (Genesis 1:2-3; 6:3; 41:38). In these references we see "the Spirit moving", "the Spirit striving", and "the Spirit interpreting" dreams of God given to Pharoah.

In Genesis One the Spirit is moving. The Spirit is brooding. The Spirit is seen hovering like a dove over the waste earth, the earth without form and void.

Just this one verse becomes a prophetic and significant verse of the whole of the Bible. A study of the Scriptures show how the Holy Spirit constantly moves in generation after generation to bring about, to prepare for, God's work of restoration and redemption. The point is: **There must be MOVEMENT of the Spirit before restoration can take place!**

2. **The Word Spoken**

The next verse in this picture of restoration says: "And God said, Let there be light, and there was light ..."

The expression "**God said**" is used at least ten times in Genesis Chapter One (1:3,6,9,11,14,20,24,26,28,29). It is the coming of the Word of God. It actually brings us to the first principle of restoration - the key to the whole Bible. The principle is this "First the Spirit, then the Word ..." "**The Spirit moved ... and God said ...**" The Spirit preceded the Word. The Spirit prepared for the Word. The Spirit made way for the Word. The Spirit and the Word work together! It is not one without the other.

"The Spirit" is mentioned once in this chapter. "God said" is mentioned ten times in this chapter. But this is Divine order in restoration. The Spirit moves and God speaks.

To understand this principle is to understand the underlying principle of the whole of Scripture, as the following examples show.

* Holy men of God spoke the prophetic Word as they were moved (energized, quickened, anointed) by the Holy Spirit. The Spirit preceded the Word. The Spirit produced the Word - the Holy Bible.

All Scripture is given by inspiration of the Spirit. The Scriptures were God-breathed (2Timothy 3:16 with 2Peter 1:20-21).

* The Sword of the Spirit is the Word of God (Ephesians 6:17).

* The Spirit of the Lord spoke by me (David) and His Word was on my tongue (2 Samuel 23:2).

Many more Scriptures could be mentioned. The Spirit works with the Word. The Spirit prepares for the Word. The Spirit and the Word agree (1John 5:7-8).

It is the first principle of Biblical restoration and it is illustrated in the first few verses of the Bible. These verses become "**the key**" to the whole Bible: The Spirit and the Word!

John confirms the activity of **THE WORD** in creation in the first several verses of his Gospel, which has some parallel with the first several verses of Genesis.

"In the beginning was the Word, and the Word was with God, and the Word was God. The same was in the beginning with God. All things were made by Him and without Him was not anything made that was made" (John 1:1-3).

Thus Elohim - Father, Word and Holy Spirit - are seen to be active in creation and also in restoration.

3. **Let There Be Light**

The next important step to see is that which pertains to light. God said, Let there be light and there was light.

The first thing the Word produced was **LIGHT**! The Psalmist tells us: "The entrance of Your Word gives light" (Psalm 119:130). God can only truly work in an atmosphere of light. God is light and in Him is no darkness at all (1John 1:5). Light is pure, transparent, clear, and light cannot be contaminated or defiled by Satan or sin. The Word always produces light.

4. **Light and Darkness Divided**

"And God saw the light, that it was good; and God divided the light from the darkness. And God called the light Day, and the darkness He called Night. And the evening and the morning were the first day". There are some important thoughts to be seen here.

(a) **Light and Darkness**

God divided the light from the darkness. This is the first thought of division in the Bible. It foreshadows the great division that exists between light and darkness. That is, the Kingdom of Light and the Kingdom of Darkness. Light and darkness can never mix. By their very nature, they are opposites and can never be united. Light and darkness bring division. Such becomes prophetic and significant of the division in mankind in time into two kingdoms: the Kingdom of God, which is the Kingdom of Light, and the Kingdom of Satan, which is the Kingdom of Darkness. Read these Scriptures which speak of "light" and "darkness" as these two prophetic streams flow through the Bible from Genesis to Revelation (Genesis 1:4,5,18; Job 38:19; John 1:5; 3:19; 8:12; 2Corinthians 4:6).

(b) Light and Darkness Named

God called or named these things. He called the light, Day, and the darkness He called or named Night. This became prophetic of the redemptive motif seen through the Word of God.

F. Creation To Redemption

To confirm the fact that this picture of restoration in creation foreshadows restoration through redemption, we turn to the apostle Paul's writings in the New Testament Epistles.

In his Epistles to the Corinthians and the Thessalonians, Paul alludes back to the scene of creation here in Genesis. Paul actually takes the language of creation and uses it as the language of redemption.

In 2 Corinthians 4:4-6 Paul tells the Corinthians that the god of this world (age) had blinded the minds of those who believe not. Satan does not want the light of the Gospel of the glory of Christ, who is the image of God, to shine on them. He then says: "For God who commanded the **light** to shine out of **darkness**, hath shined in our hearts, to give the light of the knowledge of the glory of God in the face of Jesus Christ". Here the language of creation becomes the language of redemption!

When Paul wrote to the Thessalonian believers, he again uses the language of creation in a redemptive manner; the language being that of Genesis 1:1-5.

Paul writes to the believers about the second coming of Christ. He says: "But you, brethren, are not in **darkness**, that that day should overtake you as a thief (ie., a thief in the night). For you are all the children of the **light**, and are children of the **day**. We are not of the **night** nor of **darkness**. Therefore, let us not sleep, as do others; but let us watch and be sober. For they that sleep sleep in the **night**, and they that be drunken are drunken in the night. But let us, who are of the **day**, be sober, putting on the breastplate of faith and love, and for an helmet, the hope of salvation" (Read 1 Thessalonians 5:1-9).

Where did Paul get this language? It is taken and adapted from Genesis 1:1-5. The language of creation becomes the language of the symbol, which in turn becomes the language of redemption.

All the history of the world is set forth in two kingdoms: the Kingdom of Light and the Kingdom of Darkness. All mankind are either children of the Day or children of the Night! Characteristics of those of the Day are watchfulness and soberness. The characteristics of those of the Night are drunkenness and sleep!

This first day's work prepares for the "week's work" as God's brings order out of chaos, fruitfulness out of barrenness, and order out of waste, and life out of death. He crowns His whole handiwork with the creation of man and woman, Adam and his bride, making them king and queen over the restored creation!

In Summary:

The creation and restoration of a ruined creation becomes a motif of the creation and restoration of fall mankind through redemption. Our first shadow of restoration is seen in creation and the principle of restoration is first illustrated there. Such is the inspiration of the Scriptures.

Romans 8:18-22 points to creation being restored once again because of what happened in the fall of Adam. Creation rises and falls with the man God created. When Adam fell, all creation fell with him. The present creation is groaning in the bondage of corruption, waiting the unveiling of the mature sons of God. The past points to the future restoration of creation but this restoration will be by redemption of mankind back to the image of God from which he fell.

But this brings us to the next chapter!

PART THREE

THE CREATION OF MAN

⚘

CHAPTER SEVEN

THE CREATION OF MAN

As will be seen, that which took place in creation sets forth a pattern of that which takes place in the creation of man. The principles therein are seen in Adam and his fall and then the restoration of mankind through God's redemptive work.

However, in this chapter we need to consider God's purpose in the creation of the original man before proceeding to God's plan in restoration through redemption.

A. The Original Man

In Genesis 1:26-28 we are given the account of the creation of man and woman. On the sixth day of creation we have God's "masterpiece" in the creation of man in His image and likeness. From the Genesis account, along with other supportive Scriptures, we consider God's original purpose in the creation of Adam and his wife.

God said: "Let us make man in our image, after our likeness, and let them have dominion ... So God created man in his own image, in the image of God created He him; male and female created He them. And God said unto them, Be fruitful and multiply and replenish the earth, and subdue it, and have dominion.."

The Scriptures show that man was created a triune being; spirit, soul and body, even as God Himself is a triune Being; Father, Son and Holy Spirit (1Thessalonians 5:23-24).

B. The Original Purpose

There was a fourfold purpose of God in the creation of man; these being Fellowship, Character, Dominion and Fruitfulness, which we consider here.

1. Fellowship

The first reason God created man for was for the purpose of fellowship, or, relationship. God is a Father and His desire was to have a family of children to share His life with, to get to know each other in a personal way. Fellowship, relationship and intimacy were in the heart of God when He created man. Man was created to relate to his Maker and Creator. Man was not created to be alone or to live life apart from God.

History shows that there is within every person a longing for relationship, for fellowship, for intimacy with another person. There is a deep within man that can only be filled from the deep in God. When God created man, He would have this kind of fellowship with man in the Garden of Eden, the earthly Paradise. There, in the cool of the evening, God walked and talked with man (Genesis 3:8) Man was created for relationship. This is seen in marriage relationship, in family, with brothers and sisters and so forth. The ultimate relationship of all is relationship or fellowship and intimacy with God.

2. Character

The second reason God created man for was to see reproduced in man His own nature and character. God, as Father, wanted His children to be like Him in His nature, in His moral attributes. This is seen in the fact that God said: "Let us make man in Our image, after Our likeness ..." (Genesis 1:26).

In Hebrews 1:3 Jesus is spoken of as the "express image" of God, the express image of His Father. The Greek word for "express image" is "**charakter**", from which we get the English word "character".

God created man to be a partaker of the Divine nature (2Peter 1:4-7), to be conformed to the image of His Son (Romans 8:28-29). Jesus is the express image of the invisible God and God wanted man to be in His image and likeness. God wanted His moral attributes of holiness, righteousness, love, goodness, grace, mercy, compassion, kindness and faithfulness to be in the man He created. This is character! This is the Divine nature. This is the nature and character of the Father God. Every natural father delights to see his children like him: "like father, like son". So this was the heart of the Father God.

3. Dominion

The third reason that God created man was that man should have dominion, to rule over the restored creation. God the Father wanted His children to be involved in the business of ruling the universe, of ruling the earth.

God not only proposed that man be something (character), but also that man do something (dominion). God wanted man to share in His dominion (Genesis 1:26). To do this, God told man to subdue the earth. By implication there is an enemy around that has to be subdued, that has to be conquered (Genesis 1:28). At that time, the enemy unknown and unseen to man was Satan.

Dominion, subjugation, rulership speaks of kingship. Man would be king of the human kingdom under God. He would rule over the animal kingdom. Man was created to rule under God. Man was created to have dominion under God. As the author understands it, the Garden of Eden was but a small part of the earth and man was, through his offspring, to make the whole earth as the Garden of Eden. This is rulership. This is kingship. Adam and his bride were as king and queen together, vice-regents to rule and have dominion over creation.

4. Fruitfulness

The fourth reason God created man for was that man share something of **His** creative powers. God the Father wanted His children to reproduce more children to be in the family.

The Lord told Adam and his bride to be "fruitful and multiply and replenish the earth ..." (Genesis 1:28). This spoke of reproduction and reproducing "after their kind".

When we consider that Adam and his bride were perfect and sinless, made in the image and likeness of God, we realize that this would have been the kind of offspring born. Adam and his bride would have reproduced "after their kind" - that is, they would have produced perfect and sinless children. This was indeed God's original intention.

God gave man some of His Creatorship powers; power to reproduce, to create by the union of the man and the woman, children after the image and likeness of God! What a magnificent honour God placed upon man!

This fourfold purpose of God is both progressive and interdependant. **Fellowship** with God is essential for **character** development. **Character** is required to handle **dominion**. When these are in proper order, **fruitfulness** will be the natural result! Man cannot handle dominion without character, and he cannot have character without relationship, fellowship and intimacy with God!

This was God's fourfold purpose in the creation of the man and the woman in His image. This was God's original intention for the original man and for the generations that would proceed from him.

But the Divine purpose and the beautiful story ended - for some time - there!

CHAPTER EIGHT

THE RUINED MAN

As seen in the previous chapter, God had a fourfold purpose for creating man. However, this purpose, like His purpose for earth, was brought to chaos through the entrance of sin. It is this that needs to be considered in this chapter, for SIN ruined the man made in the image of God. Let us note the details of the entrance of sin and its effect on Adam and his wife and then the whole human race.

A. The Creation of Man

The Book of Genesis provides the account of the creation of man. As seen previously, man was created as a free-will, morally responsible and intelligent creature (Genesis 1:26-28; 2:7,15-25). The creation of man was in the image and likeness of God; a triune being composed of spirit, soul and body. Adam's sinlessness was an untested kind of perfection. Adam and Eve were placed in the Garden of Eden, a perfect earthly environment, and experienced unhindered fellowship with their Creator.

B. The Probation of Man

It was necessary that man be placed under a period of probation. Man, though a free-will creation had to be placed under the law of God, especially because of the whole human race as yet to be born. Adam and Eve had to make a choice between doing God's good, perfect and acceptable will, or their own will. They had to learn dependence upon God or be an independent creature. They had to learn to be self-giving or self-gratifying. Thus God gave them one law, one commandment, with a penalty attached if violated. This commandment is recorded in Genesis 2:7. "But of the tree of the knowledge of good and evil thou shalt not eat of it, for in the day that thou eatest, thou shalt surely die". In principle this was the tenth commandment of the Decalogue which says, "Thou shalt not covet" (Exodus 20:17). Law was an absolute necessity, both in the creation and for the creature, otherwise there is lawlessness and lawlessness is chaos, disorder and eventually disaster.

C. The Temptation of Man

In Genesis 3:1-6 we have God's account of the temptation of man and the entrance of sin into the human race. The word "temptation" simply means "to test, to try, to prove". The test centered around a particular tree which was in the Garden of Eden; the tree of the knowledge of good and evil. More particularly it involved obedience to the one commandment of God as given in Genesis 2:17. Man was permitted to eat of all the trees of the garden, which also included the tree of life. Only one tree was forbidden; the tree of the knowledge of good and evil. Man was confronted with a choice; obedience or disobedience to God's will and word. He also knew the consequences of his choice would be either life or death. As a free-will creature, he had the power of choice. Deuteronomy could well have been spoken to Adam, as it was to Israel as a nation. "I call heaven and earth to record this day against you, that I have set before you life and death, blessing and cursing, therefore choose life, that both thou and thy seed may live ..."

In the testing of man, God permitted the Devil, the original sinner, to tempt him (Read also Matthew 4:3; 1Thessalonians 3:5 with Genesis 3:1-6). Satan, previously Lucifer, experienced temptation from within himself; pride leading to lust. But for man the temptation came from without, lust leading to pride. It should be remembered that temptation itself is not sin. It is yielding to temptation that is sin. We now analyze more fully the things involved in the temptation and subsequent fall of man.

1. **Tempted in Body, Soul and Spirit**

   God permitted Adam and Eve to be tempted by the serpent, to prove whether they would make the supreme consecration of their free-will to the will of God in loving obedience or stoop to self-will. The temptation of Satan was to all parts of man's being; spirit, soul and body (1Thessalonians 5:23). Satan's approach was body, soul and spirit.

   (a) Temptation to the **body** - the lust of the flesh. The tree was good for food.

   (b) Temptation to the **soul** - the lust of the eyes. The tree, pleasant to the eyes.

   (c) Temptation to the **spirit** - the pride of life. You will be as gods knowing both good and evil. It was a tree to be desired to make one wise.

   Thus man in his triune being was tempted according to the three things mentioned in 1John 2:15-17. When man fell in body, soul and spirit, he committed sins of the body, sins of the soul and sins of the spirit. It produced total depravity.

2. **Tempted to Lust, Pride and Self-will**

   When Satan (Lucifer) fell as an angelic being, his temptation was within himself. Sin began in him when he became lifted up in pride, while beholding his God-given attributes and ministry. Thinking more highly of himself than he should, he coveted God's position and set his will against God's will in rebellion.

   The beginning of sin in man was different in that temptation to sin came to him from without. Satan, the serpent, appealed first to the external part of man's being, enticing him to covet what was not rightfully his. This lust (unlawful desire) led to pride, and pride led to self-will against God's will. For Lucifer it was pride, lust and self-will while for man it was lust, pride and self-will.

   (a) **Lust** - The serpent's temptations were aimed at God-given instincts within man. Satan always seeks to exploit these basic laws of man's being. God has given man five basic instincts, which are as follows:

      1. The Law of **Self-Preservation:** enabling man to take care of himself.

      2. The Law of **Self-Acquisition:** enables man to acquire the necessities of self-support.

      3. The Law of **Self-Sustenance:** the food seeking instinct.

      4. The Law of **Self-Propagation:** the sex instinct by which man can be fruitful and multiply in the earth.

5   The Law of **Self-Assertion:** whereby man can subdue and have dominion over the earth.

Satan's initial temptation was aimed at the body when he showed the woman that the tree was good for food. It was an appeal to the desire of the flesh which was a God-given and lawful appetite. This desire could be satisfied on any other tree but not the fruit of the tree of the knowledge of good and evil. The temptation therefore was designed to make man covet or lust for the forbidden fruit (Exodus 20:17; Romans 7:7). The temptation was an exploitation or perversion of a God-given instinct, a law of man's very being. The serpent kept enticing the woman to break God's one commandment.

(b) **Pride** - The temptation also involved that which arises out of inordinate desire, even pride. Satan's statement, "Ye shall be as gods, knowing good and evil" was an appeal to the ego. It was an appeal to pride, exploiting the law of self-assertion. Lucifer himself desired to be "like the Most High", to be as God, and now his appeal to the man was to be "as Gods". The temptation appealed to man to gain wisdom and knowledge which he did not have and which was forbidden by the law of God.

(c) **Self-will** - Enticed by the serpent's appeal, the final step was an independant and deliberate act of the will. This was the whole purpose of Satan's temptation. Though all temptation is aimed at spirit, soul and body (or the "all points" of man's being), the act of sin being self-will, Satan's aim was to get to the will of man. He wanted to get man to exercise self-will against God's will, to exercise his will independantly of God. Satan fell through self-will and so did Adam.

Thus man exercised his free will; he made the choice to disobey God's will. God's law and God's word is His will and His will is His word. His word is also law. Man chose to be independant of God, to be selfish, to be a law to himself, to deify himself, to follow self-will and thus chose death for himself and for the entire unborn human race as yet in his loins (Romans 5:12-21; Psalm 51:5; Romans 7:14-24). Adam did not originate sin but fell into it by a deliberate choice. There was a response in him to the principle of sin. The seat of sin is in the will.

3.   Tempted in Relation to the Law

Another important thing to observe in the temptation in Eden, as well as in temptation ever since, was the attack on the law-word of God. The one prohibition given by God to man in Genesis 2:17 was God's law, command, word and will. The temptation was a direct attack by the Devil, the "lawless one", on the law of God that man was placed under. To break that one law was to break all laws, as is stated in James 2:10. "For whosoever shall keep the whole law, and yet offend in one point, he is guilty of all". Adam sinned when he and his wife transgressed the one law. As I John 3:4 declares, "Sin is transgression of the law".

The serpent had to undermine God's law to lead man to exercise self-will. He had to attack that law-word before he could entice the man to transgress it. We note the successive steps in this attack on the law-word.

* The serpent put a doubt into the mind of the woman concerning the law-word of God. He questioned, "Hath God said?" It was a doubt as to the authority of the spoken word. Doubt is the beginning of unbelief.

* The woman added to the word by saying that they were not to "touch" the tree.

* The woman also adulterated the word by watering it down, taking away its full effect, when she said "lest we die" (Compare Genesis 3:2 with 2:17).

* The serpent lied against the word by saying, "ye shall not surely die".

* The serpent slandered the word by attacking God's intentions, suggesting that He was withholding from them the privilege of beings "as gods to know good and evil".

* The woman was then deceived and believed the lie of Satan instead of the word of God, thus falling from faith to unbelief (1Timothy 2:13-15). Adam sinned knowingly. He was not deceived, therefore this sin was charged to the man as the seed-bearer of the entire human race (Romans 5:12-21).

D. The Fall of Man And Its Effects

Adam's sin was a deliberate act of the will against a given law. It was high treason against God and open rebellion. Not only did the Fall affect Adam, but all of his unborn descendants. We outline the immediate and far-reaching effects of the Fall.

1. **Immediate Effects of the Fall**

    (a) **Forfeited Purity** - Genesis 3:7 with 2:25. "They knew they were naked". A sense of shame fell upon Adam and Eve after their disobedience. Undoubtedly they were clothed with garments of light before the Fall (cf. Psalm 104:2). Those redeemed from the Fall will have a glorified body like Christ's in eternity which will be a Divine covering for the spirit (Philippians 3:21; 2Corinthians 5:1-5).

    (b) **Knowledge of Good and Evil** - A dual knowledge of good and evil entered their minds, but though they knew good and evil, they could only do the evil (Romans 7:18-24). It is interesting to note that the tree of the knowledge of good and evil found in Genesis is not found in Revelation, but the tree of eternal life is there restored through Christ.

    (c) **Law of Conscience at Work** - The moment man sinned, the law of his conscience began to work, "their thoughts the mean while excusing or else accusing" them (Romans 2:14-15). Conscience produced guilt.

    (d) **The Law of Works** - A guilty conscience drove them to works, to make themselves presentable to God in the cool of the evening. They sewed fig leaves together as aprons to cover themselves (Genesis 3:7).

    (e) **The Fear of God** - Sin and their guilty conscience drove them to hide themselves from the presence of God. Sin brought fear instead of love. When God came, they hid themselves among the trees of the Garden (Genesis 3:8).

(f) **The Blame of Others** - When the Lord came on the scene and called them, Adam and Eve were in hiding. God sought a confession of sin from them. However, each blamed other than themselves for their sin. Adam indirectly blamed God: "The woman You gave me ..." Adam also blamed the woman: "The woman gave me to eat ..." The woman blamed the serpent: "The serpent beguiled me and I did eat ..." This was an endeavour to balance out their guilt by blaming others (Genesis 3:9-13).

(g) **Man's Nature Corrupted** - When sin entered man, it corrupted his entire human nature; spirit, soul and body. Man became totally depraved.

> (1) **Man's spirit** - the lamp of the Lord was thrown into darkness, losing its contact with God (Proverbs 20:27).
>
> (2) **Man's soul** - the soul and faculties of mind, will and emotion, were also affected. The mind became self-centered, the emotions uncontrolled and the will bent away from God's will (Ephesians 2:1-3,4,17-19; 2Timothy 2:25-27; Genesis 6:5-12; Romans 1:18-31; 8:7-8).Sin brought moral and mental discord. Man's affections were defiled (Titus 1:15).
>
> (3) **Man's body** - the body with its senses became subject to perverted instincts, sickness, disease and death.

Instead of God's order being spirit, soul and body, it was reversed so that man's body and soul controlled his spirit. He now had the sin-principle operating in his being. Sin is an intrusion into man's nature and was never meant to be there, which explains why man seeks to be rid of it. It should be remembered that sin is not a physical thing, but a spiritual law, though expressed physically (Galatians 5:19-21; Romans 8:7; Mark 7:21-23; Genesis 6:5; Jeremiah 17:9). Sin as a spiritual law within man desires expression in sins of the spirit, sins of the soul and sins of the flesh.

It should be noted also that the seven-fold immediate effects of the Fall are included in the long-range effects on the fall of all mankind.

2. **The Long-Range Effects of the Fall**

The full effects of the Fall were not evidenced immediately in Adam and Eve but were to follow in his offspring, the human race. We summarize under two headings the long-range effects of the Fall upon mankind.

(a) **Sin passed upon all men** - Romans 5:12 clearly explains that by one man sin entered the world and all have sinned in Adam. When Adam sinned, all men sinned, for they were as yet in his loins. All were made or constituted sinners in Adam as the federal head and representative of the entire human race (Romans 5:19). In this sense, sin is both hereditary and universal. All of Adam's posterity are born in sin. All are born with sinful and depraved natures. Thus all need to be born again.

Romans 3:23. "All have sinned and come short of the glory of God". Read also Romans 3:9-18; Psalm 53:1-3; 1Kings 8:46; Galatians 3:22; Isaiah 53:6; Romans

5:12. All have gone astray. All are disobedient. (Read also these Scriptures: Psalm 124:1-3; Jeremiah 17:9;; Mark 7:21-23; Matthew 15:18-20; Isaiah 1:5-6; Psalm 51:5; Job 14:4; Ephesians 2:1-5; 1John 1:8-10; 5:19; Romans 6:17; 7:14; 1John 3:8-10; John 8:44).

Adam sold his unborn generations into slavery in Satan's kingdom of darkness, and all became children of the Devil. They all came under the curse of the law (Galatians 3:10). Though all sin is primarily against God (Psalm 51:4), Adam also sinned against the entire human race. His breaking the law brought all mankind under the wrath of God (Romans 4:15).

Man became a sinner both in original and actual sin. Original sin is inherited from Adam. Actual sin is that which man commits. Because man is sinful in nature, he is also sinful in acts. He does what he does because of what he is. He is not a sinner because he sins, but sins because he is a sinner. Man is also accountable to God for his sins, though not the sins of his fathers (Jeremiah 31:29-30; Ezekiel 11:21; 18:4,20).

The progression of sin as seen both in Lucifer and Adam became active in man. As sin began in Lucifer from within, pride leading to lust and self-will, and began in Adam from without, lust leading to pride and self-will, so man is now subject to sin coming both from within and without. In that fallen man now has self-centeredness and pride resident within him, he has lusts that arise within him and lead him to exalt his will against God's will. This is similar to the progression in Lucifer's fall. But, having the nature of Adam, man is also subject to lusts being stirred up from without that cause him to rise up in pride and set his will against God's good and perfect will.

(b) **Death passed upon all men** - As sin entered the world by one man, so also the penalty of sin. This penalty is death (Romans 5:12-21; Genesis 2:17; Romans 6:23). All sinned and all died "in Adam", the father and representative of the human race (1Corinthians 15:21-23,45-50). Death was also foreign to man. Man was created with a capacity for immortality and did not need to die. The tree of life was available to man but as sin became universal, so also did death (Genesis 3:22).

3. **Divine Judgment Pronounced and Executed**

There was a sixfold judgment pronounced and executed by God with the entrance of sin.

(a) **Judgment on the Serpent** - The serpent was cursed with an irrevocable curse. In the midst of this pronouncement, the promise of Messianic deliverance was given. The Seed of the woman would bring about the crushing of the serpent's head in due time (Romans 16:20; Luke 10:18; Genesis 3:14-15; Revelation 20:11-15).

(b) **Judgment on the Woman** - Sorrow and pain in childbearing under the headship of the husband was the judgment pronounced on the woman (Genesis 3:16 with 1Timothy 2:13-15).

(c) **Judgment on the Man** - The judgment pronounced on the man was that he would sweat in toil to earn his sustenance until death overtook him (Genesis 3:17-18).

(d) **Judgment on the Earth** - The earth was cursed with thorns and thistles. Instead of all the earth being as a Garden of Eden, it came under the curse (Genesis 3:17-18 with 2:4-6,15). This also affected the animal creation which became wild, hostile and rebellious against man's dominion.

(e) **Judgment on Sin by Death** - Romans 6:23 declares: "The wages of sin is death" (James 1:15; Jeremiah 31:30; Ezekiel 18:20). God said to Adam, "In the day you sin you will surely die". Or more literally, "In dying thou shalt die" (Genesis 2:17). The death penalty touches three areas relative to man, these being:

   (1) **Physical Death** - separation of the spirit from the body. Death began in Adam's body the moment he sinned and consummated 930 years later (Ecclesiastes 12:7; Genesis 2:17; Numbers 16:29; 27:3; Psalms 90:7-11).

   (2) **Spiritual Death** - separation of the spirit from God. This speaks of man dead in trespasses and sins, out of fellowship with God (John 5:24; Romans 8:6; Ephesians 2:11,5; 1Timothy 5:6; Romans 5:12-21).

   (3) **Eternal Death** - separation of spirit and soul from God for all eternity in the lake of fire. Death is not cessation of existence, nor annihilation, but eternal separation from God because of sin (Matthew 25:41; 10:28; 2Thessalonians 1:9; Hebrews 10:31; Revelation 14:11; 20:11-15).

(f) **Judgment by Expulsion from Eden** - The final act of God in the Genesis account was to provide a substitutionary covering by death of an innocent victim, and then drive man out of the Garden of Eden. At the gate of Eden, God placed Cherubim and a flaming sword, which turned every way to keep man from the tree of eternal life. Here He placed a manifestation of His presence where man could come for worship and sacrifice. In due time Christ would come, deal with sin, and open Paradise again, thus restoring the tree of life to man (Revelation 2:7; 22:14). Sin separated man from God (Isaiah 59:2), and must be judged before perfect fellowship between God and man can be restored.

E. The Ruined Man

In Jeremiah 18:1-6 we have, what can be used, a picture of what happened to God's original man.

The Lord told Jeremiah to go down to the potter's house and hear His words there. The potter was working a vessel on the wheels. But the vessel became marred in the potter's hands and he had to make it again another vessel. The Lord told the nation of Israel that they were like that clay in the potters hand and He could make them again another vessel.

What a picture of ruined man. God, the great Potter, made man to be His vessel, to bear His image and glory. But through sin, man became marred in the Potter's hand. Now God, the great Potter, has to make man another vessel - that is, if man will be responsive clay in His hand. Sin has marred the man God made. The Fall brought about a ruined man, a ruined creation.

Now God will come in redemption to remake the marred vessel. We see how the Fall and the entrance of sin frustrated God's original fourfold purpose for man. With relationship to this fourfold purpose and the entrance of sin we see the tragic effect.

In Summary:

1. **Broken Fellowship** - Fellowship was broken, relationship was destroyed. Sin caused man to hide from the God he once knew and loved and fellowshipped. It is sin that hinders relationship, fellowship and intimacy with God.

2. **Marred Character** - Man's character was marred by the entrance of sin. The image of God in man is a marred image. Sinfulness, unrighteousness, hatred and all kinds of evil came into man's being when the seed of sin entered him. The image and likeness of God is stained by sin.

3. **Lost Dominion** - Man lost his authority, his dominion, his rulership with the entrance of sin. Instead of ruling over creation, he became ruled over by sin and Satan, sickness and death.

4. **Sinful Fruitfulness** - Man's offspring was affected by sin. Instead of sinless offspring, Adam and Eve produced sinful offspring. The seed of sin in Adam was manifested in Cain, his firstborn son. All mankind is born in sin and so death reigns over all. Instead of reproducing after the image and likeness of God, Adam begat a son after his image and likeness - that is, a fallen, marred and sinful image (Genesis 5:1-3).

In the light of the content of this chapter, with the entrance of sin and man's fallen and ruined condition, there certainly was the NEED FOR RESTORATION!

(**Note:-** Material in this chapter adapted from "**The Foundations of Christian Doctrine**", **pages 145-150**, by Kevin J. Conner).

CHAPTER NINE

THE COVENANT OF RESTORATION AND REDEMPTION

The entrance of sin and its tragic results in Adam and mankind through Adam's sin shows the great need of restoration. Man's restoration can only come through redemption.

A. The Need of Restoration

As mentioned previously, what happened to earth is a picture of what happened to man, as the following comparison clearly shows.

EARTH	MAN
1. Earth created by God	1. Man is created by God
2. Earth created for a purpose To be inhabited	2. Man created for a purpose To be indwelt by God
3. Earth became a waste, ruin, and emptiness	3. Man became a waste, ruin, and emptiness
4. Darkness on face of the deep	4. Darkness on man's deep within
5. Entrance of sin and chaos	5. Entrance of sin and resultant chaos
6. The need of restoration	6. The need of restoration by redemption.

B. The Covenant of Redemption

The Bible is a Book of Redemption. From the Fall of man and the entrance of sin, God is seen coming in redemptive grace to restore man to that from which he fell in Adam. The shadow of this restoration through redemption is seen in Genesis 3 in the experience of Adam and Eve. It is the first covenant of redemption that God made, that is, the Adamic Covenant. Restoration through redemption is all on the basis of covenant. It is through covenant God will work to restore man back to His fourfold purpose.

But there are several things that are required to make a covenant valid: that is, Terms, Sacrifice, Priesthood and Sanctuary (Hebrews 8:1-6).

1. The Terms of the Covenant

Because man had fallen from obedience of the Edenic Covenant, the covenant of creation, God now seeks to restore man back to that obedience through the Adamic Covenant, which as noted, is the first covenant of redemption. Adam's disobedience was the result of unbelief in the penalty word of God. The emphasis therefore is a return to faith and obedience (Hebrews 11:6; Romans 14:23; John 16:8). Andrew Murray wrote words to the effect that "Christ died to bring man back to the obedience from which he fell". Faith and obedience are the terms of the covenant.

It is evident that Adam and Eve accepted God's redemptive work and their faith is seen in:

(a) Adam's naming Eve as "the mother of all living" or "the mother of the living one" (Genesis 3:15,16,20). It was an act of faith as Eve had brought death along with Adam in eating of the forbidden fruit.

(b) Adam and Eve receiving the coats of skin in exchange for their self-made covering of fig leaves (Genesis 3:21; Isaiah 64:6). They could have rejected the coats of skin provided by the death of a substitute victim and held on to their fig-leaf covering of their own works, seeking to make themselves presentable to God.

(c) Eve's response of faith in naming Cain at his birth (Genesis 3:15; 4:1). She thought that Cain was the expected and promised "seed" that would bruise the serpent's head. Even though this was not so, there was Eve's faith in the promise.

(d) Adam's communication concerning the approach to God in faith through blood and body sacrifices as given to his children, Cain and Abel (Genesis 4:1-4; Hebrews 11:4; 1John 3:12).

All these things were evidence of Adam and Eve's faith in God's promise of restoration through redemption.

2. The Sacrifice of the Covenant

After Adam and Eve fell from covenantal relationship and their conscience was awakened and smitten with guilt, as already seen, they sought to cover their sin and make themselves acceptable to God and to each other. The law of conscience drove them to the law of works (Romans 5:12-14; 3:27). These man-made fig leaves were their own attempt to cover themselves and make themselves righteous before God. God, however, judged this self-righteousness. It was God who then moved in grace to deal with man's sin and provide an acceptable covering.

Because man had broken the Edenic Covenant and was under the death penalty, death had to take place in order for his sin to be covered. God introduced a substitutionary sacrificial death in order to cover for man's sinfulness. This is confirmed in the coats of skin with which God clothed them. They were the evidence that death had taken place, and Adam and Eve were clothed in the death of another. The coats of skin came from a slain innocent animal. Thus, based upon substitutionary body and blood sacrifice, Adam and Eve were redeemed.

The innocent died for the guilty, and the sinless animal was sacrificed for sinful man. This covenant sacrifice was the first of all animal sacrifices that pointed to the New Covenant sacrifice, the body and blood of the Lord Jesus Christ (John 1:29,36; Hebrews 10:1-12).

3. The Mediator of the Covenant

It is evident from Genesis 3:21 that God Himself acted as mediator of this covenant. He slew the animals. He made the coats of skin. He clothed Adam and Eve with them. Although the Creatorship name of God (Elohim) was used in relation to the Edenic Covenant of creation before the entrance of sin, it is the redemptive name of Lord (Jehovah) that is used in relation to the Adamic Covenant of redemption after the entrance of sin. The name belonging to the covenant is "the **LORD GOD**", which embodied in itself both creation and redemption (Genesis 3:14,21,22,23).

Further Scripture reveals that the mediatorial person in the Godhead is the Lord Jesus Christ, all of which is shadowed forth here (Hebrews 9:15; 1Timothy 2:5; Hebrews 12:24).

The scene here also initiated the development of the Patriarchal priesthood. As the Lord God demonstrated His own priesthood on Adam's behalf, He set an example for Adam to follow in being the priest of his own household. This was later substantiated in that the Levitical priesthood, under the Mosaic Covenant, were given the coats of skin of certain animal sacrifices (Leviticus 7:8). Patriarchal priesthood was also seen in Job's priesthood on behalf of his own family and household (Job 1:1-5).

4. **The Sanctuary of the Covenant**

   The place where the covenant of redemption was given, the sacrifice made, and the mediatorial work of the covenantors fulfilled was the Garden of Eden. However, the focus in Genesis 3:21-24 seems to be on the place at the east of the Garden of Eden. The revelation of the sanctuary (or "Tabernacle") under the Mosaic Covenant confirms the sanctuary language of the Adamic Covenant. This is seen in the following:

   (a) God **placed** (Hebrew "caused to dwell") His presence (Genesis 3:24; 4:16 with Exodus 25:8) there at Eden.

   (b) This place was at the **east** (Genesis 3:24 with Leviticus 16:14; Ezekiel 43:1-4).

   (c) The **Cherubim** were placed there as guardians (Genesis 3:24 with Exodus 25:17-22).

   (d) A **flaming sword** was placed there also to keep the way to the tree of life (Genesis 3:24; Exodus 26:33).

   (e) This was the most suitable place for Cain and Abel to bring their **offerings** to the Lord (Genesis 4:1-4; Hebrews 12:4).

   The gate of Eden and the manifest presence of God in the Cherubim and the flaming sword constituted the sanctuary of the Lord for some time. Those of Adam's loins would come in faith and obedience with their sacrifices and know, in measure, the restoration to fellowship with the Lord through redemption.

   Having forfeited the tree of eternal life from the Edenic Covenant, Adam and Eve receive the coats of skin as tokens of their faith in the atoning sacrifice of the Adamic Covenant. Such pointed to the faith-righteousness that the Holy Spirit would bring to the New Covenant believer who accepts the body and blood of the Lord Jesus Christ (Isaiah 61:10; Romans 4:1-5).

(**Note:-** For fuller details, the reader is referred to "**The Covenants**" by Conner/Malmin).

C. The Redeemer and Restorer

The greatest promise of the Adamic Covenant was the promise of the "**seed of the woman**" that would bruise the serpent's head (Genesis 3:15).

In this verse we see two "seed-lines", and "two bruisings". There would be "the seed of the woman" and "the seed of the serpent". The seed of the serpent would bruise the heel of the seed of the woman. The seed of the woman would bruise the serpent's head.

The seed of the serpent pointed to the ungodly line. The seed of the woman pointed to the godly line. Within the promise was the enigmatic prophecy of the Redeemer, the Lord Jesus Christ, who would be the **restorer of man and redeemer of man** and give to him all that was lost in the Fall.

It was not "the seed of Adam", for all of Adam's seed or offspring would be born in sin, and shapen in iniquity and need redemption themselves. Adam was the seed bearer and no son of Adam could redeem or be the deliverer seed. It would be "the seed of the woman". The prophecy implied that the woman would bring forth a seed, apart from the aid of man, or apart from human instrumentality. It would be a supernatural act. It implied the virgin birth of the Christ-child, the absolute "new creation". This seed was to be the Redeemer, the one who would buy man back from Satan's kingdom. It would be the God-Man who would bring deliverance and restore man back to the image of God.

Many promises and prophecies were fulfilled in the virgin birth of Christ (Isaiah 7:14; 9:6-9; Matthew 1:18-25; Luke 2:1-20).

Jesus would be the **Redeemer**. He would be the **Repairer of the Breach** that sin had brought between God and man. He would be "the **restorer** of the paths to dwell in", from which man had turned astray (Isaiah 58:12). This was the whole purpose of the cross; Christ's death, burial and resurrection (Isaiah 53).

D. The Restored and Redeemed Man

All that was lost in Adam is now restored through Christ our redeemer. This is available for all mankind who will come in faith and obedience to God through Christ and the New Covenant.

1. Restored Fellowship

Through Christ man can be restored to fellowship, to relationship with the Father God (1John 1:3-6). As man walks in redemptive light, the blood of Jesus cleanses from all sin. There is fellowship with the Father, the Son and all other believers (2Corinthians 13:14). This is by the power of the indwelling Holy Spirit (John 17:16-20,23).

2. Restored Character

Through Christ, man can and will be restored to the character, the image and likeness of God, which was marred by sin. God's purpose is to conform the redeemed man to the image of His Son (Romans 8:28-29). In the new birth, believers become partakers of the Divine nature, being born again of the incorruptible seed, which is the Word of God (2Peter 1:4-7; 1Peter 1:23; John 3:1-5). It is by the Spirit of God that we shall be changed into the same image and likeness, from glory to glory (2Corinthians 3:19; 4:4).

3. Restored Dominion

Through Christ man can be restored to the dominion and rulership which he lost. The serpent will be subdued, his head will be bruised under our feet because of Calvary (Romans 16:20).

4. Restored Fruitfulness

Through Christ man can see his offspring come to God by redemption. The Lord has given promises of salvation for Adam's fallen race, Though born in sin and iniquity, all can be born again, born from above. There are promises of household salvation. Adam's race, affected by sin, can come to repentance and faith-righteousness by Christ and His redeeming blood (Romans 5:12-21). Man can also know a fruitful life in Christ, fruit unto righteousness, and the fruit of the Spirit, the Divine nature and character manifest in his whole being (1Thessalonians 5:23-24).

All that was lost in Adam can be and will be restored in Christ. Jesus is the Way, the Truth and the Life (John 14:6). In Adam we lost the way, the truth and the life but in Christ all is restored. This is the message of restoration through redemption of the fallen man.

The Adamic Covenant is a "seed" covenant which introduces the covenants of redemption that are to follow, consummating in the New Covenant. Jesus Christ as the seed of the woman fulfills this covenant in redeeming man back to perfect and eternal covenantal relationship with God.

In Conclusion:-

Restoration is only possible for mankind through redemption. Unless men and women come to repentance and faith in God through Christ, there will be no restoration. None can by-pass God's redeemer. Man can only be restored to God on His terms. There is no other way. This truth refutes the false doctrine and heresy of "Universalism".

At the beginning of this chapter, it was seen how earth and man follow, as it were, a similar pattern. Just as earth needed restoration in creation, so fallen man needed restoration, but this could only be through redemption. There could be no restoration without redemption. The following analogy continues between earth and man, and this certainly foreshadows restoration and redemption.

EARTH	MAN
1. The Spirit of God moved on the waters	The Spirit of God moved over mankind
2. God's Word brought light	Kingdoms of Light and Darkness divided
3. Light called Day, Darkness, Night	Children of the Day, Children of Night
4. A restored earth	A restored and redeemed mankind

The cycle is complete: From the creation of man, to the ruin of man, and ultimately to the restoration of man through redemption! Creation rises and falls with the man God created. As man rises through redemption, so creation will also experience restoration!

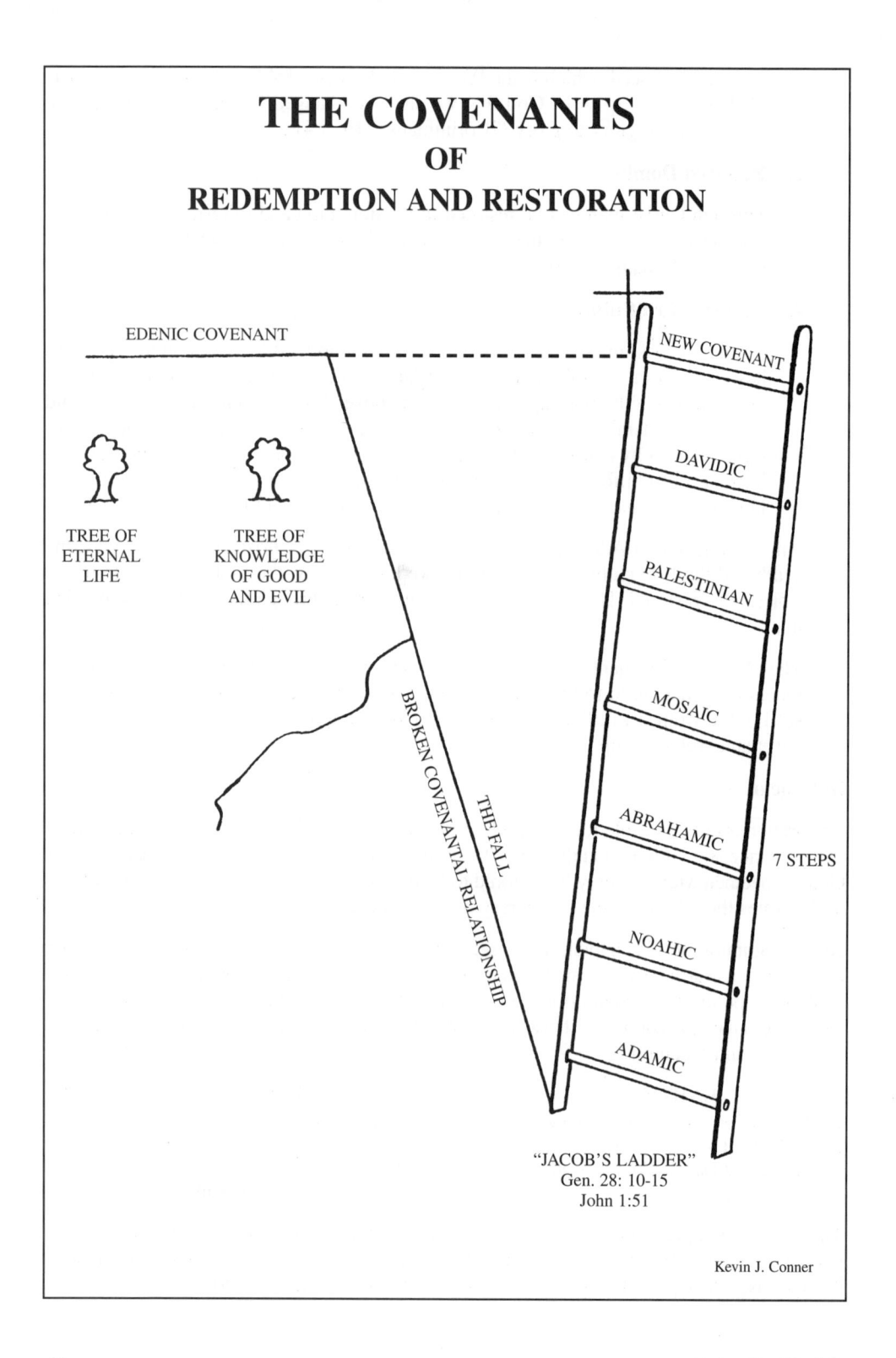

THE COVENANTS
OF
REDEMPTION AND RESTORATION

EDENIC COVENANT

NEW COVENANT

TREE OF ETERNAL LIFE

TREE OF KNOWLEDGE OF GOOD AND EVIL

DAVIDIC

PALESTINIAN

MOSAIC

ABRAHAMIC

7 STEPS

NOAHIC

ADAMIC

BROKEN COVENANTAL RELATIONSHIP

THE FALL

"JACOB'S LADDER"
Gen. 28: 10-15
John 1:51

Kevin J. Conner

PART FOUR

THE NATION OF ISRAEL

CHAPTER TEN

THE ABRAHAMIC COVENANT AND ISRAEL

An area of great controversy, confusion and misunderstanding is that which pertains to natural and natural Israel. The question arises: What about Israel, the chosen nation? What about the Jew? What about the promises of restoration concerning Israel? Some of these things were referred to in brief in an earlier chapter. Further details, within appropriate limits, will be covered in this and the next chapter.

In dealing with the subject of the restoration of natural and national Israel, such can only be dealt with in relation to covenant.

When it comes to the nation of Israel, there are five particular covenants involved, these being; the Abrahamic Covenant, the Mosaic Covenant, the Palestinian Covenant, the Davidic Covenant and the New Covenant. (The reader is referred to the textbook "The Covenants", by Conner/Malmin for fuller details which can only be dealt with in these chapters within the limits of the truth of restoration).

It will be seen that the Abrahamic Covenant is actually the most comprehensive of all covenants, including in itself the four other covenants mentioned.

A. The Abrahamic Covenant

It all began with Abraham, continued on through Isaac, and then Jacob and then on to the nation of Israel. This covenant was not only made with Abraham, but its oath was given to Isaac, and it was confirmed to Jacob, and then Israel afterwards (1Chronicles 16:15-17). These three fathers were together partakers of the one covenant, even as the three Persons in the Godhead are partakers of the one covenant (Exodus 2:24; 3:6,15). The covenant as given to these three fathers and to Israel is stated in the following passages of Scripture. These Scriptures should be read as they are too vast to be spelt out in full in this text.

1. To Abraham

Genesis 12:1-3; 13:14-18; 15:1-21; 17:1-27; 18:17-19; 21:12; 22:1-18. God gave a number of promises to Abraham here, the father of the chosen nation as well as the father of all who believe.

2. To Isaac

The promises were confirmed by God to Isaac, the Old Testament only begotten son. Read Genesis 24:60; 26:1-5,24.

3. To Jacob

The promises were also confirmed to Jacob, the third person of this trinity of men. Read Genesis 27:28-29; 28:1-4,13-22; 32:12,28; 35:10-12; 48:3-4.

B. The Promises of the Covenant

There were a number of promises God gave to Abraham in the covenant and these were also confirmed to Isaac, Jacob and then to the nation of Israel.

1. **The Personal Blessing (Genesis 12:2).**

   "I will bless thee", is God's personal blessing on Abraham. The promise was confirmed to Isaac (Genesis 26:1-5), to Jacob (Genesis 28:3) and to Israel (Deuteronomy 28:1-14).

   God blessed Abraham through Melchisedek and the communion (Genesis 14:19-20). God blessed Abraham with material prosperity (Genesis 13:2; 24:1,35). God blessed Abraham physically (Romans 4:17-21).

   This blessing was also fulfilled in the lives of Isaac (Genesis 26:12-14), Jacob (Genesis 30), and in Israel (Deuteronomy 8:18).

2. **The Blessing of Others (Genesis 12:2)**

   "I will make you a blessing", God also said to Abraham. The very purpose of God blessing Abraham personally was that he would be a blessing to others. This promise was confirmed to Isaac, Jacob and Israel. This was fulfilled in:

   * Abraham's own household being blessed (Genesis 14:14;18:19;24:35).
   * Abraham's blessing to Lot in the choice of land and his rescue of Lot from Sodom's destruction through his intercession (Genesis 13:5-9; 14:1-16; 18:16-33).
   * The blessing of healing of the Gentile Abimelech's household (Genesis 20:17).
   * The blessing of covenant relationship with a Gentile king of the Philistines (Genesis 21:22-32).

   The same promises of blessing are fulfilled in the lives of Isaac and Jacob (Genesis 30:27) as well as the nation of Israel (Deuteronomy 28:1-14).

3. **The Blessing by Others (Genesis 12:3)**

   "I will bless them that bless thee" was another promise God gave to Abraham. As a confirmation of His blessing, God promised to bless those who blessed Abraham. This promise was also confirmed to Isaac (Genesis 26:12-33), Jacob (Genesis 30:25-43) and Israel (Numbers 24:9).

   This is seen in the blessing of Rebekah's family for responding to the request of Abraham for a bride for his only son, Isaac (Genesis 24:51-53).

   This was also fulfilled in Isaac (Genesis 26), Jacob (Genesis 29,30,31) and the nation of Israel (Deuteronomy 27,28).

4. **The Blessing of Messiah (Genesis 12:3; 22:17-18).**

   God also promised Abraham, "in thee shall all the families of the earth be blessed". This was the greatest promise of blessing; that through Abraham all the nations of the earth would be blessed. This promise involved the birth of the seed, Jesus the Messiah. This was fulfilled in the New Covenant, which is the greatest promise in the Abrahamic Covenant.

This was confirmed to Isaac (Genesis 26:4), to Jacob (Genesis 28:14), to Judah (Genesis 49:8-12), and to Israel (Numbers 24:17), and finally to David (2Samuel 7; Psalm 89, 132).

It was fulfilled in Christ, who is the seed of Abraham, Isaac, Jacob and Judah as well as Israel and then through David. This was "the gospel preached to Abraham" (Galatians 3:8,16,29; Matthew 1:1; Romans 1:3; 16:20; Genesis 3:15).

5. The Blessing of a Great Name (Genesis 12:2)

God also promised "I will make your name great ..." This was fulfilled in:

* The blessing of the new name change from Abram to Abraham given at the time of the circumcision (Genesis 17:5; Acts 7:8).

* The blessing of a good reputation (Genesis 24:35).

* The blessing of association with God, as "the God of Abraham, the God of Isaac and the God of Jacob" (Genesis 24:12; 26:24; 28:13; Exodus 2:15; Mark 12:26-27).

* The blessing of many nations who would revere his name (John 8). These are three major religious groupings that honour the name of Abraham: Islam, Judaism and Christianity.

* The blessing of a name of faith as "the father of all who believe" whether Jew or Gentile (Romans 4:11-16).

6. The Blessing of Multiplicity of Seed (Genesis 22:17-18)

The blessing of multiplicity of seed was given progressively through the years to Abraham and Sarah, and Isaac and Rebekah, to Jacob and to Joseph's sons.

* To Abraham - Genesis 12:2. His seed would be as the dust of the earth (Genesis 13:16), and as the stars of heaven (Genesis 15:5). Abraham would be a father of many nations (Genesis 17:4-8). His seed would be as innumerable as the stars and the sand (Genesis 22:17-18).

* To Sarah - Genesis 17:16. Sarah would be a mother of nations.

* To Isaac - Genesis 26:4. His seed would be as the stars of heaven.

* To Rebekah - Genesis 24:60. To be a mother of thousands of children.

* To Jacob - His seed would be as the dust of the earth (Genesis 28:14), and as the sand of the sea (Genesis 32:12). A nation and company of nations would come of his loins (Genesis 35:11).

* To Joseph -Genesis 48:4. Fruitfulness and a multitude of people to come.

* To Ephraim and Manasseh - Genesis 48:16,19. Together they would grow as a multitude in the earth, then Ephraim and Manasseh would become a nation and a company of nations in the earth.

*   To Israel - Exodus 19:6. Israel would be a holy nation, and would multiply in the land (Leviticus 26:9). Israel would be blessed above all peoples (Deuteronomy 7:12-14), and would be as numberless as the sands of the seashore (Hosea 2:10).

The promises of multiplicity of seed to Abraham find fulfilment in Hagar and Ishmael; that is, predominantly the Arab nations (Genesis 21:13,18; 25:12-18). Further fulfilment is found in Israel and Judah, the chosen nations through Isaac and Jacob (Ezekiel 37:15-28). Then again, further fulfilment is seen in the nations that come from Abraham's sons of Keturah after Sarah died (Genesis 25:1-4,6).

7. The Blessing of Land

If there is seed, then there must be land in which the seed needs to dwell. God promised land to Abraham, Isaac and Jacob and Israel as the following Scriptures show. God set the bounds of the other nations according to the number of the children of Israel (Deuteronomy 32:8,9; Acts 17:26).

*   To Abraham - God promised to show him a land (Genesis 12:1,7). God would give him and his seed the land for ever (Genesis 13:14-18). The land would extend from the river Euphrates to Egypt (Genesis 15:7-21). The land of Canaan would be an everlasting possession (Genesis 17:7,8).

*   To Isaac - "All those countries" were promised also to Isaac and his seed (Genesis 26:2-4).

*   To Jacob - His seed would spread abroad north, south, east and west (Genesis 28:13-15). Land would be needed for the nation and the company of nations (Genesis 48:15-20). Canaan land would be given to his seed for an everlasting possession (Genesis 48:3-4).

The land promises find their fulfilment in Israel conquering Canaan (Joshua to David; Joshua 1-24; 1Kings 4:20-25; 2Chronicles 9:16). The Palestinian Covenant was placed alongside the Abrahamic Covenant adding conditions for maintaining possession of the land in blessing.

8. The Blessing of Victory over Enemies

After the typical offering of his only begotten son, Isaac, the Lord promised Abraham that he would "possess the gate of his enemies" (Genesis 22:17). The promise was confirmed to Rebekah (Genesis 24:60), and to Judah (Genesis 49:8-12).

This found fulfilment in:

*   Joshua's conquest of Canaan land and its kings (Joshua 11-12).

*   Judah's leadership in warfare (Judges 1).

*   David's victory over all his enemies (2Samuel 8; 1Chronicles 22:8).

9. The Blessing of Kings

God also promised Abraham and his descendants that kings would come of their loins (Genesis 17:6). It was confirmed to Sarah (Genesis 17:16), to Jacob (Genesis 35:11), to Judah (Genesis 49:8-12), to Israel (Deuteronomy 17:14-20; Numbers 23:21), and finally to David (2Samuel 7).

This found fulfilment in:

* The natural seed of Abraham in the kings of Esau/Edom (Genesis 36).

* The chosen natural seed of Abraham in the kings of Judah and Israel (2Chronicles 12:18,19; 14:15-18).

* The Davidic Covenant given later on confirmed this promise of kingship given to Abraham in the Abrahamic Covenant.

10. The Blessing of Divine Relationship

God also promised Abraham that He would be a God to him and to his seed after him (Genesis 17:7,8). This promised blessing was confirmed to Moses (Exodus 6:1-8), and then through the prophets (Jeremiah 24:7; 30:22; 31:31-34; 32:38-40; Ezekiel 11:19,20; 36:25-28). All speaks of relationship with God.

This was fulfilled in:

Old Testament saints who knew God and ultimately New Testament saints who know God through the Lord Jesus Christ and the New Covenant (Hebrew 8:6-13; Revelation 21:3).

As seen in these ten great promises of the Abrahamic Covenant, it was distinctly a covenant of blessing. There was a curse attached to this covenant when God said, "I will curse him that curses thee" (Genesis 12:3). This promise of a curse was confirmed to Isaac (Genesis 27:26-29). Even Balaam recognized that he could not curse the people of Israel whom God had blessed (Numbers 22:6; 23:8; 24:9).

C. The Terms of the Covenant

As seen previously, **faith and obedience** are the terms for receiving the promises of blessing in the covenant. Abraham believed God. He was a man of faith and becomes the father of all who believe (Romans 4:3; Genesis 15:6; Psalm 106:31; Galatians 3:6; Hebrews 11:8-19; Romans 1:17). Abraham obeyed God (Genesis 22:18; 26:5; Hebrews 11:8; James 2:20-24).

Faith and obedience are like two sides of the one and same coin. Faith is evidenced by obedience. Faith and obedience are synonymous, even as unbelief and disobedience are synonymous (Hebrews 4:11). Faith and obedience are God's conditions for receiving the blessings of the covenant.

D. The Oath of the Covenant

The Abrahamic Covenant was confirmed by God's oath thus making it an irrevocable covenant. Note the following Scriptures which speak of the oath of the covenant.

- * The oath to Abraham (Genesis 22:16-18; Hebrews 11:17-19).
- * The oath confirmed to Isaac (Genesis 26:2-5).
- * The oath confirmed to Jacob and Israel (1Chronicles 16:16; Psalm 105:8-10; Deuteronomy 7:8; 29:9-13; Jeremiah 11:5; Micah 7:20; Acts 7:17; Luke 1:72,73).

The Book of Hebrews explains that, when God made promise to Abraham, He confirmed it with an oath, that by two immutable things (God's promise and God's oath), He bound Himself irrevocably to its fulfilment (Hebrews 6:13-18). The promises of the Abrahamic Covenant can never be annulled from God's viewpoint. However, for Israel to receive the blessings of the covenant, it requires faith and obedience - as subsequent history of Israel proved!

E. The Sacrifice of the Covenant

Every valid Biblical Covenant was ratified by sacrifice: the body and blood of some victims. The sacrificial elements of the Abrahamic Covenant were progressively unfolded during Abraham's lifetime.

1. The Communion (Genesis 14:18)

The bread and wine Melchisedek gave to Abraham at the time of blessing pointed to the body and blood of the Lord Jesus Christ (Matthew 26:26-28).

2. The Animal Sacrifices (Genesis 15:7-17)

The five specified offerings offered to God in this chapter pointed to the body and blood of covenant ratification. They shadowed forth the sacrifices of the Mosaic Covenant (Leviticus Chapters 1-7). All find their fulfilment in the once for all perfect sacrifice of the body and blood of the Lord Jesus Christ (Hebrews 10:1-10).

3. The Sacrifice of Isaac (Genesis 22)

God asked Abraham to offer a "human sacrifice"; the sacrifice of his only begotten son, Isaac. After three days journey to Mt Moriah, Abraham offered typically his only son and received him from the dead in a figure (Hebrews 11:17-19; James 2:20-23).

The ram offered as a substitute pointed to the sacrifices of the Law Covenant until the offering up of God's only begotten Son, Jesus, at Calvary. All the sacrifices find their ultimate and final fulfilment in the sacrifice of Christ.

F. The Priesthood of the Covenant

Every covenant needs an officiating priesthood. If there is sacrifice, there must of necessity be a priesthood.

Abraham was of the patriarchal priesthood, following Adam, Noah and Job. The fact that altars of sacrifice were built constituted them as patriarchal priests over their families, their households.

The greater priesthood was when Melchisedek came to Abraham and blessed him. Melchisedek was a king-priest, King of Righteousness and King of Peace. He blessed Abraham with the communion as the priest of the Most High God, the priest of Jerusalem (Genesis 14; Psalm 110; Hebrews 7).

The Levitical and Aaronic priesthood was introduced in due time, but abolished at the cross. The everlasting priesthood finds its fulfilment in the Lord Jesus Christ, who is the priest for ever after the order of Melchisedek.

G. The Sanctuary of the Covenant

Covenant necessitates sacrifice; sacrifice necessitates priesthood; priesthood also necessitates sanctuary.

The patriarchal altars became God's sanctuary where He appeared to them and blessed them (Exodus 20:24-26). Each of the three fathers had their altar to God.

* Abraham's altar was where he called on the name of the Lord (Genesis 12:7,8; 13:1-4, 18; 22:9).

* Isaac's altar was where he called on the name of the Lord (Genesis 26:25).

* Jacob's altar was where he called on the name of the Lord who appeared to him (Genesis 33:20; 35:1-15).

In due time, the altar was incorporated into the Mosaic Covenant economy in the Tabernacle of the Lord (Exodus 27:1-9). The temple of Solomon replaced the Tabernacle in time with its great altar. All, however, found fulfilment in God's sacrificial altar - **THE CROSS** of our Lord Jesus Christ (Hebrews 13:10-16).

H. The Seal of the Covenant

The Abrahamic Covenant was called "the covenant of circumcision" (Acts 7:8). The rite of circumcision is spoken of a token (Genesis 17:11), a seal and a sign (Romans 4:11). It involved the cutting off of the flesh and the shedding of blood (Genesis 17:9-11). The child's name was invoked and this rite was performed on the eighth day (Genesis 21:4; 17:12; Luke 1:59; 2:21).

Without obedience to the rite of circumcision, none of Abraham's seed were entitled to the promises and the privileges and blessings of the Abrahamic Covenant. To reject or neglect this rite would be to break the covenant and to be cut off from its benefits (Genesis 17:14). Circumcision was the outward evidence of their inward commitment to the terms of the covenant.

So important was this rite that God sought to kill Moses, even after his call, because he had neglected to bring his family into covenantal relationship with Himself (Exodus 2:23-25; 3:1-6; 4:24-26). How could Moses deliver Israel on the basis of the Abrahamic Covenant when his own family did not have the seal of that covenant?

For Israel, the rite was so important that none, neither Israelite or stranger, could partake of the Passover lamb unless they had the seal of circumcision (Exodus 12:43-51).

Circumcision finds its fulfilment in the cross of Christ, and then in the circumcision of the heart of the believer in New Covenant relationship with God through Christ (Romans 2:24-29; 4:8-12; Ephesians 2:11-13; Galatians 6:15-16; Colossians 2:11-13).

In Summary:-

The Abrahamic Covenant is the most comprehensive of all covenants. Its promises were fulfilled over the centuries in the history of the chosen nation of Israel. What a blessed and privileged nation Israel was.

However, this did not continue, for the nation went the way of all nations and departed grievously from the Lord and His covenants!

CHAPTER ELEVEN

THE DIVINE PURPOSE IN ISRAEL'S ELECTION

Much has been written on the Abrahamic Covenant. This is because, for Israel, it was the foundational covenant. All other and subsequent covenants arose out of the Abrahamic Covenant. The rest of the covenants in the Bible are actually progressive unfoldings of the Abrahamic Covenant. In this chapter we need to consider more fully God's purpose in the election of Israel as a nation from among the nations.

A. Israel - The Chosen Nation

From the creation of Adam to the tower of Babel (Genesis 1:1-11:19), mankind was one race, speaking one language. The events recorded in Genesis 11 provide us the background for the division of mankind into different nations. The origin of the nations is described in this chapter. Out of these nations God chose a man for Himself and from this man - Abraham - God would bring forth the chosen nation, Israel, for His own purposes.

In the Old Testament, there are two major ethnic divisions: the chosen nation, Israel and the Gentile nations.

As has been seen in the previous chapter, God chose Abraham to be the father of the new ethnic, the chosen nation of Israel. Israel was taken by the Lord as a nation from the midst of the nations and God made them a great nation by giving them His statutes, laws and judgments (Deuteronomy 4:6-8,34). This was in fulfilment of the promise to Abraham that he would be a great nation (Genesis 12:2,3).

It is important, therefore, to understand why, and why not God chose Israel as His elect nation.

1. Not Chosen for Numbers (Deuteronomy 7:6-7).

"For you are a holy people unto the Lord your God: the Lord your God has chosen you to be a special people unto Himself, above all people that are upon the face of the earth. The Lord did not set His love upon you, nor choose you, because you were more in number than any people: for you were the fewest of all people ..." Israel was not chosen because of great numbers.

2. Not Chosen for Righteousness (Deuteronomy 9:4-6)

"Speak not in your heart, after the Lord has cast them out from before you, saying, For my righteousness the Lord has brought me in to possess the land, but for the wickedness of these nations the Lord drove them out from before you. Not for your righteousness, or for the uprightness of your heart, do you go to possess the land, but for the wickedness of these nations the Lord your God does drive them out from before you ... not for your righteousness, for you are a stiff-necked people." Israel was not chosen before of her righteousness, but because of the wickedness of the Canaanite nations.

3. **Chosen because of Divine Love (Deuteronomy 7:8)**

   "But because the Lord loved you…" This was the reason God chose the nation of Israel, it was out of Divine love.

4. **Chosen because of Divine Covenant (Deuteronomy 7:8,9)**

   "… and because He would keep the oath which He had sworn unto your fathers. Know therefore that the Lord your God, He is God, the faithful God, which keeps covenant and mercy with them that love Him and keep His commandments to a thousand generations".

   "… and that He may perform the word which the Lord sware unto your fathers, Abraham, Isaac and Jacob" (Deuteronomy 9:5c). Thus Israel was chosen on the basis of covenant made to the fathers, and because of Divine love. It was **not because of numbers and not because of their own righteousness**!

5. **Chosen to Bless all Nations (Genesis 12:2,3)**

   In Abraham and his seed, all nations would be blessed. This was one of the major reasons for which God elected Israel to be His special treasure (Genesis 17:4-7; 18:18; 22:16-18).

B. **Israel - Chosen to receive Divine Blessings (Romans 9:4,5; 3:2)**

By a careful reading of these Scriptures, we see that Paul lists nine particular blessings which God gave to the chosen nation. Paul showed the things that pertained to Israel. These things were like "**the birthright**" given to Israel as God's "**firstborn son**".

Exodus 4:22-23 "Then say to Pharaoh, This is what the LORD says: Israel is my firstborn son, and I told you, "Let my son go, so he may worship me." But if you refuse to let him go; I will kill your firstborn son."

1. **The Adoption**

   Israel was adopted as God's firstborn son from among the nations (Exodus 4:22-23).

2. **The Shekinah Glory of God**

   The visible manifestation of the glory presence of God as seen in the cloud was also a manifest blessing of God on the nation.

3. **The Covenants**

   Israel was blessed as a covenant nation. The Abrahamic, Mosaic, Palestinian, Davidic and finally the New Covenant was their portion as a covenant elect nation.

4. **The Giving of the Law**

   This involved the giving of the Law: the moral, civil, health and hygiene and ceremonial laws, all given for their protection as a nation.

5. **The Service of God**

   This involved the Tabernacle of Moses, the Tabernacle of David, and the Temple of Solomon with their respective orders of worship and approach to God.

6. **The Promises**

   These promises especially pertained to the seed that would be an innumerable as the sand and the stars; the earthly, natural and heavenly and spiritual seed.

7. **The Fathers**

   Abraham, Isaac and Jacob were particularly the three fathers of the chosen nation, although it may include the fathers of the twelve tribes of Israel (Exodus 3:6; Genesis 48:15-16).

8. **The Oracles of God**

   The sacred Scriptures of the Law, the Psalms and the Prophets were the oracles of God, and Israel, as a nation was chosen to receive and preserve the sacred writings for the whole world (Luke 24:44-45).

9. **The Messiah**

   From the elect nation, of the tribe of Judah, of the house of David, came the Messiah after the flesh, or, as pertaining to His human nature, as the Son of David (Romans 1:3).

Israel was indeed a chosen and blessed nation, chosen by the grace and love of God, and blessed for his elective purposes in the earth, chosen to bless all the nations of the earth. This was indeed a high and holy calling.

C. Israel - A Brief History

The history of Israel can only be considered in brief as it pertains to the theme of restoration.

The books of the Old Testament each present their major theme as the Abrahamic Covenant promises are fulfilled in the nation of Israel. Following we note the theme of a number of these books.

Genesis is primarily the book of covenant promises as given by the Lord to Abraham, Isaac and Jacob.

In Exodus we see Israel developing as the promised seed, the chosen nation. The book covers the prophesied deliverance from Egyptian bondage into the wilderness of Sinai. At Sinai the Lord gave Moses the revelation of the Tabernacle, His dwelling place among them, and the order of approach to His presence.

In Leviticus the Lord provides the way of sacrifice and priesthood as well as the laws for living in the promised land, and punishments if these laws are violated.

In Numbers there is the tragic rejection of the land promised to Abraham, Isaac and Jacob by that first generation. That first generation wanders in the wilderness for forty years because of their unbelief. Only Joshua and Caleb and the new generation would enter Canaan (Hebrews 3-4 with Numbers 13-14).

The book of Deuteronomy repeats the law in its fullness, with additions, to the new or second generation who would possess the promise land.

Joshua provides the account of Israel and the twelve tribes possessing the land under the directions of the Lord. This is the fulfilment of the land promises.

Judges records the failures, the lapses into idolatry and the compromise over several hundreds of years. God allowed about seven periods of servitudes to surrounding nations. Each time Israel cried to the Lord, God raised up a deliverer and judge. The book of Ruth belongs in the period of the Judges.

The books of 1 Samuel and 2 Samuel close off the period of the Judges and introduce the beginning of the fulfilment of the Abrahamic Covenant promises of kingship. David is given the covenant of the kingdom and kingship unto Messiah, who would be the greater Son of David, King of Kings and Lord of Lords.

The books of 1 Kings and 2 Kings along with 1Chronicles and 2Chronicles provide the histories of the kings of Judah and Israel. It is important to understand that Israel was a united nation from the time of the Exodus under Moses through to the reigns of Saul, David and Solomon - under whose reign the nation reached its highest glory.

After the death of Solomon, the nation was divided into two houses, two kingdoms, two nations, known as Israel and Judah (1Kings 11-12). God permitted this division in order to fulfill His distinctive purposes for each house, each nation.

It must also be recognized that, from this time on, there were two dynasties, two kingdoms and two destinies for these two houses: the house of Judah and the house of Israel.

When it comes to the books of the prophets, the major and minor prophets; they can only be understood by setting them in their proper historical context. There were prophets to the house of Israel and prophets to the house of Judah. These must not be confused. Much confusion, misunderstanding and misinterpretation result because of missing this important part of Israel's history. Some prophecies were spoken to the house of Judah and some to the nation or house of Israel. These must be distinguished as each has their destiny under God to fulfill.

Israel was a great and blessed nation as they experienced the fulfilment of the promises of the Abrahamic Covenant. Israel became a great nation. Israel possessed the promised land. Israel had kings that had victory over their enemies. Israel knew the manifest glory and presence of the Lord in the Tabernacle and later the Temple. The covenant promises found fulfilment in the chosen and elect nation.

These are the distinctive reasons why God chosen Israel to become His nation. They were not chosen because of numbers or any righteousness of their own. They were chosen because of Divine love and Divine covenant. They were chosen by God for God to deposit in them His treasures in order to prepare them to bless all the nations of the earth. This was the Divine purpose in Israel's election from among the nations. Tragically the chosen nation only fulfilled in measure their destiny!

CHAPTER TWELVE

ISRAEL'S DECLINE, APOSTASY AND REJECTION

As already seen, Israel was indeed the most blessed and privileged nation upon the face of the whole earth. Never had another nation been granted the presence of God in such a powerful and manifest way as Israel had experienced.

However, over the years of the history of the chosen nation, the record in the Historical and Prophetical books of the Bible show the rise and fall of Israel. The evidence is there of continual lapses into idolatry and apostasy. The two houses of Israel and Judah actually became worse than the surrounding nations, according to the prophets of God. For this reason, God punished both Israel and Judah by using Gentile kingdoms to take them into captivity.

Under the word of the Lord through Moses, God had foretold the nation that, as they obeyed the word of the Lord, blessing would follow, but if they disobeyed the word of the Lord, then all these curses of the law would come upon them. The reader should note carefully the "blessings and the cursings of the Law" as recorded in Deuteronomy Chapters 27-28. The details of Divine judgment are considered in brief.

A. The Desolations and the Captivities Foretold

In Leviticus Chapter 26 the Lord gave the nation of Israel what has been called "**The Seven Times Prophecy**". The words speak of the punishments and the desolation that would come upon the nation should they fall into idolatry and apostasy and fail to keep the laws of the land.

The student should note the "seven times" in verses 18,21,24,28.

The student should note "covenant" in verses 9,15,25,42,44,45.

The student should note "desolation" in verses 22,31,32,33,34,35,43.

The "seven times" punishments and plagues would come upon the chosen nation because of violations of the covenant and the end result would be desolation. These "**desolations**" would be fourfold.

1. Desolation of the Cities

The city of Jersualem and the cities of Israel and Judah would be desolated because of their sins of idolatry and apostasy.

2. Desolation of the Sanctuaries

The temple of the Lord and the various holy places would also be desolated because of their sins and hypocrisy before the Lord.

3. Desolation of the Land

The land would also be desolated. God would withhold the early and latter rains because of the abominations done in the land. The Lord told Israel that the land would vomit them out if they committed the same evils and abominations as the nations did before them. Israel also failed to keep the sabbaths of the lands and the jubilee years. Therefore God sent them into the Captivities to rest the land.

4. Desolation of the People

The people were also punished by the Lord and were cast out the land for their sins. The people of God were desolated because of the abominable practices they fell into. Backsliding, idolatry and apostasy continually surfaced in the history of the elect nation. Under godly kings the nation experienced periods of reformation and revival. Under ungodly kings, the nation turned from the Lord and became more evil than even the Gentile nations which surrounded them.

The final chapters of Kings and Chronicles, and the books of Jeremiah, Ezekiel and Daniel especially deal with the Captivities of Israel and Judah.

The two nations went into two different Captivities, to two different places, under two different world kingdoms.

The house of Israel went into captivity to Assyria about BC 721 and from there to be scattered through the nations, becoming known, generally speaking as "the lost ten tribes of the house of Israel".

The house of Judah went into captivity to Babylon about BC 604-606 and this for a period of seventy years. The house of Judah, in measure, returned from Babylon to the land after the Captivity had ended. There was a restoration of the city of Jerusalem, the temple, the land and the people. The whole purpose of this restoration was to hold the people of Judah in the land until the next promise in the Abrahamic Covenant was fulfilled - that was, the coming of the Messiah, the seed through whom all the nations of the earth would be blessed.

B. Israel's Divorce

Both Israel and Judah are likened to two women belonging to Jehovah (Ezekiel 16; Ezekiel 23). After repeated adulteries and harlotries with other gods and lovers, and after repeated calls to repentance through the prophets, Jehovah, reluctantly, has to give the elect nation "**a bill of divorce**" as the following Scriptures show.

Jeremiah 3:6-11. "During the reign of King Josiah, the LORD said to me, "Have you seen what **faithless Israel** has done? She has gone up on every high hill and under every spreading tree and has **committed adultery** there. I thought that after she had done all this she would return to me but she did not, and her **unfaithful sister** Judah saw it. I gave **faithless Israel** her **certificate of divorce** and sent her away because of all her **adulteries**. Yet I saw that her **unfaithful sister** Judah had no fear; she also went out and **committed adultery**. Because Israel's **immorality** mattered so little to her, she defiled the land and **committed adultery** with stone and wood. In spite of all this, her **unfaithful sister** Judah did not return to me with all her heart, but only in pretense," declares the LORD. The LORD said to me, "**Faithless Israel** is more righteous than **unfaithful Judah**".

Even though the Lord divorced Israel, Judah did not heed and she went and committed further adulteries with other gods. Judah was also heading for divorce by the Lord, her husband (Read also Isaiah 50:1 with Jeremiah 31:31-34).

Restoration Theology

C. Judah's Rejection

The Lord extended mercy to the house of Judah bringing a remnant of Judah back to the land until the birth of the Messiah. From Malachi to John the Baptist and the manifestation of the Messiah, there was a period of about 400 years, referred to as "the silent years". Then the Gospels present the glorious ministry of Christ for some three and one-half years. It was the greatest ministry the world had ever seen.. But as John says: "He came unto His own, and His own received Him not ..."(John 1:11-12).

Beyond Judah's former spiritual adulteries and idolatries, the nation now committed the greatest of all sins - the rejection of their long promised and often prophesied of Messiah, the Lord Jesus Christ. The cry of the nation, as a whole, was, "We will not have this Man to reign over us. Crucify Him. We have no king but Caesar. His blood be on us and our children" (Matthew 27:1-26).

The nation had filled up its cup of iniquity, and the wrath of God would come on them to the uttermost (Matthew 23:32-33; 1 Thessalonians 2:14-16).

There was a godly remnant that knew and accepted Jesus as Messiah. These would be the beginning of a new ethnic - "the church". In the Acts the gospel went to the Jew first, but, as a whole, the Jew rejected it and the gospel went to the Gentiles (Romans 1:16; 2:1-11; Acts 13:4,14,42-52). Because the house of Judah rejected their Messiah, they were rejected of the Lord. In AD 70, God allowed once again, the fourfold desolations to come on Judah. Jesus Himself foretold these very desolations as He saw His coming rejection and crucifixion.

1. Desolation of Jerusalem

Under Prince Titus and the Roman armies, Jerusalem and the cities of Judah were desolated (Luke 21:20-24).

2. Desolation of the Temple

According to Christ's prophecies, not one stone was left unturned upon another in the desolation and destruction of the temple by the Roman armies. The Father, Son and Holy Spirit forsook the material temple, and in AD 70 it was also desolated by the Romans (Matthew 24:1-2; John 2:13-17; Matthew 21:10-17; Luke 19:41-46).

3. Desolation of the Land

The Romans desolated the land, denuding it of trees as they crucified the Jews around the walls of Jerusalem (Luke 21:23,24).

4. Desolation of the House of Judah

The Jews were scattered to the four winds of heaven, scattered among the nations until the times of the Gentiles be fulfilled. Josephus, the Jewish historian tells of the terrible slaughter of Jewry in the seige of Jerusalem in AD 70, in fulfillment of the word of Jesus, and the words of Moses in the books of the Law (Deuteronomy 27-28 chapters).

All these things came upon "this generation" according to Matthew 12:34,39,41,45; 11:16; 23:36.

For about nineteen centuries, Jewry has been a desolated people; desolate of city, temple and land. They have suffered the curse of innocent blood invoked upon them and their unborn generations by those who rejected and crucified the Christ of God. What a tragic history is written in the blood of Jewry over these centuries.

D. The Present State of Jewry

What then is the present state of Jewry since the rejection of their Messiah - that is, the state of those who have not or do not accept Christ as Lord and Saviour? The following brief quotations and references from the Old and New Testaments tell the present state of the Jew, or the house of Judah, outside of Christ?

1. Jewry, like Israel, has been divorced for spiritual adulteries (Jeremiah 3:6-11).
2. Jewry, though Abraham's seed after the flesh, are not Abraham's seed after the Spirit (John 8).
3. Jewry stumbled at the stumblingstone and rock of offence in Christ. They rejected the crucified Christ as well as the faith-righteousness provided by Him, choosing rather self-righteousness by works of the Law (Romans 9:32-33; 1Corinthians 1:23). They are ignorant of God's righteousness, and go about to establish their own righteousness, refusing to submit to the righteousness of God in Christ (Romans 10:1-4).
4. Jewry can only be saved by calling on the Name of the LORD in the Name of the LORD Jesus Christ (Romans 10:1-13; 11:26).
5. Jewry, at present, is a disobedient and gainsaying (Word-resisting) people (Romans 10:21).
6. Jewry is blinded until the fullness of the Gentiles be come in (Romans 11:7,8,25).
7. Jewry has been cast away, except for a remnant according to the election of grace (Romans 1-11,15).
8. Jewry has been broken off and out of the faith-olive tree because of unbelief, and the Gentiles are being grafted into the faith-olive tree by faith in Christ (Romans 11:16-24,32).
9. Jewry has become, as far as the gospel is concerned, enemies of Christ even though God loves them for the fathers sake (Romans 11:28).

The student is encouraged to read again Paul's chapters concerning his own people, Israel, after the flesh (Romans Chapters 9-10-11).

In Conclusion:

Such is the sad situation of the chosen nation, including both the houses of Israel and Judah: divorced, cast off and out, rejected and desolated of city, temple and land. Israel and Judah both need God to come to them in grace and mercy and bring about **restoration** to Himself!

The prophets speak of this restoration that would come to both houses of Israel and Judah. It would be through the New Covenant and through the Lord Jesus Christ. However, this brings us to a new chapter!

CHAPTER THIRTEEN

ISRAEL'S NEW COVENANT RESTORATION

In the light of Israel/Judah's "divorce" and rejection by the Lord, many, many questions arise about the covenantal promises given to the chosen nation.

What about the Old Testament prophecies concerning Israel? What about the promised land which has never been possessed as "an everlasting possession"? What about Divine blessing and Israel blessing the nations of the earth? What about the restoration of Israel to Divine favour?

Expositors are divided over the matter and basically fall into three schools of opinion.

A. The "No-Restoration" School

This school of interpreters believe that Israel/Judah will never be restored to early glory and blessing as a nation. They believe that any prophecies which speak of restoration of Israel or Judah as spoken by the prophets were all fulfilled in the restoration from Babylon, as seen in Ezra, Nehemiah and Esther. They see no future restoration for Israel. They teach that, when Israel/Judah rejected Christ, all the promises of the covenants were nullified. Israel/Judah are now as other Gentile nations and there is no hope for them outside of accepting Christ. They are no longer an elect nation since the cross.

B. The "Mosaic Restoration" School

This school of interpreters teach that Israel/Judah will be restored to the early glory and blessing of former days. This school believes that there will be a new temple built, either in the end of this age or in a coming Millennial age. The Mosaic Covenant sacrifices and oblations, the Aaronic and Levitical priesthood will be restored. Sabbath days, and years, circumcision and festival days will be restored. Jewry will be restored to the land of Israel and will become the head of the nations. In the thousand years kingdom age, all nations will go to Jerusalem to keep the Feast of Tabernacles. Jewry will become the "missionary nation" to the world, and thus fulfill the Old Testament prophecies of blessing on Israel and through them to the whole Gentile world.

This view is generally known as Dispensationalism. The fact that many, many Jews have (or are) returned to the land - the Middle East - and Jerusalem, is used as proof of the beginning of a Mosaic Restoration. There are some variations in this view, but this kind of restoration is to take place in the end of the age or in a future Millennium.

C. The New Covenant Restoration School

This school basically is a balance between, what this writer believes, the two extremes of the previous schools of thought. The one school "damns the Jew" and the other "deifies the Jew". Both are extreme in the writer's understanding. The view held by this writer is to be found in the prophecies and promises of the NEW Covenant.

For the "No-Restoration" school, it should be remembered that, according to Paul, the Jew is still "beloved for the father's sake" (Romans 11:28). That is, the fathers, Abraham, Isaac and Jacob. God still remembers His covenant. God has not totally cast them away as there is a remnant saved according to the election of grace (Romans 11:1-11,5).

God is still able to graft them back again as branches into the faith-olive tree **if they abide not still in unbelief** (Romans 11:16-24,32).

For the "Mosaic-Restoration" school, it should be remembered that the Book of Hebrews shows that the Mosaic economy will never be restored in this age or any age to come. The Old and Mosaic Covenant was fulfilled and abolished at the cross. The Mosaic Covenant was temporal and revocable and was abolished at Calvary, the rent veil signifying the end of that economy. The Jew will know restoration but **NOT** to the Mosaic Covenant!

It is the "New Covenant" school of interpretation that shows the only way of restoration for the Jew is the same as that for the Gentile. The prophets, predominantly, though under the Mosaic Covenant, foretold the day when the Lord would make a **NEW Covenant** with the house of Israel and with the house of Judah. The New Covenant (Testament) writers show clearly the cessation of the Old Covenant (Testament) and the bringing in of the New Covenant realities.

D. The New Covenant

An understanding of the Old and the New Covenants in relation to Israel, as a nation, will help to bring a clearer understanding of restoration when it comes to the restoration of Israel. We consider these things in relation to these two covenants.

1. **What Jeremiah Said - Jeremiah 31:31-34**

    Jeremiah, the prophet, while under the Old Covenant, clearly foretold of a day to come when the Lord would make a New Covenant with the house of Israel and the house of Judah. It would not be according to the covenant He made with Israel at Mt Sinai, after the exodus from Egypt. It would be an entirely New Covenant with new elements in it, as this passage of Scripture clearly shows. God was a Husband to the nation at Mt Sinai, but they broke the marriage covenant, committed spiritual adulteries and ended the marriage in divorce.

2. **What Jesus Said - Matthew 26:26-30**

    There can be no mistaking the words of Jesus. Jesus Himself was born under the Law and fulfilled in Himself the Old Covenant details both in letter and in spirit. He came to redeem those who were under the Law Covenant (Galatians 4:4-5). He will redeem them by the power of the New Covenant. On the night of His betrayal, He took the bread, representing His broken body, and the cup, representing His shed blood, and said to the twelve disciples: "This is the NEW TESTAMENT (Covenant, Arrangement, Will) in My blood" (Read also Mark 14:22-26; Luke 22:17-20).

    Undoubtedly Jesus was instituting the New Covenant prophesied by Jeremiah, and undoubtedly the twelve apostles knew this even though subsequent events show they did not fully comprehend the full significance of it all! There are some writers of the Dispensational school who say that the New Covenant has not yet been made and is to be made in the Millennium with Israel. If this is so, then the Christian Church should not be celebrating the Lord's Table as often as it does, or should not even celebrate it at all!

3. What Paul Said - 1Corinthians 11:23-27

When Paul wrote to the Corinthian church concerning the table of the Lord, he clearly spelt out the fact that the Gentile believers, as also Jewish believers, are under the New Covenant. He says that he received of the Lord Himself - not from Peter, James, or John or other apostles - the revelation of that which was instituted the night the Lord was betrayed.

Paul quoted the words of Jesus in relation to the bread and the cup: "This cup is the New Testament in My blood". Paul, the great Pharisee, and apostle to the Gentiles, having been born and raised and taught under the Old Covenant now declares the revelation of the New Covenant.

4. What Hebrews Said - Hebrews 8:6-13; 10:15-17

The writer to the Hebrews again confirms the fact that the Christian is under the New Covenant. It should be remembered that the Hebrew believers, more especially, had been for years under the Old Covenant ceremonies, laws and ritualism. At the time of writing they were in the period of transition from the Old Covenant to the New Covenant. They were under great pressure from the Judaizers to return to the Old Covenant shadows.

The writer to the Hebrews shows that they were under "a better covenant", "a better testament". Everything was better under the New Covenant. In the Scriptures quoted above, he quotes to them the prophecy of the Old Covenant prophet, Jeremiah, concerning the coming of the New Covenant, as well as giving some interpretative comments. Why return to the "old" when the "new" is better?

The Scriptures are clear. The Christian Church is under the New Covenant and all that is involved in that covenant. Jeremiah prophesied it. Jesus instituted it. Paul confirmed it. The writer to the Hebrews interpreted it. Christ Himself is the mediator of it. He is the mediator of the new and better covenant (Hebrews 9:15).

E. The Old Covenant

This brings us to some important questions: What happened to the Old Covenant? Does it continue alongside the New Covenant? What is the relationship of the Old Covenant to the New Covenant?

Again, the Scriptures are specific as to what happened to the Old Covenant. We consider several passages from the New Testament Epistles that deal with this.

1. The Hebrews Epistle - Hebrews 8:6-13

The writer to the Hebrews, in the course of his quoting from the prophet Jeremiah, gave some specific interpretative comments about the Old and the New Covenants. Only the points relevant to the present context are noted here, the other points being considered in due time.

* Christ is the mediator of a better covenant or testament.

* The better covenant is established upon better promises.

* The first or old covenant was not without its faults, otherwise no place would have been sought for the second or new covenant.

* The days would come when the Lord would a new covenant with Israel and with Judah.

* It would not be like the old covenant made with them after the exodus from Egypt, that covenant that Israel failed to keep and so caused the Lord to disregard them.

* The very fact that God said He would make a **NEW** Covenant implies that the first covenant had now become **OLD**.

* That covenant which has decayed and become old is now ready to vanish away.

* In the context of things, the writer also says: "He takes away the first (the Old Covenant) that He may establish the second (the New Covenant). Hebrews 10:9.

The Old or Mosaic Covenant is spoken of as "the first covenant" (Hebrews 8:7; 9:1; 10:9). The New or Messianic Covenant is spoken of as "the second covenant". Therefore, why should the Hebrew believers and believers today, seek to go back to that covenant which had "decayed", "waxed old", and "vanished away" when the New Covenant is "new", "better" and "everlasting" in its duration (Hebrews 13:20)?

2. The Corinthian Epistle - 2Corinthians 3

A study of this chapter written to the Corinthian believers reveals that Paul is comparing the glory of the Old Covenant ministry and the New Covenant ministry.

Moses was the minister of the Old Covenant tables of law written on tables of stone. Moses had glory on his face and had to wear a veil to hide that glory. The Old Covenant was a ministration of death. In due time, Moses died, the glory was done away, or abolished.

In contrast, Jesus is the mediator of the New Covenant. His law is written on the tables of the heart and mind. His glory exceeds the glory of Moses and His glory remains as a ministration of life.

One is a ministration of the letter that kills; the other is the ministration of the spirit that gives life. Ministers of the New Covenant can be changed from glory to glory beholding the unveiled face of the Lord Jesus Christ.

The Old Covenant glory is "done away". It is "abolished". The New Covenant glory "exceeds in glory" and "remains".

Therefore why do Christian believers, Jews or Gentiles, need to restore that which has been done away or abolished? We have the more glorious covenant that eternally remains.

Restoration Theology

3. **The Galatian Epistle - Galatians 4:21-31.**

   A careful consideration of this passage of Paul to the Galatian believers also confirms the fact that the Old Covenant has been replaced by the New Covenant. Paul, in his inspired allegory, likens the **TWO SONS** of father Abraham, Ishmael and Isaac, to the **TWO COVENANTS**!

   Hagar, the bondmaid and her bondson, Ishmael, represent the Old Covenant from Mt Sinai, and the bondage of Jewry after the flesh, even though of the seed of Abraham. It spoke of earthly Jerusalem, that Jerusalem which now is.

   Sarah, the free woman, and her promised son, Isaac, represent the New Covenant from Mt Zion and the Jerusalem which is above, and the freedom of Christians, born of the Spirit, being Abraham's seed by faith.

   A reading of Genesis Chapter 21 in connection with this Galatian passage shows that, in due time, when Isaac came, Hagar and Ishmael were "cast out" for they could not be heirs together and remain in the same household with Sarah and Isaac.

The truth is evident. Once the New Covenant had been established, the Old Covenant had to be "cast out". Both covenants could not remain together in the same house, the household of faith. The Judaistic teachers tried to bring back the Hagar-Ishmael or Old Covenant and be at peace with the Sarah-Isaac or New Covenant. This was not to be. For, as Ishmael, born after the flesh, persecuted Isaac, born after the Spirit, so did the Old Covenant believers oppose New Covenant believers. They could not dwell together in the same house without there being some conflict. No wonder Paul asks: "Am I become your enemy because I tell you the truth?" (Galatians 4:16).

The Old Covenant has indeed become "old", "decayed" and "vanished away". The Old Covenant has been "done away", "abolished" and been "cast out". The New Covenant is indeed "new", "better", and it "exceeds in glory" and "remains" in the house of God as "heir" of the promises of God in Christ.

The Galatian Church, as many believers today, was bound by mixture. It was a mixture of Moses and Jesus, the bondage of the law and the liberty of grace, the Old and the New Covenant. Paul showed them clearly that they could not be under both covenants at the same time. They could not have Moses in one hand and Jesus in the other hand. They could not mix law and grace. The Old and the New Covenants will not and cannot be joined together. Hence the need to come out of any covenantal confusion.

F. **The Restoration of Israel**

   It has been necessary to consider the Old and New Covenants in relation to the restoration of Israel/Judah.

   The Old Testament prophets did prophesy of a restoration of Israel but it is NOT a restoration under or to the Mosaic Covenant economy. To say so is to contradict all that has been seen in the New Covenant passages of Scripture in this chapter.

   God loves all nations. He is not a respector of persons, neither Jew nor Gentile. If He was, He would be violating His own commands concerning partiality and showing respect to persons. He would be violating His own laws (Acts 10:34; Romans 2:11; Deuteronomy 10:17). There is no partiality with the Lord God.

The prophets prophesied of an outpouring of the Spirit in the last days on "**all flesh**" whether Jewish or Gentile flesh (Joel 2:28-30). Whosoever would call on the name of the Lord would be saved. The prophet Zechariah also foretold the fact that Judah would experience an outpouring of the Spirit upon them. Under this outpouring, the eyes of Jewry would be opened, the spirit of grace and supplication would come on them, and they would mourn as for the only begotten son - Jesus Christ, rejected centuries ago (Zechariah 12:10-14; 13:1-6; Ezekiel 39:29; Joel 2:28).

The truth of Scripture is that Israel's restoration will be by the **NEW Covenant**, by the power of the Holy Spirit. The restoration is **TO THE LORD, NOT TO THE MOSAIC COVENANT ECONOMY**!

Paul clearly sums up the "Jewish problem". It is actually everyone's problem - the sin of unbelief! Paul says that if Israel (or Jewry in our day) **abides not still in unbelief**, God is able to graft them in again to the faith-olive tree (Romans 11:16-24,32).

During this Church Age, every Jew or Gentile, who comes to repentance and faith in Christ is grafted into the olive tree and partake together of its goodness. This is the only **restoration** of which the prophets speak. Whether Israel (a remnant) returns to the land of Palestine (the Middle East) or whether Jewry remains in the various nations of the world, the issue is repentance towards God, and faith in the Lord Jesus Christ!

Although Jewry has been centuries in unbelief (since AD.70), it seems evident from the Scripture that, as a nation, they will experience an outpouring of the Holy Spirit on them, as other nations, and have their eyes opened to the Christ of God.

When this takes place, "**in Christ there is neither Jew nor Gentile**", but all become "one body, in Christ" (1Corinthians 12:13; Ephesians 3:1-12).

This is the only restoration that Scripture speaks of as far as Israel (modern Jewry) is concerned. It is not a restoration to the Mosaic Covenant economy, but a restoration to God through Christ, the Messiah and the New Covenant, in His broken body and shed blood. Any Gentile or Jew who rejects God's Christ will be eternally lost, whether in or out of Palestine or any other country or nation!

In Conclusion:

* The Mosaic Covenant economy will not be restored.
* Jewish nationalism will not be restored.
* The Palestinian Covenant as in Old Testament times, will **not** be restored.
* **Jewry will be restored to God through Christ only and the New Covenant!**

(**Note:** The reader is referred to fuller comments in "**New Covenant Realities**", by the author).

PART FIVE

RESTORATION OF THE CHURCH

☙

CHAPTER FOURTEEN

THE CHURCH - GOD'S NEW ETHNIC

Having considered (1) The Restoration of Earth, (2) The Restoration of Mankind, (3) The Restoration of Israel, we come now to (4) The Restoration of the Church, God's New Ethnic.

The word "ethnic" has to do with the basic divisions of mankind, distinguished by culture. The word is used of Israel/Judah, the Gentile nations and the Church. The apostle Paul recognized that, while God is no respector of persons, He has instituted certain ethnic distinctions. Paul noted these basic ethnic divisions in the human race in 1Corinthians 10:32. He writes: "Give none offence, neither to the **Jew**, nor to the **Gentiles**, nor the **Church of God**". Therefore, in God's mind, the three main divisions of the human race are the Jews, the Gentiles and the Church.

In previous chapters we have dealt with God's choice of Israel. Israel was God's chosen ethnic in the Old Testament times and was mightily blessed of the Lord. The Gentiles were set, as it were, on the side-lines. Odd Gentiles came into blessing because of Israel/Judah, God's chosen ethnic.

However, since the cross, this has been changed. Israel, because of rejection of their Messiah, and unbelief, is on the side-lines, while God is especially visiting the Gentiles to take out of them a people for His name (Acts 15:15-18).

It is important to understand the condition of the Gentile nations, as we have that of Israel, and see how God at and after the cross, brought about a new ethnic - the church - composed of believing Jews and believing Gentiles.

A. The Gentile Nations

1. Their Condition

In Scripture the term "Gentile" is used to refer to all nations besides Israel and Judah. It denotes all peoples not in covenant relationship with God, as was Israel. Paul aptly describes the condition of the Gentiles in Ephesians 2:11,2.

* Gentiles in the flesh - as to natural and national birth.

* Uncircumcision in the flesh - not in Abrahamic Covenant relationship.

* Without Christ - having no Saviour or Anointed One.

* Aliens from Israel's commonwealth - estranged from the rights of Israel.

* Strangers from the covenants of promises - the covenants given to Israel and the blessings therein. That is the Abrahamic, Mosaic, Palestinian, Davidic and New Covenants as given to the chosen nation.

* Having no hope - no Messianic expectation.

* Without God in the world - having general but not special revelation of God.

* Afar off - no nearness of relationship with God.

Paul, later on in the same Epistle, summarized the spiritual condition of the Gentiles as "having the understanding darkened, being alienated from the life of

God through the ignorance that is in them, because of the blindness that is in their heart" (Read Ephesians 4:17-18 and Romans 1:18-32).

2. Their Salvation

The writers of the Old Testament Scriptures were concerned primarily with the chosen nation and only dealt with Gentile nations as they related to it (Deuteronomy 32:8; Acts 17:26). However, the Scriptures also plainly declare that God is no respecter of persons (Acts 10:34,35). As already noted, Israel was chosen as a nation to eventually bless all other nations. The following Scriptures attest to this fact:

* All nations to be blessed through the seed of Abraham (Genesis 22:18).
* All families of the earth to be blessed (Genesis 26:4).
* All kindreds of the nations to worship God (Psalm 22:27,28).
* All nations to flow to the house of the Lord in the last days (Isaiah 2:2,3).
* Gentiles to seek to the Root of Jesse (Isaiah 11:10).
* Messiah to sprinkle many nations with His blood (Isaiah 52:15).
* Many nations to be joined to the Lord in that day (Zechariah 2:11).
* The name of the Lord to be great among the Gentiles (Malachi 1:11).
* The Gentiles shall trust in His name (Matthew 12:21).

The great commission involves taking the Gospel of Christ to every creature, making disciples of all nations (Matthew 28:19; Mark 16:15; Luke 24:47; Acts 1:8). The Book of Acts shows God's turning from the chosen nation to the Gentile nations in order to take out of them a people for His name (Acts 9:15; 13:44-49; 14:1,2; 15:14-18; 28:23-31).

The Scriptures clearly show that the Gentile nations would be blessed through the chosen nation by "the Seed" - Messiah. "And the Scripture, foreseeing that God would justify the heathen through faith, preached before the gospel unto Abraham, saying, In thee shall all nations be blessed" (Galatians 3:8).

B. The Church - The New Ethnic

1. Definition of the Church

The third group mentioned by Paul in 1Corinthians 10:32 is "the church of God". The word "Church" is a translation of the Greek word "**Ekklesia**", which is made up of two other words: "**Ek**" which means "**out of**", and "**Kaleo**", which means "**to call**". The word "**Ekklesia**" literally means "the called out ones". It is used in Scripture to refer to the nation of Israel and to the Christian community of believers, whether in heaven or on earth.

* Israel is called "the church in the wilderness" (Acts 7:38).
* The saints in heaven are in "the church of the firstborn" (Hebrews 12:23).

* The saints on earth are also in "the church" (Revelation 1:11).

In these references the word Church is used in its two basic senses: the church universal and the church local. The universal church includes the redeemed of all ages both in heaven and earth, and the local church is the visible expression of it. (**Note:** A fuller definition of the word "Church" will be considered in the next chapter under "**What Jesus Said About His Church**").

2. **The Calling of the Church**

God has always had a people for Himself; a company of called out ones. Being "called out" involves:

* Being called out of darkness into light (1Peter 2:9).
* Being called to a holy vocation (Ephesians 4:1).
* Being calling to a calling of hope (Ephesians 4:4).
* Being called to a high calling (Philippians 3:14).
* Being called to a heavenly calling (Hebrews 3:2).
* Being called unto eternal glory by Christ Jesus (1Peter 5:10).
* Being called to His kingdom and glory (1Thessalonians 2:12).

The Church is "the called out and assembled people of God"; called out of the kingdom of darkness, into the kingdom of light to be a holy people unto God.

3. **Composition of the Church**

The Church, as it is revealed in the New Testament, is composed of both Jew and Gentile. As God called Israel as a nation from the midst of the nations and constituted them His Church in the Old Testament, so God now calls unto Himself, out of every nation, Jews or Gentiles, and constitutes them as His Church in the New Testament. The New Testament Church is revealed as the Body of Christ composed of Jew and Gentile.

* Christ is the builder of His Church (Matthew 16:18).
* The Lord is the One who adds to His Church (Acts 2:47).
* Christ is the head of the Church, His body (Colossians 2:19).
* The Church is Christ's body in earth (Ephesians 1:22,23).
* Jew and Gentile are baptized into one body (1Corinthians 12:13).
* Jew and Gentile are one new man in Christ (Ephesians 2:15,16).
* Jew and Gentile are fellow-heirs in the same body (Ephesians 3:6).

Thus the Church, being the third major ethnic division, is a called out company, consisting of Jew and Gentile, circumcision and uncircumcision, chosen nation and Gentile nations, in the one Body of Christ. National distinctions are determined by natural birth, but by spiritual birth, all national distinctions cease to exist, for "there is neither Jew nor Greek, there is neither bond nor free, there is neither male nor female; for you are all one in Christ Jesus" (Galatians 3:28). "For in Christ Jesus, neither circumcision avails anything, nor uncircumcision, but a new creature" (Galatians 6:15).

4. **Significance of the Church**

This Church is taken out of every kindred, tongue, tribe and nation (Revelation 5:9). It now constitutes God's holy nation in earth. It is the true Israel of God entitled to the spiritual promises of the Abrahamic Covenant.

* Those in Christ are a holy nation (1Peter 2:9).
* The kingdom was taken from Judah and given to a nation that would bring forth the fruits there (Matthew 21:43).
* The prophets foretold of a righteous nation that would keep the truths (Isaiah 26:2).
* Salvation was offered to a nation not yet called by His name (Isaiah 65:1 with Romans 10:20,21).
* All those who are new creatures in Christ Jesus constitute the Israel of God, as seen in Galatians 6:15,16.
* The Gentile by faith is brought into the commonwealth of Israel (Ephesians 2:12).
* The believing Gentile is grafted into the faith-olive tree of Israel (Romans 11).
* The Israel after the flesh is not necessarily the Israel after the Spirit (Romans 9:6-8).
* The true Jew and true circumcision is of the heart and in the spirit, and not of the flesh or the letter (Romans 2:28,29).
* The believers in Christ are now Abraham's seed and heirs according to the promise (Galatians 3:16,29).

These Scriptures attest to the fact that the Church, composed of Jew and Gentile, is God's holy nation, the true Israel of God, the seed of Abraham, and the called out company. This is the "mystery" revealed to Paul, that Jew and Gentile would become one body in Christ (Ephesians 3:1-9).

In conclusion, it can be seen that the three main ethnic divisions mentioned by Paul in 1 Corinthians 10:32 are supported by the testimony of Scripture, both the Old and the New Testaments.

The Church is **God's new ethnic, God's "new thing"** promised in the Old Testament prophets.

(**Note:** The student is referred to "**Interpreting the Scriptures**", Chapter 13, Conner/Malmin, for fuller treatment of "The Ethnic Division Principle").

CHAPTER FIFTEEN

CHRIST'S VISION OF THE CHURCH

Having seen from both Old and New Testaments that the Church is **God's New Ethnic**, we need to consider in this chapter what Jesus said about the Church. What is Christ's vision of the Church? It is necessary to understand what the Church is and what the Church is not. A clear definition of the word "Church" is therefore needed.

A. What The Church Is

The Doctrine of the Church is defined as "Ecclesiology", from the Greek word **"Ekklesia"** - the Church! The word "Church" is a word that needs to be reclaimed or recaptured because its true meaning has been lost in a maze of other and unBiblical ideas, as will be seen.

The two major passages in the Gospel of Matthew provide for us the major seed thoughts in the mind of the Lord Jesus about the Church. The word "church" is used but three times in the Gospel of Matthew - the Gospel of the Kingdom. The word is not used in Mark, Luke or John. It is distinctly a word that is, first of all, Matthean.

The passages in which the word is used are quoted in full here, for it is from these passages that the seed thoughts of Christ are developed in this chapter. The first passage is found in Matthew 16:15-20.

"He saith unto them, But whom say ye that I am?

And Simon Peter answered and said, Thou art the Christ, the Son of the living God.

And Jesus answered and said unto him, Blessed art thou, Simon Barjona: for flesh and blood hath not revealed it unto thee, but my Father which is in heaven.

And I say also unto thee, That thou art Peter, and upon this rock I will build my **church**; and the gates of hell shall not prevail against it.

And I will give unto thee the keys of the kingdom of heaven: and whatsoever thou shalt bind on earth shall be bound in heaven: and whatsoever thou shalt loose on earth shall be loosed in heaven.

Then charged he his disciples that they should tell no man that he was Jesus the Christ".

The second passage is found in Matthew 18:15-20, which is quoted in full here also.

"Moreover if thy brother shall trespass against thee, go and tell him his fault between thee and him alone: if he shall hear thee, thou hast gained thy brother.

But if he will not hear thee, then take with thee one or two more, that in the mouth of two or three witnesses every word may be established.

And if he shall neglect to hear them, tell it unto the **church**: but if he neglect to hear the **church**, let him be unto thee as an heathen man and a publican.

Verily I say unto you, Whatsoever ye shall bind on earth shall be bound in heaven: and whatsoever ye shall loose on earth shall be loosed in heaven.

Again I say unto you, That if two of you shall agree on earth as touching any thing that they shall ask, it shall be done for them of my Father which is in heaven.

For where two or three are gathered together in my name, there am I in the midst of them".

Most of the following material concerning the definition of the "**church**" is adapted from "**New Testament Words**" (Pages 68-72) by William Barclay, and is arranged accordingly by the writer of this text.

"Ekklesia" is the New Testament word for 'church', and is, therefore, one of the most important of all New Testament words. Like so many New Testament words it has a double background.

1. **"Ekklesia" has a Greek Background**

    In the great classical days of Athens the **ekklesia** was the convened assembly of the people. It consisted of all the citizens of the city who had not lost their civic rights. Apart from the fact that its decisions must conform to the laws of the State, its powers were to all intents and purposes unlimited. It elected and dismissed magistrates and directed the policy of the city. It declared war, made peace, contracted treaties and arranged alliances. It elected generals and other military officers. It assigned troops to different campaigns and dispatched them from the city. It was ultimately responsible for the conduct of all military operations. It raised and allocated funds.

    Two things are interesting to note. First, all its meetings began with prayer and sacrifice. Second, it was a true democracy. Its two great watchwords were 'equality' (**isonomia**) and 'freedom' (**eleutheria**). It was an assembly where everyone had an equal right and equal duty to take part. When a case involving the right of any private citizen was before it - as in the case of ostracism or banishment - at least 6000 citizens must be present. In the wider Greek world **ekklesia** came to mean any duly convened assembly of citizens.

    It is interesting to note that the Roman world did not even try to translate the word **ekklesia**; it simply transliterated it into **ecclesia** and used it in the same way. There is an interesting bilingual inscription found in Athens (dated AD103-4). It can be read against the background of Acts 18. A certain Caius Vibius Salutaris had presented to the city an image of Diana and other images. The inscription lays it down that they are to be set up on their pedestals at every **ekklesia** of the city in the theatre. To Greek and Roman alike the word was familiar in the sense of a convened assembly. So, then, when we look at it against this background, as Deissmann puts, the Church is God's assembly, God's muster, and the convener is God.

2. **"Ekklesia" has a Hebrew Background**

    In the Septuagint it translates the Hebrew word **qahal**, which again comes from a root which means 'to summon'. It is regularly used for the 'assembly' of the 'congregation' of the people of Israel. In Deuteronomy 18:16; Judges 20:2, it is translated 'assembly', and in 1 Kings 8:14; Leviticus 10:17; Numbers 1:16, it is translated 'congregation'. It is very common in the Septuagint, occurring over 70 times.

In the Hebrew sense it, therefore, means God's people called together by God, in order to listen to or to act for God. In the certain sense, the word 'congregation' loses a certain amount of the essential meaning. A 'congregation' is a company of people 'who have come together'; a **qahal** or an **ekklesia** is a body of people 'who have been called together'. The two original words, Hebrew and Greek, put all the emphasis on the action of God.

F.J.A.Hort rightly points out that originally the word does not mean, as is so often stated, a body of people who have been 'picked out' from the world. It has not in it that exclusive sense. It means a body of people who have been 'summoned out' of their homes to come and meet with God; and both in its original Greek and Hebrew usages, that sense was not exclusive but inclusive. The summons was not to any selected few; it was a summons from the State to every man to come and to shoulder his responsibilities; it was a summons from God to every man to come to listen to and to act on the word of God.

In essence, therefore, the Church, the ekklesia, is a body of people, not so much assembling because they have chosen to come together, but assembling because God has called them to Himself; not so much assembling to share their own thoughts or opinions, but assembling to listen to the voice of God". (End quote and emphasis this writer)

In the writer's understanding, the above definition of the word "Church" is undoubtedly one of the clearest definitions of what the Church is in the mind of God and of Christ. It is certainly a word that needs to be recaptured in this day when it has almost lost its true meaning in a maze of unBiblical ideas and concepts. How different would be the assembling of God's people if they had a greater and clearer and Scriptural understanding of the **CHURCH - God's Ekklesia**!

B. What The Church Is Not

Having defined what the Church is, it will be profitable to understand what the Church is not! Some things should not have to be written but, because the word "church" has lost it true meaning for many, many of God's people today, (let alone the unconverted world!) they need to be written.

1. The Church is not a Material Building

For over two hundred years or more, the early church did not own buildings, nor were buildings consecrated for the purpose of worship. The word "church" is not used once of a material building in the New Testament. In Acts 19:37 where "robbers of churches" is wrongly used, the Greek word is "**hierosulos**" and should be translated "robbers of temples". The New Authorized Version and some others translate this correctly. The Church is the **meeting of the redeemed, NOT the meeting place**! It is a habit that is almost impossible to break in the minds of God's people that a material building is NOT the Church. Placing denominational labels on buildings has helped to rob the people of God and the world of the true meaning of the word "Church". The Church is a building, but NOT a material building!

2. **The Church is not an Extension of Judaism**

   Paul speaks how, when he was in "**the Jews religion**" (Literally, **Judaism**), he persecuted "**the church of God**" (Galatians 1:13,14). All that pertained to the externalisms, and ceremonialism of Judaism and the Law were fulfilled and abolished at the cross. It is not Moses in one hand and Jesus in the other hand. The Judaizers endeavoured to take the "new wine" of the New Covenant and put it into the Old Covenant "wineskin", and the result was schism and division in the synagogues. Christianity is not an extension of Judaism. It is the Christ of an entirely New Covenant, in which the New and the Old Covenants do not mix.

3. **The Church is not a Sect or Denomination**

   In the Gospels and the Acts there were various sects within Judaism. There was the sect of the Sadducees (Acts 5:17), the sect of the Pharisees (Acts 15:5; 26:5), and the Jews charged Christianity as being the sect of the Nazarene (Acts 24:5; 28:22).

   Sectarianism and denominationalism is contrary to the Scriptures and is evidence of Corinthian carnality, and party spirit (1Corinthians 3:1-3).These are things which divide the Body of Christ and the Lord has to deal with these things as all are theologically incorrect and do not constitute "the church" in the New Testament sense and meaning of the word.

4. **The Church is not an Individual**

   This may be simplistic, but the church is not a personal or individualistic thing. No one person is or ever can be the church. No person who truly belongs to Christ can be a 'loner'. The church is a corporate thing in the mind of God. People who isolate themselves from "the church", for whatever reasons are actually living in disobedience to God's word and the true meaning of the church. They may isolate themselves from "institutionalism" or "denominationalism" but they cannot be 'loners', isolated from some assembly of God's people. No individual can really live apart from the church. Such is a contradiction in terms. No one family even can be the church. The church is the summoned together people of God, called to assemble together to hear from God and to act for God!

5. **The Church is not a Para-Church Organization**

   Many para-church groups exist today because "the church" has failed in so many areas of ministry and these para-church groups or organizations have arisen because of this failure. They have been in the permitted will of God. Most para-church organizations depend on "the church" for their existence, for financial support and for members to carry out the vision of the para-church group. Some para-church groups (not all, thank God!) are often critical of "the church" and do not build "the church". Para-church organizations are not the church as defined in this text. It is hoped, therefore, that all who truly love the Lord Jesus Christ and understand what "church" really is, belong to some local assembly and contribute accordingly.

C. What Jesus Said About The Church

Having seen what the church is, and what the church is not, in this part we consider what Jesus said about the church. In the Scripture passages quoted at the beginning of this chapter we saw that the word "church" is used by Christ in the Gospel of Matthew three times.

The words Christ spoke here are actually like "**seed-words**" or "**seed-thoughts**" which Christ gave here. The words are actually Christ's own words and are prophetic promises of what He would do.

The "**Seed-Kingdom**" Parable in Mark 4:26-29 can be used to illustrate the New Testament revelation and progression of the truth of the church. The kingdom of heaven is like a Man sowing seed. Then comes "first the blade, then the ear, then the full corn in the ear". So it is with the unfolding and progressive revelation of the church in the New Testament. In the Gospel of Matthew, we see "**first the blade**", then in Acts, "**the ear**" (or head), and then in the Epistles, especially the Pauline Epistles, "**the full corn in the ear**". All that follows in Acts or in the Epistles actually arises out of and is all a development of the "**seed-words**" of Christ as He gave in the Gospel of Matthew, which are considered in outline form here.

1. It would be a Church He would Build

"Upon this Rock, I will build My Church ..." Christ Himself is THE Builder of the Church. It is important for all believers and leaders to keep this in mind. The Psalmist said: "Except the LORD build the house, they labour in vain that build it ..."(Psalm 127:1).

"Every house is built by some one, but He that built all things is God" (Hebrews 3:1-6). The church is built by Christ as His spiritual house (1Peter 2:5). Christ is indeed "THE wise man" who builds His house on a rock (Matthew 7:24-26; Luke 6:48-49).

Believers and ministers are "co-labourers" with Christ, and builders along with Him. But Paul warns every person to "take heed how you build". There must not be wood, hay or stubble, but gold, silver and precious stones in the material put into His house (1Corinthians 3:9b-16; Ephesians 2:20). The church grows into a holy temple in the Lord as a habitation of God by the Spirit.

Christ is the wise man, the architect, the builder. He has the plans, blueprint for the church that He is building. Moses may build the Tabernacle (Exodus 25-40), and Solomon may build the Temple (1Chronicles 1-8), but over and above and beyond all THE LORD IS THE BUILDER! So it is with the Church. Christ is THE Builder of the Church!

2. It would be His Church

"Upon this rock I will build MY Church ..." It is important for believers and all ministers to realize that the Church is HIS Church - Christ's Church. It is not "our church". We do not possess the Church. The **ekklesia** is His. How many divisions and schisms have come into the church and among the people of God because leaders held the idea that it was their church - not Christ's Church! So we have churches (or denominations, more correctly) named after some personality, or some doctrinal emphasis, or some form of government, or even a city or country, making the church a sectarian enterprize of some person. It has to be constantly kept in mind that the church belongs to Jesus. It is HIS Church! The Church is people! People is what the Church is about, that is, the people of God assembling before God to hear from God.

William Barclay brings out the three ways the word "church" is used in the New Testament. It is used of:

a. The Universal Church

"I will build My Church" (singular, not plural). The word is used of the church universal (Ephesians 1:21-23; 5:25-27; 4:4-6; Colossians 1:18; Hebrews 12:22; 1Corinthians 10:32; 12:28; Philippians 3:6). The church universal is composed of all believers, of all ages and time, and includes those believers both in heaven and earth. Christ is the head of the church - the universal church!

b. The Church Local

The word is used of a particular local church, or a church in a given locality (Acts 9:31; Romans 16:4,16; 1Corinthians 16:1,9; 2Corinthians 8:1; 1Corinthians 1:2; Galatians 1:2). The apostles wrote their letters primarily to local churches, not to individuals, but churches at Corinth, Ephesus, and so forth.

c. The Actual Assembly of Believers

The word is also used of an actual assembly or gathering of believers in a given place, met together for worship (1Corinthians 11:18; 14:19,23). Often there was "the church in the house of ..." They were **house-churches** (Romans 16:5; 1Corinthians 16:19; Colossians 4:15; Philemon 2). Christians met in New Testament times in any house that had a room large enough to accommodate them, as they did not have large buildings.

3. It would be a Church built on the Rock Foundation

"Upon this rock I will build My Church ..." The theme of the "rock/stone" is a very strong theme in the Scriptures. Christ is not only the builder, but He is also the foundation. Peter is not THE Rock. He is A rock, A stone, but NOT THE Rock, or THE Stone, as Peter himself confirms in his Epistle (1Peter 2:5-9). Note some of the major Scriptures on this theme of Christ being the stone or the rock upon which the church is built.

* Christ is the anointed stone of Bethel (Genesis 28:18-19; Luke 4:18; Acts 10:38.

* Christ became the stone of stumbling and rock of offence to the unbelieving nation of Jewry (Romans 9:33; 1Peter 2:5-9).

* Christ was the smitten stone, the rock from where the living waters of the Holy Spirit flowed (Exodus 17:5-7; 1Corinthians 10:1-4).

* Christ is the foundation stone in Zion (Isaiah 28:16). Christ is also the headstone of the Temple, the Church (Ephesians 2:20; 1Peter 2:5-9).

* Christ is the stone that will crush all who will not fall on Him and be broken in this time (Matthew 21:42-44).

Christ applied the Scriptures about "the rock" or "stumblingstone" to Himself. The religious leaders knew these Messianic prophecies. Peter himself applies it to Christ also (Acts 4:11). Jesus is the rock of revelation (Exodus 33:21-33).

Christ is the foundation of the Church as Paul clearly declares (1Corinthians 3:9b-16). All must be built upon Him in order to stand the storms of life.

4. It would be a Church against which the <u>Gates of Hades</u> could <u>not prevail</u>

"... the gates of hell (hades) will not prevail ..." One needs to understand the significance of "gates" in Scripture. The cities of the Canaanites were fenced with high walls, gates and bars that Israel had to conquer in order to possess the promised land. It involved warfare (Deuteronomy 3:5; 28:52,55,57; Judges 5:8). The city of Jerusalem had twelve gates by which the tribes would enter to keep the feasts of the Lord (Psalm 122:2; Isaiah 26:1-4; Revelation 21:12-23; 22:14).

The Lord promised Abraham that his seed would possess the gates of his enemies (Genesis 22:17; 24:60).

From "**Manners & Customs of Bible Lands**" (pages 239-240) we adapt some information about "gates" in Bible times.

"The gates of an Oriental city were of course connected with the walls; nevertheless, they were in a sense a structure by themselves. They were usually made of wood or stone, or wood that had been armoured with metal. The Psalmist speaks of gates of brass (copper), and gates of iron (Psalm 107:16). Often they were two-leaved gates (Isaiah 45:1), and were provided with heavy locks and bars (1Samuel 23:7). Sometimes a city or town had two walls and therefore two gates with a space between them. A sentinel was stationed in the tower of the first gate. When David was at Mahanaim awaiting the result of the battle with Absolom, Scripture says: "And David sat between the two gates: and the watchman went up to the roof over the gate unto the wall, and lifted up his eyes, and looked, and behold a man running alone" (2Samuel:18:24). This space between the gates was used for many purposes.

* The gateways of ancient walled cities and the open spaces near them were popular meeting places for people. They seemed like large halls that could care for great assemblies of people. Being vaulted, they provided a cool place to meet on a hot day (Proverbs 1:21).

* The city gate was used for the giving of an address or proclamation (2Chronicles 32:6)

* David spoke about people gossiping in the gates (Psalm 69:12).

* Mordecai sat in the king's gate in order to attract attention from him (Esther 2:21).

* The prophets often spoke their sermons in the gates of the city (Jeremiah 17:19).

* Gates were also used for holding court. Stone seats were provided for the judges. Lot sat in the gate as a judge (Genesis 19:1). At the gate Boaz went to redeem the estate of Elimelech and receive Ruth to be his wife (Ruth 4:1).

* David was thinking of the temple gates in Psalm 118:19, when he said, Open to me the gates of righteousness. Read also Psalms 24:9; 87:2; 100:1,4).

The gates were generally closed at sunset for protection from enemies at night.

When Jesus said that the gates of hades would not prevail against the church, the disciples understood the significance of gates. The gates of hell (or hades) speak of the unseen world, the powers of darkness, of death and Satanic forces and these would not prevail against the church. It speaks of the church being militant and triumphant - in spiritual sense! The gates of hades would not overcome the church. The church would eventually triumph. Samson took the gates of the city at the midnight hour (Judges 16:3).

When an enemy attacked a city, they would attack the gates, and try and break them down, burn them down, for, once they broke through the gates they were able to enter and conquer the city. Those within would guard the gates and do all in their power to fortify the gates against enemy attacks. Gates signified protection, safety, security and defence from enemy attacks. As Abraham and his seed would possess the gates of the enemies, so Christ in His church will conquer the gates of hades and the Satanic powers will not prevail against the church! The gates symbolize the power of the underworld to hold captives. This is the word of Christ in spite of all the attacks against the true church throughout Church history!

Other translations say: "... not even death will ever be able to **overcome**" (TEV); "And the gates of hades will not **overcome** it" (NIV); "And the powers of death will never have power to **destroy** it" (Phillips); "And the power of death shall never **conquer** it" (NEB), "And the gates of the underworld shall never **hold out against** it" (Jerusalem Bible).

The Church Christ builds will be victorious over all the onslaughts of the powers of its enemies. The Church would go forth conquering and to conquer!

5. It would be a Church having the <u>Keys of the Kingdom</u> of Heaven

"... I will give unto thee the keys of the kingdom of heaven ..."

A key is "an opener". It is an instrument that serves to unlock a door and let people in or lock the door and keep them out. The key symbolizes power to open or shut, to bind or loose, to lock or unlock. It speaks of power and authority.

The ancients believed that heaven was closed off by doors that needed to be opened; to be unlocked by the one having the keys. Jesus spoke of these keys as the keys of the kingdom of heaven. The Scriptures speak of various keys that the Lord gives to those under His authority.

* The key of knowledge (Luke 11:52)
* The key of David (Isaiah 22:21-22 with Revelation 3:7-8)
* The keys of death and hades (Revelation 1:18)
* The key of the bottomless pit (Revelation 9:1; 20:1)
* The keys of the kingdom of heaven (Matthew 16:19).

The prophetic promise here was especially spoken to Peter. In the Book of Acts we see Peter using the keys of the kingdom of heaven to unlock the door and let the Jews and the Gentiles enter into the kingdom of God (Acts 2 with Acts 10-11 chapters). Jews and Gentiles enter into the kingdom by repentance and faith and water baptism and the Holy Spirit (Matthew 3:1-2; 4:17; Hebrews 6:1-2; John 3:1-5).

The Church is the instrument in the hand of the Lord to preach and proclaim and demonstrate the power of the Gospel of the kingdom to all nations on the earth (Matthew 24:14).

6. It would be a Church that would exercise a **Binding** Ministry

"... whatsoever you bind on earth shall be bound in heaven ..." The word about binding is spoken both in Matthew 16:18-19 and also 18:18-20.

The word "bind" means "to tie together, or confine with a cord, or anything that is flexible; to fasten with a bond". It means "to constrain or restrain; as with a chain, fetter or cord, as "to bind hand and foot". It means, "to restrain in any manner". The Scriptures illustrate the whole thought of binding ministry.

* Samson was bound by the men of Judah (Judges 15:10-15; 16:5-21).
* The Hebrew youths were bound when cast into the fire (Daniel 3:20-24).
* Jesus said, First bind the strong man, then spoil his house (Matthew 12:29).
* The daughter of Abraham had been bound by Satan physically (Luke 13:16).
* In due time, Satan is to be bound in the bottomless pit for 1000 years (Revelation 20:1-10). Read also Psalm 149:8; Matthew 13:30; Mark 5:13; Acts 9:14; 22:4; Psalm 68:6.

In the Matthew 16 passage, this binding ministry seems to have more to do with the binding of Satan's powers, the demonic spirits that would seek to hinder the Church's ministry.

In the Matthew 18 passage this binding ministry seems more to do with the matter of Church discipline of unrepentant members who are bound by Church discipline.

The Church has been given the power to bind principalities and powers and wicked spirits that hold mankind captive and hinder the going forth of the Gospel. Jesus bound Satan, evil spirits, demonic powers and works. He wants His Church to continue His ministry. At Calvary, He conquered principalities and powers, triumphing over Satan's kingdom in the cross. This made possible the binding and loosing ministry in the Church.

7. **It would be a Church that would have a <u>Loosing</u> Ministry**

    "... whatever you loose on earth shall be loosed in heaven ..." The word is spoken in both passages in Matthew's Gospel (Matthew 16:18-19; 18:20).

    The binding and loosing ministry are actually both connected. Jesus manifested this binding and loosing ministry. When He ministered to the woman, a true daughter of Abraham, he said: "Ought not this woman whom Satan has **bound** these eighteen years be loosed from her infirmity?" (Luke 13:12-13).

    * The Hebrew youths, though cast bound into the fiery furnace, were loosed by the fourth Man in the fire, the Son of God (Daniel 3:25).

    * Jeremiah was loosed from chains that bound him (Jeremiah 40:4).

    * There are four angels at present bound in the River Euphrates and they will be loosed in a set time to kill men (Revelation 9:14-15).

    * There will be a company of God's people who will be loosed from death's appointment (Psalm 102:20 with Hebrews 9:27).

    The word "loose" means "to untie or unbind; to free from any fastening, to relieve from imprisonment; to liberate; to set at liberty". It also means "to free from any thing that binds or shackles". Also, "to remit, to absolve, or to free from anything burdensome or afflictive".

    When Lazarus was raised from the dead, he came forth bound in graveclothes. Jesus commanded him to be loosed (John 11:44).

    People in Satan's kingdom are bound mentally, spiritually, emotionally and physically. They have to be loosed from these things. This is the ministry of the Church. People bound by sin, sickness, immorality, drugs, habits, and wrong attitudes, as well as numerous other things, need to be loosed to serve the Lord.

    This word is used in both passages in Matthew. In the first it seems to belong to the Church's ministry of loosing people from Satan's domain. And in the second passage it deals more with loosing those who have come to repentance after being excommunicated from the church through lack of reconciliatory attitudes to offended members.

    The Amplified New Testament puts it this way. "... and whatever you bind, that is, declare to be improper or unlawful on earth **must already be bound in heaven**; and whatever you loose on earth - declare lawful - **must be what is already loosed in heaven**" (Matthew 16:19-20).

And again: "... Truly, I tell you, whatever you forbid and declare to be improper and unlawful on earth **must be what is already forbidden in heaven**, and whatever you permit and declare proper and lawful on earth **must be already permitted in heaven**" (Matthew 18:18).

This means that the Church in the earth must know the mind of Christ, who is the head of the Church and rules in heaven, which brings us to the next seed-word that Christ spoke about His Church.

8. **It would be a Church having <u>Heaven and Earth</u> connections**

"... whatever you bind on earth is bound in heaven ... whatever is loosed on earth is loosed in heaven ..." (Refer Amplified New Testament again).

This seed-word of Christ shows that the Church must have heaven and earth connections. This can only be as the Church, the Body of Christ in earth, is in touch with the Christ, the Head of the Church in heaven. Heaven and earth are united only through Christ. Where there is no heaven/earth connection, then the Church in earth is powerless.

* Jesus said, All power is given to Me in heaven and in earth ... go therefore and make disciples of all nations (Matthew 28:19).

* He taught us to pray: Your kingdom come, your will be done in earth as it is in heaven (Matthew 6:9).

* When Melchisedek met Abraham, he ministered communion to him, and he was priest of the Most High God, possessor of heaven and earth (Genesis 14:19,22).

Earth is totally dependant on heaven, in the natural, and also in the spiritual. As the early believers went forth with the Gospel, the Lord (in heaven) worked with them (in earth) confirming the Word with signs following (Mark 16:15-20). Without the power of Christ, in heaven, the Church may bind or loose all to no avail, and without results. It will be words, mere, empty and powerless words. But with heaven and earth, Christ and His Church, working together as one, then the Church will be victorious, triumphant, conquering and to conquer. Prayer is the key that connects heaven and earth together. A prayerless church is indeed a powerless church! There is spiritual warfare that takes place in heavenly places. Therefore, the Church in earth must be connected with the Christ in heaven!

9. **It would be a Church exercising a <u>Disciplinary Ministry</u> as necessary**

The passage in Matthew 18:15-20 especially has to do with Church discipline. The first Matthean passage speaks of the Church universal. The second speaks of the Church local, as the offence is of a local member. It would not at all be possible to "tell it to the church" universal!

The whole principle of reconciliation is set out here. It is a principle that very few local churches follow, and therefore the Lord in heaven cannot place His seal upon the matter of discipline.

If a member wrongs another member, then reconciliation should be done on a one-on-one basis. If this is not accomplished, then two or three others need to be brought in to effect reconciliation. If the member will not listen to them, then it needs to be brought before the Church. If the member will not listen to the appeal of the Church, then excommunication takes place.

Jay E. Adams says that the person is excommunicated, not for the original wrong but for refusing to listen to the Church, the **ekklesia**! This discipline is the "binding" of a unrepentant member, and only as he comes to repentance and reconciliation can the sin be remitted and this member be "loosed" again and restored into fellowship in the Church.

The Church is given the power of discipline under the Lord, the head of the church. The New Testament provides examples of Church discipline.

* The Corinthian fornicator was excommunicated from the Church until he came to repentance. The whole church had to take their stand with Paul's word on the discipline of immorality (1Corinthians 5).

* There was church discipline at Thessalonica for those who walked disorderly and not according to the tradition of the apostolic teaching (2Thessalonians 3:6,14,15).

* Ananias and Sapphira were Divinely disciplined for lying to the Holy Spirit over financial giving (Acts 5:1-11).

* Church leaders or elders need discipline when necessary (1Timothy 3:1-7 with 5:17-25). King David was Divinely disciplined for his sin or adultery and indirect murder of Urriah (2Samuel 11-12 with Psalm 51). He came to true repentance and restoration, but knew he was pardoned and punished in the remaining years of his life.

* Paul talks about other evils that need discipline if not brought to repentance (1 Corinthians 5:11). Divisions in the church need discipline (Romans 16:16-18). (The reader is referred to **"The Church in the New Testament"**, Chapter 30, on "Church Discipline" for a fuller treatment of this area. Text by the author).

Church discipline is an absolute necessity to keep the Church clean before the Lord. All discipline is either unto restoration or unto damnation. This is why members must judge themselves so that they be not judged by the Lord (1Corinthians 11:23-34). This is part of the teaching underlying the Lord's Table - the communion.

10. It would be a Church that Christ as Risen Head would be "in the midst"

"For where-ever two or three are gathered together (drawn together as My followers) in (into) My name, there I AM **in the midst** of them" (Amplified New Testament).

"In the midst", or "in the middle, right among you" is the thought here. Christ is central in His Church when we gather in His Name. It is the guarantee of His presence. There I AM (Exodus 3:14) in the middle of you, central among you. Jesus said: "Lo, I am with you even to the end of the age" (Matthew 28:18-20).

The Church needs to have a greater awareness of Christ "in the midst" - in the middle, and taking His place central among us. As His people agree together, or harmonize together, together make a symphony (Amp.NT), He is there in the midst of them. It speaks of unity, one accordance, harmony and a recognition of the Lord in the midst. It is the awareness of the omnipresent and risen Lord.

The theme of "**in the midst**" is seen throughout Scripture, of which we note a few brief references.

* The tree of eternal life was "in the midst" of Eden's garden (Genesis 2:9).
* The voice of the Lord came out of the midst of the bush (Exodus 3:2-4).
* The Lord was "in the midst" of the cloud (Exodus 24:16-18).
* God was "in the midst" of the camp of Israel (Deuteronomy 23:14).
* The Son of God, as fourth Man was "in the midst" of the fire (Daniel 3:25).
* Jesus resurrected stood "in the midst" of His disciples (Luke 24:36; John 20:19,26; Revelation 1:13; 2:1).
* The Lamb was "in the midst" of the twentyfour elders around the throne of God (Revelation 5:6; 7:17). Read also Zephaniah 3:17; Zechariah 2:5,10,11; John 19:18; Psalm 40:1-5; Psalm 22:22; Hebrews 2:12; Revelation 2:7; 22:2.

This is Christ's vision of His Church! The seed-thoughts given in Matthew's Gospel are watered by the Holy Spirit and develop through the Book of Acts and on into the Pauline Epistles. This is "the joy" that was set before the Lord Jesus and by which vision He endured the cross and is now set down at the right hand of the Father (Hebrews 12:1-2).

In Summary:

What kind of a church did Jesus have in mind when He gave the prophetic promise?

1. It would be a Church that He would build.
2. It would be His Church.
3. It would be a Church built on the Rock foundation.
4. It would be a Church against which the Gates of Hell would not prevail.
5. It would be a Church that would have the Keys of the Kingdom of Heaven.
6. It would be a Church that would have a Binding Ministry.
7. It would be a Church that would have a Loosing Ministry.
8. It would be a Church that would have Heaven and Earth connections.
9. It would be a Church having a Disciplinary Ministry as necessary.

10. It would be a Church with Christ as Risen Head in the midst.

This is Christ's vision of the Church! This is His prophetic promise and nothing will ever stop it coming to fulfilment. His word will not return unto Him void but it will accomplish that which He sent it unto (Isaiah 55:8-11).

As the student can see, any one of the points may be developed more fully as themes that run throughout the Holy Scriptures! May Christ's vision of His Church become our vision of what a New Testament Church should be. That is, a people summoned out of their homes, called to assemble together to hear God speak and to act for God in this ungodly world system!

CHAPTER SIXTEEN

SYMBOLS & TYPES OF THE CHURCH

Having considered what the Church is and what the Church is not, and yet to be, it is appropriate to consider in brief outline some of the numerous symbols and types of the Church.

God has, as it were, ransacked nature to give us symbols, types and pictures of the Church. It is, of course, important to realize that no one picture is the whole truth of what the Church is in the mind of God.

The Amplified New Testament says: "In **many separate revelations, each of which set forth a portion of the truth**, and in different ways, God spoke ..." (Hebrews 1:1-2). So each of the symbols, types or pictures of the Church may be looked at as "separate revelations", but each of them "set forth a portion of the truth", none of them on their own being the whole truth.

A. Pauline Revelation of the Church

Next to the Lord Jesus, the apostle Paul, no doubt, is the greatest revelator of the New Testament Church. Many of the pictures of the Church are provided for us through the apostolic writings of Paul.

It is worthy of note to see the use of the word "Church" by the New Testament writers, and it will be seen that Paul is the one who speaks of the Church the most. The word "Church" is used:

1. **By Jesus** - 3 times (Matthew 16:18; 18:17,17).

2. **By Luke** - 24 times (21 times, Church, 3 times, Assembly. Acts 2:47; 5:11; 7:38; 8:1,3; 9:31; 11:22,26; 12:1,5; 13:1; 14:23,27; 15:3,4,22,41; 16:5; 18:22; 20:17,28 and 19:32,39,41 respectively).

3. **By Paul** - 64 times in all (Romans 16:1,4,5,16,23; 1Corinthians 1:2; 4:17; 6:4; 7:17; 10:32; 11:16,18,22; 12:28; 14:4,5,12,19,23,28,33,34,35; 15:9; 16:1,19,19; 2Corinthians 1:1; 8:1,18,19,23,24; 11:8,28; 12:13; Galatians 1:2,13,22; Ephesians 1:22; 3:10,21; 5:23,24,25,27,29,32; Philippians 3:6; 4:15; Colossians 1:18,24; 4:15,16; 1Thessalonians 1:1; 2:14; 2Thessalonians 1:1,4; 1Timothy 3:5,15; 5:16; Philemon 1:2; Hebrews 2:12; 12:23(?).

4. **By James** - one time.

5. **By John** - 23 times in all (3John 1:6,9,10; Revelation1:4,11,20,20; 2:1,7,8, 11,12,17,18,23,29; 3:1,6,7,13,14,22; 22:16.

Of the 115 times the word "Church" is used in the New Testament, Paul uses it at least 64 times. Paul is indeed the greatest revelator of the Church that Jesus said He would build. Paul takes, as it were, the seed-word of Christ in the Gospels and develops it fully in the Epistles to the Churches.

Paul is the one who shows more fully that the Church is indeed the **ekklesia**, "the called out ones". The Church is:

* Called out of this present evil age (Galatians 1:4)
* Called out of darkness into light (1Peter 2:9).
* Called with a high and holy calling (2Timothy 1:9).
* Called with a heavenly calling (Hebrews 3:1).

The Church consists of those people who have responded to that call. They have been called out of their homes, summoned out of their homes, and called together by God to listen to God and act for God. Paul writes: "Unto the church (assembly) of God which is at Corinth ... with all that in every place call upon the name of the Lord Jesus Christ, both theirs and ours ..." (1Corinthians 1:2).

The Church consists of those people who "come together" for a Divine purpose. Therefore **"ek"** (**"out of"**), and **"kaleo"** (**"to call"**), and **"klesia"** (**"come together, assembling together"**): this is what the Church is - people who have been called out of the world, out of their homes, and assembling together to hear from God and to act for God. Note in 1Corinthians 11:17,18,20,33,34; 12:24; 14:23,26 how often Paul speaks of **"come together"**, or **"when the whole church is come together"**.

B. **Symbols and Types of the Church**

Because Paul is the greatest revelator of the New Testament Church, most of the symbols and types of the Church are drawn from Pauline Epistles, along with several others from apostolic writings. It is seen, however, that all the symbols and types of the New Testament Church are drawn from the Old Testament also. The nation of Israel was called "the church in the wilderness" (Acts 7:38). The things that happened to Israel become types and examples to us in this end of the age (Note 1Corinthians 10:6,11). Each of the following pictures of the Church become great studies in themselves.

1. **The Church is God's Household**

    The Church is the household of God in which Christ is the Firstbegotten Son (Ephesians 2:19; Matthew 24:45; Luke 12:42; Hebrews 3:1-6).

2. **The Church is God's Temple**

    The Church is God's Temple, God's Habitation, in which Christ is the Chief Cornerstone (Ephesians 2:20-22; 1 Corinthians 3:16-20; 2 Corinthians 6:16-18; 1Peter 2:5). The Old Covenant material Temple is replaced by God's people as the spiritual and living Temple (Exodus 25:8).

3. **The Church is God's Family**

    The Church is the Family of God, of which Christ is the Firstborn Son amongst a vast family of brothers and sisters (Ephesians 3:14-15; 2:19; Galatians 6:10). The Father always wanted a Family. This is fulfilled in the Church Family (Romans 8:25-30).

4. **The Church is the Body of Christ**

   The Church is the Body of Christ in the earth, of which Christ is the head, both universally and locally (Romans 12:4-5; 1Corinthians 12:12-13,27; Ephesians 1:22-23; 4:4,11-16; 2:16; 3:6; Colossians 1:18). This is strictly a Pauline revelation of the Jew and Gentile being one body in Christ.

5. **The Church is the Bride of Christ**

   The Church is the Bride of Christ of which Christ is the Husband, head and bridegroom (Ephesians 5:22-32; John 3:29; Revelation 21:2,9; 19:7; 22:17; 2Corinthians 11:2). The Church is spoken of as the Wife of the Lamb (Revelation 19:7).

6. **The Church is the Army of the Lord**

   The Church is the Army of the Lord, in spiritual warfare and of which Christ is the Captain of our salvation (Ephesians 6:10-18; 2Corinthians 10:4; 2Timothy 2:3). The Church is militant and triumphant against the gates of hell (Matthew 16:18-19).

7. **The Church is the Flock of God**

   The Church is the Flock of God, His sheepfold, of which Christ is the Chief Shepherd, who gave His life for the sheep. Christ is the Good Shepherd, the Chief Shepherd and the Great Shepherd of the sheep (John 10; Psalm 23; 1Peter 5:2-3; Acts 20:28,29; Hebrews 13:20). It is the sheep in the sheepfold.

8. **The Church is a Kingdom of Priests**

   The Church is a Kingdom of Priests, a royal priesthood, of which Christ is the King-Priest after the order of Melchisedek (Revelation 1:6; 5:9-10; 1Peter 2:5-9; Hebrews 7; Psalm 110; Exodus 19:1-6).

9. **The Church is God's Spiritual Israel**

   The Church is the Spiritual Israel of God, the holy nation, of which Christ is the Commander in Chief (Galatians 6:16; Romans 9:6; Ephesians 2:12; Revelation 7:4). It is through the gates of the city of the New Jerusalem that all believers enter into the twelve tribes of Israel according to their place in the Israel of God (Revelation 21-22 Chapters).

   The true Jew is not one outwardly, of the flesh, but one of the heart, one that is spiritually joined to the Lord in praise (Romans 2:28-29; Revelation 2:9; 3:9). As in the Old Testament, those only who were "in Isaac" were counted for the seed of Abraham, so in the New Testament, only those who are "in Christ" are counted as the true seed of Abraham (Galatians 4:22-31; Romans 9:6-9; Genesis 21:12).

10. **The Church is God's Vineyard**

    The Church is God's Vineyard, of which Christ is the Vine and the believers are the branches, the fruit bearing part of Christ. The Father is the Husbandman and He looks for fruit unto His glory (John 15:1-16; Isaiah 5:1-7).

11. The Church is God's Discipleship School

The Church is God's School of Discipleship making, of which Christ is the Master-Teacher. Disciples are to follow Christ in their walk and learning (Matthew 28:18-20; 10:24-25; 16:24-26). The disciples are to be as their Master, and also to make disciples of all nations.

12. The Church is God's Dwelling Place

The Church is God's Tabernacle (or Temple), God's House of which Christ is the Architect and Master Builder. The Church is God's dwelling place (Hebrews 3:1-6; 1Peter 2:5-9; 1Timothy 3:15).

13. The Church is God's Lampstand

The Church is God's Candlestick or Lampstand which is meant to give light in the midst of a darkened world (Revelation 1-2-3 Chapters, Exodus 25:31-40; Matthew 5:14; John 8:12; Isaiah 60:1-2). As Christ was the light of the world in earth, now He has left the Church to be His light in the world.

14. The Church is God's Holy Nation

The Church is God's Holy Nation in the earth, it is the new ethnic composed of believing Jews and believing Gentiles (Exodus 19:1-6 with 1Peter 2:5-10).

15. The Church is God's Olive Tree

The Church is God's Olive Tree, in which the anointing oil of the Holy Spirit dwells, in ministry, fruits, grace and gifts (Romans 11:15-25). The Church is a faith-olive tree in which all abide by faith. Unbelief causes branches to be broken off the faith-olive tree (Psalm 52:8; Isaiah 17:6; 24:13; Jeremiah 16:11).

16. The Church is God's Seed

The Church is God's Seed, the Seed of Abraham in the earth, and in which all nations of the earth will be blessed. Christ and His Church constitute the one yet many-membered Seed to bless the nations (Galatians 3:16,29; Genesis 12:1-3; Genesis 22:17-18).

17. The Church is God's Peculiar Treasure

The Church is God's Peculiar Treasure, found and hidden in the field of this earth. Israel was His Old Testament treasure, now the Church is (Exodus 19:3-6; 1Peter 2:5-9; Matthew 13:44).

18. The Church is God's Pearl of Great Price

The Church is God's Pearl of great price, which Christ came and redeemed from the sea-nations of this world (Matthew 13:45-46). The Church is bought with a great price and cost Christ His all at Calvary.

19. The Church is God's New Jerusalem

The Church is God's New Jerusalem, the holy city of God and the Lamb in which all the redeemed of all ages shall dwell eternally (Revelation Chapters 21-22; Matthew 5:14; Hebrews 11:10-16; 12:22). It is the city of refuge for all who are willing to run into it through Christ the High Priest.

The Church fulfills "Zion" of the Old Testament also, which was part of Jerusalem, the City of God (Psalm 87:1-7; 2:6; 14:7; 132:13-17; Isaiah 28:16; 1Peter 2:5,9).

20. The Church is the People of God

The Church is the People of God, who were once not a people and had not obtained mercy, but now have obtained mercy and are become the people of God. The Church is people! God has always longed to have a people who would be entirely His own people (Exodus 6:7; 17:7-8; 1Peter 2:5-10; Romans 9:23-26; 2Corinthians 6:16; Titus 2:14; Psalm 110:3). Israel was the people of God in Old Testament times. Jews and Gentiles in Christ are the people of God in New Testament times (Ephesians 2:11-18).

21. The Church is the Bread of God

The Church is God's Bread in the earth. Christ is the Bread of Life to us but now the Church becomes bread to one another and to the lost and hungry world (John 6; 1Corinthians 10:17).

22. The Church is a Mother in earth

The Church becomes a Mother in the earth as she brings forth children unto God. God is our Father, the Church is likened to being our Mother. Christ is spoken of "the everlasting Father" (Isaiah 9:6-9). By evangelism, children are brought to birth, otherwise the Church is barren. New converts feed on the milk of the Word, then mature to meat (1Peter 2:2; 1Corinthians 3:1-3).

23. The Church is a Revealed Mystery

The Church is a Mystery now revealed, though kept secret since the world began. The Church is a manifestation in time of an eternal purpose, and this great mystery was especially revealed to Paul, and to holy apostles and prophets by the Spirit (Romans 16:25-26; Colossians 1:26-27; Ephesians 3:1-9)

24. The Church is the Pillar and Ground of the Truth

The Church is the Pillar and Ground (or, Support, Stay, Foundation) of the truth in the earth. The Church is to know the truth, guard the truth, preach the truth and set people free by the truth (John 14:6; 4:24; 16:13; 17:17; 8:32-34). The Church is to contend for "the faith" once and for all delivered to the saints. Though Church History shows restoration and recovery of truths lost, there are never any additions to that truth as already revealed in the Scriptures (Jude). The Church should be the place where truth is found!

25. The Church is God's Tabernacle of David

The Church is the fulfilment of the Tabernacle of David (Acts 15:15-18). All that was set forth in the Old Testament Tabernacle of David as concerning the order of worship, the singers and the musicians and the spirit of Davidic worship finds its expression in the New Testament Church (1Chronicles 15-16-17 Chapters). Jews and Gentiles, believing, gather together to worship the Lord in this Tabernacle of David, with Jesus, who is the greater Son of David and the leader of our worship to the Father God (Hebrews 2:12).

Many other pictures of the Church could be given as found in both Old and New Testament. It should be remembered that each picture is only one facet of the glory of the Church in the eyes of the Lord. No one picture is the whole truth but each presents a fragment or portion of the truth. These things are types and examples and written for our admonition and comfort (1Corinthians 10:6,11; 1Peter 1:10-12; Romans 15:4).

In Summary:

* God has given Christ to be head over all things to the Church (Ephesians 1:22-23).

* It is through the Church that the manifold wisdom of God will be seen before principalities and powers in heavenly places (Ephesians 3:10-11).

* Glory throughout all ages will be seen in the Church (Ephesians 3:21).

* Christ is the head of the Church and the Saviour of the Body (Ephesians 5:23-24).

* Christ loved the Church and gave Himself for it, that it might be a glorious Church without spot, or wrinkle, or blemish or any such thing, but that it should be a holy bride presentable to Himself (Ephesians 5:26-27). He will cleanse it by the washing of water by the Word.

* The Lord will nourish and cherish the Church as His bride (Ephesians 5:29).

* The marriage of Christ and His Church is indeed a great mystery (Ephesians 5:32).

The apostle Paul, the greatest revelator of the New Testament Church, was willing to suffer afflictions in himself for the sake of the Church, the Body of Christ (Colossians 1:24-29). Every true minister of the Gospel will feel that way about the Church, which is the Body of Christ, His bride-to-be, and will do everything for the perfecting of that Church to be presented to Christ, the heavenly Bridegroom!

This was indeed the "heavenly vision" which Paul was not disobedient to - Christ and His Church (Acts 26:19). Every true minister will maintain the vision of Christ and His Church until the ultimate day!

CHAPTER SEVENTEEN

THE PURPOSE OF THE CHURCH'S EXISTENCE

Having considered the Church as God's new ethnic, and seeing the vision of the Church as Jesus saw it, and then looking at a number of symbols and types of the Church, we need to consider the purpose of the Church's existence! What is the purpose for the Church's existence?

In this chapter we set out the reason for the existence of the Church as being basically fivefold. God had an eternal purpose in mind when He planned both creation and redemption. This purpose was manifold in Christ, and it is an "**eternal purpose**". This great purpose is **THE CHURCH**. Nothing will be allowed to frustrate the eternal purpose of God in Christ and His Church (Ephesians 3:1-12). All things work together for good to those who are called according to His purpose (Romans 8:26-28). Let us consider this fivefold purpose for the Church's existence.

(Note:- For fuller treatment of this matter, the reader is referred to "**The Church in the New Testament**", Chapter 33, Pages 296-302, by the author).

A. Ministry unto the Lord

The chief purpose for the Church's existence is to glorify and worship God. All things were created by God and for Him and for His pleasure (Revelation 4:11).

The Church is redeemed to be a worshipping community of people (Psalm 29:1-2). The people of God are redeemed to worship Him, then to serve Him (Matthew 4:10). It is first upward, then outward; it is first God, then man. Worship always precedes service, as these Scriptures indicate (Deuteronomy 4:19; 5:9; 6:13; 8:19; 11:16; 12:32; Joshua 24:14-24). Man was created to be a worshipper. Sinners cannot worship God. Only the redeemed can. The worship must be in spirit and in truth (John 4:20-24). The worshippers are measured by the rod of God (Revelation 11:1-2). The chief end or purpose of man's existence is to worship and glorify God and enjoy Him for ever.

B. Ministry to the Saints

The second purpose for the Church's existence is to edify itself, this being done by the saints ministering to one another. This is the ministry of the Body of Christ edifying and increasing itself in love (Ephesians 4:9-16; 1Corinthians 12).

The saints are to be built up in the most holy faith (Jude 1-3,20). God has given the various ministries for this purpose (Ephesians 4:9-16; Colossians 2:7; 1Corinthians 3:10-15; 14:26). The ministries in the Body of Christ are to educate the members of the Body of Christ with the doctrines in the Word of God (Matthew 28:18-20).

The saints are to be built up as to holiness of character and conformity to the image of Christ. It is the Lord's will that the Church be holy, without spot, blemish, wrinkle or any such thing. He desires to present to Himself a glorious Church as His bride (Ephesians 5:23-32; John 15:2; Hebrews 12:10; 1 John 3:2; Revelation 19:7).

The saints are to be brought into the work of their ministry as functioning members of the Body of Christ (Ephesians 4:9-16). The Church is to be a covering and protection for the saints of God. It is His house and all that a natural home provides should be found in the house of the Lord (Isaiah 2:1-4).

The saints will minister one to another, even as the members of the natural body minister one to another (John 13:33-34; Galatians 6:2; 1Peter 1:22; 1 John 3:18). A worthy subject to study in the Word of God is the theme of "one another" as in some sample Scriptures here (John 15:12,17; 1Thessalonians 4:18; Hebrews 10:24; 3:13; Romans 14:19; 15:14; Colossians 3:13,16; 1Peter 4:10; Ephesians 5:21; James 5:16; 1Peter 4:9; 5:14; 1John 1:7 and many others).

The human body with its millions of cells and members, all working in harmony, unity and life show what can be in the members of the Church, the Body of Christ.

C. Ministry to the Sinner

The third purpose of the Church's existence is to minister the Gospel of grace to the unsaved, to the sinner, to the lost and dying world. The more effective our ministry is to the Lord, the more effective ministry is to the saints, the more effective should be our ministry to the world of the unsaved. When the saints are built up, they should multiply themselves. The Church is to preach the Gospel of the Kingdom to the world before the end of the age comes (Matthew 24:14; 28:18-20).

The promise to Abraham was that all nations would be blessed through his seed (Genesis 12:1-3). This was confirmed to Israel (Exodus 19:1-6). The inheritance promised by the Father to the Son was the coming in of the heathen to the Kingdom (Psalm 2:8; 11:6). The Church is the light in a darkened world (Matthew 5:14-16).

Signs and wonders are to follow the preaching of the Gospel (Mark 16:15-20, as the Church fulfills the great commission (Matthew 28:18-20; Acts 1:5-8; Luke 4:18-21; John 20:20-22). This is the age for the coming in of the Gentiles to be grafted into the faith-olive tree with believing Jews (Romans 11:25; Acts 13:1-4; 15:15-18). The Church is to be God's arm of salvation to a lost and dying world. He sent His disciples out to continue His ministry until out of every kindred, tribe, tongue and nation there will be those who are the redeemed (Revelation 5:9-10). The Lamb will see the fruit of His sufferings. The Church is to minister the evangel.

D. Ministry to Conquer Satan's Hosts

The fourth purpose for the Church's existence is to bring about the downfall and casting out of Satan and his evil hosts. The kingdom of Satan is to be subdued under Christ and His Church.

The Church is called to be militant and triumphant. The gates of hades are not to prevail against the Church (Matthew 16:15-20). The Church will be a victorious Church. Though there be warfare and conflict in the spiritual realm against evil spirits, principalities and powers, the Church will be more than conqueror (Genesis 22:17; 24:10). The Church will be clothed with the armour of God and give spiritual weapons for warfare (Ephesians 6:10-20; 2 Corinthians 10:1-5; Revelation 12:10-11; Psalm 9:13; Isaiah 26:2). The head of the serpent will be bruised under the feet of the Church (Genesis 3:15 with Romans 16:20).

This Church (as has been seen) will have the keys of the kingdom to bind and loose according to the will of the Christ, who is the head of the Church in heaven (Matthew 16:18-19). Repentance and faith bring people into the kingdom (Matthew 3:2; 4:16). The kingdom is entered by new birth (John 3:1-5; Colossians 1:13-14; Acts 8:12; 19:8; 20:25; 28:28-31).

It is the Church's ministry to preach and demonstrate the power of the kingdom of God. This is part of the purpose for the Church's existence.

E. Ministry and Guardian of The Truth

The fifth purpose for the existence of the Church is to be the guardian of the truth of God in the earth. The Church is "the pillar and ground of the truth", as has been listed under symbols and types of the Church. The Church is to guard the faith that was once delivered to her (Jude 1-3; 1Timothy 3:15-16).

This fifth part of the fivefold purpose of the Church's existence needs to be considered more fully, therefore, the next chapter will deal with this.

In Summary:

The purpose of the Church's existence is not for herself, but for the Lord, for the edifying of itself, to serve the Lord, to minister to a dying world, to conquer the kingdom darkness, and also to guard the deposit of Divine truth entrusted to her. This brings us to our next chapter!

CHAPTER EIGHTEEN

THE CHURCH - THE GUARDIAN OF THE TRUTH

As seen in the conclusion of the previous chapter, the fifth purpose for the existence of the Church is the Church is called to be the guardian of the truth in the earth.

In the development of thought in this chapter, it will be seen that the Church is called to be the guardian of "**the truth**" and, what the Scripture calls "**the faith**". The distinction, yet inter-relatedness of these two expressions will be seen in the course of this chapter. However, this needs to be seen in Christ, the Holy Spirit and then in the Church.

A. Christ- The Word of Truth.

The Lord Jesus Christ is the fullness of Divine truth personified. He came as the fullness of grace and truth (John 1:14-17). He Himself said: "I am THE Way, THE Truth and THE Life" (John 14:6). He is the whole truth, and nothing but the truth. All the truth that is in the Father is revealed in the Son. Jesus is the WAY to the Father. He is the TRUTH about the Father. He is the LIFE of the Father. Man's only approach to the Father is through the Son.

Jesus is THE WORD of truth (John 17:17; 18:36). To know Him as the truth, both spiritually and experientially is to be set free (John 8:31-36).

The four Gospels actually present to us the teaching of the Lord Jesus, which words He received from the Father. He said that He had not spoken of Himself but spoke the words that the Father gave Him. He said His doctrine (teaching) was not His but the Father's, who sent Him (John 7:16-17; 12:44-50). It is this word that will judge us "in that day".

Gordon Lindsay, in "**The Words of Jesus**" (Volume 1-2, 1951, now out of print), arranged all the words and sayings of Jesus in groups of sevens. The student would need to study all that the Gospels say on the words of Christ. However, the following is a list of the subjects of themes of truth that Jesus spoke in His earthly ministry, and which the New Testament recorded under inspiration of the Spirit. The list is adapted from Gordon Lindsay's notes.

1. The Promises of Jesus
2. The Commandments of Jesus
3. The Revelation of the Godhead
4. The words of Jesus on Heaven and Earth, the World and Time
5. The words of Jesus on Salvation
6. The words of Jesus concerning Sin
7. The words of Jesus on Righteousness, the Fruit of the Spirit
8. The words of Jesus on the Resurrection, Second Coming and the New Order
9. The words of Jesus on Judgments

10. The words of Jesus on Prayer, Faith and Healing
11. The words of Jesus on Life subjects
12. The words of Jesus on Government, Kingdom of God, the Church, Israel
13. The words of Jesus to the Jews
14. The words of Jesus concerning the Scriptures
15. The words of Jesus spoken during the performance of Miracles
16. The words of Jesus on Preaching the Gospel of the Resurrection
17. The words of Jesus on His Ministry and Atonement
18. The Prophecies of Jesus of the future
19. The Conversations of Jesus with individual persons
20. The Parables, Miracles and Persons to whom Jesus spoke
21. The Last or Final words of Jesus.

There is not a subject or truth that Jesus THE TRUTH did not speak about. Throughout the Gospels we have the teaching, the words of Jesus. All that Jesus spoke was TRUTH. HE is the truth. He spoke truth. His words are truth. He is THE WORD of Truth - the fullness of grace and truth personified.

B.   The Spirit of Truth

It is to be noted that, in spite of all the truth that Jesus gave to His disciples, as recorded in the Gospels, Jesus still had much more to teach them. In John's Gospel, He told them that He had many more things to say to them, but they could not at that time receive or handle them. Because of the disciple's humanness and weaknesses at that time, Jesus promised to send the Holy Spirit to complete His ministry.

He spoke of the Holy Spirit as the Comforter, and as **THE SPIRIT OF TRUTH**. The Holy Spirit would lead and guide them into **ALL TRUTH** (John 14:16-17,25; 15:26; 16:12-15).

If Jesus was THE WORD OF TRUTH, the Holy Spirit is THE SPIRIT OF TRUTH! But there is absolute unity and oneness of mind, will and purpose in the Son of God and the Spirit of God. The Word and the Spirit agree in one (1John 5:7-8).

From the outpouring of the Holy Spirit and the birthday of the Church, truth continued to flow to the apostles. The Holy Spirit was simply completing the ministry of the Son. The apostles gave themselves to "prayer and the word" (Acts 6:4). The Holy Spirit revealed the further truths to the early church. These truths came over a period of approximately 50-60 years, and were received and written down in the Books of the New Testament, in all twenty-seven books.

All the truth (truths) we need to know and receive and experience are contained in the New Testament Scriptures. The New Testament books complete the truths that Jesus wanted to give to His disciples, which they could not receive while He was with them on earth. The New Testament Scriptures, as also the Old Testament Scriptures, were inspired by God - they were "God-breathed" (2Timothy 3:15-16). This completed the New Testament canon of inspired Scriptures.

By grouping the New Testament books in the following order, we gain a brief overview of the truths that each book presents. Because we believe absolutely in the inspiration of the Scriptures, we see that there is a progression of truth revealed in the twenty-seven books of the New Testament.

1. **The Gospels**

    The four Gospels of Matthew, Mark, Luke and John present the truths of Christ's virgin birth, baptism, anointing, ministry of signs and wonders, His teaching and preaching of the Gospel of the Kingdom, His sinless life, the Lord's table, His death, burial, resurrection, commission and ascension to the Father, and His words received from the Father. These are historical books.

2. **The Acts**

    The Book of Acts is an historical book. It presents the truths of the Lordship and headship of Christ, the outpouring and ministry of the Holy Spirit, the power of Christ's name, the Apostles doctrine, and the revelation and planting of New Testament Churches.

3. **The Gentile Epistles**

    There are nine Gentile Epistles, each of them written by the apostle Paul, the apostle to the Gentiles. Each of them present distinctive truths.

    Romans - Justification by faith.

    1-2 Corinthians - New Testament Church order, Gifts of the Spirit, Love, the Communion, Body of Christ, Marriage relationships, Doctrine of Resurrection, Apostolic ministry qualifications.

    Galatians - Law and grace, Covenants, Works and Faith, Spirit and Life, Liberty or License.

    Ephesians - The Church, the great mystery of Christ's marriage, and purpose of the Church's existence.

    Philippians - Joy and rejoicing in all things; the Humiliation and Exaltation of the Lord Jesus Christ.

    Colossians - The fullness of the Godhead in Christ, the head of the Church.

    1-2 Thessalonians - The Second Coming of Christ in comfort, the Coming of the Antichrist, Apostasy, the Rapture of the Saints at the Revelation of Christ.

4. **The Hebrew Epistles**

    There are also nine Hebrew Epistles and each of them present their distinctive truths for the Church to hold to and guard.

Hebrews - The New Covenant Sanctuary, Priesthood, Sacrifices, Promises. The Order of Melchisedek as King-Priest. All things are better in Christ.

James - Faith and Works and Practical Christian living.

1-2 Peter - The Sufferings and Glory of Christ and His Saints. Grow in Grace and Knowledge. Beware of False Ministries. Watch for Christ's Second Coming and the New Heavens and New Earth.

1-2-3 John - Light, Life and Love in Christ. Discern the Spirit of Truth and Error, the Spirit of Christ and Antichrist. Know the Truth both doctrinally and walk in it experientially.

Jude - Preservation in the midst of Apostasy.

Revelation - The Book of Ultimates; the Book of Sevens - Seven Churches, Seals, Trumpets, Vials; the Christ and Antichrist; the Bride of Christ, the Harlot Church, the Great Tribulation, the Wrath of God, Coming of Christ, and the Eternal States - New Jerusalem or the Lake of Fire.

5. **The Pastoral - Personal Epistles**

    1-2 Timothy - Qualifications for Church Officers, Elders and Deacons, the Laying on of Hands, Necessity of Sound Doctrine amidst departure from the faith.

    Titus - Adorn the Doctrine of Godliness and the True Grace of God.

    Philemon - The Epistle of personal Reconciliation.

The Gospels, Acts and the Epistles cover every facet of truth that the Lord intended the Church to receive, walk in and guard. These truths were deposited in the Church.

They include Doctrinal, Ministerial, Ecclesiastical, Covenantal, Christological, Pastoral and Relational, Typical and Personal and Eschatological in their completeness. Such were the truths given to the Church.

C. **The Church - The Guardian of the Truth**

The progression of truth has been from Jesus who is THE WORD of Truth, to the Holy Spirit, who is THE SPIRIT of Truth, and now on into THE CHURCH, the guardian of the truth.

Paul writes to Timothy in 1 Timothy 3:15-16:

"But if I tarry long, that thou mayest know how thou oughtest to behave thyself in the house of God, which is **the church of the living God, the pillar and ground of the truth**. And without controversy great is the mystery of godliness: God was manifest in the flesh, justified in the Spirit, seen of angels, preached unto the Gentiles, believed on in the world, received up into glory".

Once these truths as seen in the New Testament books were given to the Church, the Church became the pillar and ground (the stay, the support, the foundation) of the truth. The Church has become God's guardian of these Divine truths. These truths are not just to be known mentally but experientially. To know the truth in this manner sets one free. To know the Son is to be set free for the Son is truth personified (John 8:31-36).

In the Old Testament times, Israel as a nation was God's repository of truth. The prophet Isaiah spoke of "the righteous nation, which keepeth the truth (KJV. Margin reference; "the truths"), entering in through the gates of the strong city of God (Isaiah 26:1-4). God gave to Israel His truth - His truths - the truth of the one true God, the truth of redemption and approach to God through sacrifice (and many other truths) as embodied in the symbolism of the Tabernacle and Temple order.

The nation of Israel was meant to be the guardian of those truths and share them with the nations of the earth. These many "fragments of truth" were given over many years until the Old Testament canon of Scripture was complete (Hebrews 1:1-2. Amplified New Testament). The same is true of New Testament Scriptures, except that this was a quicker work of the Spirit of Truth, in completing the New Testament canon.

At the beginning of this chapter, there were two expressions used which are inter-related, yet each have their uniqueness, these being (1) The Truth, and (2) The Faith.

1. The Truth

Enough has been written on the fact of "the truth". Jesus is the truth. The Holy Spirit is the Spirit of truth. The Church is the pillar and support (foundation, guardian) of the truth as given by Jesus and the Holy Spirit.

"Truth" simply means "Conformity to fact or reality", true state of facts or things. Truth is things as they really are; the real state of things; not falsity. All the things Jesus and the Holy Spirit gave and spoke of are things as they are, the real state of persons and things in the mind of God.

The believer needs a love for the truth so that he does not believe a lie and come under deception (2Thessalonians 2:1-12; John 16:13). The believer needs to discern between the spirit of truth and the spirit of error (1John 4:6).

2. The Faith

Another expression used much in the New Testament is "the faith". It seems that this expression in an all-inclusive expression of the truth. **In other words, it may be said that, "the faith" includes in itself all "the truths" that God has revealed and entrusted to the Church.**

In order to understand this expression more clearly and fully, we note how the word "faith" in the New Testament falls into several categories. These need to be understood and distinguished in order to save God's people from confusion, as is often the case on the subject of faith. The New Testament speaks of different aspects of faith and these distinctions need to be recognized.

a. Saving Faith

Saving faith is the gift of God to the repentant sinner that he might be saved (Ephesians 2:8; Luke 7:50; Acts 16:31; Hebrews 11:4). Saving faith is trusting Christ for salvation.

b. Fruit of Faith

The fruit of faith is the fruit of the Spirit that grows in a believer's life as he walks in obedience to the Word. The fruit of faith causes one to grow in grace and knowledge (Galatians 5:22; Hebrews 11:8,10,17-19,28,30,31). The "faith chapter" illustrates this aspect.

c. Gift of Faith

The gift of faith is a gift of the Spirit to speak the supernatural power of God into operation and into the area of the miraculous (Hebrews 11:29; 1Corinthians 12:1-12; Mark 11:12-14,22-26).

d. Perfect Faith

Perfect faith is the spirit of faith, full and complete faith, devoid of any shade of doubt. It is God's faith (2Corinthians 4:3; Psalm 116:10; James 2:22).

e. Doctrinal Faith

This is what Jude writes about when he says to "contend earnestly for the faith once delivered to the saints" (Jude 3).

This is "the faith" which is meant here in this section of our chapter. This aspect of faith refers more particularly to the **doctrinal revelation** of God. It is the word of the Gospel in its fullness. It speaks of the sum total of the revelation of God as given in the total Bible.

Vine's Expository Dictionary says: "The faith", by metonymy, What is believed, the content of belief".

Wuest's Word Studies in the Greek New Testament says: "The faith" here is not faith as exercised by the individual, but Christianity itself in its historic and life-giving salvation" (Jude, page 235).

"The faith" therefore is the whole Biblical revelation and doctrines that God gave to His people. Jude calls it "**the faith**" once delivered (and that, once and for all times) to the saints (Jude 3).

There are a number of Scriptures that refer simply to "**the faith**" and when used in this way speak of "**the truths**" revealed to the Church as set forth in the Scriptures. Note some of these references.

* A great company of priests became obedient to "**the faith**" (Acts 6:7).

* The disciples must continue in "**the faith**" (Acts 14:22).

* Before "**the faith**" came, we were under the law (Galatians 3:23-25).

* Some make shipwreck concerning "**the faith**" (1Timothy 1:19; 2Timothy 3:8), while Paul had kept "**the faith**" (2Timothy 4:7; Titus 1:13).

* In the last days some shall depart from "**the faith**"(1Timothy 4:1-3).

* When the Son of Man comes, will He find (Lit.) **"THE FAITH"** in the earth? (Luke 18:8).

The Amplified New Testament puts Jude 3 this way. "Beloved, my whole concern was to write to you in regard to our common salvation. But I found it necessary and was impelled to write to you and urgently appeal to and exhort you to contend for **the faith** which was once for all handed down to the saints - **the faith (which is that sum of Christian belief)** which was delivered verbally to the holy people of God".

What then were these truths - "the faith" - once and for all time give to the saints, the people of God?

D. "The Truths" in "The Faith" Once Delivered to the Saints

The writer uses this sub-title to mean "the faith" which includes in itself all the distinctive "truths" God has revealed in His Word. "The faith" is used as an all-inclusive word. "The truths" speak of the different truths God has given the Church (eg., The truth of redemption, the truth of baptism, etc, etc.,).

Following is a reasonably comprehensive list of the truths in "the faith" as given to the early apostles and the early Church. It can in no way be exhaustible.

1. The revelation of God as Father, Son and Holy Spirit (John 14,15,16,17; Matthew 28:19-20).

2. The truth of creation, angels, creation and fall of man and the entrance of sin into the universe (Genesis 1,2,3; Romans 5:12-21).

3. The doctrine of Christ - His Deity, virgin birth, sinlessness, ministry, death, burial, resurrection, ascension, mediatorial work, second coming and final judgments in the earth. It has to do with His person (who He is), His work (what He has done) and His words (what He said).

4. The Holy Spirit - His Deity, personality and ministry in the world and the Church.

5. The Fruit, the Gifts, the Operations and the Baptism of the Holy Spirit (Acts 2).

6. The Inspiration and Infallibility of the Scriptures (2Timothy 3:15-16).

7. The Gospel of the Kingdom (Matthew 10:1-10; 24:14).

8. The Ministry of Angels.

9. The Apostolic Doctrines, or, First principles (Acts 2:42; Hebrews 6:1-2). These include: Repentance from Dead Works, Faith towards God, Baptisms, Laying on of Hands, Resurrection from the dead, Eternal judgment and Perfection.

10. The Lord's Table, Communion (1Corinthians 11; Matthew 26:26-28).

11. The Priesthood of all believers (1Peter 2:5-9; Revelation 1:6; 5:9-10).

12. The life of Holiness (1Peter 1:15-16), or Justification unto Sanctification.

13. The Ministry of Divine Healing as in the Bible, the Gospels, etc.

14. The Ministry of Deliverance from demonic powers.

15. The fivefold ascension-gift ministries of apostles, prophets, evangelists, shepherds and teachers (Ephesians 4:9-16; 1Corinthians 12).

16. The Government of the Local Church under Christ, Elders and Deacons (Philippians 1:1).

17. The Church, the Body of Christ and the Headship of Christ (1Corinthians 12).

18. The Tabernacle of David - Davidic Worship (Acts 15:15-18).

19. The Feasts of the Lord: Passover, Pentecost and Tabernacles (Leviticus 23).

20. The events pertaining to Eschatology: Apostasy, Antichrist, Tribulation, Coming of Christ and the Kingdom in fullness (Daniel and Revelation).

21. The Eternal States of the Righteous and Unrighteous, the Saved and Unsaved (Revelation 20,21,22).

Other great truths could be listed, but all are comprehended in the list given here. Together these things were the truths deposited in the early Church. These are the truths that constituted "the faith" once and for all delivered to the saints. These things made the Church the pillar, ground, stay, support and foundation of the truth. These are the things that made the Church the guardian of the truths of God.

But what would happen in the days ahead? Could the Church guard the Divine deposit or would the Church come under attack by the one "who did not abide in the truth" (John 8:44)?

But this brings us to the next chapter!

CHAPTER NINETEEN

DEPARTURE FROM TRUTH-DECLINE OF THE CHURCH

As the title of this chapter shows, departure from truth meant decline of the Church. In our previous chapter it has been seen how the Church became the depository and guardian of the Divine truths and custodian of "the faith" once delivered to the saints. As long as the Church would maintain the truths of the faith, and walk in obedience to them, the Church would be a victorious Church, marching forth, conquering and to conquer.

If the enemy of the Church, Satan and his evil hosts, wanted to conquer or destroy the Church, then it would be an attack against THE TRUTH. Satan would have to draw the Church away from the ground of truth on to the ground of error, even as he did when he caused Adam and Eve to fall. He enticed them away from the original WORD God gave and deceived Eve from the ground of truth, the ground of faith and obedience, on to the ground of error, the ground of unbelief and disobedience (Genesis 3:1-6). This is exactly what happens in Church history.

Satan himself did **not abide in the truth** and now there is no truth in him (John 8:44). Satan has to attack the truth of God's Word in order to bring about departure from the faith and decline of the Church. This he did.

It is sad but true, that the Church would soon depart from the things that God had given to it and enter into a long period of decline.

In the Old Testament, the prophet Moses foretold Israel's departure from the law of the Lord and His word, as seen in Moses' final address to the nation (Deuteronomy Chapters 27,28,29,30,31).

In the New Testament, the apostle Paul, along with other writers, foretell also the departure from the faith once delivered to the saints (1Timothy 4:1-2 with Jude 3).

In the chapter under consideration, it is necessary to follow a brief overview of Church History from its early glory to its decline. The steps followed in this brief outline include Early Glory, Persecution, Syncretism, Departure and Decline into the Dark Ages.

A. The Early Glory

The Book of Acts shows the glory of the early Church, especially in its early chapters. The Day of Pentecost saw the birthday of the Church and the power of the Holy Spirit at work in the Church. Signs and wonders followed the preaching of the Gospel. The Lord added to the Church daily those that were being saved. Unity prevailed. Great power, great grace and great fear of the Lord was upon the Church. The Gospel spread from Jerusalem to Judea, to Samaria and then to the uttermost parts of the then-known world (Acts 1:8). It seemed that nothing would stop the Church as it maintained the truth of the Gospel and walked in the faith entrusted to it. The Church would go from glory to glory, victory to victory, grace to grace, faith to faith and conquering to conquer as the Lord blessed and built His Church. This was indeed the vision of the living Christ, the risen and ascended head of the Church. The Gospel of the Kingdom would reach all nations as the Lord built His Church.

B. Opposition and Persecution

This early glory was not going to continue without opposition leading to persecution by the enemy of Christ and His Church. The Church would experience opposition and persecution for the next two or more centuries, from AD100-AD300 or thereabouts.

The tactics of Satan and his hosts as the enemies of Christ and His Church have always been "divide and conquer". The motto has been: "if you cannot destroy them, join them", or, "if you cannot conquer them, corrupt them". This would happen in due time.

As has been drawn to our attention over the years, the Church would have warfare **spiritually** with Judaism, warfare **mentally** with the Greek philosophies, the Gnostics, and then **physically** with Rome in the great persecutions of the Church and martyrdom through to about AD300.

It began even in the Book of Acts. The early Church experienced opposition from Judaism which had rejected the Christ of God. The Church experienced, first of all, religious opposition from the Jews who rejected Christ. Later on the opposition came from the political world. The Roman Emperors set the persecution forward over a number of years, especially those Emperors who demanded worship as deity. Thousands upon thousands of Christians were martyred because they refused to call Caezar 'LORD'. To the Christian, Jesus was 'LORD' - not Caesar!

One of the greatest persecutions of the Church lasted for a period of ten years under Emperor Domitian (AD81-96). It was under his rule that the apostle John was exiled to Patmos as a slave of Rome. There John wrote "**The Revelation**". Just after the death of Domitian, John died, according to tradition, in Ephesus, thus closing off the Apostolic Age.

The greatest benefit from the religious and political opposition and persecution of the Church was that such helped to keep the Church reasonably pure. Very few wanted to pay the price of being a true Christian in the age of persecution. The era of opposition and persecution under the Roman Emperors continued right through to approximately AD313.

"The tenth and final persecution beneath the cruel hand of Emperor Diocletian was undoubtedly the most desolating of them all. The whole power of the Roman Empire combined in a desperate effort, not only to suppress the Scriptures entirely, but to exterminate every trace of Christianity from the earth. This final and fearful conflict between Paganism and Christianity, while adding fresh chapters of glory to the growing records of the martyrs, failed to check the germination of the seeds of corruption which the affiliation with the world had sown" ("**A Brief Synopsis of The Public History of The Church**", Page 5, by G.H.S.Price).

Emperor Diocletian endeavoured to destroy every Bible, all Scriptures everywhere, and totally exterminate Christianity and Christians off the face of the Roman Empire because they were counted as "atheists", rejecting the gods of Rome, and because they would not accept and confess "Caesar is Lord", and because they acknowledged and confessed only that "Jesus Christ is LORD!".

(The reader is pointed to textbooks that deal with early Church History, and the persecutions of the Church under the Roman Emperors. Fox's Book of Martyrs especially deals with such).

C. The Age of Syncretism

The time was about AD300. The enemy, Satan, found that "the blood of the martyrs became the seed of the Church". Sow a martyr, you plant a Church! So the method of attack changed. If you cannot destroy the Church from **without**, by opposition and persecution, then seek to destroy it from **within**, by corruption and seduction.

It was under Emperor Constantine that the greatest danger of all fell on the Church. Church Historians show how Constantine was supposedly converted to Christianity by "the sign of the cross" and that "by this sign he would conquer". He issued the "**Edict of Toleration**" for Christianity in AD313. The Church now became protected by the Roman Empire. Some good things happened but had evil effects in the Church as history would tell.

Constantine favoured Christians in every way, filled public offices with them and made Christianity the State Religion. Bibles were ordered to be printed. Sunday was made a day of worship. Church buildings, which the early Church never had, and which previous Emperors had destroyed where they had been built, were allowed to be erected. The Church became a power in politics in this unholy union of Church and State.

However, the same spirit that was in the Roman Empire came into the Church. The Church became a religious/political power. From persecution the Church came into favour. The Roman Emperor sometimes presided over the Councils of the Church.

The worst part of this era was seen in the fact that **pagans** flocked into the Church, bringing with them the doctrines of heathenism, cultic beliefs and practices, idolatry and immorality, along with gnostic and Greek philosophies. The Church adjusted to many of these things, giving them "Christian names".

This period became **"the age of syncretism" - the age of mixture!** Christianity became inter-mingled with Romanism, Heathenism, Occultism, Greek Gnosticism and a mixture of philosophies abounding at the time. It was the mixture of the worst kind.

As mentioned earlier, the enemy's tactic has always been: "If you cannot destroy them, then corrupt them", or, "If you cannot beat them, join them". This is exactly what happened in this period of Church History.

D. Departure from The Faith

As has been anticipated, there were more serious matters of concern for the Church now that the persecutions had ceased. The great problem now was not so much as from without, but the entrance of pagans with their philosophies and the trouble from within. It was the departure from "the faith" from within the Church with this mixture of Christianity and Pagan and Gnostic philosophies. The apostles had warned of this departure in the New Testament writings.

1. **Paul** warned the Ephesian elders that after his departure, grievous wolves would spoil the flock (from without), while elders (from within) would draw disciples after themselves (Acts 20:28-30).

2. **Paul** also told Timothy that the Holy Spirit had expressly said that in the latter times some would depart from **the faith** giving heed to seducing spirits and doctrines of demons (1Timothy 4:1-4).

3. **Peter** also wrote in his Epistle that false prophets and false teachers would bring in pernicious doctrines and would make merchandise of the people of God (2Peter 2:1-10).

4. **John**, the beloved apostle, wrote concerning the spirit of Antichrist that would arise in the Church and would deny the doctrine of the Father and the Son. They would deny that Jesus Christ had indeed come in the flesh and was God incarnate. They would also divide from the Church. Also the spirit of Diotrephes would arise and seek to dominate the people of God, and introduce Clergy and Laity concepts and rob the saints of the priesthood of all believers (1John 2:15-17; 3John 9-10). This is seen in the early heresies concerning the Person of Christ as the God-Man, in His Deity and Humanity.

5. **Jude** spoke of those who would creep into the Church, turning the grace of God into all kinds of lusts. Because of these who crept sideways into the Church, he exhorts the saints to earnestly contend for **the faith** once and for all delivered to the saints (Jude 1-3).

6. **John** in his letters to the seven Churches in Asia, even then speaks of the false doctrines and evil practices of Nicolaitanism, Balaamism, Jezebelism and Judaism, all of which would corrupt the Church from within (Revelation Chapters 2-3).

Carnality, leaving first love, compromise, self-will, worldliness, idolatry, immorality and lukewarmness would be contributing factors in the Church's departure from **the faith** and a corruption of **the truths** entrusted to the Church.

E. **Decline into the Dark Ages**

It is a logical sequence of events that, once departure from the faith delivered to the saints began, it would lead to decline. Departure from truth leads to decline in power, glory and influence. This is exactly what happened in Church History. Departure from the faith, corruption of truths, quickly aided the decline of the Church. The Church's decline covered a period of time from about AD313 to AD600. The following is a brief history of the Church's decline from the God-given heritage to what has been aptly called "The Church's Dark Ages". The dates given here can only be approximate. The main thing to be noted is the gradual loss of truth and decline following the departure from the faith.

1. **AD30-100**

    From Pentecost onwards, the early Church witnessed the ministry of the apostles of the Lamb. John, the beloved, was the last of the living apostles of the Lamb. With his death, the Apostolic era ceased as far as the Twelve were concerned (Revelation 21:14). The apostolic signs and wonders, on the whole, ceased.

2. **AD130**

    The doctrine of the laying on of hands became a formal ritual, losing its true purpose, power and ministry.

3. **AD140**

   With the loss of apostolic ministry, the ministry of the prophet ceased to function in the Church. Prophetic utterances became rare also in the Church.

4. **AD150**

   The baptism of the Holy Spirit and the resultant gifts of the Spirit were no longer in evidence in the Church. Evidence of the baptism of the Spirit with the speaking with other tongues gradually faded from the Church's experiences.

5. **AD160**

   The spirit of Diotrephes arose in the Church where, instead of the plurality of leadership of elders, as seen in the Acts and the Epistles, one man took power over the Church. This was the rise of the monarchical bishop, the rise of the one-man ministry, and therefore a violation of early local Church government.

6. **AD180**

   Local Church government and autonomy began to decline more and more as Rome became more of a governing power. It was the seed of denominationalism and the coming control of local churches from external headquarters.

7. **AD187**

   Water baptism of the believers by immersion began to fall into disuse. In this period (AD185) there is the first recorded account of "infant baptism", apart from repentance and faith in the Lord Jesus Christ.

8. **AD200**

   By this period of time, most Churches no longer used the Name of the Lord Jesus Christ in water baptism (as had been done in the Acts and Epistles), but only repeated the command of Christ as in Matthew 28:19-20. It has been said that it was Pope Stephen who declared baptism into the Name of the Lord Jesus Christ to be invalid, and that it must be only "in the Name of the Father, and of the Son and of the Holy Spirit". Thus the Name was denied in baptism.

9. **AD210**

   The doctrine of the priesthood of all believers was being denied as a class of priestly clergy developed. A priest-class was forming, thus the spirit of the Nicolaitans was operating ("Nico" meaning "to conquer", and "Laos" meaning "the people". Nicolaitanism is "to conquer the people"). It was the seeds of clergy/laity manifesting itself in the Church. Priests and people were separated.

10. **AD225**

    Requirements for "church membership" was now on the basis of agreement with "the creeds" of the Church and not upon genuine conversion to Christ. It was more of "what you believe" and not "who you believe" that counted. As long as one believed in "the creeds", that would be the basis of acceptance as Church members - not whether one had experienced new birth or not.

11. AD240

In various Churches, as heathen came into the Church, worldliness crept in and began to infiltrate the Church and the standard of "Holiness unto the Lord" was compromised in order to keep people in the Church. The Churches that were suffering persecution maintained much more purity of life. Some withdrew to Monasteries to solve the problem. The problem was within the heart of man, internal and not just external.

12. AD300

Monastic asceticism caused many to over emphasize "works" as a basic for eternal life. The truth of justification by faith disappeared from the Church, and so justification was possible by religious works.

13. AD313

Constantine became the Emperor of Rome and the Empire. Christianity was chosen as "the best out of all the religions" and made the State Religion. Church and State became united in an unholy wedlock. The State began to exercise control over the affairs of the Church. The unregenerate heathen were forced to consent to Christianity by the sword, as Constantine had seen "the sign of the cross" and heard the words, "By this sign conquer". Although the Emperor Constantine did many good things, such as the allowance of printing the Scriptures, religious freedom for Christians, yet much evil came out of this freedom. Heresies increased, creeds were formed under Constantine's authority and syncretism prevailed. The corruption was now within the Church.

14. AD350

Because Christianity was the "State Religion"; all those not in the Church came under persecution. Heathen people flocked into the Church rather than face the sword and were called "Christians" without any relationship with Christ through repentance, faith and new birth. Salvation by faith was virtually denied and salvation was by "joining the church". Heathenism corrupted the Church further in this age of mixture.Ritualism became the norm as the Church had form but no power.

15. AD380

During this time, Theodosius made Rome, which was already the capital of the Roman Empire, the final authority for all matters of Church doctrine and practice. The Roman Church became the final authority above the authority of the Sacred Scriptures.

16. AD392

Theodosius exercised further power when heathen worship was outlawed. The penalty of death was placed on anyone who had any other religion but the religion of the State and the Roman Church. Both heathen and heretic were persecuted now by the State/Church. What a contrast! Instead of the pagan world persecuting the Church, the Church now persecutes the pagan world!

17. **AD400**

    Water baptism by this time was now considered unnecessary and unimportant. The ordinance of Christ had already degenerated into mere formalism without any accompanying experience. In this time, many put baptism off until their death bed or never were baptized at all.

18. **AD484**

    Under this period of time, the Roman Emperor exempted the priests/clergy from tax, and many of the poorer and uneducated were brought into the priesthood or clergy ministry, rather than those who were wealthy and could cause loss of tax revenue for Rome.

Thus the Church declined in glory and power as it departed from the faith once delivered to the saints, and departed from the truths the Lord had entrusted to it. The Church lost her early glory. Opposition and persecution ceased. Corruption and mixture from within caused the Church to depart from the faith. The Church continued to plunge deeper and deeper into spiritual decline.

As "**Present Day Truths**" (Dick Inversion/Bill Scheidler, pages 36-42, and to which the reader is referred) brings out, the pagan infiltration of the Church made it easy for people to be comfortable without any relationship with Christ. They could enjoy liturgies and form of prayers. Church buildings were elaborate, built after heathen temples and ornamentations. The worship of gods under the names of saints and the apostles and Mary was an easy transfer of devotion. Material objects, pleasing to the eyes of people, images and relics all helped to keep people comfortable - but not convicted! People did not need to trust an invisible God when they could see their visible priest in sacred garments and ritualistic worship forms.

Because Rome was the capital of the Empire, exercising authority over the Empire round the then-known world, it was easy to accept the Roman Church and Supreme Pontiff as the final authority for all matters of faith and practice rather than look to the Lord Jesus Christ, the head of the Church. The relationship between the Emperor of the Roman Empire and the Supreme Pontiff of the Roman Church was simple to accept. One was the political authority, the other the spiritual authority.

In Summary:

In this chapter therefore, we have seen the early glory of the early Church, the opposition and persecution over the first several centuries, and how the Church entered into the age of syncretism and finally her departure from the faith and the loss of the Divine truths as it declined into the Dark Ages. The time from the early period was about five hundred years.

The Church now enters what has aptly been called "The Dark Ages". Martin Luther called it the period of "The Church's Babylonian Captivity". This period was going to last almost one thousand years until the period of the Reformation. As will be seen in the following chapter, it was also the Age of Substitution!

CHAPTER TWENTY

THE AGE OF CORRUPTION AND SUBSTITUTION

In our summary of the previous chapter, it was seen that the Church of the "Dark Ages" became the Church of Corruption and Substitution. Syncretism (mixture), corruption and substitution (replacement) became the order of the day. But this is best illustrated by first looking at one of the parables of Jesus as given in Matthew Chapter 13. It is the middle parable of the seven and corresponds, in principle, with the Church of the Middle Ages. In an historical setting, it would cover the period of Church History from the time of Papal Rome (The Roman Empire fell about AD478) until the time of the Reformation.

The Age of Corruption and Substitution will be considered into two parts: The Parable of the Woman and Leaven in the Meal, and then the Corrupting Leaven therein.

A. The Woman, The Leaven, The Meal

In Matthew 13:33 and Luke 13:20-21 we have the words of the Parable of the Leaven given, which reads as follows:

"Another parable spake he unto them; The kingdom of heaven is like unto **leaven**, which a **woman** took, and hid in **three measures of meal**, till the whole was leavened".

The setting of the parable is a part of the teaching of Jesus by the seaside. The people are standing on the seashore while Jesus is sitting in the boat and teaching. The rendition in Luke indicates that Jesus also told this parable in a synagogue. As we consider the parts of the parable (like the parts of a puzzle), the Scriptures interpret these parts for us as to the truth of their symbolism. The kingdom of heaven is represented by each of these parts, and no one part can be separated from the whole of the parable, even as no part of a jig-saw puzzle can be separated from the whole. The interpreter must work from whole to part and part to whole in order to understand the parable or puzzle.

1. The Woman

Most all expositors recognize that a woman in Scripture is a type or picture of the Church, whether true or false. The Scriptures confirm this fact.

* Zion in Israel is likened to a delicate woman (Jeremiah 6:2). The Lord God was married to Israel and Judah under the Old Covenant. Both houses of the nation are likened to two women who played the harlot. Israel was given a bill of divorce (Jeremiah 3:6-11,20; Ezekiel 16; Ezekiel 23).

* The false or harlot Church is called, Mystery, Babylon the Great, the Mother of Harlots and abominations in the earth (Revelation 17).

* The true Church is likened to the bride of Christ and is spoken of as the great mystery in the marriage of Christ and His Church (Ephesians 5:23-32).

Undoubtedly the woman who hides the leaven in the meal symbolizes or typifies a Church. The question to be answered is: Is she a picture of the true or the false Church? As the parable unfolds in its interpretation, the answer will be discovered.

2. The Three Measures of Meal

Meal in Scripture always speaks of good, wholesome and healthy food, generally either being barley or wheat flour. It does not represent evil in the Scripture, as the following show.

Barley meal was used in offerings to the Lord (Numbers 5:15; Judges 13:23).

The meal offering was made of fine flour and offered as the morning and the evening sacrifice on the altar to the Lord, along with appointed blood sacrifices (Leviticus 2:1-15; 5:13; 6:14-2;3; Exodus 29:41).

The prophets lamented when there was no meal offering and drink offering to be presented to the Lord (Joel 1:9,13; 2:14). Note also other Scriptures which speak of the meal used in positive sense (1Kings 17:12-16; 2Kings 4:38-41).

The disciples understood the significance of the meal and the meal offering before the Lord. The meal offering points to Christ, who, as the "corn of wheat" fell into the ground and died. It points to Christ as God's "fine flour", perfect in His nature and being. Christ is the bread of life. Christ is the meal offering accepted by God the Father (John 12:24; John 6). The Church is even spoken of as bread and called to be unleavened bread (1Corinthians 10:17; 5:6). The meal in this parable points to the food of God, the Divine meal.

The three measures of meal point to the truth of the fullness of the Godhead. The number three is the number of God, the number of the Godhead, revealed as the Father, Son and Holy Spirit. Three is the number of a perfect and complete witness and testimony, a perfect and full witness.

Two or three witnesses always completed the testimony in all cases of trial in both Old and New Testament (Deuteronomy 17:6; 19:15; Matthew 18:16; 2Corinthians 13:1; 1Timothy 5:19; Hebrews 10:28; 1John 5:8).

God Himself is three, yet one: the Father, the Son and the Holy Spirit. The number of the Godhead and the testimony of the Father, the Son and the Holy Spirit make a unified and complete witness to mankind (1John 5:7-8). The number three, therefore, is the number of God in all His fullness. It speaks of the triune Godhead.

The first mention of "three measures of meal" in the Bible is significant. In Genesis 18 we have the account of the visit of the three angels to Abraham, the father of all who believe. God was involved in the visit of these three angels. Abraham asked Sarah to make ready three measures of meal and cakes for the three angels (Genesis 18:6).

Saul met men going to Bethel with three loaves of bread and other supplies for the prophetic school (1Samuel 10:3).

The friend in the parable of Jesus came to his friend and received three loaves of bread (Luke 11:5-6).

In some of the meal offerings there had to be three-tenths of fine flour (Numbers 28:12,20.28; 29:3,4). Read also Judges 5:18-19; Leviticus 2:11.

Three then is the number of God in His fullness. The fullness of Divine revelation of God and His purposes in creation and redemption are to be found in the Scriptures, the Word of God. The Word of God is the Divine meal for the Church. The Scriptures are the food for the believer to feed upon.

3. **The Leaven**

   For many expositors, interpreting the leaven presents the most difficult symbol in the parable to interpret. Is it good or evil as used in symbolic sense here? The Scriptures interpret the symbol of leaven for us and it is always used in both Old and New Testaments in an evil sense. Only through misunderstanding the use of leaven in the Bible can it be used to represent good in this parable.

   a. **Leaven in the Old Testament**

   In the Feast of Passover leaven was forbidden. All had to be put away on pain of excommunication (Exodus 12:15-20,34-39).
   In the Feast of Unleavened Bread, all leaven was forbidden. Israel ate unleavened bread for seven days (Exodus 12:15-20; 13:1-7; 23:15; 34:18; Deuteronomy 16:3-8).
   Unleavened cakes were used in the consecration of priests to the Lord (Exodus 29:2,23; Leviticus 8:2,26).
   The meal offering was to be of fine flour mingled with oil and frankincense. No leaven or honey was permitted (Leviticus 2:1-5,11; 6:16,17).
   Leaven was permitted in the Pentecostal wave-loaves, but they must be offered with unleavened bread and blood sacrifices, or they would not be accepted of the Lord (Leviticus 23:15-21; Numbers 28:26-31 with Leviticus 7:13; Amos 4:5). A sacrifice of thanksgiving was the same. No blood sacrifice was offered with leaven (Exodus 23:18; 34:25).

   b. **Leaven in the New Testament**

   With all the references to leaven in the Old Testament, not one verse interprets the symbol for us. However, when we come to the revelation in the New Testament, it is Jesus and Paul who, especially, make no mistaken interpretation of the symbol of leaven.
   Jesus warned the disciples against the "**leaven of the Pharisees**" which is hypocrisy (Matthew 16:5-12 with Luke 12:1).
   Jesus also warned against the "**leaven of the Sadducees**" which was a denial of the supernatural (Matthew 16:5-12; Acts 23:8).
   Jesus also warned against the "**leaven of Herod**" which was the lusts of worldliness and its evils (Mark 8:15).

   Paul speaks to the Church at Corinth to purge out the leaven. The **leaven of Corinth** was sensuality and carnality in it numerous forms (1Corinthians 5:1-13).
   Paul also speaks of the **leaven of Galatia**, which was the leaven of legalism and licentiousness (Galatians 5:9).
   It is significant to remember that these were "Pentecostal Churches".

The disciples certainly came to understand more fully that leaven was used in an evil sense. Perhaps because of their Old Testament training that is the reason they did not ask Jesus to interpret this uninterpreted parable.

We ask then: What then is the spiritual meaning and significance of these things? Leaven is "that which swells up; a yeast-cake, as swelling by fermentation; that which is pungent, tastes sour, or causes fermentation (Strong Concordance 7603,7604).

Leaven (or yeast) works silently, secretly, steadily, gradually spreading its influence and power through the whole lump of dough until all is affected. Leaven is that which "puffs up", "makes sour" or "ferments". Leaven in Scripture is symbolic of evil, or human fallenness, of false doctrine, of hypocrisy, of unbelief in the supernatural, or carnality or legalistic Judaism.

Because leaven is in the Pentecostal "wave loaves", this was God's recognition of sin as yet in the Spirit-filled, yet imperfect, Church, accepted only through the perfections of Christ, THE MEAL OFFERING, without the leaven of sin or imperfection in Him.

This woman took and **hid the leaven** in the three measures of meal until all was influenced by it. The leaven is not the Gospel, for Paul says the Gospel is not to be hidden from those are lost (2Corinthians 4:3-4). The word "hidden" is "to conceal in, to incorporate with". The Gospel of the Kingdom is not to be concealed from those who are perishing.

4. **Application of the Parable**

Although Jesus left the parable uninterpreted, within the context of the whole of Scripture, we believe the truth is discovered by interpreting the symbols used in the parable. In the context of this present chapter, this is the interpretation and application used here.

As we have seen over the history of the Church, a false Church arose and by the subtil influence of false doctrine has influenced the whole of the pure meal of the Word of God.

The woman points to the "harlot church". She corresponds to the Jezebel of Revelation 2:20, and the Great Harlot who rules over many peoples as seen in Revelation 17:5. She is the one who has something to hide. It is the leaven of false teachings and corrupt practices. The true Church, the Bride of Christ, has nothing to hide. The pure meal of God's Word - the Sacred Scriptures - have been corrupted over the centuries by the injection and the hiding of this leaven until the Scriptures have been influenced with this evil leaven. The revelation of God in His fullness and the fullness of revelation in the Bible has been infiltrated with the leaven of false doctrine. This is the interpretation and the application of the truth of this parable as used in this chapter. This is what happened in the Age of Corruption and Substitution.

B. The Leaven in the Meal

Following is presented a reasonable list of things that have either been corrupted or substituted by the Church of the Middle Ages. In column form we see "the pure meal of God's Word", and then "the corrupting leaven of substitute doctrines" that have been "hidden" in the "three measures of meal" and Divine revelation given in the sacred canon of the Scriptures. The list is not in any special order.

THE PURE MEAL OF GOD'S WORD	THE CORRUPTING LEAVEN
1. The Godhead: Father, Son, Holy Spirit	Mary and the Saints
2. Heaven and Hell	Purgatory
3. Headship of Christ over His Church	Supreme Pontiff, The Pope
4. The Virgin Birth of Christ	Immaculate Conception
5. Repentance from Dead Works	Penance and Dead Works
6. Forgiveness of sin by the Blood	Absolution
7. Prayer to God through Christ	Prayers to Mary, Saints, the Rosary
8. Justification by Faith	Justification by Works
9. Worship in Spirit and Truth	Worship of Saints, Statues, Relics
10. Baptism in water by Immersion	Infant baptism, pouring, sprinkling
11. The New Birth	Baptismal Regeneration
12. Confession of sins to Christ	Confessional Booth
13. Baptism in the Holy Spirit	Confirmation by the Bishops
14. Anointing of oil for the Sick	The Last Rites, Extreme Unction
15. Christ's once-for-all Sacrifice	Continual Sacrifice of the Mass
16. Communion, the Lord's Table	Transubstantiation (Bread & Wine)
17. Gift of Tongues & Interpretation	Latin & no Interpretation
18. Raising Hands in Worship	Limited to Priests only
19. Singing spontaneous Praise	Gregorian Chant
20. Hymns of Praise to the Lord	Censer of Incense, Lighted Candles
21. Prayers for the living	Prayers for the dead
22. God is Spirit - no similitude	Sacred Heart, Crowning of Images
23. Fruit of the Spirit, Self-control	Indulgences
24. Spiritual & Living Water	Holy Water
25. Dancing before the Lord	Procession of the Priests
26. Prayer Requests to God	Mass Stipends
27. Fasting to the Lord	Imposition of Fasting Days
28. Sin-Transgression of God's Laws	Sin-Transgression of Church Laws
29. Faith in God through Christ	Superstitious Beliefs
30. Priesthood of all Believers	Orders of Priestclass, Monks, Nuns
31. Mystical Body of Christ	Christ/Head; Mary/Neck then Others
32. Mediatorial Ministry of Christ	Mary, Mother of God, Mediatrix
33. Authority of the Scriptures	Tradition & Authority of the Church
34. The Church subject to Scriptures	The Scriptures subject to the Church

35.	The Rock Foundation - Christ	Peter the Rock Foundation
36.	Bible its own Interpreter	Priests only qualified to Interpret
37.	Christ coming from the East	Priests turning to the East
38.	Atonement through Jesus' Blood	Self-Atonement through Religion
39.	The Name of the Lord Jesus Christ	The Name of the Father, Son, Spirit
40.	Kneeling before the Lord	Genuflect (Act of bending the knee)
41.	Ascension Gift Ministries	Pope, Cardinals, Archbishops, Bishops
42.	Ministry of the Body Members	Ministry of Priests only
43.	Local Church Government	Government from Rome Church
44.	Many Local Churches	One, Holy, Apostolic Catholic
45.	Gifts of the Spirit available	Natural Gifts of Unregenerate
46.	Elders & Deacons	Diakonate for Priests
47.	Marriage or Celibacy	Celibacy for Priests
48.	Empty Cross & Tomb	The Crucifix
49.	Scriptures for all Believers	Scriptures especially for Priesthood
50.	Infallibility of the Bible	Infallibility of the Pope
51.	Old & New Testaments Books	Apocryphal Books added to Bible

An extended list could be given but the above is a reasonably complete list. The list is sufficient to give some clues as to the "**leaven**" which has been "**hidden**" in the "**pure meal of God's Holy Word**".

One may think of all the great doctrines of the Bible and see how the false Church has corrupted these doctrines with leaven. The authority of the Bible has been leavened with the authority of man. The Biblical traditions have been leavened with the leaven of the traditions of the Church. Repentance has been exchanged for penance. Justification by faith in Christ alone has been corrupted with justification by works. Water baptism has been leavened by the teaching of sprinkling; the priesthood of all believers with the leaven of a priestclass, and so forth as the above list shows.

The Dark Ages indeed became the Age of Corruption and Substitution. The pure meal of the Word of God was corrupted with the hiding of the leaven of false teaching, and now the whole has been leavened. Many of the things in the Scriptures have been substituted with other extra-Biblical things. None can distinguish between what is "meal" and what is "leaven".

This mixture of good and evil, however, will continue in the kingdom in its present mystery form unto the second coming of Christ. The major lesson of this parable is in the corruption of the Word of God by evil influences of the leaven of wrong doctrine and practice. The meal is good. The leaven is evil. But both have been blended together in this syncretistic age. The mixture is there.

The period of the Dark Ages was indeed a departure from the faith and decline from the truths entrusted to the Church. The Dark Ages became the Age of Corruption and the Age of Substitution. The lamp-light of the truth had almost gone out. It was indeed a dark time for the Church and the world.

Hypocrisy, sham, formalism, corruption, tradition and evil power held sway while the truth of God was suppressed. Truth had fallen in the streets (Isaiah 59:14). Like the little horn in Daniel's vision, the truth had been cast down to the ground while evil prospered both inside and outside the Church (Daniel 8:9-12).

Truth was being suppressed in unrighteousness by religious leaders as the Scriptures were withheld from the people and the Bible became a "forbidden book" by the very Church that was entrusted with it for the sake of a lost world (Romans 1:18).

The Scribes (the theologians and hermeneuticians) of that time had indeed "taken away the key of knowledge". They would not enter into the kingdom of God themselves, through repentance and faith, and hindered, forbad, all those who desired to enter in (Luke 11:52).

The ministry of that day had become like Jeroboam of old. Jeroboam, the king, set up a counterfeit religion, a false priesthood of the lowest of the people, a counterfeit altar for sacrifice and incense, the idolatry of the golden calf, and feast days of the devisings of his own heart (1Kings 12:25-33). Such was a picture of what happened in the period of Church History in the Dark Ages.

The false Church had corrupted the pure meal of God's Word with the leaven of false teaching (Matthew 13:33). It would require someone to "**purge out the leaven**" from "**the meal of God's Word**".

But this brings us to our next chapter and the need for **REFORMATION** and **RESTORATION** of the true Church!

CHAPTER TWENTY-ONE

THE NEED AND PROMISE OF RESTORATION

The condition of the Church in the Dark Ages certainly showed the need for restoration. Because of God's foreknowledge, He foreknew, foresaw and foretold the apostasy and departure from the faith, He gave promises of restoration. There is always Divine promise to meet human need.

A. The Eight R's of Restoration

As seen in an earlier chapter, the greatest New Testament passage on restoration is found in the Book of Acts in Peter's second sermon. The passage is quoted here in full from Acts 2:17-27, especially noting verses 19-21 (Amplified New Testament).

"So **repent**-change your mind and purpose; turn around and **return** (to God), that your sins may be erased (blotted out, wiped clean), that times of **refreshing** - of **recovering** from the effects of heat, of reviving with fresh air - may come from the presence of the Lord;

And that He may send (to you) the Christ, the Messiah, Who before was designated and appointed for you, Jesus, Whom heaven must **receive** (and **retain**) until the time for the complete **restoration** of all that God spoke by the mouth of all His holy prophets for ages past - from the most ancient time in the memory of man.

Thus Moses said to the forefathers, The Lord God will raise up for you a Prophet from among your brethren as (He raised up) me; Him you shall listen to and understand by hearing, and heed in all things whatever He tells you. And it shall be that every soul that does not listen to and understand by hearing and heed that Prophet shall be utterly exterminated from among the people (Deuteronomy 18:15-19; Leviticus 23:29).

Indeed, all the prophets from Samuel and those who came afterwards, as many as have spoken also promised and foretold and proclaimed these days. You are the descendants (sons) of the prophets and the heirs of the covenant which God made and gave to your forefathers, saying to Abraham, And in your Seed (Heir) shall all the families of the earth be blessed and benefited (Genesis 22:18; Galatians 3:16). It was to you first that God sent His Servant and Son Jesus, when He raised Him up (provided, gave Him,) to bless you in turning every one of you from your wickedness and evil ways".

It will be noted that the Amplified uses eight words commencing with the letter "R". For the purpose of this chapter, we will consider them as "the eight R's of restoration". Although the message of Peter was spoken to his generation of listeners, the principles of the sermon are applicable to any generation, but probably more especially to the end-time generation who will see the restoration completed. Let us consider these eight "R's" of Restoration.

1. Repentance - A Change of Mind

Repentance is a change of mind especially with relationship to God and sin. It is a change of mind and purpose. It becomes the foundational word in the work of restoration, both personally and corporately. God cannot restore what has been lost to the unrepentant. Repentance precedes restoration.

* John the Baptist preached repentance (Matthew 3:1-8).

* Jesus confirmed the same and preached repentance (Matthew 4:17; 12:42).

* The twelve apostles preached repentance (Mark 6:7-13).

* Peter preached repentance on the Day of Pentecost (Acts 2:37-38).

* Paul also preached repentance (Acts 26:20-21).

* Repentance is the first principle of the doctrine of Christ (Hebrews 6:1-2). Read also Acts 17:30; Luke 24:49.

2. **Return - A Change of Direction**

The Scriptures tell people to turn and return ("re"-"again") to the Lord (2Chronicles 30:6). From going away from God, with one's back towards God, it is now coming towards God with your face towards Him. The prodigal son experienced true repentance (a change of mind), then return (a change of direction, as he came to himself and then to his father and home (Luke 15:15-32). See also Luke 22:31-32; Acts 28:27. If there is true repentance, then there must be return.

3. **Refreshing - A Change of Seasons**

Refreshing comes with the change of seasons. To everything there is a time and a season (Ecclesiastes 3:1,17). The Lord was refreshed after the six days of work in the creation, as He rested on the seventh day (Exodus 31:17). The feasts of the Lord governed the seasons; Passover, Pentecost and Tabernacles, for Israel (Leviticus 23). Refreshing comes upon repentance and return to the Lord (Matthew 16:1-4; 1Thessalonians 5:1-5; Ecclesiastes 3:1-11).

4. **Recovery - A Change of Climate**

Recovery is a change of climate, a recovering from the effects of heat. The summer season was hot and dry, the earth broke open and desired rain (Psalm 68:7; Deuteronomy 11:11; Psalm 65:9-10). With the early or latter rains came refreshing, recovery to the earth, to the trees and the plants. There could be no recovery without refreshing.

5. **Reviving - A Change of Condition**

Reviving is a change of condition, from a dying state back to life. The word "revive" means to bring back to life again that which was dying or had died. The reviving comes with fresh air. God revives the spirit of the humble and the contrite (Isaiah 57:15; Hosea 6:2; Psalm 85:6; Habakkuk 3:7).

This refreshing, recovery and reviving all comes from the presence of the Lord (Psalm 16:11; Isaiah 64:1-4; Psalm 51:11; Exodus 33:12-23).When the presence of the Lord withdraws from His people, then there is dearth and there is death.

6. **Receive - A Change of Place**

"And that He (God, the Father) may send to you the Christ, the Messiah (the Son) who before was designated and appointed for you, Jesus, whom heaven must receive ..."

This refers to the ascension of Jesus. Jesus was sent the first time by the Father and He came right on time. He will be sent the second time by the Father right on time and in the will of the Father. The Scriptures show that the heavens received Jesus from earth. It was indeed a change of place; from ministry on earth to His ministry in the heavens (Mark 16:19-20; Luke 24:51; Acts 1:9; Psalm 24; Psalm 110; 1Timothy 3:15-16).

7. **Retain - A Change of Position**

"Whom the heaven must receive and retain until ..." The heavens have received Jesus and will retain Him unto an appointed time. The word "retain" literally means "to hold back, keep in possession, kept from departure". It is like a retainer wall, holding Jesus back until the appointed time. So the heavens received Jesus, and the heavens will hold Him back until the Father's appointed will and time (Mark 16:19-20; Psalm 110:1; Acts 2:34-39; Hebrews 10:12-13; 1Corinthians 15:22-28).

8. **Restoration - A Change of Ownership**

The heavens are to retain (hold back) Jesus until "the times of restitution" (or, restoration) of all things spoken by the prophets since the world began".

As seen in an earlier chapter, restoration or restore means "to return, as property to the rightful owner; to replace; to put all things or persons into the former condition or right place". It means a bringing back to a former place, station and condition.

Many other synonyms are used also to define the word restoration (ie., renew, revive, recovery, re-establish, replace, rebuild, repair, regenerate, resuscitate). The word "restitution" is "the act of restoring; especially the act of restoring anything to its rightful owner; or of giving an equivalent for any loss, damage or injury; that which is offered in return for what has been lost, injured or destroyed" (Collins Dictionary). So the Church needed restoration of all that she had lost over the centuries of Church History.

B. **The Promises of Restoration**

The Lord foresaw all that would happen to His Church by the world, the flesh and the devil and He made promises of restoration to His Church.

Many of the promises given to Israel are lessons of restoration to the Church also (1Corinthians 10:6,11; Romans 15:4). The Lord restored His people from out of the Babylonian Captivity (Psalm 137 with Psalm 126). He would do the same for the Church. He would bring the Church out of its spiritual Babylonian Captivity.

Even though the Church was in this state in the Dark Ages, and the Word of the Lord was scarce, there being no open vision, God never ever let the light be totally extinguished. As in the days of the evil priest, Eli, and his immoral sons, God called the young man Samuel before the lamp of God went out in the Tabernacle (1Samuel 2:22; 3:1-21).

The Lord has always, as in the history of Israel, so in the history of the Church, preserved unto himself "a faithful remnant" as these Scriptures reveal (2 Kings 19:30-31; Romans 11:5; Ezekiel 6:8; Joel 2:32; Romans 9:27; Isaiah 1:9; Ezekiel 14:22; Amos 5:15; Micah 4:7).

The Lord would raise up His servants who would become "repairers of the breach" and "restorers of the paths in which to walk" (Isaiah 58:12). He would raise up those who would once again cry, **Restore**. He would bring His people out of the prison holes and prison houses into which they had been snared and spoiled (Isaiah 41:22).

It will be noted that Peter spoke of the "times of restoration" spoken of by the prophets. Undoubtedly the Old Testament prophets are referred to here. The restoration concerns those things that the prophets spoke since the world began. The limit of the restoration is that which is contained in the boundaries of the Scriptures and nothing outside the limits of the Bible.

Because the prophets spoke, not only to their generation, but also to our generation, we note several of the words the prophets spoke concerning restoration (1Peter 1:10-12; 2 Peter 1:20-21).

The Prophet Isaiah lamented in his time concerning the people of God. He says: "**For this is a people robbed and spoiled: they are all of them snared in prison holes, and they are hid in prison houses, they are for a prey, and none delivereth; for a spoil, and none saith, Restore**" (Isaiah 42:22).

So the true Church became a people robbed and spoiled. They became snared in religious holes and religious prison houses. God's people became a prey in the Dark Ages of Church History, no one brought deliverance and no voice cried "Restore!"

Isaiah also prophesied of one who would be a "repairer of the breach and a restorer of the paths to dwell in" (Isaiah 58:12). Jesus, as Head of the Church would indeed be that to His people. The breach (the gap) between the early church and the church in the Middle Age was certainly wide and needed to be repaired. The paths of truth needed to be restored for the people of God to walk therein.

The Reformation would begin the reparation and the restoration. The Lord would raise up the foundations of many generations.

The Prophet Joel also speaks the word of the Lord that He would restore the years that had been lost (Joel 2:25). About one thousand years had become, as it were, "lost years" in Church History, from AD600-AD1500. But the Lord promised that He would restore both the things and the years that had been lost to the Church.

The reader is also reminded of the Laws of Restitution that He gave to Israel. Things that had been lost, stolen or destroyed were, by the Laws of the Lord, to be restored to those who had lost them. Those very laws became prophetic of what God Himself would do. God did not give the Laws of Restitution to Israel that He Himself would not fulfill. The need for restoration was there. The promise of restoration was given.

In Summary:-

Repentance, Return, Refreshing, Recovery, Reviving and Restoration would be the portion of the Church while the heavens have **Received and Retain** the Lord Jesus Christ. This is the need of His Church and the promise of the Lord!

CHAPTER TWENTY-TWO

GOD'S METHOD AND PRINCIPLE OF RESTORATION

When it comes to the matter of restoration, we find that God follows His own method and principles in restoration. This may be seen in an application (though not necessarily the interpretation) of the words of the prophet Isaiah Chapter 28:9-13.

"Whom shall he teach knowledge? and whom shall he make to understand doctrine? them that are weaned from the milk, and drawn from the breasts.

For precept must be upon precept, precept upon precept; line upon line, line upon line; here a little, and there a little:

For with stammering lips and another tongue will he speak to this people.

To whom he said, This is the rest wherewith ye may cause the weary to rest; and this is the refreshing: yet they would not hear.

But the word of the LORD was unto them precept upon precept, precept upon precept; line upon line, line upon line; here a little, and there a little; that they might go, and fall backward, and be broken, and snared, and taken".

The truths given to the Church were not all lost at once, or at the same time. The departure from the faith took place over some centuries. In like manner, the truths lost would not be all restored at once. They would be restored over the centuries of Church History.

To use the language of the prophet Isaiah: "... the word of the Lord would be precept upon precept, precept upon precept, line upon line, line upon line, here a little and there a little ..."

Church History and the recovery of truth to the Church has proven the reality of the principle in this word of Isaiah.

It would have been wonderful if God had restored all truths lost at once. But God, in His wisdom and patience and knowledge of human nature knew that man could only handle a little at a time.

Even Jesus said to His disciples - the Twelve - that He had many things to say to them but they were not able to handle them at that time. He promised to send the Holy Spirit, who was the **Spirit of Truth**, to **GUIDE** them into **ALL** truth (John 16:12-15). The Holy Spirit would guide, that is, He would lead, direct and set the path of truth in which they were to walk, before them. He would not drive or force them into the truth or force truth on them. He would gently lead His own into the fullness of truth as it is in Jesus. The Spirit of Truth would reveal the Word of Truth!

This has been, and still is God's method and principle of the recovery or the restoration of lost truth. It is "here a little, there a little ..." and "line upon line, line upon line ..."

In conjunction with this principle of restoration, God always uses a channel, a human instrument in the recovery of truth. He has chosen to work in, with and through human instrumentality.

The apostle Paul in Acts 13:40-41 puts it this way in speaking to the Jews in the Synagogue. "Beware therefore, lest that come upon you which is spoken of in the prophets. Behold, ye despisers and wonder and perish. For I work a work in your days, a work which ye shall in no wise believe, though a man declare it unto you".

In the recovery of truth, God in His sovereignty, always comes to a man (or men), and uses him as an instrument to proclaim truth. The Scriptures themselves evidence this fact. Moses, Samuel, David, the Major and Minor Prophets, the New Testament apostles and writers, all wrote the truth of Scripture under inspiration of the Holy Spirit. In every step of restoration, God has used human instruments to declare principles of truth.

The Amplified Old Testament puts it this way: "Look you scoffers and scorners, and marvel, and perish and vanish away, for I am doing a deed in your days, a deed which you will never have confidence in or believe, even if someone - clearly describing it in detail - declares it to you".

So it was through Church History. God restored truth and used human vessels to declare it. Divine sovereignty and human responsibility met together.

When the Lord gave promise to Israel with regards to the possession of the land of Canaan, He said He would drive out the nations "**little by little**". They would not possess the whole land at once (Deuteronomy 7:22; Exodus 23:30), but little by little. An old Chorus put it this way:

> "Little by little He is changing me, Line upon line He is teaching me,
>
> Precept on precept, until I am free; Jesus is changing me".

This is God's method and principle of recovery of lost truth to the Church until "the faith" that was once delivered to the saints is fully restored!

CHAPTER TWENTY-THREE

THE RESTORATION OF THE SCRIPTURES

With the proliferation of the Scriptures in our day and the numerous translations of the Scriptures, it is hard for this generation to understand the priceless treasure we have in the complete Word of God, the Bible, without some brief knowledge of the history of the Bible.

The Old Testament canon of Scriptures had been completed and preserved in Jewry for some centuries, with the rejection of many Apocryphal Books. The New Testament books were completed, as far as writing was concerned, about AD96 when John wrote the Book of Revelation on the isle of Patmos.

The Early Church had no New Testament or complete Bible as we have today. The Early Church had their own collections of inspired writings, and copied or shared them with each other. Their 'New Testament' was more especially the 'Old Testament' while the New Testament writings were in the process of being written over the first century.

It was not until about AD397 that the Council of Bishops agreed and accepted as inspired the sixtysix Books of the Bible as is now in the Authorized Version (and other Translations of the same). The New Testament canon of Scriptures was only brought together and accepted after much disputation as to authenticity and inspiration.

Then from about AD600 to AD1500, approximately, over what has been called "the Dark Ages", the Bible became "a forbidden and closed Book". Many were burnt at the stake for reading or translating the Scriptures. It was the period of the Reformation that brought the change and thus the Scriptures were restored to the people of God.

The significance of this brief synopsis is what Arthur Wallis had to say in "**Another Wave Rolls In**", by Frank Bartleman, Christian Publications, Inc., (1962 VOICE).

Arthur Wallis, in dealing with "Revival and Recovery" makes this important statement: "**A return to Apostolic Christianity must of necessity be a return to the Word**". This is what this chapter is about.

In order for there to be any kind of restoration of truth and power to the Church, then there must be a return and restoration of the Word of God, the Scriptures, the Holy Bible. There could be no recovery of truth or any return to the faith apart from the Scriptures. The Scriptures must be restored to the people of God.

This can be illustrated in the history of Israel and Judah. Paul says that the things which happened to Israel happened to them for types and examples and are written for our admonition upon whom the ends of the age are come (1Corinthians 10:6,11).

An overview of Israel's history shows how God gave His Law-Word and truths to the prophet Moses. The Lord told Moses to write the words in a book (Exodus 17:14; 24:7; Deuteronomy 17:18; 28:58,61; 30:10; 31:24-26; Joshua 1:8). The Book was given to the chosen nation to walk in the Laws of the Lord. This book was in the side of the Ark of the Covenant. It was especially read in the Feast of Tabernacles as seen in the Book of Deuteronomy 31:24-26. Also, it was the responsibility of the Levitical priests to teach the Law of the Lord to the people of Israel.

Restoration Theology

Over the years, however, ungodly priests and kings and leaders in Israel departed from the Law of the Lord. The Book of the Law was neglected. Godly kings always caused the people to return to the Law of the Lord. One Godly king by the name of Jehoshaphat actually held "**teaching seminars**" on the Law of the Lord in the various cities of Judah (2Chronicles 15:1-19). But over many years, the Book of the Law was neglected and the people of Israel kept in ignorance. The resultant idolatry and apostasy was evidenced by this ignorance.

"For a long season, Israel was (1) Without the true God, and (2) Without a teaching priest and (3) Without law" (2Chronicles 15:3). When Israel was without the true God, they fell deeply into idolatry. When Israel was without the teaching priests, Israel fell deeper into spiritual ignorance and blindness concerning Divine truths. When Israel was without Law, they became a law to themselves, and lawlessness and anarchy often prevailed.

One ungodly king, Jehoiakim, when he heard the word of the Lord through the prophet Jeremiah, cut the leaves of the sacred scroll with a penknife and threw them into the fire. The king had no fear of God (Jeremiah 36:1-32).

The last of the Godly kings of Judah was king Josiah. He caused a great reformation in the land and destroyed idolatrous places. In the eighteenth year of his reign, they cleansed the Temple, the house of the Lord. In the course of the cleansing, Hilkiah the High Priest found the Book of the Law of the Lord. Great repentance was the result and when the priests read the Law of the Lord, the king and the people entered into covenant with the Lord anew. They had the greatest Passover ever since the days of the prophet Samuel. No king had ever done like this before (2Chronicles 34; 35:1-19). All kings were judged by their attitude to the Book of the Law, as the laws for kings clearly show (Deuteronomy 17:18-20).

The key to every revival in Israel or Judah's history was the discovery and recovery and return to the Book of the Law. Every **reformation** in Judah's history was always the result of a return to the Scriptures, the Book of the Law, the Law-Word of God!

It is simple enough to see the same picture in Church History (The reader is referred to texts on "**The History of Christianity**" by various authors for fuller details).

The Lord Jesus was indeed "the prophet like unto Moses" (Deuteronomy 18:15-22 with Acts 3:22-23). He was THE WORD made flesh (John 1:1-3,14-18). He promised the Holy Spirit would lead His Church into all truth as it is in Jesus (John 16:5-15). That "all truth" is to be found in the completed canon of Scripture - both Old and New Testaments, the Bible, God's Word. As mentioned earlier, the New Testament canon of Scripture with its twentyseven books were not accepted as the final canon of Scripture until the later part of the third century (AD387).

The tragic part of Church History is that "**the book**" fell into the hands of the Roman authorities and priestclass and was "**preserved**" in Monasteries, but became "a forbidden book" to the common person. The Bible was lost to the common people, under the guise that none of the common people could rightly interpret the Scriptures. Only the priests of Rome could interpret the sacred Scriptures. Instead of the Church being subject to the Bible, the Bible became subject to the Church! The Bible became a forbidden book.

Under the persecutions of the Roman Emperors, one of the greatest was when all Scriptures and sacred writings were to be systematically destroyed and burnt. It was in the Fourth

Century, AD, that Emperor Constantine professed Christianity, making it the State Religion. Whether he was a true convert or not is debatable. One good thing, however, was that he did allow the writing and promulgation of the Scriptures. The evil thing was, in making Christianity the State Religion, persecution ceased, and pagans flocked into the Church with their pagan deities and philosophies. A hierarchy arose in the Church in Rome, and the Scriptures became the exclusive property of the hierarchy.

Dr. Jesse Lyman Hurlbut gives some conclusive evidence and indisputable facts on this subject in his "**Story of the Christian Church**" (pages 141-144, 163-163), which are quoted here. The truth of the matter is that, these men became "**Forerunners**" as it were, of the **Reformation which was the result of the recovery and restoration of the Bible**!

A. **Five Great Movements**

We quote:

"During this period (The Medieval Church) and especially towards its close, gleams of religious light began to shoot over the age, foretokens of the coming Reformation. Five great movements for reform in the Church arose, and they were repressed with bloody persecution.

1. **The Albigenses**

    The Albigenses grew up to prominence in Southern France, about AD1170. They repudiated the authority of tradition, circulated the New Testament and opposed the Romish doctrines of purgatory, image-worship, and priestly claims. Pope Innocent III, in 1208, called for a 'crusade' against them, and the sect was extirpated by the slaughter of almost the entire population of the region, Catholic as well as heretic.

2. **The Waldensians**

    The Waldensians were founded about the same time, 1170, by Peter Waldo, a merchant of Lyons, who read, explained, preached and circulated the Scriptures, to which he appealed against the usages and doctrines of the Roman Catholics. The Waldensians were bitterly persecuted.

3. **John Wycliffe**

    John Wycliffe began the movement in England for freedom from the Roman power and for reformation in the Church. He attacked the medicant friars, and the system of monasticism; rejected and opposed the authority of the pope in England; wrote against the doctrine of transubstantiation, ie., that in the mass the bread and wine are transformed into the veritable body and blood of Christ; regarding them merely as symbols, and urged that the church service be made more simple, according to the New Testament pattern. In other lands, he would have suffered martyrdom, but in England he was protected by the most powerful among the nobles". The time period was about 1382.

    John Wycliffe translated England's only Bible from the Latin Vulgate into the language of the common people. The entire Bible had been translated by Jerome at Bethlehem into the Latin language, and this was completed about AD400. Now

John Wycliffe translated it into English. People were in great spiritual darkness and bondage to Rome's authority in this time. Wycliffe has been called "**the Morning Star of the Reformation**" period. As the Word of God was available for people to read, and as the Word of God was preached, light and life came to many. The unScriptural practices of the church of that day were exposed by the light of God's Word.

On into the fourteenth century, Wycliffe headed a spiritual movement known as the Lollards. They went everywhere as itinerant preachers stirring England to return to what the Bible says. Rome opposed the "poor priests" (Arthur Wallis, "**Another Wave Rolls In**", page 9).

4. **John Huss**

    John Huss, in Bohemia (born 1369), was a reader of Wycliffe's writings, and preached his doctrines, especially proclaiming freedom from papal authority. The Pope excommunicated him, and laid the city of Prague under an interdict while he remained there. Huss was condemned and burned to death in 1416.

5. **Jerome Savonarola**

    Jerome Savonarola (born 1452) was a monk of the Dominican order at Florence in Italy, and Prior of the Monastery of St. Mark. He preached, like one of the old prophets, against the social, ecclesiastical and political evils of his day, filled the great cathedrals to overflowing with multitudes eager to listen and obey his teachings. But he was excommunicated by the Pope, was imprisoned, hanged and his body burned in the great square of Florence.

History provides us with the opposition of Rome to those who translated the sacred Scriptures, putting them into the hands of the common people. People were burnt at the stake; Bibles were destroyed, Bibles were burnt. The "spirit of Jehoiakim" was evidenced in this tragic era of Church History and that by the very religious leaders who should have given the Word to the people.

B. **Foundation for The Reformation**

    "The exact date fixed upon by the Historians as the beginning of the **Great Reformation**, under the leadership of Martin Luther, is October 31st, 1517. On the morning of that day Luther nailed his ninety-five theses or statements to the door of Wittenberg Cathedral. These theses related to the sale of indulgences (pardon of sin) and struck at the authority of the pope and the priesthood. After many controversies and the publication of pamphlets which made Luther's opinions known throughout Germany, his teachings were formally condemned, and he was excommunicated by a bull (decree of a pope) of Pope Leo X in June, 1520".

The reader is directed to those textbooks which deal fully with the events of this period of time, as that is not the purpose of this chapter. Untold thousands of people were tortured, killed or burnt. In some countries the reforming tide was totally crushed. The fact of the matter is, the recovery of truth had begun and nothing would stop it. The Bible had been placed in the hands of the people. With the invention of the printing press, all this was made possible to multitudes of people.

The **foundation for The Reformation** was laid. **There could be no recovery of lost truth without a recovery of the Word - the Bible**!

As was noted at the beginning of this chapter, it is hard for us to realize that the Bible was withheld from the average person for some one thousand years! The fifteenth century dawned. The Reformation had begun. Luther, Calvin, and many other great Reformers would continue the translation of the Scriptures into their language for the people. There could be no **recovery of truth** apart from the **recovery of the Word**!

C. Light and Truth

The recovery of lost truth began about the fifteenth century under the Reformation period. Although there were glimmers of other truths in the Scriptures, it seemed that there was always some major truth that was restored over the centuries.

In each successive truth recovered, the principle of Psalm 43:3-4 was fulfilled. The Psalmist says:

"O send out thy **light** and thy **truth**: let them lead me; let them bring me unto thy holy hill, and to thy tabernacles. Then will I go unto the altar of God, unto God my exceeding joy: yea, upon the harp will I praise thee, O God my God".

As each step of restoration took place, God sent out His **LIGHT** and shone it upon His **TRUTH**! The truth was in the Scripture of truth but it needed Divine light to shine on it before anyone could see it. The Spirit of truth had to illumine the Word of truth. Illumination had to come upon the revelation given by inspiration. Once light shone upon truth, this light and truth would lead those who accepted such to the "altar of God". That is they would consecrate themselves to walk in the light and walk in the truth. The end result would be that they could take the harp and rejoice before the Lord. Light and truth were committed to hymns and songs as they were reinforced into the hearts and lives of people. This has been true of every truth recovered to the Church. God's Word is Truth. The entrance of God's Word brings Light - Light and Truth meet together as the Spirit of truth shines light on the Word. Unless this happens, none can see the truth that is in the Scripture.

There could be no recovery of truth without the restoration of the Scriptures, and there could be no recovery of truth without the Holy Spirit shining light on the truth. The people of God need to pray constantly: "**O send out Your LIGHT and TRUTH, let them lead me, let them bring me to Your holy hill ... then will I go to the altar of God, unto God my exceeding joy; upon the harp will I praise You, O God**".

CHAPTER TWENTY-FOUR

RESTORATION-JUSTIFICATION BY FAITH

It all began basically in the year AD1505 when Martin Luther was 22 years of age. Martin Luther and a friend of his were caught in an electrical storm. A sudden clap of thunder and lightning hit the ground. His close friend was struck dead while Luther himself narrowly escaped death.

Luther came under deep conviction of soul and great fear of death. The surest way to salvation in his time was the Monastic life. He left Law studies and enter Monastic life. He did everything his Church - Roman Catholic - told him to do in order to make himself holy before God and find peace of mind.

His asceticism was extreme, involving self-flagellation, watchings, fastings, scourgings, confessions and all forms of self-denial and penance. All this was to no avail.

Once Luther visited Rome, "the holy city". There he climbed the steps of St. Peter's Cathedral on his hands and knees, repeating the traditional Lord's Prayer on every step in order to deliver his grandfather from purgatory. At the top of the stairs, the question flashed across his mind, "Who knows whether this is true?"

Luther became frustrated with such a tyrannical and hard-hearted God; he himself doing so much in religious works and finding no peace with God.

The Superior in his order suggested that Luther give himself to the study of the Scriptures and perhaps he might find his peace with God this way. It was indeed the best advice he ever received from the Church authority. Little did the Church realize that this would lead to the beginning of the Reformation.

After about two years in the Monastery, he was ordained in AD1507 at the age of 24 years. Four years later, Luther became the professor at the University of Wittenburg. It was during his years here as a Research Professor of Biblical Studies that the spirit of revelation ("illumination on the revelation given by inspiration", to be more precise!) came.

The Lord, by His Spirit, shone "**light on truth**" (Psalm 43:3-4) as he read Romans 1:16-17. "**The just shall live by faith ...**" Luther, through Romans, discovered that salvation could not be earned by works, religious works or otherwise, which were dead works. Luther discovered that no one is saved by "works of righteousness which we have done, but according to His mercy". He discovered that it was "by grace you are saved, through faith, and that not of yourselves, it is the gift of God" (Ephesians 2:8).

Luther found peace with God through **FAITH alone in the Lord Jesus Christ apart from any works, religious or otherwise**. He knew he was justified -made righteous- in Christ (Romans 5:1-2). Unbeknowns to him, the Reformation had been born in his heart and experience.

As Luther compared the teachings of the Roman Catholic Church with the New Testament Church and the Book of Acts, he saw many things that were not Biblical. Being a professor, he preached and lectured for more than four years on the revelation of "**justification by faith**", preceded by repentance from dead works (Hebrews 6:1-2).

In AD1517, a man by the name of John Tetzel, convinced by the reigning Pope, Leo X, came to Germany selling indulgences. The Pope needed much money to complete St. Peter's church building at Rome. The Certificates, signed by the Pope himself, guaranteed release from purgatory of both dead and living the moment the money was dropped into the chest. No repentance, no penance, no confessions, no priestly absolutions would be needed.

Luther preached vehemently against Tetzel's selling of pardons and the Pope's authority to issue indulgences. He took definite steps to rectify the situation.

Luther wrote 95 Theses and nailed them to the door of the Castle Church in Wittenburg, Germany, on the eve of All Souls Day, October 31st, 1517. The Reformation had begun - in earnest! His action spread like wild-fire throughout Europe.

Martin Luther's main objective was to rectify the Church's abuse by the use of indulgences, relics and other extra-Biblical and unScriptural practices. Luther did not want to break away from the "one true Catholic Church" and start a new denomination. He simply want to reform the Roman Church.

However, in AD1520, Luther was called to recant of his "heresies", or the death penalty would be carried out. Luther defied Pope and Councils and was excommunicated from the Roman Catholic Church. Confusion, chaos, and even riots, revolution and wars took place in the European countries between Catholic and Protestant.

The "old wineskin" could not receive the "new wine" and the schism became evident. The Roman Catholic Church experienced division as Protestantism spread in European countries and nations.

The major points of the doctrine Luther taught which were contrary to that of the Roman Church were:

1. The Church could not forgive or remit sins or remit sentences which it had inflicted. Christ alone was the one Mediator between God and man (1Timothy 2:5).

2. Indulgences could not affect souls in a so-called purgatory nor remove guilt.

3. Truly repentant and believing Christians could receive forgiveness from God through Christ, without indulgences or penance (Acts 4:12; 1 John 1:9-10).

4. Neither the Pope nor the clergy had any supernatural priestly powers. All power was in the name of Jesus (Acts 4:12).

5. All Christians are priests unto God and all have access to God through Christ apart from Pope or Roman priests (1Peter 2:5-9; Exodus 19:6; Revelation 1:6).

6. Any true Christian, having the Spirit of God, could search and understand and interpret the Scriptures without the Pope or Roman priesthood (2 Timothy 2:15; 2Peter 1:20).

7. True repentance from dead works, religious works, and faith towards God through Christ, were the Biblical foundation for salvation. Salvation was by grace through faith, not of works lest any one should boast (Ephesians 2:8-10; Romans 1:16-17).

Under Martin Luther and a number of other Reformers, the **foundational truths** restored to the people of God were (1) **Repentance from dead works**, and (2) **Faith towards God**. It is not the purpose of this text to be a textbook on Theology itself, but it is profitable to bring into the appropriate chapters some outline of the doctrines recovered to the Church over these centuries. Hebrews 6:1-2 counts repentance from dead works and faith towards God as "foundational principles". Both are considered in brief outline form here because of their importance in the beginning of the Reformation period. The significant thing is that the last truth lost to the Church is the first truth restored to the Church.

A. **Repentance from Dead Works**

Repentance is the first word of the Gospel of Jesus Christ. The second word is the word "believe" (or faith) (Mark 1:15).

1. John's first message was repentance (Matthew 3:1-8).

2. Christ's first message was repentance (Mathew 4:17).

3. The twelve apostles preached repentance (Mark 6:7-13).

4. The first message of Peter at Pentecost was "repent" (Acts 2:38).

5. Paul's message also involved repentance (Acts 20:20-21).

Repentance is the first step in a believer's life. God commands it. If this foundation stone is not properly laid, the whole structure will be shaky, unable to stand the tests and trials that come. God commands all men everywhere to repent (Acts 17:30). It is indeed a foundational principle.

It is also important to understand some of the false concepts about it. Repentance is not:

1. Conviction of sin. Conviction precedes repentance, but not all who are convicted repent (Genesis 6:3; Acts 24:24-25).

2. It is not worldly sorrow. This is simply being sorry for being caught, not for the sin itself (2 Corinthians 7:10).

3. It is not mere reformation. Many in Luther's time made some reformation but not of the heart. It was reformation often without true repentance.

4. It is not being religious. The Pharisees in Christ's time (as numerous people in Luther's time) were extremely religious, yet they were hypocrites. They never came to repentance, but ended up crucifying Christ (Matthew 5:20; 3:7-12).

5. It is not "only believism" or mental faith. Mental faith is merely a mental acceptance and assent to a set of creeds or doctrines, without any change in the life. This is dead faith (James 2:19-20).

True Biblical repentance involves both **root and fruit** (Matthew 3:8). Repentance is a change of mind, or a change of heart and attitude, and this in particular concerning God and sin. It is a complete about turn, a change of direction. From running away from God, with one's back towards God, it is coming to God with your face towards Him.

The Fall brought about in man a mind in rebellion against God and His law; a mind which desires to go its own way (Ephesians 2:3; Colossians 1:21; Isaiah 53:6; 2Corinthians 11:1-3). Man needs to repent, to change his mind. This is what Luther experienced as he was performing dead works.

It has been defined as "Repentance is the informing and changing of the **mind**; the stirring and directing of the **emotions** to urge the required change, and the action of the **will** in turning the whole man away from sin and unto God".

The first principle is "repentance from **dead works**". Luther in the Roman Church, along with millions of others, knew what "**penance of dead works**" was all about. Dead works are religious works done to gain salvation. A person who is "**dead in trespasses and sins**" can only produce "**dead works**", be they religious or what ever. Dead works need to be repented of and the blood of Jesus is needed to cleanse the conscience of dead works. Works done before salvation, or done to earn salvation are all dead works (Hebrews 6:1-2; 9:14). Luther and the Reformers came to know this.

Fruits of genuine Biblical repentance are:

1. Godly sorrow for sin (2Corinthians 7:9-11)

2. Confession of sin (Psalm 32:1-5; 1John 1:9).

3. Forsaking of sin (Proverbs 28:13).

4. Hatred of sin (Ezekiel 36:31-33).

5. Restitution where possible (Leviticus 6:1-7; Luke 19:8).

Without these fruits being manifested, there is no genuine repentance. If there is the root of repentance, then there will be fruit of repentance. John called for fruits of repentance. Paul spoke of corresponding works of repentance (Matthew 3:8 with Acts 26:20). The prodigal son, when he came to himself (which was repentance, or a change of mind), came to his father (which was a change of direction (Read Luke 15:11-24).

B. Faith towards God

Luther also came to genuine faith in God through Christ. The message of justification by faith included in itself repentance - a change of mind towards God and sin. There could be no genuine, saving faith apart from genuine repentance. One precedes the other.

It could not be faith in one's own good words, religious works, or faith in oneself. It must be faith in God through Christ, and Christ alone. "The just shall live by faith" became the "battlecry" of the Reformation period.

The Bible shows that the second word of the Gospel is "believe" (Mark 1:15; Acts 20:21; Hebrews 6:1-2). Faith is the foundation of the entire Christian life. Without faith it is impossible to please God (Hebrews 11:6; Romans 1:17; Habakkuk 2:4). Nothing can be known or received of God apart from faith.

The very word "faith" in its noun form, means "belief, firm persuasion, assurance, firm conviction, honesty, integrity, faithfulness, truthfulness". In its verb form, it means "to trust in, put faith in, confide in, rely on a person, or thing, have a mental persuasion, to entrust, commit to the charge of power of".

Biblical faith is created by the Word of God (Romans 10:17). The heroes of faith in Hebrews 11 all received a word from God and their faith was in that word (Read Hebrews 11 and Romans 4:16-22).

Scriptural faith is a condition of the heart, not of the mind. It is in the present, not only in the future. It produces a positive change in the life and behaviour of the one who knows it.

Luther and the Reformers came to know the truth of "faith towards God". Faith, and faith alone, in God through Christ, apart from dead works, became the message of truth in the period of the Reformation. Martin Luther did teach that true faith was accompanied by good works, but works before salvation were dead works. Works **after salvation** should be **good works**, as one lets their light shine before men to glorify the Father in heaven (Matthew 5:16).

Such was the great emphasis and truth in the Reformation. "The just shall live by faith", not trying to earn or merit salvation. It was salvation by grace, through faith, and that not of ourselves, but all was the gift of God.

What was the result?

1. Truth was **recovered** to Luther and the Reformers.
2. Truth was **received** by those who accepted the Word of God..
3. Truth was **rejected** by the religious leaders of that generation.
4. Truth was also **perverted** and by those who fought bitterly against the truth of justification by faith, apart from dead works. There were those who deceitfully handled the Word, wrested it to their own destruction (2Corinthians 2:17; 4:2; 2Peter 3:16; 2Timothy 2:15).

In due time, against Luther's intention, the Lutheran Church was formed and spiritually camped around the truth of justification by faith in Christ alone.

But God had yet more truth to recover and restore to the Church. Repentance and faith were but the beginning, the foundation principles of the doctrine of Christ. More was yet to be restored. Every true Christian should, however, make sure these foundation stones are securely laid in their experience.

CHAPTER TWENTY-FIVE

RESTORATION - WATER BAPTISM

Within a few short years, the next important truth that was recovered and restored to the Church was **water baptism by immersion**.

It was not that there was no form of baptism at all in the period of the Roman Church. It was in the fact that water baptism, according to Biblical standards and requirements was not fully practised. Hence the need for restoration of this truth. While repentance and justification were truths experienced in the heart and mind, or internal, water baptism was a truth and experience that touched the outer man, the external also.

By the time of Tertullian, in the third century AD, baptism had long been separated from the initial experience with Christ. Various innovations had been introduced into baptism by the Church in those early centuries.

According to various textbooks on **"The History of the Christian Church"**, (Refer Bibliography), these unScriptural innovations changed the Biblical ordinance of water baptism by immersion into magical rites, which examples are given here.

Those wanting baptism had to give their names forty days beforehand. The candidates were subjected to various exorcisms, which meant, "standing barefoot on sackcloth of goats hair, then kneeling with face veiled, head bowed, hands outstretched, and outer garment removed, one of the ministers breathed on the candidates to fill them with a purifying fear and, to drive away the devil; they heard words by which they were freed from Satan's power ..." It was repeated several times in their various examinations. Then there was one last dramatic exorcism by a Bishop to ensure they were purified.

Augustine is known to have congratulated candidates who were "ascertained to be free from unclean spirits". In Rome, at the commencement of the fifth century, this was repeated three times.

The candidate had to attend to daily instruction in Scripture, then in the Creed. The actual occasion of the baptisms was also very ordered. The very entry to being baptised was a whole rite in itself.

The Western Church had a ceremony where the Bishop touched the nose and ears of the candidate, believing that the person who understood the ceremony would share in "a good odour of Christ". Then the act of stripping - the women had a separate baptistry for this. This was to symbolize Christ's naked entry into life and the discarding of the old life by the candidate. The whole body was anointed with olive oil. This was also to drive away the demons. Then there was the renunciation of the devil himself, and everything connected with him. In the East they actually said the words, "I renounce you Satan!" Then there was the pledge of loyalty to Christ. The baptismal water was blessed, the water also being exorcised, and then the power of God was called on the water. A sign of the cross was made, and then, the immersion - at last!

It seems that even at this time, the practice was still to immerse the candidate three times in the water as they named the three persons of the Trinity.

Restoration Theology

There were some different formulas used, with questions before each immersion in reference to the particular person of the Trinity being named. However, it still was not finished. The person was anointed with oil again. The feet were washed. They were dressed in a white garment, and the rite of confirmation was followed which was associated with the reception of the gift of the Holy Spirit. In some places, the person was given a lighted candle to carry.

Through history, down to the present time, these things have either become worse or more complicated. It has been over-simplified for fear of all that kind of ritualism, or so mysterious that few can understand the truth and meaning of baptism.

Augustine, for example, said that baptism ought to be delayed until near death, so that the person involved may receive forgiveness in association with baptism; hence the Roman Catholic rites at death. Augustine himself was not baptized until late in life.

The first mention of infant baptism was not until about AD185. There were some variations in the ritual of baptism. But, as can be seen, these ritualistic administrations of baptism were a far departure from New Testament water baptism.

Over several centuries, the Roman Church taught and practiced infant (or child) baptism by sprinkling. Various men in the Reformation began to doubt the validity of infant baptism or adult baptism. If salvation was by repentance and faith, how could an infant repent and have faith in God through Christ?

Through the study of the Scriptures, some of the Reformers saw that baptism **followed** repentance and faith. This group pulled away from the Reformation and were primarily known as the Ana-Baptists (meaning "re-baptizers") in AD1524. The Ana-Baptists believed:

1. That they should hold aloof from Civil office and war.

2. That the Church was a group of regenerated persons and Church and State should be separated. Both Catholic and Protestant Churches still held the concept that Church and State were one.

3. That true Christianity was more than mental faith and verbal confession. It involved discipleship and transformation of life.

4. That brotherly love should rule the lives of believers, sharing their wealth and having all things in common.

5. That the Church would not be reformed but should be restored to the glory of the early Church.

6. That infant or adult baptism had no saving grace without a prior repentance and confession of faith.

7. That water baptism should be by total immersion. Those who had been baptized by sprinkling did not have a valid baptism and needed to be re-baptized. Only those who were adults could be baptized, upon genuine repentance and faith - not infants (Matthew 3:16; Acts 8:38; John 3:23; Acts 19:1-6; Matthew 28:19; Romans 6:1-4,16,17; 5:19).

The Ana-Baptists would rebaptize any Lutheran (Germany), Anglican (England), Catholic or Presbyterian (Scotland) who had received baptism by **sprinkling** as an infant. Since they denied the validity of infant baptism, the nickname was inappropriate, and "Baptists" would have been more the proper designation.

Protestants and Catholics joined together to destroy the Ana-Baptists. History records the horrible persecutions and tortures that the Ana-Baptists received at the hands of both Catholic and Protestant Churches and leaders. Thousands of Ana-Baptists were put to death. They were drowned, in hideous parody of their belief in water baptism by immersion. They were put to death by the sword. Membership in any Ana-Baptist group was punishable by death. All were called heretics. Some were burned at the stake, others were exiled and many were publicly executed. The persecution was far greater than that which the Lutherans has experienced by Catholic hands.

Several groups managed to survive in Europe beyond the sixteenth century: "Brethren" in Switzerland and southern Germany, the Menonnites in the Netherlands and north Germany, and the Hutterites in Moravia.

Most of the descendants of the Ana-Baptists are called "Mennonites", after their leader, Mene Simon. In England they would be called "Baptists", migrating to America and maintaining the same name.

The Baptist Church was founded in Rhode Island in AD1639. The Baptist Church of the following centuries would become the greatest promoters of Ana-Baptist teachings.

Once again, as in the restoration of justification by faith, so it was in the restoration of water baptism by immersion. The principle of John 1:10-12 was true. "He came unto His own, His own received Him not, but to as many as received Him, to them He gave ..."

The persecuted of the previous truth now became the persecutors of the next recovered truth. The Lutherans, with the Catholics and other Protestants persecuted the Ana-Baptists. Not only so, but, those who before were at enmity with each other now join hands to persecute and destroy the Ana-Baptists.

Like Herod and Pilate, who were enemies before and hated each other, and then became "friends" to crucify Jesus, so now the Catholics and Protestants, who were at enmity before, now become "friends" to get rid of and exterminate the Ana-Baptists (Luke 23:11-12). As has often been said, "the only thing we learn from history is that we never learn from history!"

Those who had heard what God had said before rejected what God was saying now! The leaders of the previous visitation became the persecutors of the next visitation - only worse in their tortures. They kill and destroy the people of God with "a Bible under their arm" to justify the slaughter. So did the Priests, Scribes, Pharisees, Sadducees and religious leaders in Christ's time do to Him when He violated their Talmudic and traditional interpretations of the Scriptures, the Word of God! But then, water baptism by immersion was striking at the very traditional foundations of the institutionalised systems.

The truth of baptism, however, was recovered. Those who accepted it experienced the truth of Proverbs 23:23. "**Buy the truth and sell it not ...**" They paid a great price for the truth and would not sell it at any price! Thousands paid for it with their lives! This was the next of the principles of the doctrine of Christ (Hebrews 6:1-2).

As in the previous truth, so it is with this truth. Only an outline of the major points of baptism can be noted as it is not the purpose of this text to expound fully on the subject.

Water baptism is not merely a form or a meaningless ceremony, but a definite experience in the life of a New Testament Christian, as recorded for us, not only in the Gospels, but also in the Acts of the Apostles and the Epistles.

1. The word "baptism" means "to dip, to plunge, to immerse" (Mark 1:5; John 3:33; Acts 8:36-39). By definition and usage, the word means "to put into or under water so as to entirely immerse or submerge".

The translators understood the meaning of the Greek word and, therefore, transliterated it "**baptizo**", rather than translate its proper meaning. This was done more especially to appease denominational interpretation, so each could "baptize" the way they wanted to, by sprinkling or immersion. Baptism was by immersion, not sprinkling as the Scriptures show.

2. Baptism was in obedience to the command of Christ. Jesus commanded His disciples to baptize (Mark 16:16; Matthew 28:15-20).

3. Jesus Himself was baptized (Matthew 3:13-17).

4. The apostles commanded baptism (Acts 2:37-47; 10:44-48).

5. Repentance and faith in the Lord Jesus Christ is validated by water baptism (James 2:17-18). Jesus said, "If you love Me, keep My commandments" (John 14:15).

6. It is believer's baptism (Mark 16:16; Acts 8:12-15, 35-38; 10:47-48; 19:4,5). An infant is not able to repent and come to faith in Christ. If a person is baptized, and they are not genuine believers, then they simply go down "a dry sinner" and come up "a wet sinner!" (Read also Acts 9:17-18; 16:30-34; 18:8).

7. Water baptism though not essential to salvation is essential to obedience. It is not an optional extra. To refuse water baptism is to live in disobedience to the revealed Word of God.

8. Water baptism involved a confession of faith in the Lordship of Christ (Acts 8:36-39; Romans 10:9-10). The pre-requisites of baptism are repentance, faith and one's confession of Christ as Lord and Saviour.

9. Water baptism is a symbolic yet real spiritual experience. Water baptism is into

   (a) His Death (Romans 6:3,4,5,11).

   (b) His Burial (Colossians 2:12);

   (c) His Resurrection (Colossians 3:1; Romans 6:4,5).

By baptism we stand as "dead" to the old life; by immersion we bury the "dead", and by rising up out of the water, we rise to walk in newness of life.

10. Baptism is part of the sanctifying process in a believer's life. The water is symbolic of a cleansing from the former sinful self-life (Romans 6:2-5).

11. Baptism is also a circumcision of the heart as the believer comes into New Covenant relationship with the Father through His Son (Colossians 2:11-12).

12. Baptism was to be into the Name of the Father, and of the Son and of the Holy Spirit (Matthew 28:19).

(**Note:** Williston Walker in "**A History of the Christian Church**", **page 87**, has this to say: "With the early disciples, generally baptism was 'in the name of Jesus Christ'. There is no mention of baptism in the name of the Trinity in the New Testament, except in the command attributed to Christ in Matthew 28:19. That text is early, however. It underlies the Apostles Creed, and the practice recorded in the **Teaching (Didache)**, and by Justin. The Christian leaders of the third century retained the recognition of the earlier form, and, in Rome at least, baptism in the name of Christ was deemed valid, if irregular, certainly from the time of Bishop Stephen (AD254-257)".

More will be seen on this in a later chapter. So far in the recovery of the lost truth we have (1) Repentance from dead works, and (2) Faith towards God, and now (3) Water Baptism by immersion. All these are foundational principles of the doctrine of Christ as spelt out in Hebrews 6:1-2. These things are the "word of the beginning" (Hebrews 5:12-14 with 6:1-2).

But the Lord still had further truth to recover and restore to the Church. Once again, denominations were formed around this particular portion or fragment of truth. The Lord however, would continue to visit His own, even if it meant stepping over the walls they had erected to protect that fragment of truth. The Lord intended to restore to the Church all truths that had been lost, in order to bring His people back to "the faith once and for all delivered to the saints" (Jude 3). Believers who have not been baptized need to obey the Word of the Lord and experience the truth of this recovered truth!

CHAPTER TWENTY-SIX

RESTORATION-SANCTIFICATION

It would be some two hundred years or so before another major truth would be recovered and restored to the Church.

Over the years, from the fifteenth to the seventeenth centuries, both the Catholic and the Protestant Churches had come to some measure of the toleration of each other. The threefold cycle of recovered truth always seems to be (1) Rejection, and (2) Opposition and persecution, and then eventually (3) Toleration by those who do not accept freshly recovered truth.

The Protestant denominations (Lutheran, Episcopalian and Presbyterian) settled down on their lees spiritually. They fenced themselves in and fortified their doctrines as the foundations for their denominations. The Protestant Churches which accepted and practiced water baptism did the same.

The situation at this time was, many people had experienced repentance, justification by faith and water baptism but failed to live a correspondingly holy life.

Various believers in different places began to realize that there was something more than salvation by faith, and water baptism. There was something more than doctrinal correctness and formalism of Church attendance. They began to hunger and thirst after the living God. Theology must be experienced to produce and manifest the life of Christ.

It was in the seventeenth century that great soul stirrings began to take place in the hearts and lives of certain believers. It was quite evident that God was at work again in the hearts of the hungry.

In Germany, the movement became known as the Pietist Movement. Philip Jakob Spener was a major voice on the fact that the Christian life begins with a conscious awareness of the forgiveness of sins, and a definite witness of the Spirit within. The believer is adopted into the family of God. However, the experience of **justification by faith** must be balanced out by the evidence of a holy life; that is, **sanctification**!

The truths of Pietism sparked off the Moravian Revival in AD1727. In the next number of years, Moravian missionaries went to various foreign countries. It was under the instrumentality of Moravian missionaries that John and Charles Wesley came to conversion.

The Wesley brothers, because of their methodical ways of Bible study, prayer and Christian practices, came to be known as the **Methodists**. John graduated from Oxford and was ordained to the Anglican ministry. According to John and Charles Wesley, however, they did not experience regeneration until May, 1738. It took place in a Moravian Society meeting at Aldersgate Street in London.

According to "**The Holiness-Pentecostal Movement**", page 16, by Vinson Synan, who writes: "Wesley's slow and painful conversion from sacramental Anglicanism to evangelical Methodist Christianity came to a climax on May 24, 1738, while attending a reading of Martin Luther's Preface to Romans at a religious society meeting on Aldersgate Street in London. Entering the service with a "strange indifference, dullness, and coldness" after experiencing months of "unusually frequent lapses into sin," Wesley felt his heart "strangely warmed". This was his famous conversion experience, simultaneously conscious, emotional and empirical. Yet he did not feel that he had attained his goal of holiness of Christian perfection in this Aldersgate experience, preferring to believe that for him perfect holiness lay in the future".

John Wesley maintained the truths of repentance from dead works and faith towards God, but still held **sprinkling** to be a valid form of water baptism according to Anglican tradition.

Because John Wesley became one of, if not, the major voice on the doctrine of sanctification, or "Holiness unto the Lord", this chapter deals more especially with his emphasis on sanctification.

One of the most prominent tracts that Wesley wrote on the subject was "**A Plain Account of Christian Perfection as Believed and Taught by Mr John Wesley**". It was issued and repeatedly revised as a tract over the years 1739 until 1777. In one sense, it is the manifesto for all holiness and perfectionist groups which have separated from Methodism over the years since.

Vinson Synan, in "**The Holiness-Pentecostal Movement**" (page 18), in dealing with Wesley's teaching on sanctification from Wesley's writings, and other histories of the Methodist Movement puts it this way.

"In 1740, Wesley's ideas on theology were fairly well cast in the permanent mould that would shape the Methodist Movement. Succinctly stated, they involved two separate phases of experience for the believer: **the first, conversion, or justification, and the second, Christian perfection, or sanctification.** In the first experience, the penitent was forgiven for his actual sins of commission, becoming a Christian but retaining a "residue of sin within". This remaining "inbred sin" was the result of Adam's fall and had to be dealt with by a "second blessing, properly so-called". This experience purified the believer of inward sin and gave him "perfect love" toward God and man.

Wesley never taught "sinless perfection" as some have charged. "Imperfect judgment, the physical and mental passions common to men, temptation, and the freedom by which, through wilful disobedience, he might fall again into sin, would remain real".

The perfection which Wesley taught was a perfection of motives and desires. "Sinless perfection" would come only after death. In the meantime, the sanctified soul, through careful self-examination, godly discipline, and methodical devotion and avoidance of worldly pleasures, could live a life of victory over sin. This perfection, Wesley taught, could be attained instantly as a "second work of grace" although it was usually preceded and followed by a gradual "growth in grace".

The truth that was sent forth into spiritual orbit in the Church was the truth of "**Holiness unto the Lord**". The believer must know and experience both **justification AND sanctification**! This was the message.

John Wesley was the preacher. Charles Wesley was the singer. What John preached, Charles put into song. Untold thousands of hymns were written and sung in the Methodist Revivals. The songs were clothed in the language and experience of holiness. The hymns evidenced the language of deep longings after God, after holiness of life.

The Holiness Movement shone the brightest in the years 1750-1850, climaxing about AD1800. It was the message of the hour for those hungering and thirsting after God.

Many men could be mentioned with regards to the Holiness Movement, but John Wesley stands out among them all. The Methodist Church became the banner of the truth of sanctification - the life of holiness!

While the previous movements of God emphasized **justification by faith**, the Methodist Movement emphasized **sanctification**. Various terms were used to describe the sanctifying experience. It was spoken of as:

"The second blessing",

"The second work of grace",

" The blessing of holiness",

"Sinless perfection",

"Wholly sanctified",

"Perfect love", or "Christian perfection",

"The blessing of a clean heart", and various other terms were used.

The basic tenet was that the two separate experiences for the believer were: (1) Conversion, or justification, the forgiveness of sins, and (2) Christian perfection, or sanctification, the removal of "inbred sin". Sinless perfection would come after death, but there was a perfection of a believer's motives and desires while on this earth. It was possible to live a life of holiness on this earth, Wesley taught.

Sanctification of the soul and separation from the world was the holiness message of the time. A redeemed person must be a holy person. Believers are redeemed unto holiness.

The Methodist revival brought great conviction of sin and powerful manifestations were seen as result of this conviction. Many books give accounts of these revivals and their manifestations; spiritually, mentally, emotionally and physically, as people were slain under the convicting power of the Holy Spirit.

During those years, hundreds of Church groups were established, all preaching and teaching some expression of holiness or sanctification. Although the terminology varied, and the ways to the experience varied, the underlying truth was: "God wants a **justified people to be a sanctified people!**"

The reader is referred to those textbooks that deal with the theology of Sanctification or Holiness unto the Lord. Sufficient for this chapter is to note some important Scriptures which clearly teach that God wants His people to be holy and live a life of holiness.

"Sanctification" is defined as "the setting apart of something or someone to a particular use or service. Theologically it speaks of God setting apart the believer for Himself, from all evil use, to be wholly used for Himself and His service".

1. Days and seasons were sanctified (Genesis 2:3; Joel 1:14; Nehemiah 13:19-22).
2. Places were sanctified (Leviticus 27:14-22; Hebrews 12:20).
3. The Tabernacle was sanctified (Exodus 29:27,33,36; Leviticus 8:10).
4. The priests were sanctified before service (Exodus 29:4-9; 40:12-13).
5. The nation of Israel was sanctified (Exodus 19:5,6,10).
6. Believers in Christ are to be sanctified (1Thessalonians 5:23).
7. Believers are sanctified by (a) The blood of Jesus, (b) The Word of God and (3) the Holy Spirit (Hebrews 13:12; Ephesians 5:26; 1Corinthians 6:11).

The key word to Israel is found in Leviticus 11:44. "For I am the Lord your God: ye shall therefore sanctify yourselves, and ye shall be holy; for I am holy ..." The word is also used for believers in the New Testament by the apostle Peter in 1Peter 1:15-16. "But as He which hath called you is holy, so be ye holy in all manner of conversation (conduct); Because it is written, Be ye holy, for I am holy".

Many other Scriptures could be given, but the reader is referred to the Bible and those textbooks on Theology dealing with the subject (Read also Hebrews 2:11; John 17:17-19; 1Thessalonians 5:22-24; Hebrews 12:10). The Scripture teaches, "Without holiness no man will see the Lord".

The truth of justification and sanctification had been restored to the Church. God wants a forgiven and justified people to be righteous and holy people! This is His will and His Word for all generations.

History, however, repeated itself. There were those believers who would not accept the truth of "Holiness unto the Lord" as a distinct or second work of grace. They believed in a "finished work", a once-for-all work that was done at the moment of justification. There was no need of any "second blessing" or "second work of grace". These believed that the moment a person was justified, they were also sanctified, using Paul's word to the Corinthians to confirm this "once-for-all finished work". "And such were some of you: but ye are washed, but ye are sanctified, but ye are justified in the name of the Lord Jesus and by the Spirit of God" (1Corinthians 6:11).

Many also believed that no one could live a sanctified life in this world and perfection could not come until death. The justified opposed the sanctified!

Undoubtedly, the most tragic thing is the divisions, both fundamental and schismatic, among those who believe and teach "Holiness unto the Lord", or the doctrine of the sanctified life. The bitterness, fightings, wars, carnalities, lack of love, and schisms among those who are sanctified prove the opposite to the truth they profess to proclaim and live! But this was the enemy's subtle attacks on the truth of sanctification. As has been facetiously said "the two brothers who argued so bitterly over the "blessing of holiness" and sanctification, both proved they did not have it!"

There are multiple divisions in the Holiness Movement, yet all claim to be justified and sanctified! This is certainly a grief to the Lord and the Holy Spirit who revealed the truth and necessity of sanctification.

In spite of the opposition, the criticism, the rejection and ostracism and divisions in the Church, the truth of holiness or sanctification was restored to the Church. Untold thousands of believers have come to know the Lord, not only as their Justifier, but also their Sanctifier (Hebrews 2:11). One of the great redemptive names of the Lord is in Exodus 31:13, "The **Lord our Sanctifier**". Santification is walking in relationship with Him who sanctifies us unto Himself and His service. It is not only a doctrine of Scripture, but, a living and personal relationship with the risen Lord and Christ.

In Conclusion:

Regardless of the carnal and the sinful divisions in the Holiness Movements and Churches today, the truth remains. God is holy. He wants to have and will have a Church that is holy, without spot and blemish, to present as a bride to His Son (Exodus 19:6; Leviticus 11:44; Ephesians 5:25-32). The Lord wants His people, not only to **know the truth of sanctification but also to experience the truth of sanctification**!

But there still remained other truths that the Lord wanted to recover and restore to the Church. His truth continues to march forward!

CHAPTER TWENTY-SEVEN

RESTORATION-PRIESTHOOD OF ALL BELIEVERS

It would be remiss to overlook, briefly, the truth of the restoration of the priesthood of all believers.

On into the 1800's, there were different movements in the purposes of God, but one movement needs to be mentioned here, and that is what became known as, the Brethren Movement.

The Brethren Movement began about AD1830. According to the accounts, a sort of simultaneous movement all over the world, but particularly in England and Ireland, began among persons totally unknown one to another. This fact proved, as it had done three hundred years earlier at the Reformation, that God Himself was at work. There was an independant work of the Spirit in the hearts and consciences of many faithful followers of Christ, among them being more prominent than others was J.N.Darby.

Dissatisfied with the state of the Established Church, they were led to separate from it and come together, in all simplicity as disciples, to partake of the Lord's Supper and not to wait on any pulpit or minister. This was the commencement of the so-called Brethren.

The distinctive truths recovered by the Brethren Movement were the truths of the priesthood of all believers, the one Body of Christ, and the all sufficiency of Scriptures for all the affairs of the Church. The Brethren had no ordained ministers and encouraged sharing in the worship meetings.

The period since the Reformation had not particularly emphasised the priesthood of all believers, which the Roman Churches, along with Lutheran and Anglican had failed to do, or else usurped the believers priestly ministry by an ordained ministry or priestclass. The headship of Christ as our Great High Priest had been usurped by the Pope. The priesthood of all believers had been usurped by a priestclass.

The priesthood of Christ and the believers certainly took on much more of an emphasis in the Brethren Revival Movement.

The Brethren Movement embraced primarily previously recovered and restored truth, as well as more fully the truth of all believers being priests unto God. The movement was strong in sound doctrine and objective truth. Christ was indeed loved and honoured as the head of the Church.

The Church as the one Body of Christ with many members was taught in order to deal with the sectarianism so prevalent in the Church as a whole. The Movement was strong in its emphasis on **"the recovery of truth"**. J.N.Darby's numerous writings include a booklet on **"The Faith Once Delivered To The Saints"**.

The Scriptures used to confirm the priesthood of Christ and all believers and the unity of the Body of Christ were seen in the emphasized truths as given here.

1. Christ is the Great High Priest after the order of Melchisedek (Hebrews 5,6,7).

2. All believers are called to be kings and priests to God (Revelation 1:5-6; and 5:9,10; 1Peter 2:5-9).

3. All believers are called to offer up spiritual sacrifices to the Lord as members of the holy priesthood (1Peter 2:5-9).

4. The Church is the Body of Christ in the earth, and all members are called to be functioning members (1Corinthians 12; Romans 12).

5. The Lord's Table is for all true believers, of which Christ is the head (Matthew 26:26-28 with 1Corinthians 11:23-34).

6. The Word of God is infallible and inspired by the Holy Spirit and is in itself sufficient for all matters of faith and practice (1Timothy 3:15-16).

7. The Church must contend for the faith once delivered to the saints (Jude 3).

8. The heavenly calling of the Church or Assembly is to be separate from evil, both ecclesiastic as well as moral, and the simplicity and joy of the early days of Church History were to be a hall-mark of "the little flock" gatherings through out the world.

Much precious truth came from the Brethren Movement. Their writings show much insight into their devotion to the Lord and His redemptive work and mediatorial ministry. But, regretful to say, as in all previous movements of the Spirit, carnal divisions surfaced and the Brethren Movement became fragmented. Fragmentation, schisms and carnal divisions came over personalities, doctrinal emphases as is evidenced in our day. Objective and positional truth supplemented many times subjective and experiential truth. Doctrine became more a thing of the head than of the heart. Doctrine became more of understanding and intellectual than spiritual and experiential for many. The movement became more of the letter than of the spirit, and so the Lord moved on.

Although the Lord loved His people, and continued to bless them, even as He did Israel in the wilderness, there was still further truth to be recovered to the Church. The Lord wanted to bring His Church into the fullness of the promised land and its inheritance as set forth in the Scriptures.

The reader is referred once again to those textbooks that deal with the history of the Church. Satan was not inactive in this revival. There were many grievous and severe attempts to overthrow or to compromise the truth. This was seen in the introduction of many sects whose foundations are entirely unScriptural, with plausible teachings yet sometimes "doctrines of demons" influencing them (1Timothy 4:1-2).

In conclusion, it should be constantly kept in mind that, God always preserved unto Himself "a faithful remnant" who maintained, in the measure they could, the truths that the Lord was recovering to the Church over the centuries. Even in the Reformation, some truths had been seen but certainly not emphasized or practiced. Such was the truth of the priesthood of all believers!

The Lord's will, however, was not for the Church to camp around this portion of truth and build denominational walls about it. His will was to bring His own into further lost truth. His will was that the believer come to repentance from dead works, faith towards God through Christ, be water baptised, and live a sanctified life and fulfill priestly ministrations unto Himself!

CHAPTER TWENTY-EIGHT

RESTORATION-DIVINE HEALING

More years would pass by in Church History before another great truth would be recovered and restored to the Church. This was the truth of Divine Healing - Healing in the Atonement!

Though many names could be mentioned, one of the major instruments God used was a man by the name of Albert Benjamin Simpson, the founder of the Christian and Missionary Alliance Church (AD1844-1919).

Dr. Bill Hamon, in "**The Eternal Church**" (pages 203-204 quoting from Moyer, page 374), has this to say. "Albert Benjamin Simpson founded the Alliance Church. He was a Canadian of Scottish Background, educated at Knox College, Toronto. Fresh out of College, called in 1865 to become pastor of the Knox Presbyterian Church, Hamilton, Ontario. During nine years in this Church, 750 members were received into the communion. Near the close of the year 1873, he entered upon a new charge, the Chestnut Street, Presbyterian Church in Louisville, Kentucky. Here he promoted a revival and the building of a new building. During the revival under the ministry of D.W. Whittle and the singing of P.P.Bliss, A.B.Simpson came into a new Christian experience, the fulness of the blessing of Christ, or sanctification through faith in the provision of the atonement. He served the Church with success in Louisville until 1880, when he resigned to accept a call to the Thirteenth Street Presbyterian Church, New York City"

During this time, through overwork, his already weak body gave in. The doctors gave him only a few months to live.

Dr. Bill Hamon writes: "It was during this time that he began to search the Scriptures in regards to the nature of man, the nature of sin, and our position as believers in Christ. He saw man consisted of a twofold nature. He saw him as being both a material and spiritual being. Both areas had been equally affected by the Fall. His body was corrupted by disease and his soul was corrupted by sin. Through his intensified study of the Scripture, the Holy Spirit illuminated his mind with the reality that Jesus had made provision for the Divine healing of our bodily ailments as He had for the forgiveness of our sins.

With that revelation, his faith laid hold of the promise of God. He had been taught that "by whose stripes you were healed" (1Peter 2:24), and other such Scriptures were only for the healing of man's sinful soul. But now he realized it was also for the healing of the body. God confirmed his revelation and faith by supernaturally healing his body and by extending his ministry for another thirty-five years".

The basic doctrines of the Alliance Movement centered around what was called "**The Fourfold Gospel**" - "Jesus the Saviour, Sanctifier, Healer and Coming King".

A.B.Simpson preached and wrote much about what the Lord had shown him in the Scriptures. God blessed the healing campaigns which he conducted.

In "**Present Day Truths**" (Dick Iverson/Bill Scheidler, pages 179-181), the following principles of healing are taken from A.B.Simpson's book, "**The Gospel of Healing**".

Restoration Theology

1. The causes of disease and suffering are distinctly traced back to the Fall and sinful state of man. If sickness were part of the natural constitution of things, then we might meet it wholly on natural grounds, and by natural means.

2. If the disease be the result of the Fall, we may expect it to be embraced in the provision of redemption.

3. In Christ's life on earth, we see a complete vision of what Christianity should be, and from His words and works we may surely gather the full plan of redemption.

4. But redemption finds its center in the Cross of our Lord Jesus Christ, and there we must look for the fundamental principles of Divine healing.

5. But there is something even higher than the cross. It is the resurrection of our Lord. There the Gospel of healing finds the foundation of its deepest life. The death of Christ destroys sin - the root of sickness, but it is the life of Jesus which supplies the source of health and life for our redeemed bodies.

6. In Christ there must be a wholly new life. If any man be in Christ, he is a new creature.

7. Physical redemption that brings Christ is not merely healing, but also life.

8. The great Agent in bringing this new life into our life is the Holy Spirit. This is why so many find it hard to meet the Healer. They do not know the Holy Spirit.

9. This new life must come, like all the blessings of Christ's redemption, as the free grace of God, without works, and without distinction of merit or respect of persons.

10. The simple condition of this great blessing is faith without sight. As with Abraham, an act of faith is required to appropriate the gift.

11. Is not the Gospel of salvation a commandment as well as a promise? And is not the Gospel of healing of equal authority?

Another great truth was restored to the Church. Other notable men of God were also stirred in this truth and ministry of Divine healing. Names such as A.J.Gordon, F.B.Meyer, Andrew Murray and R.A.Torry are listed among these names, and their writings set forth their teachings and understanding of Scripture on the subject of Divine healing.

The reader is again referred to numerous books written on the subject of Divine healing. For the purpose of this chapter, we note some of the important references and comments on healing. The Lord is indeed "Jehovah Rapha" - "The Lord that healeth" (Exodus 15:25-26).

1. The covenant of healing was first given to Israel in Exodus 15:25-26 with Psalm 105:37.

2. The Bible shows that sin and sickness are a curse, not a blessing (Deuteronomy 28:1-61; Romans 5:12-21; Galatians 3:13). Christ was made a curse for us that we might be blessed through Him.

3. The Lord is the forgiver of sins and the healer of sickness (Psalm 103:2-3).

4. The great Messianic chapter, Isaiah 53, shows that Jesus took our griefs and our sorrows in His body on the tree (Isaiah 53:4-5 with Matthew 8:16-17; 1Peter 2:24).

5. As we discern the Body of the Lord, we can know health, strength and life, as Paul teaches in 1 Corinthians 11:30.

6. The Church is the Body of Christ and the Lord desires to have healthy members in His Body (Ephesians 5:27-30).

7. The Holy Spirit is the One who quickens our mortal bodies as He quickened the body of Jesus in resurrection power (Romans 8:11).

8. The sick are encouraged to call for the elders of the Church to anoint them with oil in the name of the Lord and pray the prayer of faith over them, and the Lord will heal them (James 5:14).

9. Jesus said that the signs of salvation, healing and exorcism would follow the preaching of the word of the Gospel (Mark 16:15-20).

10. Jesus Christ is the same yesterday, today and for ever. His ministry has never changed. He is still the forgiver of sins and the healer of sickness, and continues His ministry in the Church in the earth (Hebrews 13:8; Acts 1:1).

There are many examples of healing in the Old Testament, in the Old Covenant Church (Acts 7:38). The same ministry continues in the life of the Lord Jesus in the Gospels.

* The Passover Lamb and healing (Exodus 12; Psalm 105:37; 2Chronicles 30:20).
* The brazen serpent and healing (Numbers 21; John 3:14).
* The covenant of healing (Exodus 15:26).
* The healing ministry of Christ (Luke 4:18-19).
* The healing ministry of the Twelve (Matthew 10:1-11).
* The healing ministry of the Seventy (Luke 10:1-24).
* The ministry of the early Church (Acts 5:12-16; 19:11-12).
* The anointing of oil for healing (James 5:14).

In the Book of Acts, the Church continues the ministry which Jesus "began both to do and teach" (Acts 1:1). This truth was lost over the centuries of Church History but is now recovered and restored in the eighteenth century through notable men of God.

But, like each previous visitation, recovery and restoration of truth, there was again much opposition, resistance, and rejection of the truths these men of God proclaimed. Many rejected the Biblical truth of Divine healing.

A study of Church History over this period of time shows extremes on the matter of healing in some, as well as extremes of those against it, by those who rejected it. Divine healing in very extreme cases was branded as "of the Devil" and that by believers who really loved the Lord and His Word. Divine healing, as well as gifts of the Spirit, were branded as "heresy", "false doctrine", and numerous other unkind things were said. It is almost unbelievable to see and read what believers said about these things. Truly the enemy's tactics again was "to divide and conquer" the Church, if not from without, then from within!

History has proven the greatest enemies of truth are its "friends" - God's people. Again the Lord had come to His own, and His own received Him not, but to those who did receive, He gave ... (John 1:11-12).

It is important also to note the difference between "faith-healing" and "Divine healing". The first is used much in "healing cults", but the second believes that the source of healing is Divine, that healing was in the atoning work of Christ on the cross. It is by His stripes we are healed. Faith is the channel to receive healing, but faith is not the source of healing. The cross of Jesus and His stripes are the source.

Of course, there are numerous questions concerning why some are healed and other people are not. Only God Himself has the answers to these questions. The last enemy to be destroyed is death (1Corinthians 15:26). Until then, the Lord desires to grant Divine healing, and also Divine health to His people.

In spite of extremes, rejection and opposition, the truth of Divine healing was recovered and restored to the Church, the people of God.

But once again, there was still more truth to be restored to the Church. God would continue to move in restoration to bring His Church back to the glory of the early Church, back to the Scriptures! His will is for His own to know Scripturally and experientially the truths He has so far recovered to the Church!

CHAPTER TWENTY-NINE

RESTORATION-THE BAPTISM IN THE HOLY SPIRIT

It was early into the nineteenth century that the Lord recovered and restored to the Church the truth of the baptism in (or of) the Holy Spirit, with the initial evidence of speaking with other tongues.

There are a number of books written on what became known as "The Pentecostal Movement". For the purpose of this text, a few of the most important facts with the recovery of this truth will be mentioned. The student is referred to the Bibliography.

The Holiness Movements, in many areas, had declined from true holiness of heart and had degenerated into legalism. From the internal purity of heart and life, many had slipped into external rules and regulations of the outer man. Things such as theatre, dance, ball games, jewellery, make-up, smoking, drinking, and many other things had become enforcements and outward signs of holiness.

In various places, there ascended to the Lord a deep cry for a fresh visitation of the Holy Spirit - "another Pentecost". Various believers in different places began to fast and pray and seek the Lord to come to them in a fresh away. The Psalmist said that the Lord visits the earth and waters it after He makes it to desire rain (Psalm 65:9-10). The Lord makes the earth to desire rain by allowing things to become dry and break open, in the natural. So He did this in the spiritual, in the hearts of many of His people.

Two of the major places in America that experienced this "fresh Pentecost" were Topeka, Kansas, and Azuza Street, Los Angelos. Though some details in the accounts vary, the testimony is basically the same.

A. Topeka, Kansas

At a Charles F. Parham's Bible School in Topeka, Kansas, he challenged the students to search the Scriptures diligently to see if there was any consistent Biblical evidence of receiving the "Baptism" or "Gift of the Holy Spirit" (Matthew 3:11; Acts 1:5; 2:4,38,39).

At the conclusion of their research and study, they all answered that "speaking with other tongues was the Scriptural evidence of the Baptism in the Holy Spirit." None of these students had experienced such a thing themselves, and neither had Charles Parham.

At a Watchnight prayer service in December 31st, 1900, a student (Agnes N. Ozman) asked Charles Parham to lay hands on her to receive the Baptism of the Holy Spirit with the evidence of speaking with tongues. He laid hands on her and she began to speak in an unknown language. She was unable to speak in English for three days, and when she tried to communicate by writing, she wrote in Chinese characters.

Later on, the rest of the students sought the Lord and received the same experience. Charles Parham also received the Baptism in the Holy Spirit and began to preach this in all his meetings. It is this event that is generally regarded as the beginning of the Pentecostal Movement in the United States of America.

B. Azuza Street, Los Angelos

According to the various books written on the history of the Pentecostal Movement, it was in AD1906 that the Movement was launched into the world at large at the Azuza Street Revival in Los Angelos.

A student of Parham, who had been a Baptist minister, and was now a Southern Negro Holiness preacher, became God's instrument to proclaim this truth. His name was simply Brother Seymour.

Brother Seymour was used much over these years of continuous Pentecostal revival at Azuza Street. People came from all over the world to seek God and the Baptism in the Holy Spirit, evidenced by speaking with other tongues, as the Spirit gave them utterance.

Although there has always been a faithful remnant through Church History, who maintained truth, and even evidenced speaking in tongues in smaller groups, God's movement in this time began to affect the Church in a worldwide sense.

Around this period of time, there were those in the Holiness Movement who did speak in tongues. Edward Irving, in his Presbyterian Church, London, AD1831, had occasions of "tongue speaking".

In Dwight L.Moody meetings in AD1875, some experienced this phenomena. In the Welsh Revival, under Evans Roberts, which broke out in AD1904-5, there were sporadic manifestations of the power of the Holy Spirit with speaking in tongues. It was actually out of the Welsh Revival that the Pentecostal Movement was born, with its emphasis on "the baptism", or "the fullness", or "the gift of the Holy Spirit".

Over in Mukti, India, a missionary by the name of Pandita Ramabai, was praying with a group of Hindu girls. They spent days and nights in prayer. Suddenly the Holy Spirit was poured out on them as at Pentecost. Visible fire was seen on one of the girl's bed, and when the other girls went for water to extinguish the fire, they discovered it was the fire of the Holy Spirit. It was like the bush Moses saw - burning yet not consumed. Those Hindu girls received the Holy Spirit and spoke with tongues as the Spirit gave them utterance. One girl spoke in English, of which she knew absolutely nothing.

According to the accounts, all about this same period of time, the Holy Spirit was being poured out, in U.S.A., England, Canada, Africa, India, on missionaries in China and in the Islands of the Sea. The Holy Spirit moved quietly and quickly and those who received the Holy Spirit baptism spoke in tongues as the Spirit gave them the utterance.

In this recovery of truth, people were taught the truth of the baptism of the Holy Spirit, that it was a definite experience, at or subsequent to, and different from justification and sanctification. It was taught that the **initial evidence** of receiving the baptism in the Holy Spirit was **speaking with other tongues as the Spirit gave the utterance**. This was what happened at the original, historical Pentecost in the birthday of the Church in the Book of Acts. This is what should happen to every true believer in the Church in their "personal Pentecost".

The teaching was primarily based on these Scriptures:

1. The Lord promised He would pour out His Spirit on all flesh in the last days (Joel 2:28-32 with Acts 2:16-18; Isaiah 28:11-12).

2. John the Baptist pointed to Jesus as the One who would baptize with the Holy Spirit and fire. Water baptism was the shadow of the Holy Spirit baptism (Matthew 3:11-12; Mark 1:7-8; Luke 3:16).

3. The Lord Jesus was endued with the power of the Holy Spirit at His baptism in the River Jordan (Matthew 3:16; Mark 1:9-11; Luke 3:21-22).

4. Jesus spoke of the Baptism of the Holy Spirit in teaching His disciples (John 7:37-39; Mark 16:17; Acts 1:5-8; Luke 24:49). He said that "speaking with tongues" would be one of the signs that would follow believers.

5. The disciples received the Baptism of the Holy Spirit on the day of Pentecost and all spoke with tongues as the Spirit gave them the utterance (Acts 2:1-4).

6. Peter, when speaking to the thousands who came to Christ that day, told them that the promise of the Holy Spirit was for them, and for all that the Lord God would call in the days ahead (Acts 2:38-42).

7. The Samaritans received the Holy Spirit through the laying on of the hands the apostles, Peter and John. They had received Christ under the evangelist Philip. Now they receive the Holy Spirit under the apostles (Acts 8:14-18).

8. The Holy Spirit fell on Cornelius and his household as Peter was preaching the word of the Gospel to them. The evidence was seen in them speaking with tongues (Acts 10:44-48).

9. Paul laid hands on the Ephesian believers and they received the baptism of the Holy Spirit and spoke with tongues and prophesied (Acts 19:1-6). This took place some twenty or more years later than the original Pentecost.

10. God commands all to be filled with the Holy Spirit. God will give the Holy Spirit to them that ask Him (Ephesians 5:18; Luke 11:10-13).

11. In the Baptism of the Holy Spirit, the Lord tames the untameable member - the tongue - as the believer speaks with other tongues and as the Spirit gives utterance (James 3:1-11; Acts 2:4).

12. Paul said he spoke in tongues more than all (Acts 9:17 with 1Corinthians 14).

13. Speaking in tongues is personal edification in order that the Church may be edified (1Corinthians 14:4,14,15; Ephesians 6:18; Jude 20; Romans 8:26).

14. Paul provides the Divine order for the operation of the twin gifts of speaking in tongues with interpretation when it comes to Church gatherings (1Corinthians 14).

The teaching concerning the Baptism in the Holy Spirit was founded upon the Scriptures as in this list.

About the same time as the outpouring of this "fresh Pentecost", there was a measure of reception of the gifts of the Spirit as enumerated in 1Corinthians 12. There were a number of believers and ministers who began to be used by the Lord, after the baptism in the Spirit, in the operation of various gifts of the Spirit. This was a matter of sequence. How could believers operate the gifts of the Spirit if they did not have THE GIFT of the Spirit - the Giver Himself - the Holy Spirit? It is the Holy Spirit who gives gifts and therefore, it is sequential to have the Spirit Himself.

Untold thousands of lives were changed in this outpouring of the Holy Spirit upon the Church.

But, once again, "He came unto His own, but His own received Him not, but to as many as did receive, to them He gave ..." (John 1:11-12).

History repeats itself. More than any other movement of the Spirit and recovery of truth, the truth and experience of the Baptism of the Holy Spirit, with the accompanying evidence of speaking in tongues, received the greatest opposition - and that, from the Church, from believers!

The previous recoveries of truth appealed more to the **mind** and **heart** of man. They touched more the s**pirit** and **spiritual** experience of truth. But the Baptism in the Holy Spirit touched the **heart** and **spirit** of man, but by-passed the **mind**, and manifested itself in the **physical** realm - speaking with other tongues!

This was something people did not understand. Paul says in 1Corinthians 14:2,4,18, about "praying in the **spirit**, but not with the **understanding**, the understanding being unfruitful". Speaking in tongues was something the natural man or carnal believer could not understand with his natural mind. Human nature wants to "figure God out", or filter God through the human mind and reason before accepting anything that could be super-natural. Speaking in tongues was treated in this way by those who rejected "tongues" as the evidence of receiving the baptism of the Spirit.

This caused violent reactions from those Christians that could not, did not and would not accept the baptism of the Holy Spirit with the initial evidence of speaking in tongues.

The doctrine of the baptism (or fullness) of the Spirit could be accepted as **a doctrine**, but to have some **physical evidence - speaking in tongues -** that was beyond human grasp and comprehension; that was beyond human mentality! It had to be accounted for on some other grounds than being something from God.

Preachers and teachers along with believers, their congregations, branded the speaking in tongues as "wild fire", "emotionalism", "hypnotism", or psychological self-inducement. Others were more vehement in their denunciation of "tongues". It was branded as "heresy", ""mere gibberish", "of the Devil", "Satanic counterfeit", and even "the three unclean spirits like frogs". The experience of the baptism in the Spirit was branded as Satanic manifestations spued out of hell! Numerous other evil things were said of this experience.

Books were written against it, along with numerous tracts being distributed. Sermons were preached against it. All were designed to frighten people away from the baptism on the Holy Spirit, especially that which was accompanied with speaking in tongues. Some of the most hateful, cruel and evil things were said and done, as well as written in many, many articles by leaders in the denominations. Those who themselves professed to be "Spirit-filled" at their conversion manifested anything but the "fruit of the Spirit". Such carnality, such hatred, such vehemence and intolerance, such unChrist-like attitudes and behaviour were manifested against "the tongue-talkers". It was hard to believe that this kind of behaviour was evidenced in those who were truly born again and loved Christ.

Undoubtedly for some it was out of the sin of ignorance. For others it was bordered closely to blasphemy against the Holy Spirit The same evils that manifested themselves in the Pharisees and Scribes of Christ's time, when they attributed His Divine works and words to the power of Satan, to Beelzebub, these things surfaced in the period of time of the restoration of the baptism in the Holy Spirit with speaking in tongues. It is still true of some great leaders in denominations today.

For some leaders, preachers, teachers and theologians, arguments like, "tongues are not for today", and "tongues ceased once the New Testament canon of Scripture was complete", or "tongues were only for the early Church", and others like these, were put to their congregations in order to try and settle the issue. These arguments were those of the School of Cessationists - that tongues, gifts of the Spirit, and the supernatural ceased with the death of the last apostle, John, closing off the apostolic era.

The persecuted of the previous visitation now become the persecutors of this next visitation. Those who received the previous portion of truth now opposed, fought and rejected those who received the next portion of truth.

As has often been said, "the only thing we learn from history is we never learn from history". The persecuted participants of the previous restoration of truth become the main persecutors of the next restored truth.

Dr. Bill Hamon in "**The Eternal Church**" (pages 227-228) says: "The Jews persecuted Jesus, Judaism persecuted the Christians; the Catholics persecuted the Protestants, the Historic Protestant Churches persecuted the Holiness Movement, and the Holiness Movement persecuted the Pentecostals and (regretfully) the Pentecostals persecuted the next restorational truth movement".

Rejection of a newly recovered truth generally comes because denominations become "old wineskins", hard, dry, stiff, brittle and inflexible! The wineskin bursts. The new wine truth is rejected.

Rejection of a newly recovered truth also comes because God often moves in and through someone else, or moves somewhere else, beyond those who may believe and preach previously recovered truth.

The Jews missed the Christ of God because they missed Nazareth. They missed Nazareth because they missed Bethlehem.

Many, many believers were excommunicated from their denominations once they became "tongue-talkers". Resistance, rejection, opposition and excommunication became the order of the day for the Pentecostals.

As in previous visitations, there indeed were extremes and excesses in behaviour among some Pentecostals. Much was attributed to the Holy Spirit that was of the flesh, and human emotions. Only by sound teaching of the Word of God would those extremes and excesses be handled. Paul had to deal with such in the Corinthian Church with regards to the speaking in tongues and interpretation (1Corinthians 14).

Both **THE WORD and THE SPIRIT** had to be brought together. The Pentecostals had to learn that the Spirit never contradicts the Word. The Spirit is governed by the Word and He would not cause behaviour that would contradict the Word He inspired.

The Pentecostals attracted many people because of the life, and moving of the Spirit, but because of a lack of sound theology, many drifted into extremes in various realms of teaching.

Most Pentecostals, however, maintained the truths which had previously been recovered to the Church. Repentance from dead works, Faith towards God (Justification), Water baptism by immersion, the life of Holiness (Sanctification), the Priesthood of all believers, Divine healing - all these previously recovered and restored truths were and are held in the main by the Pentecostals. The next truth of the Baptism in the Holy Spirit was added to these already recovered truths.

Within the Pentecostal streams (which are indeed numerous, and often the result of "Corinthian carnality"), there is variation in the proclamation of these truths, but the basics are fundamentally the same. With the outpoured Spirit, and the blessing brought, much carnality surfaced with all of its bad fruit, until the Pentecostals today, in many areas, are indeed like the Corinthian Church - gifted, Spirit-filled, yet carnally divided over personalities, doctrines, experiences and forms of Church government. Such things are not the evidences of the Spirit-filled life!

An interesting cycle that seems to occur and recur in each recovery of truth is seen in he following:

1. The routineness and 'status quo' of the people of God.
2. God breaking forth in recovery of further truth.
3. Rejection of the fresh truth and resultant division.
4. Opposition and persecution of those who receive fresh truth.
5. Resistance, isolation and fortification by those who accepted truth.
6. Tolerance over time by the persecutors.
7. Acceptance by some who were once persecutors of fresh truth.

This has been seen over the centuries and is seen in the attitude to the truth of the Baptism in the Holy Spirit. In this present period, fifty to sixty years later (1990's), after the Pentecostal outpouring, untold millions of believers, in almost every denomination under the sun, have received their personal Pentecost and speak with tongues as the Holy Spirit gives utterance.

That which was once bitterly rejected, opposed, persecuted and resisted in time seems to become tolerated over time and then accepted by the many. There are, however, many that still reject and oppose the truth for theological, denominational or personal reasons. But the **truth keeps marching on**!

C. Holy Spirit Catechism

It seems profitable to conclude this chapter with a short Catechism on the Baptism of the Holy Spirit. "Catechism" simply means "to instruct by asking questions and providing the answers". Several of the most important questions that are raised concerning Holy Spirit are answered here.

1. Is the 'Baptism in the Holy Spirit' a Scriptural term?

The answer is 'Yes', as seen in these references. John the Baptist used this expression (John 1:33). Jesus also used it (Acts 1:5). Peter also used it when speaking of the outpouring the Spirit on the Gentiles (Acts 11:16). Just as it is Scriptural to speak of 'Water Baptism', so it is to speak of 'Holy Spirit Baptism'.

Other terms are used also, each expressing some different facet of truth regarding the Baptism of the Holy Spirit. It is spoken of as being:

"filled with the Spirit"(Acts 2:1-4),

"sealed with the Spirit" (Ephesians 1:13),

"the earnest of the Spirit" (Ephesians 1:14),

"the anointing of the Spirit" (1John 2:20,27; 2Corinthians 1:21), and

"the firstfruits of the Spirit" (Romans 8:23).

2. What is the Biblical Initial Evidence of Receiving Holy Spirit Baptism?

If a person only had the Book of Acts, and not the diverse books that men have written, then they would, by a study of Acts, come to the conclusion that the speaking with other tongues was the initial evidence of receiving the Baptism in the Holy Spirit. In each of the following passages, "speaking in tongues" is evidenced, or, at least, implicit in the context of New Testament writings.

(a) The initial evidence of the baptism in the Holy Spirit on the Day of Pentecost was speaking with tongues as the Spirit gave utterance (Acts 2:1-4).

(b) Simon 'saw' some evidence of the Samaritans receiving the Holy Spirit by the laying on of hands of Peter and John that made him desire 'this power'. He had not desired 'the power' that the evangelist Philip had manifested (Acts 8:1-24). The Samaritans 'received Christ' under Philip's ministry. They 'received the Holy Spirit' under Peter and John's ministry.

(c) The apostle Paul spoke with tongues more than all, and he received the Holy Spirit by the laying on of hands under Ananias (Compare Acts 9:17-19 with 1Corinthians 14:18).

(d) The Gentiles spoke with tongues as Peter preached the Word of the Gospel to them. This was evidence to Peter and his company that the Gentiles had been accepted of God unto salvation. Peter commanded water baptism when he saw this evidence (Acts 10:44-48; 11:15-17). The Gentiles received the 'like gift' as the Jews had at Pentecost some years later.

(e) The Corinthian believers had received the Holy Spirit, and later on Paul had to teach them the regulations concerning public speaking in tongues with interpretation. Here he deals with the gifts of the Spirit (Study Acts 18:1-11 with 1Corinthians Chapters 12,13,14).

(f) The Ephesians believers received the Holy Spirit and this was evidenced to Paul and the Ephesians themselves by speaking in tongues and prophesying. They had been baptized with John's baptism, but after receiving further light, they received Christian baptism, and Paul laid hands on them and they received the Holy Spirit baptism, speaking with tongues and prophesying (Acts 19:1-7 with Ephesians 1:13). This also was some years later than Pentecost. Both Jews and Gentiles experienced their Pentecost in the Book of Acts.

(Note also Isaiah 28:11-12 with 1Corinthians 14:21).

3. **How does a Person receive the Baptism in the Holy Spirit?**

We receive the Holy Spirit by:

(a) Repentance and faith in the Lord Jesus Christ (Acts 2:38).

(b) The hearing of faith and a Scriptural understanding of God's promise to all believers (Luke 11:13; John 7:37-39).

(c) Seeing the necessity of being filled with the Spirit (Ephesians 5:17-18). Understanding that the experience is for all times (Mark 16:17; Acts 2:38).

(d) Hungering and thirsting after the rivers of water of the Holy Spirit (John 7:37-39).

(e) Asking the Lord in faith to baptize. Jesus is the Baptizer (John 1:30-33),

(g) Knowing that the Scriptural evidence of receiving is speaking in tongues as the Spirit gives utterance (Acts 2:4; 10:44-46; 19:6; Mark 16:15-17).

(h) Knowing that the Holy Spirit is the gift of God, and is to be received by faith, not by works (Acts 2:38-39; Galatians 3:2; Luke 11:13).

A person may receive the baptism of the Holy Spirit immediately from the Lord Jesus Himself, or the Lord may use the ministry of the laying on of hands. In the Book of Acts, there were two sovereign outpourings of the Holy Spirit; one on the Jews at Pentecost, and the other in the house of Cornelius (Acts 2, Acts 10-11). Every other case of receiving the Spirit in the Book of Acts was by the laying on of hands (Read again Acts 8, Acts 9, Acts 19).

4. **Is there a Distinction between being Born of the Spirit and being Baptized in the Spirit?**

Yes! It is important to understand the distinction and difference between being "born of the Spirit" and being "baptized in the Spirit". The baptism of the Spirit, however, is an experience that may be received at, or subsequent to being born of the Spirit, as these Scriptures teach.

(a) Jesus was born of the Spirit, then thirty years later filled with the Spirit (Luke 1:35; Matthew 1:23; 3:11-17; Luke 4:18).

(b) The disciples were 'saved' with Old Testament salvation before the cross, then 'born of the Spirit' after Christ's resurrection, and then at Pentecost they were baptised in the Spirit (Read John 15:3; Matthew 10:1-20 with John 20:20-23; Acts 1:5,8; 2:1-4).

(c) The Samaritans were saved (or born again) under the ministry of evangelist Philip, and then they received the baptism (or filling) of the Spirit under the ministries of Peter and John (Acts 8:1-8,15-19).

(d) The apostle Paul was saved (or born again) on the Damascus road, yet was water baptised and filled with the Spirit in Damascus under the ministry of the servant of God, Ananias (Acts 9:1-22).

(e) The Gentiles were saved and filled with the Spirit in one operation under the ministry of Peter (Acts 10; 11:14-18). They must have experienced the two distinct operations of the Spirit at the same time. When Peter saw this, then he was willing to baptize them in water.

(f) The truth is also typified in the Feast of Passover (new birth), and then in the Feast of Pentecost (Holy Spirit baptism), in Israel's history (Exodus 12 with Leviticus 23).

It may be said, therefore, that there is a distinction between being born of the Spirit and being filled or baptized with the Spirit. These are two distinct operations of the one and same Holy Spirit, one being the impartation of life, and the other being the spiritual impartation of power for service.

5. **What is the Holy Spirit's connection with Christ and His Church?**

A study of these Scriptures clearly show that the same Holy Spirit who was at work in Christ in His earthly ministry wants to continues the same work in the Church, which is the Body of Christ in the earth.

The student should read the corresponding Scriptures for Christ, the Head and then for the Church, His Body.

Christ-The Head	**The Church-His Body**
(a) Born of the Spirit - Luke 1:35	John 3:1-5; 1Peter 1:22,23
(b) Filled with the Spirit - John 3:34	Acts 1:8; 2:4; Ephesians 5:18
(c) Led by the Spirit - Matthew 4:11	Romans 8:14
(d) Preaching by the Spirit - Luke 4:18	1Peter 1:11-12
(e) Exorcised demons - Matthew 12:28	Acts 8:5-7
(f) Anointed by the Spirit - Acts 10:38	1John 2:20,27
(g) Crucified by Spirit's power - Hebrews 9:14	Romans 12:1-2
(h) Resurrected by the Spirit - Romans 8:11	Romans 8:2,13
(i) Gave commandments - Acts 1:2	Acts 15:28-29

Jesus totally depended upon the Holy Spirit for all He was, all He said and all He did. He wants His Church, His Body, to totally depend upon the Holy Spirit also for His continued ministry in the earth (Acts 1:1-2).

The reader is referred to those textbooks that deal more fully with the person and ministry of the Holy Spirit, along with books on the theology of the same. Enough has been written in this chapter concerning the restoration of the truth of the **Baptism in (or of, or with) the Holy Spirit, with the accompanying evidence of speaking in other tongues as the Spirit gives the utterance.**

As the Amplified New Testament says: "And they were all filled - diffused throughout their souls - with the Holy Spirit and began to speak in other (different, foreign) languages as the Spirit kept giving them clear and loud expression (in each tongue in appropriate words).

The Church is living in the dispensation of the Holy Spirit. Joel prophesied that this outpouring was to be in the "**last days**", and the Spirit would be poured out on all flesh. Other prophets also foretold of this glorious movement of the Spirit (Isaiah 28:11-12; Joel 2:28-32; Ezekiel 11:19-20; 36:26-27). Those days are upon the earth.

The truth has been recovered and restored to the Church. It is now the responsibility of all genuine believers to hunger and thirst after the Holy Spirit and be filled according to the promise of Jesus (John 7:37-39).

Once again, however, there is still further truth to be recovered as that which was seen in the early Church. The Lord will continue to move on in restoration and recovery of lost truth - "the faith once delivered to the saints".

CHAPTER THIRTY

RESTORATION-THE TRIUNE NAME IN BAPTISM

Closely related to and following the outpouring of the Holy Spirit in the Pentecostal realm in the early 1900's was the recovery and restoration of the truth of the triune Name of the Lord Jesus Christ relative to water baptism.

In Chapter 25 we considered the recovery and restoration of the truth of Water Baptism itself, especially according to the Scriptural practice by immersion. But, what was not recovered there was the matter of "The Name" that was used in baptism as in the New Testament. The matter of a baptismal formula was not an issue there. In the early 1900's it became a great issue. It is this restored truth that is being considered here in this chapter. This truth touched more especially the Pentecostal world.

The subject of "**The Name**" to be used in a water baptismal formula became a great issue in the early 1900's, not long after the recovery of the truth of Holy Spirit baptism with the accompanying evidence of speaking with other tongues.

The grievous thing is that the truth of "The Name" became a great issue over the doctrine of God, the eternal Godhead, as well as an issue over a formula for water baptism. These two truths became confused and a great point of contention and division.

When this truth was recovered, though apparently not fully and clearly seen, it divided the then-known Pentecostal world into two groups; the "**Trinitarians**" and the "**Oneness**" groups. Although both groups accepted the truth of water baptism by immersion, the trouble began when it came to what was believed should be the proper formula for baptism.

The "**Trinity Pentecostals**" maintained that the Scripture revelation of God was Father, Son and Holy Spirit - one God but three distinct persons. They also believed that water baptism should be administered in the triadic formula of Matthew 28:19-20; that is, "in the Name of the Father, and of the Son, and of the Holy Spirit".

The "**Oneness Pentecostals**", fearful of Tritheism (the worship of three separate Gods), tipped the scale of Scriptures the other way, and emphasized the oneness and unity of God. There was only one true God who was Jesus. They taught that Jesus was the one and only true God, who manifested Himself, first as the Father, then as the Son and now as the Holy Spirit. They emphasized three manifestations of the one true God, and not three persons in the Godhead.

And again, because the "**Oneness Pentecostals**" saw that all references in the New Testament were performed in the name of the "Lord", "the Lord Jesus", "Jesus Christ" or the "Lord Jesus Christ", and never in "the name of the Father, and of the Son, and of the Holy Spirit", they baptized "in Jesus Name". There were some slight variations in the presentation of the doctrine but the basic understanding of the doctrine of God was as seen here. There were those in the "Oneness" group who said that "JESUS" was "the name of the Father, and of the Son, and of the Holy Spirit". Hence, they were called or referred to as the "**Jesus Only**" people.

In "**The Eternal Church**" (page 233-234), Dr. Bill Hamon provides an account of a National Convention which took place in AD1913. He writes: "Both Oneness and Trinity brethren attended the Hot Springs, Arkansas, National Convention in 1913. The Oneness brethren had hoped that the oneness doctrine and baptismal formula would be accepted as part of the Statement of Faith. The majority voted for the trinitarian doctrine and triadic formula. In order to practice their own beliefs, the Oneness ministers separated and started their own group. Approximately one-fourth of the Oneness ministers separated from the Convention that formed the Assembly of God organization and that percentage remains today".

As already noted, the Trinity group formed their own denomination(s), and used Matthew 28:19 as their baptismal formula, and this was especially done to reinforce the truth of the trinity, as Father, Son, and Holy Spirit. The doctrine of the Godhead and the baptismal formula became interwoven almost as one and the same thing. They were branded as "Trinity" or "Three Gods people".

The Oneness group used Acts 2:38 as their formula for water baptism, with its emphasis on "Jesus only" as the one true God. They were branded as "Oneness Pentecostals", "Jesus Only" or "Jesus Name" people. For them, as long as the "Name of JESUS" was used in baptism, then that was sufficient. They did not understand fully the revelation of the TRIUNE Name of the Lord Jesus Christ, because they misunderstood and rejected the truth of the TRIUNE God.

Endless arguments and controversies arose over "oneness", or "twoness" or "threeness". It is to be seen that, as a matter of sequence, how one understands the Biblical doctrine of God, or the Godhead, affects how one would baptize repentant believers. The two are linked together by their very nature.

Both groups rejected each other and preached against each other, condemning each other as heretics.

Some Oneness groups became very militant and extreme in their teachings on the oneness and unity of God. Some Trinitarian groups went to extreme in their teachings on the threeness of God and lapsed into tritheism - the worship of three separated and individual Gods: God the Father, God the Son and God the Holy Spirit.

The amazing thing is that God seemed to bless both Trinitarian and Oneness groups in saving souls, people being water baptized and also filled with the Holy Spirit! It seems that, many times, doctrine can become a thing of the head, but God sees the heart and blesses more according to a person's heart than a person's head. This however, must not become an excuse for unsound doctrine!

A. Historical Data on "The Name" in Baptism

Here it will be appropriate and profitable to go back to history in the Book of Acts as well as early century Church History and consider data on "The Name" in baptism. It is not the purpose of this text to give a full exposition on the Doctrine Of God or Water Baptism, but enough needs to be covered to see the significance of the recovery and restoration of the truth of "The Name" in baptism.

1. Baptism in the Gospels

Baptism was commanded by Jesus to be "in (Grk.eis, "into") the name of the Father, and of the Son and of the Holy Spirit" (Matthew 28:19).

Baptism was also to be administered to believers only. "He that believeth and is baptized shall be saved"(Mark 16:15).

2. **Baptism in the Acts**

   There are seven important occasions of baptism in the Book of Acts. It will be seen that, not once did the apostles "quote" the command of Jesus as given in Matthew 28:19. It was always in "the name of Jesus Christ", or "the Lord Jesus" or "the Lord Jesus Christ".

   a. **In Jerusalem - Acts 2:36-41**

   Peter commanded the thousands to repent and be baptized in the name of Jesus Christ.

   b. **In Samaria - Acts 8:12-16,35-38**

   Philip baptized the Samaritans in the name of the Lord Jesus.

   c. **In Damascus - Acts 9:5-18; 22:16**

   Paul was baptized, calling on the name of the Lord.

   d. **In Ceasarea - Acts 10:48**

   Peter commanded the Gentiles to be baptized in the name of the Lord. (Lamsa, Duouy Versions = "In the name of the Lord Jesus Christ").

   e. **In Philippi - Acts 16:14-15,31-34**

   The jailer "believed on the Lord Jesus Christ" and was baptized "believing in God".

   f. **In Ephesus - Acts 19:1-6**

   Although the Ephesians had received John's baptism, this became invalid once Christian baptism came in effect. The apostle Paul baptized the Ephesians again in the name of Jesus Christ ("In the name of the Lord Jesus Christ", Lamsa and Duoay Versions).

   Manuscripts vary a little, but when brought together, it is seen that in Acts, baptism was always in the name of the Lord, the Lord Jesus, Jesus Christ, or the Lord Jesus Christ. According to notable authorities, the triune name was always used. The apostle never quoted the command of Matthew 28:19 in the Acts. This is not to say that Matthew 28:19 were not the words of Jesus. But the apostles did not quote the command, they invoked "the Name", and the name in part represented the name in the whole.

3. **Baptism in the Epistles**

   There are also seven important references to water baptism in the Epistles as listed here.

a. **Romans - Romans 6:3-4**

   Paul shows baptism is into the death, burial and resurrection of the Lord Jesus Christ.

b. **Corinthians - 1Corinthians 1:10-17**

   Paul reminds the Corinthians that they were not baptized in his name, but it was Jesus Christ who was crucified for them, and unity was to be in "the name of the Lord Jesus Christ".

   Paul also speaks of the nation of Israel being baptized unto (or,into) Moses, the mediator of the Old Covenant (1Corinthians 10:1-3).

c. **Galatians - Galatians 3:27**

   Paul reminds the Galatian believers that they were baptized into Christ, or, "in the name of Christ".

d. **Colossians - Colosians 2:11-12**

   Paul reminds the Colossians believers that they were buried with Christ in baptism, and experienced the circumcision of heart. In the Old Covenant rite of circumcision, the name of the child was invoked on them the eighth day. New Covenant baptism replaces the Old Covenant rite of circumcision (Genesis 17).

e. **James - James 2:17**

   James in writing to the twelve tribes scattered abroad speaks of "that worthy name by the which ye are called". Amplified New Testament says: "The precious name by which you are distinguished and called, the name of Christ invoked in baptism".

f. **Peter - 1Peter 3:20-21**

   Peter's reference to baptism says: "The like figure whereunto baptism doth also now save us, not the putting away of the filth of the flesh, but the answer of a good conscience toward God by the resurrection of Jesus Christ".

It will be seen by these references to baptism in the Gospels, the Acts and the Epistles that baptism was always into the name of the Lord, the Lord Jesus, or Jesus Christ, or the full triune name of the Lord Jesus Christ.

On the surface reading, it would seem that there is some discrepancy between the command of Jesus in Matthew's Gospel and the Acts and the Epistles. It is unthinkable to say that the apostles disobeyed the command of Jesus. The alternative is to see and understand that the disciples did not merely **quote the command** of Jesus; they **obeyed it**! This would mean that the **invocation** of the **triune name** is their interpretation and understanding of the **triadic formula**!

B. **Baptism in the Early Centuries of Church History**

   There are enough textbooks on the **History of the Early Church** which show that the formula of baptism in (or into) the name of the Lord Jesus Christ continued on through the first century of Church History. The reader is referred to Bibliography and those texts that deal with the same. For the purpose of this present chapter, some notable, historical quotations and documentation are quoted.

It will be seen that the early Church, especially in the first century, baptized in the name of the Lord Jesus Christ. As heresies arose over the Godhead, Matthew 28:19 became the Scriptural defence against these heresies and eventually became the formula for baptism while the name of the Lord Jesus Christ fell into disuse. The truth and glory of "the Name" was lost to the Church amidst the great heresies that arose and in the battle for defence of the truth.

1. **"A History of the Christian Church"**

    Williston Walker, in this text (pages 87, 55) writes:

    "With the early disciples, generally baptism was "in the Name of Jesus Christ". There is no mention of baptism in the Name of the Trinity in the New Testament except in the command attributed to Christ in Matthew 28:19. That text is early, however. It underlines the Apostles' Creed, and the practice recorded in the Teaching (The Didache), and by Justin. The Christian leaders of the third century retained the recognition of the earlier form, and, in Rome at least, baptism in the name of Christ was deemed valid, if irregular, certainly from the time of Bishop Stephen (AD254-257)".

    "To Christian thought at the beginning of the second century, the Holy Spirit was differentiated from Christ, but was classed, like Him, with God. This appears in the Trinitarian baptismal formula, which was displacing the older formula of baptism in the name of Christ. Trinitarian formulae were frequently in use by the close of the first and the beginning of the second century".

2. **"A Remarkable Biblical Discovery"**

    This textbook is out of print and seems to be unobtainable but it is a very challenging book and worthy of several quotations here.

    William Phillips Hall, in "A Remarkable Biblical Discovery", or "The Name of God according to the Scriptures" (pages 61,63,64,76-78) has this to say.

    "For some eighteen hundred years, the Church in its various branches has ministered the rite (of baptism) with the use of the words, "I baptize thee ... in the Name of the Father, and of the Son and of the Holy Spirit." But these words were never used in baptism by the original apostles or by the Church during the early days of its existence according to the record of the Acts of the Apostles and the Epistles of the New Testament. According to that record, in the earliest manuscript readings and versions, all baptisms in those early days were commanded to be or stated to have been performed in, or with the invocation of, the Name of the Lord Jesus Christ" (Page 61).

    "The Church of the apostolic age used the Name of the Lord Jesus Christ ... All manuscripts and versions of Matthew's Gospel, without exception contain the words as recorded in Matthew 28:19" (Page 63).

"Assuming therefore, that the words of Matthew 28:19 were actually spoken by the Lord Jesus Christ, how can that be reconciled with the obvious fact that, according to the Acts and the apostolic Epistles, Christian baptism in the apostolic age was invariably commanded and performed in the Name of the Lord Jesus Christ? The answer to this question, which has remained unanswered for some 1800 years, will be found in the original apostolic interpretation of the words, "The Name of the Father, and of the Son, and of the Holy Spirit" (Page 63).

"Although the Lord Jesus Christ commanded His original disciples to "disciple all nations, baptizing them in the Name of the Father, and of the Son, and of the Holy Spirit (Matthew 28:19, Greek Text), neither they nor the Church of the apostolic age ever literally repeated the words of that command in baptizing anybody, so far as the New Testament bears witness. So far as the New Testament shows, the rite of baptism during the apostolic age was commanded, and took place, "in" and "into" the Name of "the Lord" (A.V. and D.V.), or "Jesus Christ" (A.V.,R.V.,and D.V.), or "the Lord Jesus"(A.V.,R.V.,and D.V.), which, as we shall show, are in each case and every instance but abbreviations of the full Name of the Lord Jesus Christ, or of the Lord Jesus, the Christ. There are no exceptions recorded. Any person can verify the accuracy of this statement by reading Acts 2:38; 8:16; 10:48; and 19:5 (A.V.,R.V., and D.V.) - (Page 64).

"And now may it be distinctly noted that the Lord Jesus Christ did not command His disciples to baptize in the Names (plural) of the Father, and of the Son, and of the Holy Spirit, but in the Name (singular) - "Father, Son and Holy Spirit". The Spirit of truth, according to the Scriptures, revealed to the apostles and disciples and to the Church of the apostolic age the fact that "the Name of the Father, and of the Son, and of the Holy Spirit" is the Name Lord, revealed to mankind, and therefore invokable in prayer, and otherwise primarily and always for salvation by mankind only in and through the Name of the <u>Lord Jesus Christ</u>, the Son of God.

Baptism was never commanded nor performed during the apostolic age, in (or, with, that is, with the invocation of) any other Name than the Name of the **LORD, IN AND THROUGH THE NAME OF THE LORD JESUS CHRIST**, the Son of God".

"Saul persecuted the Christians in those days because he believed them to be guilty of idolatry and blasphemy in calling on or invoking in prayer for salvation the Name ("Lord") of God the Father, **in and through the Name of the Lord Jesus Christ**" (Pages 76-78).

3. **"Dictionary of the Apostolic Church"**

Professor Kirsopp Lake, D.D., in Vol I, page 29, of this text says: "There is no doubt that the writer of Acts regarded baptism as the normal means of entry into the Christian Church. There is also no doubt that he represents baptism at an early stage of Christian practice in which baptism was 'in the Name of the Lord Jesus' (or 'of Jesus Christ'), not in the triadic formula (Acts 2:38; 8:16; 10:48; 19:5).

4. **"The Latin Vulgate"**

   Jerome, who gave to us the translation, from the Latin Vulgate, known as the Duoay Version records the Triune Name of the Lord Jesus Christ in the records of baptism in Acts 8:16; 10:48 and 19:5.

5. **Dr. A.C. Gaebelein**

   A Trinitarian and noted Bible expositor writes: "I rather think inasmuch as baptism is into the death of Christ, that the formula 'In the Name of the Lord Jesus Christ' is the correct one.

6. **F.B. Meyer**

   Lange dissents from Meyer when he maintains that the passage (Matthew 28:19) is "improperly termed the **baptismal formula**", assigning as reason that Jesus does not, assuredly, dictate the **words** which are to be employed in the administration of baptism.

   He does quote Meyer as further saying that "No trace is to be found of the employment of these words by the Apostolic Church ..." (Lange, John Peter; "**The Gospel According to Matthew**", Translated from the Third German Edition, with additions by Philip Schaff. New York, Charles Scribner's Sons, 1899).

7. **"Names and Titles of the Holy Spirit"**

   From "**Jones Catholic Doctrine of the Trinity**", Pages 57,83, Vol II, we quote the following:

   "The disciples of Christ were commanded to baptize in the Name of the Father, and of the Son and of the Holy Ghost". And without doubt, the baptism they administered was in all cases agreeable to (with) the prescribed form. Nevertheless, we are told of some who were commanded to be baptized in the Name of the Lord (Acts 10:48), and particularly in the Name of the Lord Jesus (Acts 8:16), so that there was a strong defect either in the baptism itself, or in the account we have of it; or, the mention of One Person in the Trinity implies the Presence, Name and Authority of Them All; as the passage is understood by Iranaeus, ie.,

   > "By Baptism in the Name of Christ, is to be understood, He who anointed, and He who was anointed, and the anointing itself by which He was anointed; in other words, **FATHER, SON AND HOLY SPIRIT**".

   (Iranaeus. 50.3 and 100.20).

8. **"The Didache" - The Teaching of the Twelve**

   In Didache 7:1, which was of the earliest writings of the early post-apostolic Church, and which held great authority in early times says:

   "Concerning baptism, baptize in this way. Having first rehearsed all these things, baptize in the Name of the Father, and the Son and Holy Spirit in living water ..." "Let none eat or drink of your Eucharist save such as are baptized into the Name of the Lord".

9. **"Christianity in the Apostolic Age"**

   Professor George T. Purves, D.D., Page 56) in this book says: "The first record of their use (that is the use of the words, "the Name of the Father, and of the Son and of the Holy Spirit") in baptism is in The Teaching of the Apostles (about AD100)". This is noted in the Didache.

10. **Testimony from the Fathers**

    B.F. Smith, in "**Christian Baptism**" (Nashville, Tennessee: Broadman Press, 1970, and, Pages 74-76), lists a number of the names of Church Fathers who admit that the customary mode of baptism in the third and fourth centuries was by immersion and all listed testify to immersion with a trinitarian formula.

    Cyril, Bishop of Jerusalem. AD315-385.

    Ambrose. AD340-397.

    Jerome. AD340-420.

    John Chrysostom. AD345-407.

    Augustine. AD354-430.

    Pelagius. AD363-365

11. **Britannica Encylopedia, 11th Ed, Vol 3, Page 365**

    Baptism was changed from being in the name of Jesus Christ, the Lord, to Father, Son and Holy Spirit.

12. **Hastings Dictionary of the Bible, Page 88**

    It must be acknowledged that the threefold title of Matthew 28:19 does not appear to have been used by the first church in the Book of Acts (or on the Day of Pentecost). Matthew 28:19 was not an actual baptism, but it was showing how.

    Many other quotations could be given. Baptism was always administered in the name of the Lord Jesus Christ, or words to that effect. (So also **Hastings Encyclopedia, Vol 2, Page 377**, and many others). The student is referred to those texts in the Bibliography which deal with "**The Name of God**".

It can be seen that, from the early outpouring of the Holy Spirit in Acts, the apostles and leaders of the Church baptized in the Name of the Lord Jesus Christ, into His death, burial and resurrection. Baptism signified identification with Christ in this triune redemptive work. Baptism was in His Name, or, the Triune Name, over the first century and further on into the second century.

It can also be seen from a study of Church History that great heresies arose over the Godhead (the Trinity), especially the person of Christ and the Holy Spirit. Because of the great heresies concerning the Godhead raging at this time, the Trinitarian formula of Matthew 28:19 became a powerful bulwark of defence against such heresies. Matthew 28:19 was used much in the defence of the co-equality of the persons in the Godhead, and became used more and more in water baptismal formulae, and thus, the Name of the Lord Jesus Christ in baptism fell into disuse at the close of the third and fourth centuries.

The revelation of the glory in that **Triune Name** was almost lost, as were so many other truths given to the early Apostolic Church. In the 1900's the Lord desired to recover that "lost truth" to Church.

But we return to the situation in the early 1900's and the issue which divided the Pentecostal world then and ever since.

In one way, the conflict was a fear of a revival of ancient heresies. The "**Trinity Pentecostals**" feared that the doctrine of the Trinity was being denied; being an ancient heresy of Arianism and Sabellianism. So they vehemently reinforced the "Trinitarian formula" for baptism according to Matthew 28:19, to confirm the doctrine of the Godhead as Father, Son and Holy Spirit.

The "**Oneness Pentecostals**" feared that the doctrine of the Godhead was a lapse into the heresy of Tritheism, the worship of three separate Gods. So they vehemently opposed that and maintained water baptism in the name of "Jesus only" (or, Lord Jesus, Jesus Christ, or Lord Jesus Christ), seeing "Jesus" as the name of God and Jesus being the one true God.

Over these years of controversy and division, a man by the name of W.H.Offiler was one of a number of ministers who believed that both groups could be reconciled and come to a balanced agreement between possibly two extremes.

He held and taught that God was indeed triune, and that there was a triune name for the triune God which could be used in baptism. This truth he saw was presented over the time, hoping that both the Trinity and the Oneness groups would accept it and reconcile over it, and avoid the extremes.

Without presenting the full treatise of the truth as given by W.H.Offiler (Refer to his book,"**God and His Name**"), following is a summary outline of the same.

1. The revelation of the God of the Bible is Father, Son and Holy Spirit. The God of the Bible is **triune** in nature and being; one God, not three separate Gods. The extremes to avoid were over-emphasis on the **unity of God** and falling into oneness or unitarianism. The other extreme to avoid was over-emphasis on the **threeness of God**, and falling into tritheism - the worship of three separate Gods.

2. A water baptismal formula, which hopefully would satisfy both groups, was proposed. It was a formula that would bring both Matthew 28:19 and Acts 2:38 together in one formula. It included three verses of Scriptures; one from the Gospel of Matthew, one from the Book of Acts and one from the Epistle of Romans. It ran like this:

   To the candidate

   "On confession of your faith, I baptize you into the Name of the Father, and of the Son, and of the Holy Spirit, into the Name of the Lord Jesus Christ, into the likeness of His death, that like as Christ was raised from the dead by the glory of the Father, even so you also shall rise to walk in newness of life" ("**God, and His Name**", W.H.Offiler, Page 94).

In the light of these Scripture references, it was felt that the formula, composed of these three verses, would satisfy both groups. This formula:

1. **Quotes the Triadic command** and words of Jesus in Matthew's Gospel.

2. **Invokes the Triune Name** of the Lord Jesus Christ, as used in the Acts.

3. **Declares the spiritual truth** and significance of baptism into the death, burial and the resurrection of Christ as in the Romans Epistle.

(**Note:-** If only Peter had, on the Day of Pentecost, at least **quoted the command** of Jesus in Matthew 28:19 for water baptism, or, if there was but one reference in the Acts and the Epistles of this command, what controversy and division it would have (may have!) saved in the centuries of conflict in Church History!!!!

We dare not, however, say that Peter was wrong. He was "filled with the Spirit". He had been given "the keys of the kingdom". **The point of the matter is, this writer believes, that the first revelation the Holy Spirit gave to Peter was the revelation of the triune name for the triune God to be used in water baptism! After all, it is the Holy Spirit who reveals God and His Name!**)

3. W.H.Offiler clearly taught: "Moreover, nowhere in the Scripture is the single Name of Jesus shown to be the Name of the Father, the Son, and the Holy Spirit. This is one of those dangerous pitfalls laid by Satan for the feet of the unwary, and has in these last days led thousands of people astray. For this reason, the Name of the Godhead cannot be separated without a perversion and wresting of the truth. If the single Name of Jesus is the Name of the Father, Son and Holy Ghost, as many say, then the wonderful Names of **LORD and CHRIST**, which were added to the Saviour at His ascension (Acts 2:36) are meaningless and void, which God forbid!" ("**God, and His Name**", Pages 85-86).

Brother Offiler tried to balance out what he believed were extremes. His emphasis was on a **TRIUNE GOD** having a **TRIUNE NAME**! The Name of the LORD JESUS CHRIST was not the Name of "Jesus only" but, because the fullness of the Godhead was in the Son, the fullness of the Godhead Name was in the Son. This did not make Jesus the Father, or the Holy Spirit. The Father is eternally the Father, the Son is eternally the Son and the Holy Spirit is eternally the Holy Spirit. One God in three persons, one name in a triune name!

However, both groups, Oneness and Trinitarians, did not accept this and therefore each established their own denominations. This actually created a third group in the Pentecostal world who believed in the Triune God, but also in a Triune Name to be used in a water baptismal formula. It is because both groups did not (or do not) understand what the third group believes that both reject or brand this third group as being in false doctrine or some form of heresy.

Group One:

"**The Trinity Pentecostals**" believe in the one true God of the Bible, who is revealed as Father, Son and Holy Spirit. This is confirmed and reinforced by it's use of the triadic formula of Matthew 28:19 for water baptism. They brand this next group as "Jesus Only" or "Oneness" because of "Jesus Name" used in baptism and because of their teaching on the Godhead.

Group Two:

"**The Oneness Pentecostals**" believe that Jesus is the one true God, and that Father, Son and Holy Spirit are simply three manifestations of Jesus as the one true God. Because of this they baptize in the Name of "Jesus" (or include other parts of the name). They teach that this name is the Name of the Father, Son and Holy Spirit. They do not see or understand that the triune name involves the triune God. As noted earlier, one's belief about the Godhead affects one's practice in water baptismal formula.

This group brands the first group as "Tritheists" or "Three Gods people" because of the triadic use of Matthew 28:19 in baptism.

Group Three:

"**The Triune God and Triune Name**" group believe in the Godhead, and that the God of the Bible is revealed as Father, Son and Holy Spirit. This group are sound Trinitarians but not Tritheists. In this truth they join with the first group. But they also believe that there is a Triune Name for the Triune God, and this Name is the Name to be used in a baptismal formula. It is the Triune Name of the **Lord Jesus Christ**. Baptism is not in the Name of "Jesus only ". They disagree strongly with the second group here, but believe they see part truth in "the Name", not the full truth. This is because the second group have faulty doctrine on the Godhead, the triune God, therefore they do not comprehend the triune name! Faulty doctrine on the Godhead will produce faulty doctrine on any formula for water baptism.

The Name of the Lord Jesus Christ is a compound name involving the Father, Son and Holy Spirit. Interpret the parts of the triune name and interpret the persons behind that name. The Father is **Lord**. He has placed His name upon His Son. The Son is also **Lord**. The Son is **Jesus**, the name of His humanity. It is never the name of the Father or the Holy Spirit. The Holy Spirit is seen in the name **Christ** as anointing upon the Son. The Holy Spirit is the **anointing** (Grk.; **Chrism, Oil**), and it was the Holy Spirit's anointing on the Son that made Him "Jesus Christ" - the Saviour Anointed!

A study of the Triune Name will reveal that the Triune God, as Father, Son and Holy Spirit is involved in "the Name".

In Conclusion:-

Our chapter must be brought to a conclusion. As usual, Church History shows much dissension, division and enmity. Hatred, bitterness and charges of heresy arose between the groups.

One group pitted the Gospels against the Acts. The other group pitted the Acts against the Gospels. The third group combined the Gospel, the Acts and the Epistles. The subject became a theological issue over the Godhead as well as an issue over baptism. Both are inter-related.

Catholics, Presbyterians, Methodists, Anglicans, Baptists and most Pentecostals all use the triadic formula of Matthew 28:19, following the close of the second, and including the third and fourth centuries, and following the Roman tradition. All are Trinitarian in their understanding of the Godhead and for this reason use the Triadic formula.

The Oneness and Jesus Only use or adapt Acts 2:38 because of their faulty understanding of the Godhead.

The third group combined the truth of the Gospels, the Acts and the Epistles, and endeavoured to balance between what, sometimes, were two extremes. This group recognized that no doctrine of Scripture can be built on one reference but all references to any given subject should be brought together and compared, and then the answer is discovered.

On the subject of baptism, there was only **one reference** to water baptism in the Name of the Father, Son and Holy Spirit. There were about **fourteen references** to water baptism in the Name of the Lord Jesus Christ (or variations, part representing the whole). Therefore, proper hermeneutics would teach that these **fourteen references on baptism must be the interpretation of the one reference of baptism**! This is remarkable that the Church has built a water baptismal formula on one reference, and ignored the fourteen references on water baptism in "the Name".

It is in the light of all these Scriptures and context that water baptism is administered in the formula of Scripture as given here. Scripture must interpret Scripture. The Triune Name of the Lord Jesus Christ is the Name of the Triune God. Both are right when put together. It is not one without the other. One without the other is incomplete. One is the interpretation of the other.

While denominations may and will contest these things, the truth of "The Name in baptism" has been revealed. There are those who walk in obedience to further light. There are those who, for whatever reasons, reject it.

The truth of water baptism by immersion was recovered and restored to the Church about the 15th century. The truth of the triune name for baptism was recovered in the early 1900's. It is significant that (1) The baptism of the Holy Spirit with the evidence of speaking in other tongues, and (2) The Name for water baptism was revealed about the same period of time. The two are connected, as the Day of Pentecost revealed. The Baptism of the Holy Spirit was received, and the revelation of the triune name was revealed to Peter on that same day.

Once again, God, however, still had further truths to break forth on His people. While denominations built their walls to keep truth in and keep error out, they could not lock God within their four walls. God stepped over the walls and moved on. Those who wanted to move on with the Lord followed!

CHAPTER THIRTY-ONE

RESTORATION-THE LAYING ON OF HANDS

In setting forth "Restoration Theology" as in this Chapter and the text as a whole, it must be remembered that any or all of these truths were never totally eradicated from the true Church - the faithful remnant. God has never ever let the light of the lamp of His Word of truth ever go fully out. He has always called someone to be His Word-bearer before that light went out (1Samuel 3:1-3) He has always had a faithful remnant, no matter how small, who have maintained these truths even in some small measure. It is just that God, in the recovery of lost truths, did this in a fuller way, that in due times, would touch the world and His Church in a worldwide manner.

In the 1940's, various Pentecostal ministers began to seek God in a greater way for His power and glory to be manifested. There came a great move in evangelism with "signs following the preaching of the Word" (Mark 16:15-20).

Great tents and auditoriums were filled with thousands of people being saved, filled with the Holy Spirit, and many amazing and remarkable healings and miracles taking place. These days were known under "**The Voice of Healing**" Ministry Magazine days.

So many names could be mentioned of those who moved in "**Healing and Deliverance Ministry**" over the years 1940-1950 and onward. "**The Voice of Healing**" Magazine carried their stories until most of these established their own ministry and magazines.

Richard Riss, in "**Latter Rain**" (page 47) gives a report of the early years of this salvation and healing move of the Holy Spirit. He writes:

"In Pentecostal circles, a major emphasis came to be placed upon healing during this time. David Edwin Harrell, Jr., has written of the Healing Revival that, "A generation grew up that would never forget the ecstatic years from 1947 to 1952, years filled with long nights of tense anticipation, a hypnotic yearning for the Holy Spirit, and stunning miracles for the believers performed by God's anointed revivalists."

Two of the earliest and most influential healing evangelists of the mid-twentieth century were William Branham and Oral Roberts. Other important figures included T.L.Osborne, Jack Coe, William Freeman, A.A.Allen, and David Nunn. Gordon Lindsay, who had helped to bring the ministry of William Branham into widespread recognition, used his talents to supply the movement with a needed element of cohesiveness.

The healing ministry of William Branham began in the spring of 1946. On May 7th of that year, according to Branham, an angel had visited him and said to him, "Fear not, I am sent from the presence of Almighty God to tell you that your peculiar life and your misunderstood ways have been to indicate that God has sent you to take a gift of Divine healing to the people of the world. IF YOU WILL BE SINCERE, AND CAN GET THE PEOPLE TO BELIEVE YOU, NOTHING SHALL STAND BEFORE YOUR PRAYER, NOT EVEN CANCER." Branham said that he was told by the angel that he would be able to detect diseases by vibrations in his left hand.

During the Sunday evening service at which he first spoke of what had happened, he received a telegram from a friend, Robert Daugherty, requesting that he come to pray for his sick daughter in St.Louis. Branham went to St. Louis and prayed for her, and Daugherty's daughter's health improved. He returned to Daugherty's Church to conduct a healing revival from June 14 to June 25, 1946. His reputation spread throughout the United Pentecostal Church, and he was soon invited to hold a revival in the Bible House Tabernacle in Jonesboro, Arkansas, pastored by Rex Humbard's father, "Dad" Humbard, where he was reported to have raised a dead man. According to Gordon Lindsay, 25,000 people had come to those meetings from twenty-eight States."

William Branham was a notable minister at this time. He was a Baptist minister who had this angelic visitation and revelation that launched him into the ministry of a prophet-evangelist. He ministered in the supernatural and gifts of the Spirit. He laid hands on the sick, moved in the word of knowledge and word of wisdom, as well as discerning of spirits and the gift of faith (1Corinthians 12:1-11). He inspired many ministries to move into the "Healing Ministry".

William Branham was like "A Morning Star" ministry and "Elijah-type" who stirred other ministers to greater consecration to the Lord and His will in the realm of the super-natural.

Gordon Lindsay, as William Branham's manager, featured many ministries in his magazine. Ministries such as T.L.Osborne, Oral Roberts, Tommy Hicks, Jack Coe, William Freeman, A.A.Allan, Kathryn Kuhlman, Paul Cain, Kenneth Hagin, O.L.Jaggers, Louise Nankervell, A.C.Valdez, David Nunn, W.V.Grant, Velmar Gardner and many others whom the Lord anointed during these years. W.J.Ern Baxter was William Branham's teaching ministry for years in his great campaigns.

The sad part was that many of these ministers went into false doctrine, some into immorality, some into drinking problems, some into money manipulation and other questionable behaviour and methods of ministry. Others started their own followings and drew people to themselves. Much became competition and not recognition. Within twenty years or so most had passed from the scene. It seemed as if God entrusted His power to ministries for a period of time, but found many had "charisma" but lacked the "character" to handle such.

(Note:- There are books and magazines that tell of these wonderful days as also some of the tragic ending of some of these ministries, which the student is encouraged to find and read).

The ministry that has a great bearing on this chapter is that of William Branham. Although Branham began teaching some questionable doctrines (he did have faulty understanding of the Godhead), and some extremes before he died, his ministry and gift was reasonably, and generally accepted in the Pentecostal world at that time. Some did not accept it at all. Following are some reports and comments from various booklets or books as well as some verbatim reports of those who write on what happened in what became known as "**The Latter Rain Movement**".

After witnessing the Lord's ministry through William Branham, some students and teachers believed God had much more to reveal to the Church about the operation of the gifts of the Spirit. Various students began to pray and fast and seek the Lord in a great way and intensified manner, some more days than others. In February of 1948, God broke forth in the Bible College and revival, recovery and restoration of truth took the next step forward. But we let George Warnock tell the story of how it began, as he wrote in "**The Feast of Tabernacles**", which became, as it were, a 'textbook' of "Latter Rain teachings". William Branham seemed to be the ministry that "seeded" the Latter Rain movement.

> "In the beginning GOD ..." So it was that in the spring of 1948 God came forth in answer to the prayer and fasting of His children, poured out the gifts of the Holy Spirit, and revealed the fact that now at this time He would bring His Body together, and make

of His Church one glorious Church without spot or wrinkle. It was a day long treasured up in the counsels of God. On February 12 and 13, 1948, the Revival started. An eyewitness testifies as follows:

"Three buildings on the Airport at North Battleford, Saskatechewan (Canada), composed Sharon Orphanage and Schools at its beginning in the fall of 1947. About 70 students gathered to study the Word of God, and fast and pray. After about three months the Revival suddenly began in our largest classroom where the entire student body was gathered for devotional exercises. One young man told me that when he was five years old, God gave him a vision of that classroom. Everything in it was identical. He saw God moving in a way he could not understand."

"I shall never forget that morning that God moved into our midst in this strange new manner. Some students were under the power of God on the floor, others were kneeling in adoration and worship before the Lord. The anointing deepened until the awe of God was upon everyone. The Lord spoke to one of the brethren, 'Go and lay hands upon a certain student and pray for him.' While he was in doubt and contemplation, one of the sisters who had been under the power of God went to the brother saying the same words, and naming the identical student he was to pray for. He went in obedience, and a revelation was given concerning the student's life and future ministry. After this a long prophecy was given with minute details concerning the great thing God was about to do. The pattern for the Revival and many details concerning it were given. To this day I can remember the gist of the prophecy, and will try to repeat some things here as they were spoken.

"These are the last days, My people. The coming of the Lord draweth nigh, and I shall move in the midst of Mine own. The gifts of the Spirit will be restored to My Church. If thou shalt obey Me, I shall immediately restore them ... But oh, My people, I would have you to be reverent before Me as never before. Take the shoes from off thy feet for the ground on which thou standest is holy. If thou does not reverence the Lord in His House, the Lord shall require it at thy hands ... Do not speak lightly of the things I am about to do, for the Lord shall not hold thee guiltless. Do not gossip about these things. Do not write letters to thy nearest friends, of the new way in which the Lord moveth, for they will not understand ... If thou doest disobey the Lord in these things, take heed lest thy days be numbered in sorrow and thou goest early to the grave ... Thou hast obeyed Me, and I shall restore My gifts to you. I shall indicate from time to time those who are ready to receive the gifts of My Spirit. They shall be received by prophecy and the laying on of the hands of the presbytery."

"Immediately following this prophecy, a sister who was under the power of God gave by revelation the names of five students who were ready to receive. Hands were laid upon them by the presbytery. This procedure was very faltering and imperfect that first morning, but after two days of searching the Word of God to see if we were on Scriptural grounds, great unity prevailed and the Lord came forth in greater power and glory day by day. Soon a visible manifestation of gifts was received when candidates were prayed over, and many as a result began to be healed, as gifts of healing were received."

"Day after day the glory and power of God came among us. Great repentance, humbling, fasting and prayer prevailed." (George Warnock, "**The Feast of Tabernacles**", The Foreword).

Richard Riss, in "**Latter Rain**" (page 64) gives another account of the beginning of the Revival as given by a brother George R.Hawtin. His brother, Ern Hawtin, is named as the one who gave the long prophecy. George reports:

> "It was on the 12th day of February that ... my brother Ern, my youngest brother, rose to prophesy. All the students were kneeling in the classroom. He prophesied by the Spirit of God for about half an hour. During the prophecy, he called the whole school to holiness, to great reverence before God, and that we must walk in the fear of God. Then there was a warning that we should not mention what was transpiring in letters, because people would not understand the things that were going on at the school at the time. But as the prophecy went on, these words were given by the Spirit of God: "I will at this time restore the nine gifts of the Spirit to My Church, and they shall be restored by prophecy, with the laying on of the hands of the presbytery."
>
> This we know, was according to the Word of God; but we had not been able to see it until that moment when the Spirit of God revealed it to us. The prophecy went on to say, "I will indicate from time to time certain ones who are prepared to receive the gifts from the Spirit of God."
>
> During the next day, February 13th, we searched the Word of God practically all day in the classroom to see if these things that had been prophesied were according to God's Word ... On the 14th of February - I can never begin to describe the things that happened on that day. It seemed that all heaven broke loose upon our souls, and heaven came down to greet us. The power and glory of God was indescribable."

Although the major truth of "**The Latter Rain Movement**" (so-called, and branded), was "**the laying on of hands and prophecy**", there were other truths that were associated with the new wine outpouring of the Spirit.

From one who was there at that time, we quote his testimony and experience and witness of the occasion.

In "**The 1948 Revival & Now**", (pages 1-3), Milford E. Kirkpatrick writes:

> "In the providence of God, I was there when the great outpouring of the Spirit came upon us".
>
> "First of all, I should lay down the setting and how all this came about and what the conditions were. At this particular time in Saskatchewan, Canada, a number of we pastors, evangelists and workers longed to see a move of God in our churches and meetings. We became alarmed at the spiritual decline and coldness and the lack of spiritual hunger among the people. We were anxious to do something about it, but things seemed to have grown steadily worse. No one seemed to have the answer. The general consensus of opinion from those who were over us in the Lord was that we were not to expect revival because we were living in the closing days of time and things were going to grow worse, and we were to hold on to the bitter end. We often heard quoted, 'Except those days be shortened there should no flesh be saved'(Matthew 24:22). This only brought more depression into our spirits so we were at the point of despair.
>
> So many of us in this large Pentecostal group, because of our desperation and hunger for God, began to fast and pray. Some fasted three weeks and one brother fasted 42 days. This was even new to us.

(**Note:** Apparently Franklin Hall's book on '**Atomic Power with God through Prayer and Fasting**' had much influence on George and Ern Hawtin and others. It was felt that the truth of prayer with fasting was another recovered truth).

Many of us gathered in this one place, through a chain of circumstances that is not necessary for us to tell here. God brought us together through a sovereign act at this particular time.

> "The year 1948 was the year when many things we could mention began. It was the year the Jews became a nation, the year when Unions made themselves known. There seemed to be a general quickening in every department and in every country around the world.
>
> "One particular day a brother stood to his feet and began to prophesy. Until that time, we had not heard much prophecy nor very little about the ministry of a prophet. For over one-half hour God spoke through him about visitation. Because of the heavy anointing we knew God had spoken to us through the honest brother. God spoke to us about restoration days and that He would pour out His Spirit upon all flesh. This thrilled our hearts, having lived in an atmosphere of defeatism. It was refreshing, for now we were assured of visitation from God. What joy swept through the camp; what faith and hope were planted in our hearts. **God said He would restore all that the Church had lost**"

Milford Kirkpatrick makes mention in his booklet of the fact that there were seven principles or seven major truths that the 1948 Revival emphasized. Many times, the prophetic word admonished them not to depart from the things the Spirit had given them. In brief, Brother Kirpatrick says there were seven truths which they were to follow.

A. Seven Main Visitation Truths

1. Reverence

The prophetic word said,"If My people will reverence My Name, My Presence and My House, I will begin to restore that which has been lost to the Church" (Proverbs 1:7). Prayer, brokenness, confession and cleansing were strong in these days.

2. Restoration

The Lord indicated through the prophetic word that He would restore to the Church all that had been lost (Acts 3:21; Joel 2:28). The Lord wants a glorious Church without spot or wrinkle or any such thing. He wants to be joined to a holy Church in holy matrimony.

3. Unity

The Lord's Prayer of John 17 took on rich and fuller meaning. Sectarianism and carnality and divisions were great evils in the Church. The unity would be around the name of the Lord Jesus Christ and not the sectarian names men had created in the schisms of the Church (1 Corinthians 1:10-13; 3:1-9).

4. Laying on of Hands

Though laying on of hands was generally accepted for the healing ministry, the laying on of hands was not really accepted with presbytery and prophetic utterances (Hebrews 6:1-2; Mark 16:18; Acts 13:1-4; 1Timothy 1:18; 4:14; with 2Timothy 1:6). Also, the laying on of hands was not the usual custom for receiving the baptism in the Holy Spirit. Most Pentecostal groups still believed that "tarrying meetings" were God's method for receiving Holy Spirit baptism.

Milford Kirkpatrick, on pages 9-10 of his paper, speaks about the restoration of the laying on of hands as brought forth in the 1948 visitation of the Spirit. He says:

"This was new to us in many respects. We had laid hands on the sick, but when the prophet spoke of laying on of hands and prophecy, this sent every one to their knees, faculty and students alike. In those days we sought the Lord to see if those things were Scriptural. We took time off for three whole days. All went to their rooms to pray and search the Scriptures. On the fourth day all came out with their findings, and everyone, without exception said, 'It is absolutely Biblical and Scriptural.' They quoted Hebrews 6:2. This speaks of it as a doctrine. Acts 13:1-4 shows that the early Church practiced it. 1Timothy 1:18; 4:14; and 2Timothy 1:6 shows that Paul believed in the laying on of hands and prophecy. Mark 16:18 says, 'They shall lay hands on the sick.' So far as far as we were concerned, the doctrine of laying on of hands and prophecy was accepted and we believed the Biblical record.

On pages 15-16 he further writes:

"It was rather amusing how in the beginning the laying on of hands got started. The question was - Who would have the faith to start doing it? Like anything new in the Spirit, it takes faith to begin. God spoke to the brother that gave the first prophecy. He was a bit afraid to lay hands on anyone. At that moment someone in the back of the congregation said, 'My servant- what the Lord has told you to do, do it, do not be afraid.' So who do you think he chose? I was sitting in the middle of the front seat and we were only halfway through the service when he walked over to me and took me by the hand. I thought this was a peculiar time to shake hands, but when he took me by the hand, I felt the glorious anointing. I might say God had prepared my heart. I had been in prayer the night before and for the first time in years was slain by the power of God, and when the brother took me by the hand, I felt the same anointing. Then he began to prophesy and mentioned the ministry of an apostle, which of course means a missionary, or sent one. Then he said, the gifts of the Spirit would come into operation when needed. This was of course, a confirmation as we had already been doing some of this type of work" (End Quote).

5. Not To Justify Ourselves

The prophetic word said: "Do not justify yourselves, by word, letter, telegram or by telephone". This was the wisdom of God because of the endless controversy that arose over this fresh visitation. However, many who were blessed in this move of the Spirit did not either know or obey this word, and caused much damage to the "Latter Rain" truths.

6. **Whose Battle Is It?**

   The prophetic word also said: "I will fight your battles for you." This was to restrain the fightings of carnality that would arise over this freshly recovered truth (2Corinthians 10:4; Zechariah 4:6). The Lord would fight for them as He did for Jehoshaphat (2Chronicles 20).

7. **World-Wide Vision**

   Evangelism and Missions became real burdens on the heart of those touched by the prophetic word (Luke 4:18-20; Acts 2:17).

Numerous people were touched and ministered to in prophetic presbytery and laying on of hands both in Canada and America. Signs and wonders, miracles and healings took place. Many were filled with the Spirit according to Acts 2:4. Much release and illumination on the Word of God came out in conferences and meetings over the immediate years from 1948-1951 or thereabouts.

Without doubt, the most controversial truth was the truth of "the laying on of hands and prophecy and presbytery". This was the most severely criticised of the doctrines of the "Latter Rain" visitation.

The Pentecostals, as a whole, accepted the laying on of hands for praying for the sick and for deliverance. Divine healing was part of the Pentecostals "tenets of faith". But "**the laying on of hands with prophecy and presbytery with the impartation of spiritual gifts**" was revolutionary. This teaching and practice caused the greatest controversy among the Pentecostal Churches.

History repeated itself. The major Pentecostal denominations, who had received the previously recovered truth of the baptism in the Spirit, now generally became the bitterest opponents of this freshly recovered truth. The intense opposition and rejection of this truth caused some of the worst kinds of carnality to surface among the Pentecostals.

The movement of the Spirit was called "Latter Rain/Scatter Rain". The leaders were charged with "giving out gifts", and "spiritual fortune-telling", and many other things. The doctrine was branded as heretical. It brought the greatest opposition and persecution, especially among the Pentecostalists. Ministers and congregations were excommunicated from denominations or else withdrew. Tracts and booklets were written against this truth.

As in every previously restored truth, there were undoubtedly those who went to extremes, violated Scriptural principles, manipulated and exploited people, and ruined lives, bringing this beautifully restored truth into great reproach.

But, in spite of rejection, opposition and reproach, both within and without the Pentecostals and the Latter Rain Movement, there were thousands who were touched by the Lord in this present truth. The truth had been recovered. God had restored to the Church another portion of "**the faith once delivered to the saints**" (Jude 3)

B. **The Doctrine of Laying on of Hands**

   A reasonable outline is given here of the truth relative to the laying on of hands as came out in the 1948 move of the Spirit.

The doctrine of the laying on of hands is found in both the Old and New Testaments. It is a real and blessed ministry ordained of God in the Church for the purpose of ministering to people. It is a means of imparting God's grace and His blessing. It is not a mere form, or a dead empty ceremony. Its distinctive truths are identification, impartation, substitution and confirmation. It is impossible to impart without the anointing and power of the Holy Spirit. The sovereignty of God and the responsibility of man are both involved in this ministry.

1. **The Old Testament**

    (a) Laying on of hands was seen in identification in the offering of Old Testament sacrifices (Leviticus 1:4; 3:2,8,13; 4:15,24,29,33; 8:14-22; 16:21).

    (b) It was used in the ordination of the priestly tribe of Levi for the ministry to the nation of Israel (Numbers 18:10-27).

    (c) Laying on of hands was involved in the inauguration of the ministry of Joshua to replace Moses as the successor under God (Numbers 27:18-23; Deuteronomy 34:9-10; 31:7-8,23).

    (d) Jacob ministered by the laying on of hands and prophecy to his twelve sons, as also Ephraim and Manasseh (Genesis 48-49 chapters).

2. **The New Testament**

    (a) The doctrine of the laying on of hands is one the first principles of the doctrine of Christ (Hebrews 5:12-6:1-2).

    (b) Jesus used the ministry of laying on of hands for the healing of many who were sick. The apostles continued the same ministry and this was also given to believers to follow (Mark 1:31,41; 6:2,5; 7:31-37; Matthew 8:15-17; Mark 16:18; Acts 3:7; 5:12; 9:17; 14:3; 28:8; Luke 5:13; 13:13; 22:51; Acts 19:11).

    (c) It was used in the prayer for baptism in the Holy Spirit (Acts 8:14-25; 9:17; 19:1-7). It is worthy to note that in Acts 2 and Acts 10 there were only two sovereign outpourings of the Spirit, all the rest being through the ministry of laying on of hands. For many Pentecostals, the "tarrying meeting" was the main way of receiving the Holy Spirit baptism, even though in Azuza Street times the first one to receive the baptism received through the laying on of hands, according to accounts. In the visitation of 1948, many 'chronic seekers' received the baptism through this ministry.

    (d) The laying on of hands was used to bless children (Matthew 19:13; Mark 10:16).

    (e) This ministry was also used in the impartation of spiritual gifts, both in Old and New Testaments (Deuteronomy 31:7-8,23; 34:9-10; Acts 19:1-7; Romans 1:11; 1Timothy 4:14; 1:18-20; 2 Timothy 1:6,14).

    (f) The laying on of hands was involved in the appointment of deacons (Acts 6:1-6), and the ordination of elders (Acts 14:23,26-28; 1Timothy 5:22), as well as the setting apart to ministry (Acts 13:1-4).

(g) Paul and the presbytery ministered to Timothy by the laying on of hands and prophecy, and there was impartation of some spiritual gift through that ministry (1Timothy 4:14-16; 2Timothy 1:6; 1Timothy 1:18-20 with Acts 16:1-4).

(h) Paul warns Timothy against the hasty laying on of hands without following proper Biblical principles (1Timothy 5:22).

Much more could be written on this truth, but these Scriptures are the most important ones on the doctrine of the laying on of hands and the truth recovered to the Church under this wave of the Holy Spirit.

The laying on of hands is a Divinely appointed ministry in the Church. It is not to be profaned or lightly esteemed. Paul exhorts Timothy in 1Timothy 5:22, "Do not lay hands on anyone hastily, nor share in other people's sins; keep yourself pure" (NKJV). Ministers and leaders need to have (1) Holy hands (1Timothy 2:8), and (2) A pure heart (Psalm 24:4; 26:6; Lamentations 3:41).

Like every other truth, it suffered much at the hands of "its friends", but it is much more accepted now by a number of Pentecostals as well as other Charismatic groups.

The Roman and Anglican Churches have generally accepted the laying on of hands, in some form or another, for "Confirmation". Presbyterian, Methodists, Baptist and other mainline denominations have used the laying on of hands generally for "prayer and ordination" to the ministry at times.

The rejection and opposition to this ministry was not so much as the truth of it in general, but it was the emphasis on "**laying on of hands and prophecy with impartation**" that became the issue. It is to be admitted that lack of wisdom and grace brought this ministry into reproach oftentimes by some who administered it.

Rejection, opposition, tolerance and acceptance once again became the cycle for this truth as for other truths in the years following 1948. For fuller details regarding "**The Laying on of Hands & Presbytery**", the reader is referred to the Bibliography).

In the 1948 visitation and several subsequent years, there were a number of other truths that were, so to speak, "**seeded**" by the Holy Spirit in the hearts of minstries that were instruments of the Lord over this period of time. The following chapter will be given to a consideration of these truths in brief for the purpose of this text on Restoration Theology. The emphasis in this chapter has been especially upon the recovery and restoration of the truth and doctrine of "the laying on of hands".

CHAPTER THIRTY-TWO

SEED TO THE SOWER - BREAD TO THE EATER

The prophet Isaiah provides a challenging word to Israel in his generation. Because truth is truth in every generation, and therefore applicable to all time, Isaiah's word is truly appropriate for the contents of this chapter. In Isaiah 55:6-11 we have these words:

> "Seek ye the LORD while he may be found, call ye upon him while he is near:
>
> Let the wicked forsake his way, and the unrighteous man his thoughts: and let him return unto the LORD, and he will have mercy upon him; and to our God, for he will abundantly pardon.
>
> For my thoughts are not your thoughts, neither are your ways my ways, saith the LORD.
>
> For as the heavens are higher than the earth, so are my ways higher than your ways, and my thoughts than your thoughts.
>
> For **as the rain** cometh down, and the snow from heaven, and returneth not thither, but watereth the earth, and maketh it bring forth and bud, that it may give **seed to the sower**, and **bread to the eater:**
>
> **So shall my word** be that goeth forth out of my mouth: it shall not return unto me void, but it shall accomplish that which I please, and it shall prosper in the thing whereto I sent it."

The Lord through this word exhorts His people to forsake their own thoughts and ways, which are so contrary and opposite to God's thoughts and ways. God's thoughts and ways are as high as the heaven above the earth and above man's thoughts and ways. The Lord desires His thoughts and ways to become our thoughts and ways.

Here the prophet speaks of God's Word being like rain that comes down from heaven. It waters the earth, and it brings forth **SEED TO THE SOWER and BREAD TO THE EATER.** He says that His Word, like the rain, will not return to Him void but it will accomplish the purpose God sent it to, and it will prosper in all that the Lord desired.

In the 1948 visitation of the Holy Spirit, these verses were evident. God gave much "**seed to the sower and bread to the eater**". There was plenty of **SEED for sowing ministries** to put in their baskets, and there was plenty of **BREAD for feeding ministries** to put in their baskets also. Read also 2Corinthians 9:10 where Paul takes Isaiah's prophecy up and speaks of both "seed" and "bread".

In several of the Parables of the Lord Jesus Christ, He mentions "the seed". There was seed in the Parable of the Sower. There was seed in the Parable of the Wheat and Tares. There was seed in the Parable of the Mustard Tree. There was the seed in the Parable of the growth of the Kingdom (Matthew 13:1-43 with Mark 4:26-29).

Luke's Gospel provides for us an interpretative key. He tells us that "**THE SEED IS THE WORD ...**" (Luke 8:11).

So it was in the movement of the Spirit in 1948 and some years onwards. Besides a major emphasis on the restoration and recovery of the truth of the laying on of hands and prophecy, there were a number of other truths that were seeded in this visitation of the Lord. Although some things had been heard of in the Pentecostal movement, the 1948 move of the Spirit brought these **seed-truths** to the fore-front. They were watered and developed in Scripture research until they touched much of the Church world as never before. New light shone upon old truths, truths that had been in the Word of God but not seen by the people of God. God sent out His **light and truth** again and led His people further on into His will (Psalm 43:1-3).

The purpose of this chapter is to note some of the major "seed-truths" that came out in this visitation. They can only be considered in brief, but to the earnest and diligent student, they provide seed that can be watered and developed more fully by research into what the Scriptures teach on these subjects. All the potential is in the life of that seed and the SEED is THE WORD!

A. The Spirit and The Word

A very significant thing in the so-called "Latter Rain" movement was how the truth of the Laying on of Hands was recovered.

It was recovered to the students who heard the prophetic word and utterance of the Spirit through the brother who spoke on that eventful morning of February 12th, 1948. The students, let alone the teachers, did not really believe in those things that were prophesied. After hearing the prophetic utterance, students and faculty spent two or three days studying the Word to see if these things were according to the Word. They had to be like the Bereans, who, "**received the word with all readiness of mind, and searched the Scriptures daily whether these things were so**"(Acts 17:11). Even though the apostle Paul had spoken these things, the Bereans still checked out what he said by the Scriptures.

As Kirkpatrick said: "It sent everyone to their knees, faculty and students alike". All prayed in their rooms and on the fourth day they came out with their findings. Everyone without exception said it was absolutely Biblical and Scriptural" ("**The 1948 Revival & Now**", page 9-10).

The seed-truth here is this. In this case, it was **the Spirit** that brought forth **the Word** and then the hearers checked out "the prophetic word" with the inspired and infallible Word and found it to be so.

In previous visitations, the Spirit quickened something in the written Word and those who received it believed it and experienced it accordingly. In other words, it was first **THE WORD** and then the experience of that Word. Here it was first **THE SPIRIT**, and then **THE WORD**! "The Spirit moved ... and God said ..." (Genesis 1:1-2. Though it cannot be equated exactly as the receiving of the inspired and the infallible Word of God, the principle was: "holy men of God spoke as they were moved by the Spirit ..." (2Peter 1:19-21). The Spirit moved, and God said.

Here the prophetic word, given by the Spirit, drove those who did not quite believe or understand these things, to the written Word. This was an unusual movement of God in the recovery of lost truth.

The seed-truth is this. Sometimes it is "first the Spirit, then the Word", and sometimes it "first the Word, and then the Spirit". The Book of Acts illustrates the truth of these things. God is sovereign. He will do what He wills to do in recovery of lost truth. Which ever way, the Spirit and the Word, or the Word and the Spirit, will always work together. The Spirit and the Word agree (1John 5:7).

B. The Latter Rain Outpouring

Another "**seed-truth**" which the Holy Spirit watered was the truth of the latter rain outpouring of the Holy Spirit in the last days.

Richard Riss (in "**Latter Rain**", page 75) notes that the brethren in Canada (George and Ernest Hawtin, Percy Hunt and later on George Warnock) did not call themselves "Latter Rain". All believed this would just become another sectarian and divisive name in the Body of Christ.

However, spiritual songs were born which spoke of the promise of the coming "Latter Rain". This expression comes from the Scriptures in Joel 2:23-32; Deuteronomy 11:14; James 5:17; Proverbs 16:15; Jeremiah 3:3; Hosea 6:3 and Zechariah 10:1. These Scriptures speak of both natural rains in Israel and point to the spiritual rains which would come on the Church in the last days. All pointed to the final outpourings of the Holy Spirit, as He would come in refreshing and reviving power after dry seasons and drought.

Many Churches that were touched by the visitation of the Spirit did call themselves "Latter Rain" Churches, which did not help the situation but further added another sectarian flavour in the Body of Christ

It is worthy of note that the expression, "latter rain" was not a new term. In the early Pentecostal outpouring in the 1900's, Pentecost was called "The Latter Rain Movement". The term, therefore, was not new, just repeated, and became more crystallised as a teaching.

The truth is that, "former and latter rains" in Scripture, naturally, pointed to the spiritual rains, the outpouring of the Holy Spirit in the early Church and then in the last day Church. All this would be fulfilled before the second coming of the Lord Jesus Christ. The rains were necessary to bring in the final harvest of souls in the nations of the earth.

One of the Scripture passages that brought much blessing was 1Kings 18:41-46. It was after the manifestation of the Lord, the God who answered by FIRE, that Elijah sought the Lord in deep and earnest prayer for RAIN. After the "seven times" looking of the servant of Elijah, he saw a cloud the size of a man's hand, and then there was the sound of the abundance of rain.

The visitation of 1948 was seen but as "a little cloud". The size of a "man's hand" was linked in thought to the restoration of the laying on of hands. The "sound of abundance of rain" pointed to the coming, final and full outpouring of the Holy Spirit on dry land, on dry Churches and denominations!

The sad thing which happened was, many "Latter Rain" Churches were estranged, disassociated from their denominations, or simply resigned, many of them being well-known and highly respected leaders.

The "**seed-truth**" of the "Latter Rain Outpouring" of the Spirit provides truth worthy of much research in the Scriptures.

C. Apostles and Prophets

In this move of the Holy Spirit, greater attention was given to, what has been called, "the five-fold ascension-gift ministries" of Ephesians 4:9-16. This became another great "seed-truth" which the Holy Spirit watered.

It was not as if this was altogether "new". The Apostolic Church of Wales (UK) had certainly emphasized the foundational ministries of "apostles and prophets". The Pentecostals, as a whole, rejected such as being "not for today". In fact, such teaching was branded as 'heresy' in most Pentecostal denominations, as also in Protestant denominations. Belief in apostles and prophets was relegated to the early and first century of Church History only. This was the Cessationists view.

The Church, in general, accepted evangelists, pastors and teachers as "for today", but "apostles and prophets" were "not for today".

In the 1948 movement, the Holy Spirit once again brought attention to and clarity on these foundational ministries. The teaching was that all fivefold ascension gift ministries were given for the perfecting of the saints, for the work of the ministry and for the building up of the Body of Christ. These were given until the Body came to the measure of the stature of the fullness of Christ, until we came to a mature and perfect man. They were also given until Christ returns the second time (Ephesians 4:9-16).

Other Scriptures were used to confirm the importance and necessity of the apostolic and prophetic ministries in the Body of Christ (1Corinthians 12:28,29; Ephesians 2:20; 3:5; 4:11; Revelation 18:20; Luke 11:49; 2Peter 3:2). Much wonderful teaching was provided on the ascension gift ministries in "**The Sharon Star**" paper and "**The Sharon Studies**" publications.

There is much wider acceptance of these foundational ministries in the Pentecostal and Charismatic world today than in those days. All ministries, be they apostles, prophets, evangelists, shepherds or teachers, must be tested by the Word of God and according to character, not only charisma. As always, there are true and false ministries in the Church and all must be tested by the Word of God. Just because there is counterfeit, this does not justify rejection of the true.

Textbooks are available that deal more fully with these gifted ministries. However, the "seed-truth" was brought to the forefront more fully for many of God's people in the visitation of the Spirit. Once again, there was much "**seed-truth**" given in the visitation.

D. The Gifts of the Holy Spirit

The Pentecostal revival, during the 1900's movement, had accepted the fact that the gifts of the Spirit were available through the baptism of the Holy Spirit. Many of the early Pentecostalists had seen these gifts of the Spirit in operation in a reasonable measure. But the majority of the Pentecostals had allowed the gifts of the Spirit to fall into disuse by the time of the 1948 visitation. This was not totally so, but indeed in the majority of cases, this was true.

Many Churches had seen the gifts of the Holy Spirit in William Branham's ministry. This created a greater hunger for these gifts to be restored more fully to the Church. Much prayer and fasting and brokenness of spirit took place as people sought the Lord.

The prophetic word in February 12th, 1948, was that the Lord would restore these gifts by the laying on of hands, as the Spirit would indicate from time to time. Many testimonies are given in the accounts of the early days of the 1948 visitation. Gifts of the Spirit came into immediate operation in many, many cases, and in Churches open to the visitation of the Spirit. As noted earlier, teachers and students alike searched the Scriptures to see if these things were so, and all were in harmony with the Bible. All found it to be so.

Scriptures seen to speak of impartation of gifts of the Spirit with the laying on of hands were 1Timothy 1:18; 2Timothy 1:6; Romans 1:11; 1Corinthians 12:8; 1Timothy 4:14-16.

This was counted 'heretical' by the main Pentecostal denominations and came under the greatest criticism and controversy. There were those, of course, who brought much reproach on this ministry, and caused further rejection of this truth by their extremes and unjudged "laying on of hands and giving out of gifts". Such unScriptural conduct caused many to reject the truth of the visitation on this matter.

As Dick Iverson wrote in, "**Present Day Truths**" (page 59, 1975 Edition, Center Press, Portland, Oregon, USA):

> "Unfortunately, the movement was judged on the basis of the most radical element which used the gifts and callings of God for their own gain. Hence, many have looked with consternation on what took place in those years, letting the abuses and fanaticism of a few blind them to the spiritual truth God wanted to reveal ... This, then, is precisely what happened in the early 1950's. Many who were involved in this original move went into extreme fanaticism and religious racketeering. Hence, the whole movement was considered negatively."

George R.Hawtin set forth excellent teaching on "The Nine Gifts of the Holy Spirit" in a publication of Sharon College (1948-1949). There are also many more textbooks available in our time on the gifts of the Spirit, from both the Pentecostal and Charismatic world. As previously, there was also much "**seed-truth**" given in the visitation of the Spirit concerning the gifts of the Spirit.

E. **Local Church Government**

Another "**seed-truth**" that was watered much in the 1948 visitation was the truth of "Local Church Government". Much teaching came out over this time. Much teaching concerned the carnality of sectarianism and denominationalism in the Body of Christ. These things were shown as things which destroy the unity of the Body of Christ. Such divisions were "Corinthian carnality"; divisions over doctrines, personalities, lack of the fruit of the Spirit, and numerous other things.

The teachers saw that the Churches in the New Testament were locally governed by elders and deacons, not by any centralized 'headquarters'. The local Churches were blessed by the fivefold ascension gift ministries. It seems that the great Church in Stockholm, Sweden (Lewis Pethrus) had much influence on the truth of local Church government.

The book "**Church Government**", by George and Ernest Hawtin (Sharon Publication, 1949) set out the teaching of the visitation at Saskatchewan, Canada.

This is not to say that all Churches that were touched by the move of the Spirit accepted or followed this teaching. It is simply to say that the truth of local Church government was greatly emphasized.

The whole subject of "Church Government" has been a matter of strong debate and controversy for centuries, and has certainly torn the Body of Christ apart. It has set denominations and fellowships into grouping of autocratic, bureaucratic, democratic or hierarchical forms of government. Undoubtedly the issue will not be settled until Jesus returns. But numerous fellowships do see that local Church government is New Testament order and seek to uphold the autonomy of the local Church under the headship of Christ.

The reader is directed to those textbooks which deal with the various forms of Church Government, whether centralized headquarters or localized government under Christ's headship. Many denominations declare their form of government by their name, whether Roman Catholic, Episcopalian, Presbyterian, Apostolic, Congregational and so forth.

F. **The Prophetic Presbytery**

Strong teaching concerning "the laying on of hands, prophecy and presbytery" was given, as based on 1Timothy 4:14. This was a major "**seed-truth**" that was watered much in the visitation of 1948 in Canada.

This was particularly emphasized when it came to ministry for the impartation and release of the gifts of the Spirit in a person's life. There were those in the Pentecostal world who did recognize and accept presbytery in a local church, but not "a travelling presbytery", moving around the local Churches in ministry.

In the "original prophetic word", the Spirit gave strong warning. They were warned not to lay hands on anyone and everyone, but only those who the Spirit indicated from time to time. The warning went unheeded by many who had been touched by the visitation, and many people were hurt and great reproach was brought on the truth of "the presbytery".

In spite of this, there were those Churches who kept safeguards around this precious ministry, whether for local or translocal presbytery kind of meetings. Several textbooks are available that deal more fully on the subject of "Laying on of Hands, Presbytery and Prophecy".

G. **Restoration of All Things**

The word "restoration" became another "**seed-truth**", or "**seed-word**" in the move of the Holy Spirit from 1948 and onward.

The original prophetic word spoke of the fact that the Lord said He would **restore** the gifts of the Spirit to His Church. The teachers searched the Scriptures and the whole theology of restoration was discovered and preached where-ever Conferences were held.

Joel 2 and Acts 3 became significant Scriptures as teachers and preachers saw that it was God's will to restore all things that had been lost in the decline of the Church as well as that which was lost in the fall of Adam. God would restore to His Church the years that had been lost over the "Dark Ages" of Church History.

The tragedy was that some took the message of restoration to its heretical extreme. They taught that the restoration of "all things" included the restoration of the Devil, fallen angels and all mankind, repentant or otherwise. The message and truth of restoration was brought into reproach and therefore, rejected of many leaders and people because of these unScriptural teachings. For some, even in the present time, the word "restoration" has unsound connotations because of these errors which crept in during the early years. The reader is referred to Chapter 5 of this text where "Things Not To Be Restored" were dealt with in reasonable length.

The "**seed-truth**" remains. God is restoring the Church to her early glory. He is also restoring man back to the image of God from which he fell in Adam. Restoration can only take place, for Jew or Gentile, "in Christ" and that by the power of Christ's redemptive work. This is the purpose of this text on "Restoration Theology".

H. **Prophecy, Tongues and Interpretation**

In the visitation of 1948, another "**seed-truth**" was brought to the attention of the leadership as well as the people of God in those years.

Whereas "**tongues**" was prominent in the Pentecostal movement, and "**healing**" was prominent in the great Evangelistic tent and auditorium meetings of that time, "**the gift of prophecy**" became much more prominent in the "Latter Rain" movement.

The teachers found that much of what was called "tongues and interpretation" was not really the case. They found that much tongues speaking simply released prophecy and people and leaders often took the prophecy to be the interpretation!

A study of 1 Corinthians 14 certainly emphasizes prophecy as the better gift and especially if tongues is not interpreted, or if there is no interpreter in the Church. Paul limits tongues with interpretation to three at the most, but, on the other hand, he says, **all may prophesy**! Prophecy was the gift, therefore, that was encouraged as the better gift in the years of the visitation.

In "Latter Rain" (pages 87-88) Richard Riss quotes some evidences of miraculous manifestations of the "gift of tongues". He writes:

> "At the invitation of Reg Layzell in Vancouver, B.C., the North Battleford party held meetings at Glad Tidings Temple on November 14-28, 1948. The speaking party from North Battleford had been scheduled to include George and Ernest Hawtin, James and Phyllis Spiers, Milford Kirkpatrick, and Roy and Lillian Borders. Two meetings were held daily and three each Sunday.

> "The main auditorium was always well filled. In the evenings the temple was always full and on Sundays it was jammed. James Watt wrote of a man from Toronto that, "as soon as he came in the door he knew by the Spirit that God was in the place". The Vancouver meetings were known for miraculous manifestations of the **gifts of tongues**:

> For the first time in our lives we saw the real manifestation of the Gift of Tongues and Interpretation in its full sense. Those who attended these meetings went away thoroughly convinced by experience that the Gift of Tongues is actually the gift of languages. Those possessing this marvellous gift can actually preach the gospel in foreign languages without any foreign accent, and have the ability to use every idiom and axiom of the tongue.
>
> While brother Taylor spoke to us, God led him to speak in tongues. The language he spoke was Chinese. When he finished speaking, his wife interpreted the message. She began quoting Isaiah 55:6. Sister Patsy Spence was with us on the platform at the time but neither brother nor sister Taylor were aware she could understand Chinese. As soon as sister Taylor finished speaking, sister Patsy got up and testified as follows:
>
> "As soon as brother Taylor began to speak, I recognized John 3:16 and I also immediately recognized Isaiah 55:6." She said the interpretation given by sister Taylor was accurate ..."
>
> This is not a passing event, for brother Taylor can speak Chinese at will. He holds street meetings for the Chinese every week. His language is so perfect. The Chinese cannot believe that he never learned the tongue.
>
> To the glory of God we wish to say that during the Vancouver meetings we laid hands especially on four missionaries bound for China and asked God to give them the language. In every case they broke out in Chinese and were understood by those in the room who understood the language. Seven or eight actually were understood in this tongue. Others were understood in Swedish, German, Dutch and Hindustani".

Reports like this caused great controversy. Fears arose because of the potential danger of sending people as missionaries to different nations, and their expecting to speak the language by miraculous empowerment, along with the devastation it could bring if not actualized.

The fact of the matter is, however, that God did show the potential and possibility of the miraculous gift of tongues with interpretation which could be given to someone, as the will of God determined.

Neil J. Hutchins, Yellowknife, N.W.T. provided this testimony, which was published in **"The Sharon Star"** paper, August 1st, 1950, pages 3,4.

> "It has been an amazing thing to many that the Scriptural ability to speak a foreign language by the guidance of the Holy Spirit has seemed to have had so little practical use in the Church. The Scriptural example seems to be otherwise.
>
> On the Day of Pentecost, a great crowd of onlookers, gathered from many different languages and nations, listened to God's people, all Galileans, speaking of the wonderful works of God in numerous understandable languages. Now, as the work of restoration in the Church begins to take place, this ability is also to be restored, the ability to speak in other languages and to be understood and real benefit derived thereby. Several instances of such occurrences have taken place in our midst which I will pass on for your encouragement.
>
> A lady came to us seeking salvation, and her understanding of English was limited. After some time, we laid hands on her and prayed for her that she might receive assurance of sins forgiven. As we prayed, we were understood by her, as we spoke in her native tongue, Cree Indian, giving her assurance of the remission of her sins.
>
> At another time, during a period of prayer, two of the men of the Assembly were understood by a sceptical onlooker, as they conversed in the Ukrainian tongue.

Again, while visiting a Christian home here, I became engaged in conversation with an unsaved European man, who was making a study in all European languages. I asked him if he could understand any European language if he heard it, and he said he could. I then spoke in a strange tongue to him by the Spirit, and when I had finished, he asked me where I had learned to speak Finnish, as that was the language I had spoken, telling him of the wonderful works of God.

Another man in the congregation, while singing in the Spirit, was understood singing "Stand up, Stand up for Jesus" in Chinese.

One of the girls of the Assembly, twelve years old, was speaking to her friend, a little Dogrib Indian girl, and telling her about the services at the Mission. While in conversation, our little twelve year old began to speak in Dogrib Indian and was understood by her friend, also by a group standing by listening. We were delighted at this account, but rather amused also when she told us that she then became frightened at her own boldness and ran out without "following through".

These incidents to us are signs that the restoration has begun and henceforth we may look forward to many more evidences of the Gifts of the Spirit being restored to the Church of Jesus Christ".

Note:- Over the years of the Pentecostal History, incidents similar to these things took place and have been recorded. Mary Woodworth Etter ("**Signs & Wonders**", page 393) tells of an incident where a worker spoke in "an unknown tongue", and the worker knew who this word in tongues was for. The end result was that the worker had spoken in pure Hebrew and a Hebrew man received Christ as His Messiah and Saviour as a result of this word. Many incidents have been recorded in Pentecostal history, but there seemed to be a greater manifestation of the "gift of tongues and interpretation" in this manner from 1948 for some period of time.

(This writer's brother-in-law was a Missionary for many years in Africa and one time experienced these twin gifts in an unusual manner. As he was preaching in the English language, through two interpreters (Zulu), the Holy Spirit fell on him. He preached for about two hours in the Zulu language and also understood what he was preaching about. The interpreters sat down! The Zulu people naturally wanted him to be "their missionary". The incident never occurred again).

The challenge is, that, in the light of this section of our "**seed-truths**", God may have much more in mind on the whole area of the gifts of the Spirit, when it comes to "tongues and interpretation" than Pentecostal/Charismatic people understand! This is especially in the light of the tongues and ethnic groups that are yet to be reached with the Gospel of the kingdom (Matthew 24:14). The visitation of 1948 saw signs of what the Lord could do in this area of the gifts of the Spirit.

It was in the light of these things, that the gift of prophecy was encouraged in the meetings more than tongues with interpretation, especially if the tongues and interpreters had not been "proven" as having a gift for public use in the Church.

I. First Principles of the Doctrine of Christ

As a result of the outpouring and move of the Spirit over 1948 and years onward, the passage in Hebrews 5:12-6:1-3 became a foundational teaching platform in the visitation.

Hebrews 5:12 speaks of the things listed here as being "the first principles of the oracles of God". In Hebrews 6:2 they are spoken of as being "the first principles of the doctrine of Christ". Altogether, there were seven principles expounded upon, some more, some less, in the teaching series that arose out of this passage. There are some textbooks that deal with each of these principles, providing much "seed to the sower and bread to the eater". The seven principles were outlined as follows:

1. Repentance from dead works,
2. Faith towards God,
3. Doctrine of baptisms, including water baptism, Holy Spirit baptism and then baptism into the Body of Christ,
4. Laying on of hands,
5. Resurrection from the dead,
6. Eternal judgment, and
7. Perfection.

Many other teachers have taken these principles and written on them in greater or lesser degree. Each of these are seen to be foundational principles that every believer should experience, and every New Testament Church should teach. As in the building of a building, the inspector generally inspects the foundation before he gives "the permit" to go on building. So Christ Jesus as the inspector and builder of the Church checks the foundation principles in the lives of individuals and Churches to see if the foundations are right. Only then does He give "the permit" to continue the building of a New Testament Church according to His pattern.

Each of these principles are indeed "**seed-truths**" that can be watered by the Holy Spirit and diligent research of the Scriptures and produce good fruit in the lives of the people of God.

J. The Heavenly Choir

Another "seed-truth" which received much emphasis in the visitation was that which was called "**The Heavenly Choir**", or "**Singing in the Spirit**".

It was not as if such had never been seen or heard before, for it had. In early Pentecostal days and in Mary Woodworth Etter's meetings, many of these things took place, as recorded in her book, "**Signs and Wonders**".

In the book (page 393) she writes:

"The singing in the Spirit is one of the manifestations of frequent occurrence. Sometimes many joined with "other tongues" in the heavenly choir, which only the redeemed of the Lamb can sing. It would rise to bursts of praise like the sound of many waters or sink to the sweetness of the dove-note, and then rise again to greater heights like the incoming waves. It was indeed the heavenly Dove singing and calling for its mate. Untrained voices joined with a purity of tone and harmony surpassing that of expert vocalists ... We have heard a brother sing a sacred hymn to God in other tongues, as a solo, in which the tone-placement, tone-purity, and tone-colour was fully equal to that of grand opera singers, and yet he never had the slightest training in singing."

On pages 261-263 she again describes the heavenly music and singing in the Spirit. She writes of this occasion:

"Suddenly there fell upon my ear - for the sound, strange to say, all seemed to pour into my right ear - a song of the most wonderful description. It did not at all appear like human voices, but seemed much more like the tones of some wonderful instrument of music, such as human ears had never heard before. It began on the right side of the audience, and rolled from there over the entire company of baptized saints in a volume of sounds resembling in its rising and falling, its rolling and sinking, its swelling and receding character, the rolling waves of the ocean when being acted upon by the wonderful force which produces the tides ... Sometimes the sounds would rise to the highest possible pitch for human voices to utter, on the one hand, while at the same time in the company that went down to the lowest notes which could be sounded on a good organ. It was not simply the singing of four parts of music such as we do when we sing hymns, for, according to the notes we listen to, there is no telling how many parts is being sung, and it seemed to me there must have been scores of them. Such blending of tones, such perfect harmony of sounds, such musical strains, my ears never before heard, and I never expect to hear again in this world under any other circumstances, not even from the most perfect band of music, which human ingenuity can provide, and yet all these sounds were produced by a company of people which had that day gathered from all over the continent of North America, very few of whom had ever seen each other".

She goes on to speak of the "heavenly anthem", and that this is what the apostle meant when he said he would "Sing with the Spirit and with the understanding also" (1Corinthians 14:14-15). She also speaks of "Dancing in the Spirit" and "Playing on Harps of Gold" and other "strange acts" of God among His people (pages 394-395). Read also Isaiah 28:21.

James Watt, who was greatly influenced by Mary Woodworth Etter's book, in his interview with Richard Riss, describes "**the heavenly choir**" in the 1948 visitation onwards as follows:

> "Heaven's strains filled the whole Church. It was as a mighty organ, with great swelling chords, and solo parts weaving in and out, yet with perfect harmony. Those who heard it some blocks away said that it did something to their souls that no power on earth had previously touched" ("**Latter Rain**", page 82).

George Hawtin described the phenomenon as follows:

> "We have heard vague rumours of the so-called Heavenly Choir in association with the outpouring of the Spirit which occurred around the turn of the century and have longed to hear it. But having heard it, we must confess that it completely beggars not only description but also in large part both appreciation and understanding ... A deep consciousness of the Spirit of Worship and Song always pervades the meeting as a prelude to the choir ... The most outstanding thing about it is the amazingly complicated depth of harmony ... From a little distance it sounds like a master choir accompanied by a matchless symphony orchestra. It seems difficult to credit that such sound could be reproduced by human vocal organs. There is such order and timing as the mighty chords swell and roll that one is forced to concede that there is an unseen conductor ..." ("**Latter Rain**", page 82-83).

George Warnock to Richard Riss reports:

> "I recall how James Watt had ministered on the matter of spiritual song from the Scriptures ... And how he exhorted the people to expect its restoration and how God would restore it as His people waited before Him, and sought Him concerning it. It seemed he was about to sit down, having thus ministered, when suddenly he burst forth in prophetic song.

Immediately after, the Spirit of prophecy rested on others in the congregation, who sang forth prophetic utterances, and then the whole congregation joined in, with spiritual anthems of praise.

It was a very sovereign ministry that came forth; preceded, nevertheless, by Scriptural teaching concerning it, and from that day forth Scriptural song became part and parcel of ministry that came when the body came together" ("**Latter Rain**", pages 83-84).

Sufficient to say that, over the years from 1948 onwards there was a greater increase of "singing in the Spirit", or "spontaneous praise", or "singing praise", and "the song of the Lord" - as it is variously described. Numerous Churches around the world, in the Pentecostal/Charismatic world often praise the Lord in this manner. As had been said often, it is the voice of the bridegroom, Christ, and the voice of the bride, His Church, responding in love song to each other, in anticipation of that day when the marriage of Christ and His Church takes place. All heaven will indeed be filled with the songs of the redeemed, spontaneously sung from the heart and with the understanding (Revelation 5:9-10). It will be "a new song".

K. The Unity of the Body of Christ

Great emphasis and teaching came forth about the unity of the Body of Christ. The "**seed-truth**" sown was that the Bible shows that there is only one body and every true believer, regardless of denominational affiliation was in that one body.

The prayer of Jesus "that all may be one as we are one" was expounded upon many times in conferences (John 17). It affected attitudes of many ministers and Churches and caused much repentance for the sectarian evils, and carnal divisions and attitudes to one another who were in the same body, yet did not believe "exactly like us". Many came to the realization that the Lord allowed different expressions of worship and all had different measures of understanding of the truth. No one has perfect doctrine or full understanding of the inexhaustible Word of God. Oftentimes doctrine was a thing of the head, but God looked upon the heart.

Many realized that a person could be faulty in their doctrine but right in their spirit before God, and others could be right in the doctrine but have wrong attitudes and they are a grief to the Lord. God's ideal is to have right doctrine and right attitudes to members of the Body of Christ.

Paul encouraged the Ephesian believers to maintain the "**unity of the spirit**" until we come unto the "**unity of the faith**" (Ephesians 4:1-16). There was great hope and faith that the prayer of Jesus would be answered in these last days, that the world would indeed see a Church that is one. Jesus prayed that His disciples would be one "that the world might believe", and "that the world may know" that the Father had sent Him into the world to seek and save the lost.

The Book of Acts showed that one of the keys to the power of the Holy Spirit working in their midst was that the early believers were of "one accord", and unity was a major theme (Acts 1:13-14; 2:1-4; 4:31-32). Divisions, sectism were evidence of "Corinthian carnalities" and needed to be repented of before the Lord.

It should be remembered that, every truth that the Lord brings forth to the Church, Satan will seek to oppose. Satan seeks to constantly destroy the unity of the Church by carnal divisions, over doctrine, forms of Church government, personalities and sinful and carnal behaviour of believers. But the Lord's prayer will be answered as God's people humble themselves and come to an experiential revelation of the unity of Christ's Body in the earth.

L. The Victorious and Glorious Church

Around this period of time, there was much defeatist mentality about the Church. The teaching was that the Lord would come any moment and rescue His Church from the evil world. The Church was looked upon as a failure and would end in great apostasy, except for a faithful remnant.

Ultra-Dispensational teaching saw the Church as a parenthetical invention of God because of Jewish rejection of the king and the kingdom of God. The Jew was seen to be the ultimate of the purposes of God in the earth once the Church was removed by a secret translation. People were defeated and discouraged because of the spiritual state of the Church.

In the 1948 visitation, the Spirit of God began to blow afresh upon such passages as Matthew 16:15-20 and Ephesians 5:23-32. These passages became important "**seed-truths**" and were greatly watered by the Spirit and intense research into the Scriptures. It was seen that the will of the Father and the Son was to have a Church that was spiritually militant, victorious and triumphant in the warfare against Satan and his kingdom. The gates of hades would not prevail this Church.

It was also seen that God's ultimate intention was to have a bride for His Son, a Church that would be without spot or wrinkle or blemish, or any such thing. It would be a holy Church, suitable to be joined to Christ, the bridegroom, in holy wedlock. Christ could not and would not be married to a Church inferior or unequal to Himself. He would be "unequally yoked". Therefore, the work of sanctification was to increase in the Church to make her a fit bride for Himself. The Church was seen to be in the eternal purposes of God and not a parenthetical invention because of Jewish failures (Ephesians 3:1-12).

This Biblical concept and understanding of the Church revolutionized the mentality of numerous ministers and congregations. The Lord was not coming back for a defeated Church. The Church existed for Divine purpose and that purpose would be fulfilled. Nothing would frustrate the word that had gone forth out of the mouth of the Lord. His word would accomplish the purpose it was sent unto (Isaiah 55:8-12).

M. The Feast of Tabernacles

One of the ministers touched in the early days of the 1948 visitation was James Watt. In the course of speaking one time, he dropped the "**seed-word**" or "**seed-truth**" into the heart of George Warnock concerning the Feast of Tabernacles. He mentioned that this Feast had never been fulfilled.

The Holy Spirit watered that "**seed-word**" and as a result George Warnock searched the Scriptures and wrote the book entitled, "**The Feast of Tabernacles**" (1951). The book has been a major source of truth to numerous Churches throughout the world.

In the book, it is clearly shown that the Feasts of Passover and Pentecost have been fulfilled historically in Christ and the Church. The Feast of Tabernacles has not seen any historical fulfilment in the Church. It is yet to be fulfilled in the end of this present age. It is a Feast of Harvest, a Feast of Ingathering after the final rains. It includes in its pages things that pertain to "The Tabernacle of Moses" and "The Temple of Solomon". Entrance within the veil is made possible for the believer since Christ caused the veil of the material temple to be torn in two, from the top to the bottom. This is the teaching of the Book of Hebrews (Hebrews Chapters, 6,7,8,9,110).

George Warnock shows that the Feast of Tabernacles is:

1. The Feast of Unity
2. The Feast of Joy
3. The Feast of Ingathering
4. The Feast of Rest
5. The Feast of Glory
6. The Feast of Restoration
7. The Feast of Christ's Appearing.

Woven throughout the book are various truths taught in the visitation of those years. Although everyone who reads the book may not totally agree with everything in it, there is much that is challenging truth to be considered in these last days.

Ultra-Dispensationalism had robbed the Church of the truths of this Feast as it was either (1) Postponed until a coming Millennium, or (2) Restricted as a Feast entirely for the Jewish nation and not for the Church.

Warnock's book became a kind of "textbook" to most all of those people who accepted the visitation of the Spirit of 1948 onwards. The study of the Feasts of the Lord has certainly been a much neglected area of God's Word. But the move of the Spirit caused much more interest and study on these great truths, all to be fulfilled in Christ and His Church.

N. The Communion Table

One of the "**seed-truths**" or, "**seed-words**" that also came in the early years of the visitation was about the Lord's table, or the Communion. Not all ministers or congregations touched by the move of the Holy Spirit picked up this "seed-word". This, undoubtedly, was because of the infrequency of commemorating the Lord's Supper, or Communion.

Richard Riss tells of George and Ernest Hawtin and Milford Kirkpatrick's ministry at Emmanuel Temple, Los Angelos, with Dr. A.Earl Lee. George Hawtin described the meetings at Emmanuel in the following:

> "The revival broke out here the day following Brother Lee's visit to Portland during the revival there last February. When we arrived, the Church was already aglow with the glory

of the outpouring of the Spirit, some of the gifts of the Spirit were in operation, and the people were in splendid condition to receive the message we brought. One of the highlights of the entire meeting was the bringing of a new revelation of the Lord's Supper by Brother Earnest Hawtin. When this truth was received by the Church, one lady, somewhat impotent in her feet, was healed as she partook of Communion" (Richard Riss in "**Latter Rain**", page 114).

Some accusations were made that "Latter Rain" teaching on Communion was transubstantiation. But, as Richard Riss confirms, there is no evidence of this in any of the available sources.

In "**The Sharon Star**" paper (February 1st, 1950), George Warnock writes an article on "**The Royal Priesthood & The Lord's Supper**" (pages 2-3). He has this to say about the Communion.

> "So it has been then with the truth of the Lord's Supper. When Satan could not rob the Church of the truth concerning it, he sought to pervert it. Consequently, on the one hand we have those who partake of the Table merely as a memorial service, in which there is no consciousness of real anticipation in the Lord's body and blood, and on the other hand, we have those who partake of the Table as if they were literally and actually feasting upon the broken body and the shed blood.
>
> How beautifully significant is the thought that, when Abraham was returning from the battle, with the spoils of victory, Melchisedek brought forth "bread and wine"- symbols of life and of a sacrifice which is eternally efficacious! His was not a sacrifice of death - but perfect symbols of the once-for-all sacrifice of Jesus Christ, of which we are partakers. Jesus said, "This cup is the new testament (covenant) in My blood" (1Corinthians 11:25). The New Covenant is a covenant of life-not of death. And if "this cup" was given to the saints of the New Covenant, we know that it was given as part of the ministration of the New Covenant - that His Divine life and glory might flow through us.
>
> How unlike the dead sacrifices of the Old Covenant - which indeed was nothing more than a ministration of death and condemnation (2Corinthians 3:7,9). How unlike the carnal ordinances of the Law which served only to bring sins to remembrance: "For in those sacrifices there is a remembrance again made of sins every years" (Hebrews 10:3). How wonderful to recollect that every time we partake of the Lord's Supper in truth and sincerity, we are not remembering SINS, but we are remembering CHRIST! We are not calling sins to mind, but we are calling CHRIST to mind - yea, and to our hearts also, and to our spirits and bodies.
>
> Said He not, "For this cause many are weak and sickly among you and many sleep ..." - because they discerned not the Lord's body? Whereas, if there is genuine remembrance of the Lord as we partake of His Supper, and a due appreciation of the members of His body - then there is an impartation of health and strength and vitality. Many are the saints who have testified of this truth as they have feasted upon Christ in the bread and the wine. Certainly, if we partake of these emblems of His sacrifice with a sin-conscience, or with a lack of due appreciation for the body of Christ, we fail to receive of its benefits; but as we determine in our hearts and souls to REMEMBER CHRIST - and not the wafer or the wine - and to appropriate the Spirit and not the flesh, we shall find life to our bodies and souls. "For it is the Spirit that quickeneth, the flesh profiteth nothing"(End Quote).

As can be understood, for many, many Churches, the Lord's Table, or Communion, was not fully appreciated nor was there much insight into the reality of the ordinance as

Christ instituted it. For most it was simply "a memorial service" - "Do it in remembrance of Me"- only. Through various fears, most ministers would teach the people that there was "nothing in the bread and the cup", and because of that people got "nothing" out of the Table of the Lord.

In the move of the Holy Spirit, greater insight and more of a true "discerning of the Lord's body and blood" came to some leaders and congregations, as these articles confirm.

One other quotation is worthy of consideration. In **"The Sharon Star"** (August 1st, 1950, page 2), George Hawtin has this to say about the Lord's Supper in the article, **"Discerning the Body"**.

> "It is wonderful to discern the Body of Christ at the Communion Table, when we participate in the body and blood of the Lord Jesus Christ; for His Word has declared, "The cup of blessing which we bless, is it not the communion (or, to understand it better, 'Is it not participation') of the blood of Christ; the bread which we break, is it not the communion (or, participation) of the body of Christ? (1Corinthians 10:16).
>
> It is wonderful to discern that, and it will bring us healing indeed. But we will never discern that as we ought to discern it until we have discovered that every man and woman who names the Name of Christ, has by one Spirit been baptized into the Body, and is a member to me to such an extent that his grief is mine, his need is mine, and that I cannot hate or despise him or neglect him even in the least degree. For what man ever "hated his own flesh, but nourisheth it and cherisheth it, even as the Lord the Church".

Undoubtedly, the most important insight and **"seed-word"** about the Lord's Table, or Communion, was that of truly **discerning the body of Christ**! Discerning the Lord's body was (1) First, the discerning of His physical body, broken for us, and by whose stripes we were healed (Isaiah 53; Matthew 8:16-17; 1Peter 2:21-24), and then, (2) Second, the discerning of the Lord's spiritual Body, the Church, and one another as members of His Body (1Corinthians 10-11; Matthew 26:26-28).

As a result of receiving and understanding this truth, numerous people testified of the Lord's healing power at the Communion table, as they came and ate and drank in faith of Christ's redemptive work on Calvary. Also, many were healed as they had right attitudes of forgiveness and love for members of the Body of Christ, and truly discerned other members of the Body of Christ.

As already noted, this **"seed-word"** of the Lord's Table and discerning the body, was not developed overly much by many ministers. Infrequency of celebration, fear of lapsing into a mere form, fears of faulty concepts of the bread and cup -- these things have robbed many Churches of the blessing that is in the Lord's Supper. In this present time, there certainly does not appear to be much insight into the Table of the Lord, or the Communion, as was seeded in the early years of visitation. But the truth is there for those who want to know the truth that sets us free (John 8:31-34). That truth is personified in the Lord Jesus Christ Himself (John 14:6).

Much more could be written on the Communion, but the student is referred to these Scriptures for further study.

* Abraham received the Communion from Melchisedek and gave him tithes of all his spoils (Genesis 14:18).

* The body and blood of the Passover Lamb pointed to the body and blood of THE Passover Lamb, Christ Himself (Exodus 12; Mark 14:12; John 1;29,36).

* The Table of Shewbread in the Tabernacle of Moses pointed to the Table of the Lord in the Church (Leviticus 24:5-9; Numbers 28:7; Exodus 25:23-30).

* The early Church continued in the apostles doctrine, fellowship and breaking of bread. It seems that this was done on each first day of the week, the day of Christ's resurrection and outpouring of the Holy Spirit (Acts 2:42-47; 20:8).

* There is life and healing in the Lord's Table. It is the children's bread (Matthew 15:25-26; John 6:54-57). The flesh profits nothing. It is the Spirit that gives life.

* Together as members of one body, we bless the bread and the cup as we share together at His Table (1Corinthians 10:16).

(The student is also referred to "**Table Talks**", by the author, in Bibliography).

In Summary:-

A number of Churches and ministers touched by the Holy Spirit in this visitation have maintained balance on the truths and principles recovered to the Church. Others have departed from them, some more and some less. Some went to extremes and have destroyed their Churches or become isolated from the larger Body of Christ and have become introverted accordingly.

Some of the Historic Pentecostal Churches and denominations have either adopted some of the principles and truths recovered, while still others totally reject anything of the "Latter Rain" visitation. This is either because of extreme practices on the part of some who accepted it, or, simply unbelief on their part as to the veracity of these truths. Some of these extremes are noted here.

1. Extreme emphasis on prophecies that were not judged according to Scriptures and the spirit of the utterances, which, according to the apostle Paul, must be judged.

2. Extreme teaching on apostles and prophets and their authority in the Church, and not balancing this out with the Scripture that the Church is built on the foundation already laid by the apostles and prophets in New Testament times, and the fact that all ministries must be tested by the infallible Word of God.

3. Extreme emphasis on the laying on of hands and prophecy and oftentimes the control of peoples lives through the prophetic words. The balance is that all words must be tested by THE WORD and must be a confirmation to a person's live.

4. Imbalance about the impartation of the gift of languages as special equipment for missionary service. The balance is that these things are given as the Spirit wills, and not as man wills.

5. Extreme teaching on "the manifestation of the sons of God", presuming ahead of the time-table of the Lord according to Romans 8.

6. Extreme teaching and claims in some places of possessing "a redemption body", and again presuming ahead of God's time-table on this inheritance promised to the saints who are alive and remain at the coming of the Lord.

7. The exploitation and manipulation of peoples lives through abuse of the laying on of hands and prophecy and impartation of gifts by some ministries who were unaccountable to other ministries.

8. The extreme teaching on the "restoration of all things", and the lapse into heresy on the restoration and reconciliation of the Devil, fallen angels, unrepentant and unredeemed mankind. The doctrine of "ultimate reconciliation" caused many people to reject the truth of restoration.

All these extremes, and sometimes sinful behaviour, robbed many ministers, Churches and congregations of accepting what was restored truth in this great wave of the Holy Spirit.

In hindsight, it could be said; that there never was there so much "**seed-truth**" and "**seed-word**" given by the Spirit in any previous visitation as in this movement, but, never was there such a fast decline into extremes or error of a revival from God that took place in a few short years. Nevertheless, the truth remains for those who are hungry after God and the restoration of lost truth to the Church!

To finish this chapter on a more positive note, we quote from J.Preston Eley's "**Kingdom Bible Studies**" (Part IV, page 10, 9176, "The Battle of Armageddon):

> "In 1948 - the very year that Israel became a nation - another great deluge fell from heaven, a mighty revival then called the "Latter Rain". In this Restoration Revival, God did a work which far transcends the work started in the Pentecostal outpouring of more than forty years before. All nine gifts of the Spirit, the fivefold ministries of apostles, prophets, evangelists, pastors and teachers, spiritual praise and worship, and the end-time revelation of God's purpose to manifest His sons, a glorious Church, to bring in the kingdom of God, all of this and much more was restored among God's people.
>
> And now the great dealings of God, the purgings, the processings, depths of revelation, edification and strengthening, understanding of the ways of the Lord, faith in the promise, waiting upon the Lord, developing of the nature and character of God - all of this is being laid upon a people who have received the fruit of that second great visitation of God and thus they are being prepared for the coming THIRD OUTPOURING which shall finally bring the FULLNESS, a company of overcoming sons of God who have come to the measure of the stature of the fullness of Christ, to actually dethrone Satan, casting him out of the heavenlies, and finally binding him in the earthlies, bringing the hope of deliverance and life to all the families of the earth. This third great work of the Spirit shall usher a people into full redemption-free from the curse, sin, sickness, death and carnality" ("**Latter Rain**", page 142-143).

Surely these words are prophetic words for that generation who will be alive unto the coming of the Lord Jesus Christ to receive for Himself a glorious Church without spot of wrinkle or any such thing!

(**Note:-** The reader of this text will understand that each of the "**seed-words**" can be or have been developed more fully into complete papers. They are condensed within reason for the purpose of this already lengthy chapter. The Bibliography lists some of the texts or books that may be obtainable for fuller treatment of the things listed in this chapter).

(**Note:-** This writer is indebted to Richard Riss for kind permission to quote, use and adapt material, especially in this chapter, from his excellent book entitled "**Latter Rain**". This book is a must for all interested in Restoration Theology in the light of recent decades of Church History).

Finally, it may be said, that, just because there are extremes or even error, this is no reason to reject TRUTH that the Lord restores to the Church. It is impossible to have heresy apart from truth. There can never be a counterfeit without the genuine. The genuine always comes first; the counterfeit follows. The writer's definition of heresy is: Heresy is taking a fragment or portion of truth to its extreme, out of proportion with the whole body of truth! Let us "buy the truth, and sell it not". Let us keep Divine and Scriptural balance in truth so that the Body of Christ can come to full maturity.

CHAPTER THIRTY THREE

THE SACRIFICE OF PRAISE

One of the truths recovered and emphasized about the time of the "Latter Rain" visitation (AD1946-1950's onwards), as already referred to in the previous chapter, was "Singing in the Spirit". There were various designations of this expression. Sometimes it was spoken of as "the heavenly choir", or "singing in the Spirit", or "singing praise", or "the song of the Lord", or simply, "free or spontaneous praise.

Again, it must be remembered that it was not as if these things had not been seen or heard before. But here we speak of this truth being emphasized by the Spirit, and coming to the forefront more. In subsequent years, this aspect of truth was spread around the world, and touched thousands of Churches, even reaching across some denominational barriers.

By the accounts, one of the major instruments who God used in this area of truth was a brother by the name of Reginald Layzell. In a number of Churches throughout America, Brother Layzell was recognized as "the apostle of praise and missions" ("**The Eternal Church**", page 261, Dr.Bill Hamon).

From Reginal Layzell's book, "**Unto Perfection**" (The Truth About The Restoration Revival, 1979), we gather the following information.

It was in the years AD1946-1947 that the great truth of "**the sacrifice of praise**" was restored to the Church. On pages 3-4, Layzell has this to say:

> "The **sacrifice of praise**" brought with it continuous revival. While pastoring the Pentecostal Assembly of Canada in Mission, British Columbia, I was asked by Rev.P.S.Jones, District Superintendant, to go with him on a series of Prayer Conferences throughout the Prairies. When ministering in Terrace, he met George Hawtin, who was the evening speaker at the Camp Meeting. I was the afternoon speaker, and I was impressed with Brother George Hawtin's teaching ability. We had some good discussions regarding God's kingdom. During the balance of 1946 and early 1947, the Church in Mission enjoyed a real visitation of God around "**the sacrifice of praise**".

Following every meeting, many young people sought the Lord at the altar. Other pastors from the surrounding area came to see what was going on, and were stirred by the effect the message had upon the young people. Other Churches asked us to visit them with the message that had been spoken in the place here".

Reginal Layzell continues to tell how in the Fall of 1947, William Branham came to Vancouver for healing meetings. Many Churches co-operated and were impressed with Branham's ministry. Layzell met other of the brethren from North Battleford, Saskatchewan. They discussed the moving of the Lord and make a covenant to seek God in greater measure in the days ahead, and contact each other accordingly.

In late Spring, 1948, a phone call came from North Battleford. God was visiting the students in the Bible College there. Reg Layzell's Church, during the winter months, sought the Lord in hours of prayer, for revival and restoration of the gifts of the Spirit.

Brother Layzell taught on 1Peter 2:5 and four important truths in that verse.

1. Believers are lively stones, and all true believers are alive in Christ.

2. Believers together are a spiritual house. The Old Testament house was the Tabernacle of Moses, or the Temple of Solomon. The New Testament house is the Church, the Temple of the Holy Spirit. Christ lives in His Church by the Holy Spirit (John 14:12).

3. Believers are a holy priesthood and all believers are called to function in their priestly ministry unto God.

4. Believers as priests are called to offer sacrifices. No one can function as a priest without offering sacrifices. The New Testament priests offer up to God "spiritual sacrifices". Christ has already offered up the one sacrifice for sins for us, for ever, as the Lamb of God (John 1:29,36). We now offer up "**spiritual sacrifices**." "**The sacrifice of praise**" is spoken of in Hebrews 13:15.

Bill Hamon, in "**The Eternal Church**"(page 261) writes:

"Dr. Reginald Layzell is recognized among most of those in the movement as the apostle of praise and missions. He preached Psalm 22:3 and Hebrews 13:15 at the yearly Crescent Beach Conferences during the 1950's until the message of those Scriptures was birthed within many a minister and congregation. Most of those who came into the movement were Pentecostals. They were accustomed to praising God from their feelings. Pastor Layzell taught that the sacrifice of praise was the "fruit of your lips" giving thanks to Jesus. Feeling has nothing to do with it. One praises God because "God inhabits the praises of His people." It is one of the "spiritual sacrifices" that the **priesthood believer** has the privilege of offering to the Lord. It is not just an emotional response but one of the greatest forces of protection and instruments of warfare ever given to the Church."

There was also much teaching on "sacrifices of joy" and the joy of the Lord. A number of Scriptures speak of joy and singing praise (Jeremiah 31:12,13; 33:10-11; Nehemiah 8:10; Isaiah 12:3; 2 Samuel 23:50; Psalm 147:1; 2Chronicles 5:11-14; Psalm 89:1). (End Quote).

In the Old Testament, the Israelites had to offer to God the morning and evening sacrifices (Exodus 29:30-42). The priest in his appropriate garment would offer it on the altar to God, morning and evening.

The Scriptures speak of those things which took place at "the time of the evening sacrifice".The fire of God fell when Elijah offered "the evening sacrifice" (1Kings 18:29-39). The angel Gabriel appeared to Daniel at the time of "the evening oblation" (Daniel 9:21), and gave him the notable "seventy weeks prophecy". Note also Ezra 9:4-5; Psalm 141:1-2; Daniel 9:26. Sacrifice costs something!

On pages 11-13 of Brother Layzell's book, he tells how the whole message on "the sacrifice of praise" came to him.

He was in business for many years. In December of 1945, he was invited to hold meetings in the West Coast on the Baptism of the Holy Spirit. He desired to do so over the three months of winter. In January 1946, he came to a small Church in Abbotsford, B.C. The minister was seriously ill and Brother Layzell was left to handle the meetings. The meetings were poor. During the week he sought God in prayer and fasting. As he was praying, Psalm 22:3 came to his mind. As he sought God, it was quickened to him that God does indeed "**inhabit (lives in) the praise of His people**". Regardless of feelings, he went around every pew in the building, hands up in the air, and praising God. He went through all the rooms offering "the sacrifice of praise".

As the meeting began that evening, the Lord was there. He writes:

> "Prior to this time, we had praised in the prayer room, but never in the open Church. We had never offered "the sacrifice of praise". So quietly I continued to praise the Lord. The meeting started and I announced the hymn, "There is Power in the Blood". I will always remember that. We sang the first verse, the second verse, and then the chorus. Suddenly a girl on one side of the Church threw her hands up and began to speak in tongues. About five minutes later, a sister on the other side began to shout and speak in tongues. Then someone in the center aisle. They were baptized in the Holy Spirit. This was the first time I had ever seen anyone baptized in the Holy Spirit in a public meeting during the song service. Thus was born the message of praise, which is the secret of continuous revival. He lives in the praises of His people!"

Four major Scriptures used in teaching on the restoration of the sacrifice of praise were:

1. **Jeremiah 33:11**

    "The voice of joy, and the voice of gladness, the voice of the bridegroom, and the voice of the bride, the voice of them that shall say, Praise the LORD of hosts: for the LORD is good; for his mercy endureth for ever: and of them that shall bring **the sacrifice of praise** into the house of the LORD. For I will cause to return the captivity of the land, as at the first, saith the LORD."

2. **Jonah 2:5-10**

    "The waters compassed me about, even to the soul: the depth closed me round about, the weeds were wrapped about my head. I went down to the bottoms of the mountains; the earth with her bars was about me for ever: yet hast thou brought up my life from corruption, O LORD my God. When my soul fainted within me I remembered the LORD: and my prayer came in unto thee, into thine holy temple.

    They that observe lying vanities forsake their own mercy. But I will **sacrifice unto** thee with the **voice of thanksgiving**; I will pay that that I have vowed. Salvation is of the LORD. And the LORD spake unto the fish, and it vomited out Jonah upon the dry land."

3. **Acts 16:23-25**

    "And when they had laid many stripes upon them, they cast them into prison, charging the jailor to keep them safely: Who, having received such a charge, thrust them into the inner prison, and made their feet fast in the stocks. And at midnight Paul and Silas **prayed, and sang praises** unto God: and the prisoners heard them."

4. **Psalm 50:23**

> "Whoso **offereth praise** glorifieth me: and to him that ordereth his conversation aright will I shew the salvation of God." The Dannish translation reads: "Whosoever offers the sacrifice of praise glorifies Me, and prepares a way whereby I shall show forth My victory".

After the restoration of the sacrifice of praise, prayers and fastings were greatly intensified (2Chronicles 7:14).

It was after this that Reg Layzell went to North Battleford and saw what God was doing in the "Latter Rain" visitation of the Spirit.

The truth of the matter was that God was working simultaneously in the restoration of "the sacrifice of praise" and "the laying on of hands". This emphasis was seen over the years of 1946-1950's and onwards, and this "spontaneous praise" or "singing praise" has spread through the earth, touching numerous Churches, who otherwise, would not receive other truths of the 1948 revival.

For many, many years, hymns had been sung, and in some places, the Psalms had been sung in some form or another, but now God was reviving **"Psalms, hymns and spiritual songs"** as people made melody in their hearts to the Lord (Ephesians 5:18; Colossians 3:16).

Many other Scriptures on the subject of **"praise"** could be given. But further things related to this will be seen in the next chapters.

CHAPTER THIRTY-FOUR

COVENANT, TEMPLE, PRIESTHOOD & SACRIFICE

Arising out of the truths seeded in the previous chapter came further and fuller development of the things involved in the believer's relationship with the Lord. This was seen in the inter-relatedness of the words: Covenant, Temple, Priesthood and Sacrifice.

The Epistle to the Hebrews clearly shows the inter-relatedness of these four things. If there is a Covenant, then there must be a Sanctuary (Tabernacle or Temple) in which covenant finds fulfilment. If there is a Sanctuary, then there must of necessity be a ministering Priesthood, and if there is a Priesthood there must of necessity be the offering of Sacrifice or sacrifices. This is the development of thought in Hebrews Chapters 5,6,7,8,9,10. We follow these things in this order.

A. The Covenant

The Bible reveals that God is a covenant-making and a covenant-keeping God. He desires His people to be in covenantal relationship with Himself (Psalms 111:5,9).

God made covenant with Adam (Genesis 3).

God made covenant with Noah and the whole of mankind (Genesis 8-9).

God made covenant with Abraham, Isaac and Jacob (Genesis 12:1-3; 22; Hebrews 6:13,18; Genesis 28).

God made covenant with the nation of Israel (Exodus 6; 19; Deuteronomy 4-5).

God made covenant with David (2 Samuel 7; Psalm 89).

The final covenant God made was the New Covenant (Jeremiah 31:31-34). The Lord Jesus confirmed it with His own body and blood sacrifice (Matthew 26:26-28; Hebrews 8:6-13).

All true believers are in covenantal relationship with God through Christ. The word covenant speaks of an agreement between God and man. It is a testament, a will, a contract, drawn up by God and presented to man. Man can either accept it or reject it but he cannot change it. It is available for all who believe on God through Christ, and come into faith and obedience.

Biblical covenants involves (1) Promises (Hebrews 8:6-13), (2) Sacrifice of body and blood (Hebrews 9:14-18), and (3) A Seal (Ephesians 1:13; Hebrews 13:20). The New Covenant will never be replaced by any other covenant (Galatians 3:14-16,29). It is as a person is in covenant relationship with God that they can receive the promises, privileges and benefits of the covenant. All believers in Christ are in that covenant relationship with God and with each other.

B. The Temple

When God made covenant with the Patriarchs, and with the nation of Israel through Moses, it necessitated a Sanctuary in which covenantal ministry could take place. The Patriarchs built their altars, and this constituted 'sanctuary' before God for them. Here the Lord appeared to them and received their sacrifices and worship. For the nation of

Israel, the Tabernacle of the Lord (Tabernacle of Moses), became God's Sanctuary. Here the Lord dwelt among His redeemed people.

In the Tabernacle of Moses, the "daily ministrations" were fulfilled. In the outer court, there was the brazen altar and the brazen laver. In the holy place there was the golden lampstand and the golden altar of incense, and the table of shewbread. The priests fulfilled their daily ministries around the particular articles of furniture. In the most holy place, there was the Ark of the Covenant. Here the very presence and glory of the Lord dwelt. The ministry took place here on the annual Day of Atonement (Exodus Chapters 25-40; Leviticus 16).

In due time, the Temple replaced the Tabernacle. The Temple became God's place of dwelling among His own. Here the Lord placed His Name and Glory over the Ark of the Covenant in the Holiest of All (1 Kings Chapters 1-8 with 2Chronicles 5-7 Chapters also).

In the New Testament, the New Covenant Temple is now the Church. The Old Covenant Temple pointed to the New Covenant Temple, the spiritual house of the Lord, which is the Church (1Corinthians 3:16-17; Ephesians 2:19-22).

Jesus referred to Himself as God's Temple. He spoke of the Temple of His body (John 2:19-21). The Church is now the Body of Christ in the earth, and therefore it is God's habitation by the Spirit. Christ is the builder of the Church, His holy Temple (Matthew 16:18-19; Zechariah 6:12-13). The Church is built on the foundation laid by the apostles and prophets, and Christ is the chief cornerstone of the building (Ephesians 2:20-22; Isaiah 28:16).

The believers, corporately, are lively stones in this spiritual house (1Peter 2:5 with 1 Kings 5:17-18; 6:7). Believers are to be fitly framed together in God's Temple in order to become the habitation of God by the Spirit. No one believer can be the whole Temple of God (Ephesians 2:19-22).

C. The Priesthood

The sequence of truths continues. If there is Covenant, then there must be a Temple, and if there is a Temple, there must of necessity be a ministering Priesthood as Hebrews 8:1-5 outlays for us.

God called Israel as a nation to be "a kingdom of priests"(Exodus 19:1-6). He wanted them to be His peculiar people, a kingdom of priests and an holy nation. In other words, God's original intention was that Israel be after the order of Melchisedek or, literally, a kingdom of priests. Israel fell from that calling of grace, and God brought in another priesthood. This was the order of Aaron. The tribe of Levi was chosen to be the priestly tribe for the nation of Israel. The household of Aaron was chosen to be the high priestly house (Exodus 28-29 with Leviticus 8-9; Numbers 1-4 chapters).

The Aaronic and Levitical priesthood was never God's perfect will but a substitute for it. God used it as shadow of things to come.

When Jesus died on the cross, He abolished the Aaronic and Levitical priesthood. Jesus introduced the priesthood after the order of Melchisedek. Christ and His Church together constitute the Melchisedekian priesthood. It is a royal priesthood. The Aaronic and Levitical priesthood was an order of priests only. The Melchisedek priesthood is an order of kings and priests; both offices combined in one, both the head (Christ) and the body (Church). Read Revelation 1:6; 5:9-10 with 1Peter 2:5-9.

The priesthood to which God calls the New Testament believer is that which is after the order of Melchisedek. Christ is the head of that order, as the Book of Hebrews shows (Hebrews 2:17; 4:14; 6:20; 5:8-9; Psalm 110:1-2).

Hebrews Chapters 5-6-7 deal with Christ's Melchisedek priesthood and the change from the order of Aaron to this new order.

The apostle Peter, along with John, confirms the fact that believers are a royal priesthood, or kings and priests unto God (1Peter 1:5-9; Revelation 1:6; 5:9-10). It is a many-membered body. Christ is the High Priest and believers are fellow-priests. The rent veil of the Temple signified the abolition of the Aaronic and Levitical priesthood and the introduction of the Melchisedek priesthood. The order of Aaron and Levi is changed and finished for ever! All believers, both men and women, are called to be priests in the New Covenant order.

D. The Sacrifice

Again, the sequence of events is: If God makes Covenant, then covenant requires a Temple, and if there is a Temple, there must be a Priesthood, and if there is a Priesthood there must of necessity be Sacrifice!

If Christ Himself is a priest, then He must of necessity have something to offer. If the Church, His Body, is a priesthood, then they must of necessity be able and willing to offer sacrifices. Both Old and New Testament confirms this truth.

1. Old Testament Sacrifice

The sacrificial system of the Old Testament begins in Genesis and continues on through every book of the Old Testament unto the coming of Christ. Sacrifices and oblations were ordained of God. The message is primarily atonement from sin by the body and blood of substitutionary sacrifices. Without the shedding of blood there was no remission of sins. It was the blood that made atonement for the soul (Leviticus 17:11-14; Hebrews 9:22).

(a) The coats of skin provided for Adam and Eve came from the death of the substitute victim (Genesis 3).

(b) The sacrifice of Abel brought in faith to the Lord was accepted by the Lord (Genesis 4 with Hebrews 11:4).

(c) The altar of sacrifice built by Noah was a covenant altar (Genesis 8).

(d) The altar and fivefold sacrifice that Abraham offered was according to the word of the Lord (Genesis 15).

(e) The altars of Jacob were built to the Lord (Genesis 28; 35).

(f) The Passover Lamb was a redeeming sacrifice (Exodus 12).

(g) The five Levitical offerings and their intricate details were ordained of the Lord in Israel (Leviticus Chapters 1-7).

(h) The sacrifice of the red heifer was a special offering (Numbers 19).

(i) The two goats on the Day of Atonement were special also (Leviticus 16).

(j) The offerings for the Sabbaths and the Festival occasions were all ordained of the Lord (Numbers 28-29; Leviticus 23).

This variety of sacrifices, with all their intricate details concerning presentation to the Lord were given to the priesthood and all have the same basic thread connecting them. That is, they have to do with redemption through the body and blood of sacrificial and substitutionary offerings. Sin brought about man's fall. Man needed redemption from sin. Only substitutionary sacrifices could make redemption possible.

For approximately 4000 years, and more especially the 1500 years of the Law Covenant, the altars of God flowed with sacrificial blood. The time would come when Christ would come and cause all such to cease by the sacrifice and oblation of His own body and blood. This brings us to the New Covenant sacrifices as seen in Christ and His Church.

2. New Testament Sacrifice

Once again, we turn to the Book of Hebrews, the great interpreter of the Old Covenant, Sanctuary, Priesthood and Sacrifice. The New Covenant sacrifices are seen in Christ and the Church. But we consider Christ's unique sacrifice which was for our sin, and for redemption. No sacrifice of the believers are equal to this once-for-all sacrifice of Christ for our sin.

The sacrifice of the body and blood of the Lord Jesus Christ on the altar of Calvary's cross was the supreme sacrifice for time and eternity. It for ever abolished animal sacrifice. His body and blood for ever replaced and superseded the body and blood of animals. Hebrews Chapters 9-10 speak of the body and blood of Jesus Christ and how such supersedes all Old Covenant sacrifices. Christ's sacrifice is THE New Covenant sacrifice. It was offered once only and once for all time. This is in contrast to the Old Covenant sacrifices that could never take away sin, as the following comparison shows.

Old Covenant Sacrifice	New Covenant Sacrifice
Animal sacrifices	Divine-Human sacrifice
Body and blood	Body and blood of Jesus
Animal nature	Divine-Human natures
Unwilling sacrifice	Willing sacrifice
Offered by a priest	Jesus both priest and sacrifice
Offering and offerer separated	Offerer and offering united
Inferior sinless substitute	Superior sinless one
Offered daily, many sacrifices	Offered once for all, one sacrifice
Never take away sins	Take away sins, remember no more
Shadows and symbols	Substance and reality
Fulfilled and abolished	Eternally remains
Temporal in time	Eternally efficacious

Even under the Old Testament, the Lord foretold the fact that Christ's sacrifice would for ever abolish animal sacrifices and oblations. Though God ordained these animal sacrifices, He was never pleased with them (Psalm 40:6-8 with Hebrews 10:5-10; Isaiah 1:10-15; 66:1-4; Psalm 50:10-14; Micah 6:6-9). When Messiah came, He would cause all sacrifice and the oblation to cease by His once-for-all perfect and sinless sacrifice (Daniel 9:24-27; Hebrews 10:1-2).

As John saw Jesus coming to baptism and he cried, "Behold, the Lamb of God who takes away the sin of the world", the Father also confirmed it by saying, "This is My beloved Son, in whom I am well pleased" (John 1:19,36; Matthew 3:13-17). Since His sacrifice, His death and burial and resurrection and His ascension, Christ now sits at the right hand of the Father, waiting for all His enemies to be made His footstool (Hebrews 10:1-14). No other creature could make the perfect sacrifice for sin.

E. The Sacrifices of The Church

It is now upon the basis of Christ's sinless sacrifice for the redeemed, that the believer can offer to God "spiritual sacrifices", acceptable to God through Christ Jesus, our risen Lord (1Peter 2:5-9).

If believers are part of the royal priesthood, as already mentioned, it is necessary that they have something to offer to God. Christ is our great high priest. He has offered Himself to God as the supreme sacrifice for sin. This kind of sacrifice the believer can never offer. Believers, however, are kings and priests to God and do have other sacrifices to offer to the Father through Christ, the great high priest.

Peter tells us that believers are a spiritual house, a holy and royal priesthood and are therefore, called to offer up **"spiritual sacrifices"** acceptable to God through Christ Jesus (1Peter 2:5-9). What then are the sacrifices that believers offer to God through our great high priest, Christ Jesus? What are these **"spiritual sacrifices"**?

Undoubtedly the best Scriptural definition of sacrifice is that found in 2 Samuel 24:24 and 1Chronicles 21:24. David said he would not offer to the Lord **that which cost him nothing! Sacrifice costs something! If it costs nothing, then there is no sacrifice at all!**

Following is a list of "spiritual sacrifices" from the Scriptures, both Old and New Testaments. Even under the Old Covenant offering of animal sacrifices, there were also spiritual sacrifices offered by those who had true insight into the truth of sacrifice. Under the New Covenant, the animal sacrifices are abolished at the cross, but all **spiritual sacrifices** remain! The student is encouraged to read the relevant Scriptures.

1. The Sacrifice of Thanksgiving

The Scriptures speak of the sacrifice of thanksgiving which was offered to the Lord from grateful hearts. This sacrifice comes from an attitude of gratitude for all that the Lord has done (Psalm 107:22; 116:17; Jonah 2:19; Leviticus 7:11-15; Ephesians 5:10; 1 Thessalonians 5:18).

2. The Sacrifice of Joy

The natural man seeks for happiness. Happiness is often dependant on one's circumstances. Joy is dependant on the Lord regardless of circumstances. Paul was in prison when he wrote to the Philippian believers, telling them to "rejoice in the Lord!" (Philippians 3:1; Psalm 27:6; Luke 6:22-23). The joy of the Lord is our strength (Nehemiah 8:10).

3. The Sacrifice of Praise

The student is referred to Chapter 33 on "the sacrifice of praise". Paul and Silas prayed and praised the Lord under the worst circumstances in prison (Acts 16:25). The sacrifice is the fruit of our lips (Hebrews 13:15-16; Jeremiah 17:6; 33:11). It is not given when we feel like it but whether we feel like it or not. It is not dependent on circumstances, good or bad. God is worthy of all praise, at all times, in all circumstances (Psalm 18:3; 50:23; 63:3,4; 67:3; 92:1-4; 102:18).

4. The Sacrifice of Righteousness

It is easy to follow in the way of unrighteousness. The way of righteousness is that which pleases the Lord. It is the sacrifice of the old flesh life and walk to walk in the way of truth and righteousness. This sacrifice pleases the Lord (Psalm 4:5; 51:19; Deuteronomy 33:19).

5. The Sacrifice of Obedience

The prophet Samuel told Saul that "obedience was better than sacrifice". Above animal sacrifices that Saul said he would offer to the Lord, God wanted plain and simple obedience to the Word He gave. Christ came to bring us back to the obedience from which Adam fell (Romans 5:12-21; 1Samuel 15:22; Isaiah 1:19-20).

6. The Sacrifice of a Broken Spirit

David saw beyond the need of offering animal sacrifices for his sins. He knew that the real sacrifice God wanted was that of a broken and contrite spirit. God would not despise this sacrifice of the spirit. It would indeed be a spiritual and real sacrifice (Psalm 51:16-19; Isaiah 57:15; Micah 6:6-8).

7. The Sacrifice of Hospitality

Ministering to one another, to the saints or to strangers is a sacrifice with which God is well pleased (Hebrews 13:16). This can be the giving of our substance to those in need; the ministry of hospitality, even as Israel was commanded to help their poorer brethren in need (Deuteronomy 15:7-18).

8. The Sacrifice of Lifted Hands

The Psalmist says that the offering of our prayer is like the offering of incense, and the lifting of our hands is like the evening sacrifice. It is an act of surrender to the Lord (Psalms 141:1-2; 134:1-3). We are to lift holy hands to the Lord without wrath or doubting (1Timothy 2:8-9).

9. The Sacrifice of Tithes & Offerings

The Lord commands us to bring our tithes and offerings to His house that there may be food in His house (Malachi 3:8-12). Giving freely to the Lord of our tithes and/or offerings is a sacrifice that pleases God and brings His blessing on the giver.

10. The Sacrifice of Time

Time represents all we are as we are creatures of time. The Lord tells us to number our days so that we can apply our hearts to wisdom, and that we also redeem the time. People sacrifice their time and life to temporal things. Time sacrificed to the Lord in eternal things is rewarded eternally (Psalm 90:12; Ephesians 5:16; Colossians 4:5). As we put the kingdom of God in first and top priority, everything else is added to us (Matthew 6:33).

11. The Sacrifice of Giving

Along with the giving of tithes and offerings, there is the sacrifice of giving to those in need. Paul thanked the Philippians believers, and the Corinthians for their material help and gifts to support him in times of need (Phil 4:13-19; Hebrews 13:16; 2Corinthians 8-9 Chapters).

12. The Sacrifice of our Bodies

The believer is commanded, by the mercies of God, to present his body as a living sacrifice, wholly, and acceptable unto God, which is his reasonable service That is, it is his priestly obligation and worship. As the Israelites presented the bodies of the animal sacrifices to God, dead bodies, the believer presents his body to God, living, for Divine service (Romans 12:1-2; 6:13). King Solomon presented himself as "a living sacrifice" on the brazen scaffold he had built in the outer court for the dedication of the Temple. This brazen scaffold was the same size as the brazen altar of sacrifice in the outer court of Moses Tabernacle (Compare 2Chronicles 6:13 with Exodus 27:1-8).

A consideration of these "**spiritual sacrifices**" show that with such sacrifices God is indeed well pleased. God will never be pleased with animal sacrifices again, but with these sacrifices of the saints to His will and purpose.

The Palmist said: "Gather My saints together unto Me; those that have a covenant with Me by sacrifice" (Psalm 50:5).

The New Testament believer agrees with the Psalmist when he also says: "I will freely sacrifice unto Thee: I will praise Thy Name, O Lord, for it is good! (Psalm 54:6).

God's people are a covenant people, a spiritual house, a spiritual and royal priesthood and are called indeed to offer up spiritual sacrifices, acceptable to the Father through His blessed Son!

These wonderful truths arose out of the truth that was seeded in the years of 1946-1950's and onwards to this time.

CHAPTER THIRTY-FIVE

THE TABERNACLE OF DAVID

It was in the AD1965 that Rev. David Schoch of Bethany Chapel, Long Beach, California (USA) was invited to speak at a Convention in New Zealand. In the course of one of the preaching and teaching sessions, he had cause to refer to the Scripture in Amos 9:11 where God said, "In that day will I raise up the Tabernacle of David that is fallen, and close up the breaches thereof; and I will raise up his ruins, and I will build it as in the days of old".

He mentioned in a passing moment that it was not "The Tabernacle of Moses" that God said He would build again as in the days of old, but "The Tabernacle of David". The writer in talking since to Brother Schoch came to see that even he did not understand the full significance of that Scripture or his own statement and what would become of it.

However, as a prophet of God, he had dropped a **Divine seed** that would be watered by the Spirit in time and grow into another great truth that was already in the Scriptures but not recognized by most of God's people. Several of the brethren in New Zealand caught this "seed", and the Spirit of God began to water it, and the Scriptures opened up a whole new area of neglected truth pertaining to worship under this title, "**The Tabernacle of David**".

This writer had the privilege of fellowshipping with these brethren and saw that there was something there. However, there were many questions unanswered and much uncertainty on the subject. This caused many hours of research to be done in the Word of God and out of this was born the textbook on "**The Tabernacle of David**".

For many years the glorious truths of "The Tabernacle of Moses" had been taught and majored upon. But, "The Tabernacle of David" - What was that? Why was there a need for "The Tabernacle of David?" Did it contradict that which was set forth in "The Tabernacle of Moses?" Can both of them be reconciled? What did it all mean?" Most did not even know if David had a Tabernacle. Some preachers and teachers spoke of this truth as heresy and a distortion of the Scriptures given to natural and national Israel.

As research was done on this subject, the writer found that this became a most suitable, and a Scriptural title on which to found many things that had come out over the years from 1946-1948 and onwards. A great reservoir of truth relative to worship and to praise was found. Numerous Scriptures and passages opened up by the discovery and use of this "**Key of David**" (Revelation 3:7).

Over the years, as the writer has moved around in ministry in many Minister's Conferences, National Workers Conventions and Seminars, as well as local Churches, he has considered the various forms and expressions of worship and longed for some solid foundation in Scriptures upon which such could be founded. This desire was fulfilled in the study of "The Tabernacle of David".

The response of God's people has been enthusiastic and enlightening. It has answered many questions pertaining to expressions of worship in the Church. Above all, it has given a **Scriptural foundation** for the things which may be done in a New Testament Church which the New Testament does not necessarily address as far as local Church order of worship is concerned. In the writer's measure of understanding, one of the richest avenues of approach to Divine worship, whether for Old Testament or New Testament saints, is to be found in a presentation of "The Tabernacle of David".

For many Churches, the various expressions and terminology such as "praise and worship", "the sacrifice of praise", "singing in the Spirit", and the clapping of hands, lifting of hands, spiritual songs, instruments of music, spontaneous praise, dancing and rejoicing before the Lord, etc.,have created questions. Most of these things could not and are not found as such in a New Testament Church "order of service".

Because of this it seemed that what was needed was some Biblical and Scriptural foundation on which these things could be laid and built. "The Tabernacle of David" became that.

(**Note:** The reader is referred to the textbook, "**The Tabernacle of David**" by the author as the following material is either adapted or taken from sections and chapters in that textbook because of its appropriateness in "**Restoration Theology**").

A. The Tabernacle of Moses

For several hundreds of years, Israel had gathered to the Tabernacle of Moses in their approach to God. All were familiar with the structure and its Divinely ordained furnishings. The outer court with its brazen altar, and brazen laver; the holy place with its golden lampstand, golden altar of incense and table of shewbread, and then the most holy place with its lone article of furniture, the Ark of the Covenant -these were the distinctions in the places of Moses' Tabernacle. All pointed the way of approach to God.

The Levitical priests served in the outer court and the holy place, but into the most holy place only the high priest went once a year, "not without blood" (Hebrews Chapters 9-10).

None dare approach God without Divine order except on pain of death. The officiating priesthood offered the Divinely prescribed sacrifices and fulfilled the festival occasions. The details of the whole Mosaic economy are to be found in Exodus Chapters 25-40; Leviticus 16 and 23 chapters.

This order continued through to the time of Samuel the prophet and the anointing of David to be king. But things were to change. The Lord was about to move on again in His full purposes. (For studies in the Tabernacle of Moses, the student is referred to Bibliography).

B. The Tabernacle of David

In 1Chronicles 17:5 the Lord told David how He had dwelt in a tent and gone from one tabernacle to another tabernacle. Now the Lord was going to move on from the Tabernacle of Moses into the Tabernacle of David. It is under David that a whole new approach to God was established. Between the Tabernacle of Moses and the Temple of Solomon came the revelation of the Tabernacle of David. For the purpose of this text, the following outline is given, as full details are in the textbook of David's Tabernacle.

1. The Old and New Testaments both speak of the Tabernacle David (Amos 9:11-13 with Acts 15:15-16).

2. The historical setting of the Tabernacle of David is found in 1Chronicles Chapters 13,14,15,16,17 along with 2 Samuel 6:17-19.

3. The Ark of the Covenant, which had for many years been in the Tabernacle of Moses was never ever returned there again after its journeys in the land of the Philistines (1Samuel Chapters 3,4,5,6,7). It is placed by David in the Tabernacle or tent which he pitched for it.

4. In David's time, there were actually two Tabernacles functioning at the same time. The Tabernacle of Moses was at Gibeon and the Tabernacle of David was at Zion.

5. There were also two companies of priests ministering at the same time at these respective Tabernacles. One company was at Gibeon (1Chronicles 16:37-43; 21:28-30; 2Chronicles 1:1-13), and the other company was at Zion (2Samuel 5:7; 2Chronicles 5:2; 1Chronicles 16:1-6; 2Chronicles 1:3-6,13).

6. Mt Zion takes on special significance from now on and is seen so in both Old and New Testaments, as these Scriptures exemplify.

    (a) Old Testament Scriptures on Zion (Psalm 2:6; 9:11-14; 48:1-12; 132:13-18; Psalm 110; Isaiah 4:3-5; 12:6; 33:14-24; 16:1-5; 28:16; Joel 2:1; Micah 4:2-4).

    (b) New Testament Scriptures on Zion (Romans 9:33; Hebrews 12:22-24; 1Peter 2:6; Revelation 14:1-5).

7. There is a whole new order of worship established in the Tabernacle of David in Mt Zion. Singing and singers, instruments of music, praise, worship and thanksgiving are the order of worship there (1Chronicles 15:28; 16:4; 23:5-6). This is in marked contrast to that order in Mt Gibeon and the Tabernacle of Moses, as will be seen in the appropriate part of this chapter.

C. The Theology of the Tabernacle of David

It is important to understand the theology of the Tabernacle of David in order to appreciate the order that is seen in Davidic worship and expressions of praise to the Lord.

The theology of the Tabernacle of David is seen in the list of truths set out here. A principle of understanding and interpreting the Word of God is this. **God often got people to do typically in the Old Testament what He Himself was going to fulfill actually in the New Testament!**

David, therefore, was establishing and shadowing forth the New Covenant times. The believing Jew and Gentile would gather together to worship the Lord in the Tabernacle of David. The Tabernacle of David shadowed forth the New Covenant of grace. The Tabernacle of Moses shadowed forth the Old Covenant of law. The Gentiles, according to James, who quotes Amos, would come into the Tabernacle of David, into grace through faith, by the New Covenant, and not into the Tabernacle of Moses, into law, by the Old Covenant. This is the truth and theology shadowed in the Tabernacle of David.

1. **The Tabernacle of David** was the Old Testament type and shadow of the New Testament antitype and reality.

2. **The Tabernacle of David** shadowed forth in the Davidic Covenant the New Covenant. Christ was David's Son as to His humanity, but David's Lord as to His Divinity.

3. **The Tabernacle of David** had only spiritual sacrifices of praise and worship offered in it by the priests, after the initial and dedicatory animal sacrifices had been offered. This shadowed forth Christ's once and for all initial and dedicatory sacrifice of His own body and blood, after which, believer priests offer only the spiritual sacrifices to the Lord (1Peter 2:5-9).

4. **The Tabernacle of David** shadowed forth the priests having "access within the veil" and before the very Ark of God. It signified the truth that, under the coming New Covenant, believer priests would have access within the veil before the throne of God (Hebrews 6:19-20).

5. **The Tabernacle of David** shadowed forth the transference of the Holiest of All from the Tabernacle of Moses. It pointed to a whole new order of worship This took place once the veil of the Temple was rent. Believers can enter into the Holiest of All by the new and living way, the blood of Jesus (Matthew 27:50-51 with Hebrews 10:19-20).

6. **The Tabernacle of David** shadowed forth the coming in of the Gentiles along with the Jews (Israel), into one and the same Tabernacle apart from any Mosaic Covenant ceremonialisms, sacrifices and oblations.

7. **The Tabernacle of David** shadowed forth the order of Melchisdek, the order of king-priests. David was a king and touched priestly ministrations. Believers in Christ belong to the order of Melchisdek and are kings and priests unto God (Revelation 1:6; 5:9-10; 1Peter 2:5-9).

8. **The Tabernacle of David** shadowed forth in earthly Mt Zion and the earthly city of Jerusalem what was to find fulfilment in the heavenly Mt Zion and heavenly Jerusalem (Hebrews 12:22-24).

9. **The Tabernacle of David** shadowed forth Mt Zion politically, as the city of the great king, in which was the throne of David and his kingdom. All this is fulfilled in Christ, David's greater Son, in heavenly Mt Zion and the throne and kingdom of His Father (Luke 1:30-33; Revelation 14:1-2).

10. **The Tabernacle of David** shadowed forth Mt Zion ecclesiastically in the Tabernacle of the priests ministering before the Lord. The Tabernacle of priesthood is fulfilled in Christ. David was king of Judah, touching priestly ministrations relative to the Ark of the Lord. Jesus is king of the tribe of Judah, but is also God's priest in the throne of the Lord.

11. **The Tabernacle of David**, in its new order of worship without animal sacrifices, shadowed forth the New Testament Church and its worship in spirit and truth apart from animal sacrifices (John 4:20-24; Ephesians 5:19; Colossians 3:16).

12. **The Tabernacle of David** is seen in the Book of Hebrews which uses the "comparative mention principle" and compares the whole of the Mosaic Covenant

economy and the New Covenant economy. Each chapter is comparative and contrastive. Christ is "**better**" than Moses, and Aaron, and the earthly Tabernacle, and the animal sacrifice, and Mt Sinai and Levitical priestly ministrations. Mt Zion and the New Covenant is better than everything, for it is eternal and ministers in the power of an endless life, the order of Melchisedek.

The writer tells us that we are not come to Mt Sinai (ie., The Tabernacle of Moses), but we are come to Mt Zion (ie., The Tabernacle of David). Read carefully Hebrews 12:18-24 for the contrast between these two mountains, Mt Sinai and Mt Zion.

The purpose of this chapter has been to see the origin in our time of the "**seed-word**" that was brought to light over the years. The prophet Amos spoke of **restoration of the Tabernacle of David** which had fallen down in his time and gone into ruins. It was a type of what happened in Church History. The early Church understood the Tabernacle of David and Davidic worship. Over the centuries the Davidic worship had fallen and come into ruins. The Lord said He would restore to the Church all that had been lost.

In the years of 1946-1948 and onwards, the Lord has indeed been recovering the truth of Davidic worship. It has progressively been restored under designations like "The Sacrifice of Praise", and "The Covenant, Temple, Priesthood and Sacrifice". In a fuller way it has been restored under the title of "The Tabernacle of David".

This now brings us to the next chapter dealing with "**The Restoration of Davidic Worship**" as set out in David's Tabernacle.

CHAPTER THIRTY-SIX

RESTORATION OF DAVIDIC WORSHIP

It is recognized that there is no "order of worship" given in the New Testament for the Church. Christ taught His disciples that He would fulfill in Himself and His Church all things that were written in the Law, the Psalms and the Prophets (Luke 24:44-45 with Matthew 5:17-18; 11:13).

Just a cursory glance over the New Testament quotations from Old Testament Scriptures reveal how much the early believers made of the Old Testament, by their use of the Law, the Psalms and the Prophets.

The Psalms of David figure much in New Testament writings. The early Church has no New Testament as yet, so they continually appealed to the Old Testament writings for all that God was doing in their midst.

When Amos said that the Lord would restore (build again) the Tabernacle of David that was fallen down and raise up its ruins, he certainly is not talking about the material tent in which the Ark of God was. He did not mean that the Gentiles would come into any material tent. He is talking about the kingdom and throne of David, as also the worship in the Tabernacle of David, for both king and priest are counted one in the person of Christ, the Son of David (Amos 9:11-15; Acts 15:15-18).

There are a number of great saints in the Old Testament, each of them manifesting some important character quality with which the Lord was pleased with. When we speak of Abraham, we think of a man of faith. When we think of Moses, we think of the quality of meekness. When we think of sorrow, we think of Jeremiah, the weeping prophet. If we talk of Samuel, we think of a man of prayer. But when it comes to the subject of worship and praise, our minds immediately go to David. David is mentioned numerous times in the Old Testament and also in the New Testament.

It may be asked why this chapter speaks of the restoration of Davidic worship. It is because David was a worshipper, a singer and an anointed musician, as well as a man after God's own heart. The Lord Jesus Christ, David's greater Son and also David's Lord, is leader of the worship of God's people. He says, "In the midst of the Church will I sing praise to You" (Hebrews 2:12 with Psalm 22:22). As David was a leader and commander in Israel so is the Lord Jesus the leader and commander in His Church (Isaiah 55:3-4).

Old Covenant and Mosaic economy sacrifices, oblations, Sabbath days, festival days, the Tabernacle and the Aaronic and Levitical priesthood - all were fulfilled and abolished at the cross. But, when it comes to the matter of **worship** of the Davidic kind, worship was not abolished at the cross. It simply moves into a higher order and a higher spiritual realm. This is why it can be said there is a restoration of Davidic worship in our generation.

Over the centuries, the Church drifted from Davidic expressions of worship and praise as in the early Church. Denominations set out "forms of worship" and established "order of worship" hymn-books and prayer-books. For some, these have been followed out very meticulously over decades of years. If David attended a service in our generation, he would be surprized many times by the formalism, ritualism and lifelessness of so much that is called "worship". The reverse is also true. If we attended "a service" in David's Tabernacle, it undoubtedly would be a spiritual shock to our set ways and forms.

Every true revival and awakening in the history of Israel under Godly leadership was always a return to the **order of Davidic worship**, as seen in these Scriptures here.

1. The foundation of Davidic worship was laid in Zion (1Chronicles 15-16; 2Samuel 6).

2. The dedication of the Temple saw the glory of God amidst Davidic worship (2Chronicles Chapter 5).

3. Godly king Jehoshaphat employed the singers in battle (2Chronicles 20).

4. Amos prophesied of the restoration of the Tabernacle of David which had fallen into ruins in his time under the reigns of ungodly kings (Amos 9:11-15).

5. Godly king Hezekiah restored worship after the Davidic order in the cleansing of the Temple, the house of the Lord (2Chronicles 29-30).

6. Under Godly Josiah there was a measure of restoration of Davidic worship (2Chronicles Chapter 35).

7. Ezra, the scribe and priest, along with the governor, Nehemiah, restored Davidic worship in the rebuilding of the house of the Lord after the Babylonian Captivity (Ezra 3; Nehemiah 12; Psalm 127; Psalm 137).

So it may be said, the beginning of Davidic worship and song was under Martin Luther when he brought back into the Church singing, and then in measure over the succeeding centuries under each awakening of the Spirit. Each movement of the Spirit has clothed its message in song, as seen in the Methodists, the Salvation Army, the Pentecostals as well as other denominations. In this generation, there is certainly an increased fullness of Davidic worship in the Church as never before.

In the light of these things, we consider, at least, eighteen expressions of worship and praise as in David's time or in the Book of Psalms, which was Israel's "National Hymn and Worship Book".The student is referred to "**The Tabernacle of David**" (Chapter 17) by the author for much of the content of this chapter.

A. Worship in Spirit and in Truth

The greatest passage in Scripture about worship is that which Jesus spoke to the woman at the well (John 4:20-24). The word "worship" is mentioned about ten times in this passage, providing some profound truths about the reality of worship before the Father.

The word "worship" means "to honour, revere, adore, pay homage, render devotion and respect" to someone, specially to God. It is used in this chapter in its broadest sense to encompass all ministry to the Lord. All service to the Lord should spring out of a true spirit of worship and praise. Worship also means to bow down, to bow prostrate before the Lord.

The Lord Jesus said that the Father was seeking those who would worship Him "in spirit and in truth" (John 4:24). Man was created to be a worshipper of God. Of himself, man does not know how to worship God, yet he longs to worship. It is for this reason that man designs forms of worship or some sort of program for religious services and then asks God to bless this program. Also, because man does not know how God desires to be worshipped, he develops a variety of different forms. People generally congregate to the particular form that suits their tastes, their spiritual disposition and which does not offend their mentality.

It is worthy to ask ourselves what Jesus meant when He said that the Father desired us to worship in spirit and in truth. How can we worship in spirit? How can we worship in truth?

1. **Worship in spirit**

   To worship "in spirit" is to allow the Holy Spirit to move upon the believer's redeemed spirit, causing love, adoration, devotion, honour and respect to ascend to God. The believer is born again in his spirit by the Holy Spirit (John 3:1-5). His spirit is to be in union with the Spirit of God (Romans 8:16 with 1Corinthians 6:17). As the Holy Spirit moves upon the redeemed spirit, then worship "in spirit" is possible and ascends to God (John 4:20-24). How can one who is not "born of the Spirit" worship God, who is Spirit, "in spirit"?

2. **Worship in truth**

   To worship "in truth" is to worship according to the Word of God. Jesus said, "Sanctify them through Your truth; Your Word is truth" (John 17:17). God has laid down in His Word how we are to worship Him. He has shown His acceptance of a variety of expressions of worship and praise from those who truly love Him. To worship "in truth" is to worship God according to the Word of God. It is to be real. A true worshipper is a real worshipper, and not one who worships God after the traditions of men with their heart far from the Lord (Mark 7:1-7; Isaiah 29:13).

To "worship in spirit and in truth" involves the believer honouring and adoring God by the quickening of the Holy Spirit and according to the Word of the Lord. The Spirit and the Word are both needed in proper worship. Both must be there. If the Spirit is not there, then worship is dead, lifeless. It is according to the letter that kills. All becomes empty form. If the Word is not there, then the worship can become mere sentimentalism, emotionalism or fanaticism. There is need of the Spirit and the Word in true Biblical worship. There is nothing wrong with Divine form and Divine order.

In Genesis 1:2, as seen in an earlier chapter, the earth was in a state of being without form and void and darkness was upon the face of the deep. The Spirit of God moved on the face of the deep and then God spoke. By the ministry of the Spirit and the Word order was brought out of chaos, light out of darkness, form out of disorder (Genesis 1:1-5). Thus, Divine worship is dependant upon the Spirit and the Word operating in the midst of the worshipping congregation.

B. **Davidic Expressions of Worship & Praise**

   Following are a number of expressions of worship and praise associated with the Tabernacle of David, as well as in the history of Israel over the years. It should be recognized that each of these can become mechanical, lifeless forms unless the life of the Holy Spirit is maintained by the congregation. It is easy for man to carry on anything that the Word says or the Spirit quickens and for it to become mere habit, without any quickening of the Spirit in it. Human nature can move from spiritual things into carnal and human ruts very easily.

Also, as these expressions are considered, it is not to say that all of these have to be in every service. Those responsible in leading worship will be sensitive to the Spirit of God and dependent upon the mind of the Lord for any particular service. The leader will follow the flow of the river of the Spirit of God for that service, so that the river of the Spirit does not end up in marshes and tributaries of lifelessness or extremes.

The variety of ways of ministry before the Lord as seen here are briefly commented on and will be done by way of contrast to the "old order" of that which took place relative to the Tabernacle of Moses.

1. **Ministry of Singers and Singing- 1Chronicles 15:16-27; 25:1-7**

    David appointed certain Levites to be singers in the Tabernacle of David. The ministry of the singers in the song of the Lord was very prominent here in contrast to the Tabernacle of Moses, where no singers sang songs to the Lord. The New Testament shows the use of the Psalms, Hymns and Spiritual Songs as believers make melody in their hearts to the Lord (Ephesians 5:18-19; Colossians 3:19). The word "Psalm" means "an ode or song of praise accompanied by a harp or a musical instrument".

2. **Ministry of Musicians with Instruments- 1Chronicles 23:5; 25:1-7**

    King David also ordained musicians with a variety of instruments to play and sing before the Lord in His Tabernacle. No musical instruments were ever played in the Tabernacle of Moses. The musicians were to prophesy before the Lord and His people with harps. Music can release the prophetic word.

    Hezekiah gave songs to be sung to stringed instruments in the house of the Lord (Isaiah 38:20). Elisha had a minstrel play as he waited for a release in the prophetic word (2Kings 3:15). The Psalmist says we are to play to the Lord on (a) Wind instruments, (b) Stringed instruments and (c) Percussion instruments (Psalm 150). As David played before Saul, the evil spirit departed from troubling him (1 Samuel 16:17). Playing before the Lord and his people needs both skill and anointing (Psalm 33:3; Ezekiel 33:32; 2 Samuel 23:1-2).

3. **Ministry of the Levites before the Ark of God- 1Chronicles 16:4,6,37**

    The Levities were appointed to minister before the Ark of the Covenant continually by day as every man's work required. This was indeed in great contrast to the order of the Tabernacle of Moses. Only the High Priest on the great Day of Atonement ever dared to enter into the Holiest of All and stand before the Ark of God. Then it was in great silence and solemnity. If any other had dared to presume into the Most Holy Place, judgment would have fallen on them. But here in David's Tabernacle stood a group of Levites before the Ark of God. It will be remembered that the Tabernacle of David signified the transference of the Holiest of All from the Tabernacle of Moses to Mt. Zion. Thus these Levites had access "within the veil", so to speak, and foreshadowed the entrance within the veil for New Covenant believers (Hebrews 6:19-20; 9:7-9; 10:20-21). The dividing veil was rent when Jesus died on the cross (Matthew 27:50-51).

4. **Ministry of Recording- 1Chronicles 16:4; 28:12,19**

King David set Levites in his Tabernacle "to record". The word "record" means, "to set it down so it can be remembered". It involved the ministry of the scribe. Many of the Psalms, especially those which concern Zion, must have been given by the inspiration of the Holy Spirit in connection with the Tabernacle of David. The title of Psalm 80 as well as the whole Psalm is an example of this. Asaph prayed a prophetic prayer as he stood before the Ark of the Covenant and the Shepherd of Israel who dwelt between the Cherubims (Psalm 80:1). The Psalms would be recorded by the Levitical scribes and thus set down so that they could be remembered. What a vast treasure would have been lost if the Psalms had not been recorded. Moses was the only one who wrote inspired Scripture in relation to the Tabernacle called by his name. Psalms 90-91 have been attributed to Moses. In the Tabernacle of David many Levites wrote Psalms, as well as king David.

5. **Ministry of Thanking the Lord- 1Chronicles 16:4,8,41**

David appointed the Levites to thank the Lord also. Many of the Psalms exhort God's people to thank the Lord for His mercy. Giving thanks is an expression of gratefulness and appreciation to the giver of all things. Unthankfulness is a sign of the last days. Those who were set in the Tabernacle of David were to give thanks continually for all things (Psalms 116:17; 2Chronicles 29:30-31 with 1Thessalonians 5:18). Under the Tabernacle of Moses, Israel could render a voluntary "thank offering" to the Lord (Leviticus 7:12,13).

6. **Ministry of Praise- 1Chronicles 16:4,36**

Part of the order in David's Tabernacle was to praise the Lord for His goodness and mercy. There were always Levites in their respective courses praising the Lord. One just needs to check the Concordance and count the numerous references to "praise" to realize the importance of this ministry to the Lord.

7. **Ministry of Psalms- 1Chronicles 16:9; Psalm 98:6**

On the day of the dedication, David delivered a Psalm to the singers and the musicians. The Tabernacle of David was characterized by the writing and the singing of Palms. The greater majority of the Psalms are linked with David's Tabernacle. This is seen by the many references to Zion. This is in contrast with the Tabernacle of Moses, where only one or possibly two Psalms were written, these being the Psalms attributed to Moses (Psalms 90-91. Title). The New Testament exhorts believers to sing the Psalms (Colossians 3:16; Ephesians 5:18-19; James 5:13; 1Corinthians 14:26), thus continuing the ordinance of David. The Church in general recognizes that the Psalms are an integral part of worship, either chanting or singing them in Divine service. Many centuries of history show that often the Psalms were chanted or sung. In this generation, many Psalms and Scripture songs are being put to music and being sung through the Church world in a new and fresh way.

8. **Ministry of Rejoicing and Joy- 1Chronicles 16:10,16,25-31**

    Joy and rejoicing characterized the order of the Tabernacle of David also. The Canaanite religions as well as most religions outside of Christianity had no real joy. Even the Tabernacle of Moses was characterized by great solemnity, not the joy of David's Tabernacle. Numerous Scriptures exhort the believer to joy and rejoice in the Lord, not in circumstances, whether good or bad (Philippians 3:3; 4:4). Joy is an infallible sign of God's presence. When one loses victory in the Lord, they lose joy. The kingdom of God is righteousness, peace and joy in the Holy Spirit (Romans 14:17).

9. **Ministry of Clapping Hands- Psalm 47:1; 98:8; Isaiah 55:12**

    One of the Psalms for the sons of Korah exhorts the people to clap hands. One of the most natural of all human responses to joy and appreciation is the hand clapping. It is a sign of applause to someone who has done something great and needs to receive appreciation. From the baby in the cradle, to the youth, to the adult, clapping of hands is an expression of happiness, thanks, appreciation, and joy. How much more shall God's people clap their hands unto the Lord as they did in Bible times? There was no such expression of joy seen in Moses' Tabernacle.

10. **Ministry of Shouting- 1Chronicles 15:28; Psalm 47:1,5; Isaiah 12:6**

    When the Ark of God was taken into David's Tabernacle, there was much shouting unto the Lord. A number of Scriptures speak of shouting in Israel's history. When Israel shouted on the seventh day on the march around Jericho, God caused the walls to fall down flat (Joshua 6:5). There are times when a shout is just an empty noise (1Samuel 4:5-9), but when God is in it and it is an act of worship unto the Lord, then God works with the shout of His people. The Lord Jesus will return for His people the second time with a shout and the sound of the trumpet (1Thessalonians 4:16).

11. **Ministry of Dancing before the Lord- 1Chronicles 15:29;2 Samuel 6:14**

    There was an expression of dancing before the Lord at the dedication day of the Tabernacle of David. Michael despised David dancing before the Ark of the Lord, and the result was physical barrenness (1Chronicles 15:10,27-28). There is a time to dance and time to refrain from dancing (Ecclesiastes 3:4). Most of the Canaanite dancing was sensuous, lustful and done amidst the orgies of idolatrous festivals. The world has corrupted much of the dance. Every culture in the world has some form of dancing. For the nation of Israel, dancing was to be joy, praise and done as a part of worship unto the Lord (Psalms 30:11; 149:3; 150:4). Young and old are to dance and rejoice together before the Lord (Jeremiah 33:12-13). Dancing for Israel was especially associated with festival seasons. Miriam and the women with her danced before the Lord at the deliverance from Egypt after the crossing of the Red Sea (Exodus 15:20). The elder brother refused to enter into the music and dancing at the return of the prodigal son and brother, and was robbed of the joy of the feast (Luke 15:25). The lame man leaped with joy before the Lord at his healing (Acts 3 with Isaiah 35:6). In much of the restoration of worship and praise, there is spontaneous dancing unto the Lord. Some speak of it as "dancing in the Spirit", but it is probably more "dancing and rejoicing before and unto the Lord".

12. Ministry of Lifting Hands- Psalms 134:141:2

The Levites in their courses in Zion also lifted up their hands as an act of worship to the Lord in David's Tabernacle. Lifting hands in Scripture has several suggested meanings. It is an act of surrender, of a person taking a vow before the Lord, of prayer and worship. It is part of Old and New Testament worship (Genesis 14:22; Leviticus 9:22; Luke 24:50; 1Timothy 2:8). In the Psalms it says, "Let my prayer be set forth before You as incense, and the lifting up of my hands as the evening sacrifice" (Psalm 141:2). Only Aaron in the Tabernacle of Moses lifted up his hands in blessing. In the Tabernacle of David all could lift their hands to the Lord. So it is today. All believers are to be ministering priests and may lift their hands in worship. We are to lift up our hearts with our hands (Lamentations 4:21). Read also Psalm 63:3-4; 134:1-2; 28:2; 88:9; 119:48; 143:6; Hebrews 12;12.

13. Ministry of Worship- 1Chronicles 16:29; Psalms 29:1-2; 95:6

Although the word "worship" is being used in this chapter in its broadest sense, in its strictest sense, the word means "to bow down, to stoop very low, to prostrate oneself".The Levites in David's Tabernacle were not only to sing, praise, play instruments, clap hands, lift hands to the Lord, they were also to worship. There was a bowing down before the Lord, a prostration of themselves in deep adoration and devotion. This aspect of worship is the very highest expression before God of all expressions of worship in spirit and in truth (John 4:20-24; Revelation 4). All believers should experience times of deep prostration of the spirit before God in the Holiest of All in this aspect of worship (Revelation 11:1-2; Matthew 28:9,17). At Mt Sinai, the people had to worship afar off (Exodus 24:1-2). In the Tabernacle of David, worship was near to God. Much nearer is it in New Testament times through the blood of the Lord Jesus Christ.

14. Ministry of Seeking the Lord- 1Chronicles 16:10-11; 2Chronicles 7:14

David exhorted the Levites to seek the face of the Lord in his Tabernacle. This is also part of worship; seeking God's face with our whole heart.Only those who seek Him with their whole heart will find Him. We are to rejoice as we seek the Lord (Psalms 27:8; 63:1-2; 70:4). The Tabernacle was a place where priests and Levites sought the Lord. There is never a time in any generation when we are to cease seeking the Lord.

15. Ministry of Spiritual Sacrifices- Psalm 27:6; 1Peter 2:5-9

David's Tabernacle was a place where spiritual sacrifices were offered to the Lord by priests and Levites. In a previous chapter, it was noted that animal sacrifices were offered to the Lord by the priests at the dedicatory service, but after that, only spiritual sacrifices were offered in the Tabernacle of David. This was in great contrast to the continual animal sacrifices in the Tabernacle of Moses order. (The reader is referred to the "**Spiritual Sacrifices**" already considered in the previous chapter).

The sacrifices of joy (Psalm 27:6), the sacrifices of thanksgiving (Psalms 116:17; Leviticus 7:12; Jonah 2:9), and the sacrifices of praise (Jeremiah 17:26; 33:11;

Hebrews 13:15-16), the fruit of our lips, these are the spiritual sacrifices with which God is well pleased. These sacrifices are offered to the Lord by the royal priesthood in the spiritual house, the Church. No animal sacrifices are needed since the once-for-all sacrifice of the body and blood of Jesus. The New Testament believer, as a ministering priest unto the Lord, offers his body (Romans 12:1-2), his praise (Hebrews 13:15) and his substance to the Lord (Hebrews 13:16), to the Father, through Christ.

16. Ministry of Standing before the Lord- Psalm 134:1; 135:1-2

The Levites also, at times, just stood before the Lord in His house. It signified the standing in the presence of the King of Kings and Lord of Lords. King Hezekiah told the Levites the Lord had chosen them "to stand before Him, to serve Him, to minister unto Him, and to burn incense (offer sacrifice)" (Read 2Chronicles 29:11). There are times in a service when it good for believers just to stand before the Lord in a spirit of worship and praise.

17. Ministry of Kneeling before the Lord- 2Chronicles 6:13-14; Psalm 95:6

When Solomon dedicated the Temple later on, incorporating into its services the Davidic order of worship, he built a brazen scaffold in the outer court. He stood on it, then knelt before the Lord as he made the dedicatory prayer The end result was the glory-fire of the Lord consumed the sacrifice and filled the Holiest of All. The Psalmist calls us to bow down before the Lord, to kneel before His presence, before the Lord our Maker. Many times saints are seen in the position of kneeling before the Lord, bowing the knee in prayer and worship (Daniel 6:10; Mark 10:17; Luke 22:41; Acts 7:60; 9:40; 20:36; 21:5). There is a time to stand, to dance, and there is a time to kneel before the Lord.

18. Ministry of Saying "Amen"- 1Chronicles 16:36

In Hebrew the word "Amen" means "Sure". It is translated "Amen, so be it, truth". It involves faithfulness and truth. In Greek the same word means, "Firm, trustworthy" (so be it), and is translated "Amen, Verily". The saying of "Amen" from the heart is an expression of support, approval of faith, of certainty that the thing spoken is true, and it shall come to pass.

It is worthy to note that Israel only responded with "Amen" to the curses of the Lord in Deuteronomy 27:15-26 and Numbers 5:22. In the Tabernacle of David it was the "Amen" of blessing. This is an Old Testament and New Testament expression of worship also (Nehemiah 5:13; 8:6; Psalms 89:52; 106:48; with Ephesians 3:21; Revelation 7:12; 1Corinthians 14:16).

The various expressions of worship related to, or in, David's Tabernacle have been briefly considered. Any or all of these may be in a given service. They are all very Scriptural. They are all a part of God's Word. Both Old and New Testament believers may enter into these expressions of worship and praise. It is vain to say that these things are only for Old Testament Israel and not for the New Testament Church because some of these things are not expressly mentioned in the New Testament.

The New Testament Church arose out of the Old Testament Church (Act s 7:38). The early believers continually appealed to the Psalms as well as the rest of the Old Testament, in their teaching, preaching and worshipping. The New Testament does not write off the Old Testament. The New interprets the Old. The New Testament does show that animal sacrifices and the Mosaic Covenant economy were all abolished at the cross. But nowhere does it say that worship was abolished, nor these expressions of worship. It is inconsistent to accept some of these expressions and reject others, for all are Scriptural expressions unto the Lord. Worship is lifted into a greater and higher realm in the New Testament because of the cross of Jesus and the power of the Holy Spirit, and because the New Testament believers are called to be kings and priests unto God through Christ, after the Melchisedekian order.

The New Testament Church worshipped the Lord as set out in the Psalms. If these things be not so, then the Church today should not accept anything of the Psalms as being applicable to our times. However, the Psalms are generally a revelation of Christ in the midst of a worshipping Church. "In the midst of the Church, will I sing praise unto You" (Hebrews 2:12 with Psalms 22:22-31). "Is any merry, let him sing Psalms" (James 5:13) "Singing to yourselves in Psalms, Hymns and Spiritual Songs, and making melody in your heart to the Lord" (Ephesians 5:18,19; Colossians 3:16).

The following diagram and its respective columns bring into sharper focus the contrast in the orders of the Tabernacle of Moses and the Tabernacle of David, and the expressions of worship as briefly considered in this chapter. The distinction between both of the Tabernacles is clear. The student should read the Scriptures on the right hand column and notice how the New Testament confirms the Old Testament order as shadowed forth in David's Tabernacle.

ORDER OF WORSHIP ESTABLISHED

The Tabernacle of Moses - Old Testament Church Mt. Sinai	The Tabernacle of David New Testament Church Mt. Zion
1. No Singing	1. Singers with Singing (1Chronicles 15:16; Colossians 3:16)
2. No Music	2. Instruments of Music (1Chronicles 23:5; 25:1-7; Ephesians 5:18-19)
3. High Priest only before Ark	3. Levites minister before the Ark (1Chronicles 16:37; Hebrews 6:19-20; 10:19-21)
4. No Recording	4. Recording (1Chronicles 16:4; Psalm 80:1; Revelation 1:10-11)
5. No Thanking	5. Sacrifice of Thanksgiving (1Chronicles 16:4,8,41; 1Thessalonians 5:18)
6. No Praise	6. Sacrifice of Praise (1Chronicles 16:4,36; Hebrews 13:15)
7. Psalms of Moses	7. Psalm Singing (1Chronicles 16:7; Ephesians 5:18-19; James 5:13)
8. Commanded to Rejoice	8. Rejoicing and Joy (1Chronicles 16:10,27,31; Acts 13:52)
9. No Clapping	9. Clapping to the Lord (Psalms 47:1; 98:8)

10. No Shouting (Jericho only)	10. Shout to the Lord (1Chronicles 15:28; 1Thessalonians 4:16)
11. No Dancing (Only Exodus 15)	11. Dancing before the Lord (1Chronicles 15:29; Psalm 149:3; Luke 15:25)
12. No Lifted Hands (Aaron only)	12. Lifting Hands unto the Lord (Psalms 134; 1Timothy 2:8)
13. Worship Afar Off	13. Worship "within the veil" (1Chronicles 16:29; John 4:20-24; Hebrews 6:19-20)
14. Sought to the Tabernacle	14. Seeking the Lord and His Face (1Chronicles 16:10-11; Acts 15:17)
15. Animal Sacrifices	15. Spiritual Sacrifices (Psalms 27:6; 116:17; 1Peter 2:3-5; Hebrews 13:16)
16. Standing Afar Off	16. Standing in the Presence of the Lord (Psalm 135:1-2; 2Chronicles 29:11; Revelation 7:11)
17. Kneel before the Lord	17. Kneeling and Bowing before the Lord (2Chronicles 6:13-14; Psalm 95:6; Mark 10:17)
18. Said "Amen" to Curses	18. Said "Amen" in Blessing (1Chronicles 16:36; 1Corinthians 14:16).

In Summary:

The truth of the Tabernacle of David is indeed a wonderful truth, and it is a great foreshadowing of the Gospel Age. It is a truth that has been, either not seen or neglected over many years. Some of the expositors of previous decades have seen this truth and its foreshadowing of the Church Age and the coming in both Jews and Gentiles into the kingdom of God through Christ.

For the diligent student, reference is made to various textbooks and commentaries that deal with the Tabernacle of David as a foreshadowing the Gospel Dispensation.

Philip Mauro - "**The Hope of Israel**"

Jamieson, Fausett & Brown, **Commentary on the Whole Bible**

Matthew Henry, **Commentary on the Whole Bible**

The Pulpit Commentary.

The truths pertaining to "the sacrifice of praise", and the various expressions of worship and praise may all be found in the typical/symbolic and prophetic foreshadowings as in the Tabernacle of David. Into it both Jews and Gentiles come and worship together in spirit and in truth!

CHAPTER THIRTY-SEVEN

A CATECHISM OF "WORSHIP AND PRAISE"

Closely related and belonging to the whole truth of "**The Sacrifice of Praise**", and the "**Restoration of the Tabernacle of David**" is the area of "Worship and Praise".

Many of the Churches which entered into the visitation of 1948 and the relevant truths were grouped as "Revival Fellowship Churches, especially along the West Coast of America. Out of that Fellowship of Churches came "**A Catechism of Worship and Praise**" which was used in most of, if not all of their congregations.

It is indeed one of the most important subjects in Scripture because God created man for worship and for His pleasure (Revelation 4:11). The times of worship and praise became a great key in the services, because true worship and genuine praise made way for the Lord to manifest His presence and release His power in the services. It was because of this that the "**Catechism of Worship and Praise**" was developed.

The word "Catechism" (SC 2727, "**Katecheo**") means "to sound down into the ears, ie., by implic. to indoctrinate ("catechize"), or, gen. to apprize of" and it translated in the AV as "inform" (Acts 21:21,24), "instruct" (Luke 1:4; Acts 18:25; Romans 2:18), and "teach" (1Corinthians 14:19; Galatians 6:6,6).

Abraham had 318 servants "trained" ("catechized") in his own house for battle against marauding tribes (SC 2593); that is "initiated, practised. trained". Abraham used these servants trained in his own house to rescue Lot in the battle of kings.

Collins' Dictionary defines "Catechism" as meaning "to instruct by asking questions and correcting the answers", especially in religious doctrine. It is a elementary book containing a summary of facts or principles in the form of questions and answers. The purpose of this chapter is to set out the general form of catechism that has been used in these Churches for instructing the congregations in the truth of worship and praise to the Lord.

A. Is Worship and Praise Important?

1. Yes! God created man to be a worshipper and to praise Him (Matthew 4:10; Isaiah 61:3; Revelation 1:6; 20:6; Exodus 19:6.

2. Satan knows the value of worship and desired to receive worship that is only due to God. He tempted Jesus to worship him (Matthew 4:10). The world ends up in the Book of Revelation in Devil worship. This is evident by the numerous Satanist Churches in our generation (Revelation 13).

3. Paul confessed that he worshipped God according to how the Old Testament Scripture taught (Acts 24:14).

B. How are we to Worship and Praise God?

1. We are to worship in spirit (John 4:20-24).

2. We are to worship in truth (John 4:24; 8:32; 17:17).

3. We are to worship with the whole heart (Psalm 111:1; 9:11).

4. Worship is not to be after the traditions of men (Mark 7:7-9).

C. **What does Worship and Praise Signify?**

1. It signifies that believers are called to be priests unto God (2Chronicles 29:11; 1Peter 2:5; Revelation 1:6; 5:9-10).

2. It signifies that as priests, believers are to offer spiritual sacrifices to God through Christ (1Peter 2:5; Romans 12:1; 2Samuel 24:24). The reader is referred to the spiritual sacrifices in a previous chapter.

D. **How should we Worship and Praise God?**

1. God Himself has ordained the way to come into His presence. He tells us to enter in through the gates of praise (Psalm 100:4; Isaiah 60:18; 62:7).

2. God inhabits ("lives in" or "is enthroned in") the praises of His people (Psalm 22:3).

3. Our praise ascends as incense to the Lord (Psalm 141:1-2).

4. Worship brings the presence of God and His refreshing to the people of God (Job 36:27; Psalm 89:15; 2Chronicles 5:13-15; 20:19-21).

5. Worship and praise glorifies God (Psalm 50:23).

6. Worship and praise fulfill the prophetic word (Psalm 102:13-18; Isaiah 12:4).

7. This is a sign that God has released His people from spiritual captivity (Jeremiah 33:11; Psalm 126; Psalm 137).

8. True worship changes the worshipper into the image of God (Psalm 115:8; 106:19-20; Romans 1:21-23; 2 Corinthians 3:18). The principle is: We become like the God we worship!

9. The Lord promised to meet with His people in the sacrifice of praise, as they offer it in true heart to Him (Exodus 29:41-42).

10. Praise is God's garment to us (Isaiah 61:3), and has a purifying power in the life of a believer (Proverbs 27:21; Malachi 3:2,5).

E. **Why should we Worship and Praise the Lord?**

1. Because it shows forth God's praise (Psalm 9:14).

2. Because God is worthy to be praised (Psalm 18:3).

3. Because praise glorifies God (Psalm 50:23).

4. Because of God's loving kindness (Psalm 63:3-4).

5. Because all God's people are called to praise Him (Psalm 67:3)

6. Because it is a good thing to sing praise (Psalm 92:1-4).

7. Because God creates generations to praise Him (Psalm 102:18).

8. Because praise is the gateway into God's presence (Isaiah 60:18; 62:10-12; Psalm 87:2; 100:1-4).

9. Because praise wins battles under God (2Chronicles 20:21-22; Acts16:25-26).

F. **Who is to Worship and Praise God?**

1. The servants of the Lord (Psalm 134:1; 113:1; 103:21).

2. The nations of the earth (Psalm 117:1; 22:23,26; 132:9; 145:10; Nehemiah 12:43)

3. The heavens and the earth (Psalm 69:34; 89:5).

4. The living who breathe are to praise Him (Psalm 150:6; 115:17; Isaiah 38:19).

G. **When are we to Worship and Praise the Lord?**

1. At all times (Psalm 34:1).

2. Continually (Psalm 35:27; Hebrews 13:15; Luke 24:53; Ephesians 5:18-20).

3. Every day (Psalm 146:1-3).

4. While we have any being (Psalm 146:1-3; 45:17; 70:4; 71:6; 104:33; 119:164).

H. **Where are we to Worship and Praise the Lord?**

1. In our homes (Psalm 149:5).

2. In the congregation (Psalm 22:22; 35:18; 100:2-4; 111:1; 134:2; 135:1-2).

3. In the world, even before unbelievers (Psalm 40:3; 126:2; Acts 16:25-34).

I. **In what Ways are we to Worship or Praise the Lord?**

We are to worship and praise the Lord according to His Word (Psalm 119:25,37). We are to love the Lord with all our **heart** (spiritually), and **soul** (emotionally), and **mind** (intelligently) and **strength** (physically). The whole being is to be involved in worshipping God (Matthew 22:36-40; Mark 12:28-31).

The Psalms, as well as other Scriptures, provide nine ways and expressions by which we can praise or worship the Lord.

1. **The Mouth**
   - (1. Audible Praise (Psalm 34:1; 40:3,16; 42:4; 66:9; 149:6).
   - (2. Singing (Psalm 47:6; 33:3; 61:8; 100:4; 104:33; 147:1).
   - (3. Shouting (Psalm 5:11; 27:6; 32:11; 35:37; 132:9; Isaiah 12:6).

2. **The Hands**
   - (4. Lifting Hands (Psalm 63:4; 141:2; 119:48; 2Timothy 2:8).
   - (5. Clapping Hands (Psalm 47:1; 98:8).
   - (6. Musical Instruments (Psalm 33:2,3; 57:8; 150; 2Chronicles 5).

3. **The Body**
   - (7. Standing (Psalm 133:2; 134:1; 135:1-2).
   - (8. Dancing (Psalm 30:11; 149:3; 150:4; Luke 15:25).
   - (9. Kneeling, Bowing (Psalm 95:6).

Restoration Theology

It is possible for a congregation to fall into the use of religious cliches, where Biblical words become meaningless to believers. This is true when it comes to the matter of worship and praise. It is necessary and helpful to understand the distinctions as well as the inter-relatedness of "worship" and "praise". By understanding these distinctions, it will be seen that it is possible to be "a praiser" but not "a worshipper". The Lord wants both worship and praise from His people. The ultimate purpose of praise really is to lead one to worship! Let us consider these distinctions as seen in Old and New Testaments.

1. **The Old Testament**

    In the Old Testament there are a number of words translated "**praise**". The most prominent words are:

    (a) "**Yadah**" (SC 3034), meaning "to use or hold out the hand, to revere, to worship with extended hands" (Psalm 118:19,21;28; 138:1,2).

    (b) "**Towdah**" (SC 8426, which comes from SC 3034), meaning, "an extension of the hand, by implic. avowal, or usually adoration, specially a choir of worshippers. It is translated by the words "confession, sacrifice of praise, thanksgiving and thank-offering" (Psalm 42:4; 50:23; Jeremiah 17:26).

    (c) "**Shabach**" (SC 7623, 7624), meaning "to address in a loud tone, to adulate, to adore" (Psalm 117:1; 147:12).

    (d) "**Zamar**" (SC 2167), from the idea of striking with the fingers, to touch the strings or parts of a musical instrument; ie., play upon it, to make music; accompanied by the voice, hence to celebrate in song and music. The word is translated, "give praise, sing forth praises, psalms" (Psalm 9:11; 47:6; 98:4,5).

    Two important words in the Old Testament translated "**worship**" are:

    (a) "**Shachah**" (SC 7812), meaning, "to depress, ie., prostrate, in homage to royalty, to God. It is translated as "bow self down, crouch, fall down flat, humbly beseech, do reverence, make to stoop, worship" (Exodus 33:10; Zechariah 14:16-17).

    (b) "**Cagad**" (SC 5457, as SC 5456), "to prostrate oneself (in homage), to fall down, worship" (Daniel 3:5,6,10,11).

2. **The New Testament**

    The major words for "praise" in the New Testament are:

    (a) "**Aineo**" (SC 134, 133, 136), and simply means "to praise God, a praising, a thank-offering" (Luke 2:13,20; 19:37; Romans 15:11; Revelation 19:5; and Hebrews 13:5.

    (b) "**Humneo**" (SC 5214, 5215), meaning, "to hymn, ie., sing a religious ode, by implic. to celebrate God in song". It is translated, "sing a hymn" ("praise unto"). Read Hebrews 2:12; Matthew 26:30; Acts 16:25; Ephesians 5:19; Colossians 3:16.

    The major word for "worship" in the New Testament is:

(c) **"Proskuneo"** (SC 4352), meaning to kiss, like a dog licking his master's hand; to fawn or crouch (lit. or fig.), prostrate oneself in homage (do reverence to, adore), and is translated "worship" (Revelation 7:11; 11:1,16; 19:4; John 4:20-24). Every worship scene in Revelation depicts this prostration before the Lord.

Over the years of "Pentecostal" styles of worship and praise to the Lord, there were different opinions as to whether saints should shout or sing their praises to the Lord. Some would shout "Praise the Lord", or shout "Hallelujah". The 1948 visitation onwards brought out "Singing praise" to the Lord, or, "Spontaneous praise" from the heart. Saying praise and singing praise are both Scriptural. It is worthy to note that the Psalms speak of **"singing praises"** to the Lord about seventy times (Psalm 47).

In Summary:

1. **Praise** = The expression of thanks, gratitude and applause for the goodness of God. Praise is appreciation to the Lord **for all He has done**. Praise finds expression in most of the nine ways (or other) as listed above.

2. **Worship** = The adoration and devotion of the heart, and the deep prostration of the spirit before the Lord. It is the bowing down in total love and reverence before Him. Worship is loving God, not just for what He has done for us, but entirely **for who He is**.

The congregation should be both a praising and a worshipping people. There should be times of praise, and times of worship. As mentioned earlier in this chapter, it is possible to be "a praiser" but not "a worshipper". Many times God's people praise the Lord for what He had done for them, but not always worship Him just for who He is! The Lord wants both, but all praise should ultimately lead to worship!

Restoration Theology

CHAPTER THIRTY-EIGHT

RESTORATION-KINGDOM TRUTH

It was over the years, AD1960-1970's and onwards into the '80's that the Holy Spirit moved afresh on many hungry people. This time, however, it was among mainline and historic denominations. This became known as "the Charismatic Movement".

Also, inter-related with this fresh movement of the Spirit, there was another fresh emphasis on truth, a truth with its many facets, a truth which had been misunderstood, misplaced and had suffered much misinterpretation. This was truth pertaining to the Kingdom of God. But these things are for our consideration in this present chapter.

A. The Charismatic Movement

Dr. Bill Hamon noted in **"The Eternal Church"** (pages 269-280):

* The Protestant Movement mainly affected the Catholics; the Holiness Movement mainly affected the Historic Protestants; the Pentecostal Movement ("Early Rain") mainly affected the Holiness Movement, and the "Latter Rain" Movement mainly affected the Pentecostal Movement.

But what became known as the "Charismatic Movement" actually affected all groups to a greater or lesser extent. The ripple effect of the movement of the Holy Spirit touched many groups. The rain of God's Spirit was being poured out on "all flesh" regardless of denomination (Joel 2:23; Acts 2:17). This was seen in the many who received the Holy Spirit baptism with the accompanying evidence of speaking in other tongues (Acts 2:4).

It was during the 1960-1970's and onwards, that it seemed that God allowed "the word of the Lord to come a second time" to the older denominations who had once rejected the outpouring of the Holy Spirit as in Acts 2 (Note: Jonah 2:1-2). The Lord used various ministers from the Pentecostal stream to have input into these various denominations. God moved by His Spirit and touched Historic Churches such as, the Episcopal, Lutheran, Reformed, United Methodist, Catholic, Baptist, as well as other denominations. Leaders in these historic denominations were baptized in the Holy Spirit and spoke with other tongues, and these are too many to mention by name here.

Dr. Bill Hamon, in his textbook, goes on to mention that most of the leaders who received the Holy Spirit according to Acts 2:4, did not want to be associated or branded with the "Pentecostalists speaking in tongues". They, therefore, coined other words and used Greek words, **"Charismata"**, for the gift of the Holy Spirit, and **"Glossolalia"** for speaking in tongues. They described themselves "as those who had received the "charismata" of the Holy Spirit accompanied with "glossolalia" (Bill Hamon, page 273). A new vocabulary was used. "Speaking in tongues", and "other tongues", or "baptism of the Holy Spirit" became "prayer and praise language", or "the language of the Spirit", or "praying with the Spirit". It was the same experiential truth but different terminology was used to explain the gift of the Holy Spirit.

Thousands of people from the historic denominations flocked to Charismatic Conferences with a variety of notable speakers from various denominations, Protestant, Catholic and Pentecostal.

For a number of years, there were groups within these historic denominations, such as, Methodist Charismatics, Lutheran Charismatics, Presbyterian Charismatics, Catholic Charismatics, Baptist Charismatics, Salvation Army, Charismatics, Episcopal and other charismatics. These Conferences were spoken as "Charismatic or Renewal Conferences" and many of these denominations had "renewal services" in their own settings. For many of them it was like the Lord pouring "new wine" into the "old denominational wineskin" (Luke 5:36-39). This however, was not to last, as will be seen.

B. Kingdom Truth Emphasis

No only was there a fresh outpouring of the Holy Spirit on so many mainline and historic denominations over these years (not all accepting it, of course), there was, as already mentioned, another emphasis on a lost, forgotten or neglected truth. This was the emphasis which came on the "**Kingdom of God**" and relevant truths and the responsibility of the Church in that Kingdom!

There were a number of men in the whole of the Charismatic scene, but five men in particular became notable men amidst great controversy that was caused over the emphases relative to the kingdom of God teaching. These men were Charles Simpson, Don Basham, Derek Prince, Bob Mumford and Ern Baxter. All five men were for some years situated at Ft. Lauderdale, Florida.

The major truth emphasized was the Kingdom of God and interwoven with this were other related truths, such as Demonology, Discipleship, Church Structure, Cell Groups, Covenant Relationships, Shepherding, the Church and the Kingdom! These truths were preached and taught and propagated by conferences, tapes, books and magazines, such as "New Wine" and "Restore" magazines.

The Pentecostal Church world, as well as the mainline historic denominations, basically believed in some of these things. At least they saw Biblical base for them. However, the great controversies, confusion and chaos that resulted was, not necessarily from the **truth** but the **methods** used and applied to people's lives!

All Bible believing Churches believe in the truth of discipleship, but it is or was the method of discipleship which created problems. All Bible believing Churches believe in the truth of shepherding the people of God. It was many of the methods used to shepherd people that became the area of much chaos and confusion. The same is true of covenant relationship. All true believers know the Bible is a covenant book, and God desires covenantal relationship between Himself and His people. The issue is, all believers are (or should recognize) that they are already in New Covenant relationship, and there is no need to make any extra-Biblical covenant. It was by this latter method of covenant-making that many people were hurt and lives ruined.

The area of demon deliverance probably was one of the most controversial areas, especially when it came to the matter of truly born-again and Spirit-filled believers being "possessed by demons". Many lives, however, were helped by some of the areas of teaching. At the same time, many became confused because of it.

There was much misunderstanding about the kingdom of God, and the relationship of the Church to the Kingdom. Ultra-Dispensationalism had robbed the Church of the aspect of the "kingdom now" by postponing it to the future. The Church has been robbed of kingdom truth by reason of teaching that "the Church is a Gentile" thing, and the "kingdom is a Jewish" thing.

It was under these ministries as well as others, that these truths were given fresh emphasis. But as has happened in Church History, much was taken to extreme by implication doctrinally, and then in method and the practical application of these facets of the kingdom of God. It has to be remembered, that truth is still truth, regardless of extreme positions that may be taken, and it is the truth that must be sought after.

It has taken some years for these issues and extremes in teaching and in practice to be "ironed out"and come to a more Biblical balance in approaching these subjects.

As can be understood, each of these teachings are vast areas in themselves, but for the purpose of this text, each will be considered in brief and as they are linked to the major theme - the kingdom of God

1. The Kingdom of God and Discipleship

Over the 60's-70's there was a great emphasis on "discipleship". Much extreme and immaturity was seen in, what was called "the Discipleship Movement". Much controversy took place and while many lives were changed, many people were hurt and sometimes destroyed by these extremes. As said before, it is not necessarily the truth of discipleship, but the methods of discipleship use that became the problem. It is more the application of truth that is the problem, not the truth itself. In due time, balance came back, reconciliation was made, and most of the extremes settled. Discipleship, however, is a truth in God's Word.

(a) The Great Commission is to "teach" or make disciples of all nations, as Jesus said to His disciples (Matthew 28:15-20).

(b) John the Baptist had disciples (John 1:35-37).

(c) Jesus had disciples (Matthew 10:1-10; Luke 14:27).

(d) The early Church discipled many people (Acts 14:21, "teach").

(e) Old Testament prophets, at times, had disciples (Isaiah 8:16).

The word "disciple" means "one that is taught, or trained; a learner, a pupil". It involves being enrolled as a scholar, to be instructed, to be taught. It speaks of one following a teacher, one that accepts the instruction from another.

It is training which develops self-control, character, submission, orderly conduct and discipline (Mark 4:34; Luke 10:23-24; 6:40; Matthew 10:24-26).

New Testament discipleship involves (1) Counting the cost, (2) Self-denial, (3) Taking up the cross, and (4) Following Christ whole-heartedly (Luke 14:25-33; 9:57-62; John 8:31; Mark 6:1; Matthew 16:24-25). Every believer is called to be a disciple of Christ, and leaders are to train and teach disciples to follow Christ. This is the fulfilling of the great commission.

2. The Kingdom of God and Demon Deliverance

During the 60's-70's there was an emphasis on the matter of "deliverance from demons". Great controversy came over whether a truly born-again and Spirit filled believer could be "demon possessed" or not, and if so, they would need deliverance. In some situations, every evil thought, word, deed or motive was attributed to some demon. Other leaders believed that it was not possible for a truly born-again and Spirit filled believer to have demonic possession, as they were protected by the blood of Jesus Christ. "In due time, by the mid 1970's most Charismatics had developed a balanced doctrine and practice concerning demonology" (Bill Hamon).

The Scriptures do speak of the ministry of deliverance.

1. Jesus was anointed to bring deliverance to the captives. This was also part of His ministry as He Himself declared in Luke 4:18-19.

2. He delegated His authority to the Twelve also (Matthew 10:1-8; Luke 9:1; Mark 3:15; 6:7,13).

3. He delegated His authority to the Seventy also (Luke 10:18-19).

4. He delegated authority to the Church and to believers individually to cast out demons and heal the sick as the Gospel is preached (Mark 16:15-20; Acts 19:13-18; Matthew 28:15-20).

The Gospel of the kingdom is to preach the Word, heal the sick and cast out demons (Matthew 2:14). With the increase of Satan worship, the occult, many unsaved will indeed need deliverance from demonic powers as they come into the kingdom of God.

The Christian may be oppressed (Acts 10:38), or bound (Luke 13:16), or even be deceived and troubled by evil spirits (1Samuel 16:14; Matthew 24:4,5,11,24), but truly born-again and Spirit-filled believers cannot be demon possessed. It is the word "possession" that is the issue.

Christ conquered Satan and all principalities and powers. A Christian is to be clothed in the whole armour of God, and use his spiritual weapons of warfare to overcome Satan and the demonic realm. God has given His Word, His blood, His name, His Spirit, His power and His gifts in order for the Christian to be victorious in the midst of a lost world.

3. The Kingdom of God and Shepherding

Inter-related with Discipleship, Deliverance was the whole subject of the "Shepherding Community". This facet touched the whole of Church structure, the caring for people, as the flock of God.

It was seen that the traditional "one-man" ministry in trying to care for numerous sheep was not God's will. The emphasis came upon smaller groups, "cell-groups", where people could be cared for, shepherded, on a smaller scale. This also was branded as "the Shepherding Movement".

As with the other facets of truth, many extremes developed. People were both blessed and some destroyed. In due time, balance in doctrine and practice came. But shepherding the people of God is still a Biblical truth.

The greatest chapters in Scripture on "Shepherding" are to found in Ezekiel 34; John 10; Acts 20; Psalm 23 and 1Peter 5.

All ministers should have the heart of THE Shepherd-Christ, and care for the people of God, without control. Not only do shepherds care for sheep, sheep care for the lambs they bring to birth. In these great chapters, the Lord spells out the responsibility of both shepherd and sheep.

There are many textbooks written on the role of the pastoral or shepherding ministries.One of the key chapters in the whole of the shepherding-teaching was Exodus 18. This is spoken of as "the Jethro principle", Here Moses, by a word of wisdom from Jethro, set rulers over the tens, the hundreds, the thousands of Israel. Some were over thousands, some over hundreds, some over fifties, and some over tens. The rulers were entrusted with as many people as they could handle, according to their ability. So the Lord entrusts His leaders in this day with as many sheep as they can handle.

Emphasis came on the "cell-meeting", or "the house-church". This concept was "seeded" back in the 1960's. It is an increasing concept and practice in the Church on a worldwide manner. Korea, South America, Latin countries, as well as the Western world - all have taken the concept and are seeking to follow it in practical care for the people of God. No one ministry can meet everybody's needs and feed everyone. This makes room for the need of under-shepherds.

Jesus was **preaching and teaching** the Gospel of the kingdom, and **healing** the sick. He was moved with compassion on the multitudes when He saw them as **sheep without a shepherd** (Matthew 9:35-38). There were plenty of religious leaders; the scribes, the Pharisees, the priests and elders of the synagogues, but they did not have a shepherd's heart and they exploited the sheep. Jesus saw the need of shepherding relative to the kingdom of God message.

The early Church met in the temple (the corporate gathering), and from house to house (the smaller gathering). Paul also taught publicly and from house to house (Acts 2:42-47; 20:20). The early believers did not have large buildings but had numerous "house-churches".

So in a number of nations, in this generation, God is confirming these things as practical ways of shepherding the flock of God. The kingdom of God and the truth of shepherding the people of God is a Biblical concept, and can be believed, taught and practiced with blessing and life, as long as it is done within Biblical safeguards.

4. The Kingdom of God and Covenant

Inter-related with Discipleship and Shepherding was woven the concept of "Covenant relationships" - another Biblical truth. As with the other facets of truth, so with this. Every time God recovers or quickens aspects of truth, human nature takes it to its extremes. The pendulum of the clock swings to either extreme both in doctrine and in practice. The truth of "covenant" was no exception. Many people entered into "covenantal relationships" with each other or their leaders.

Don Basham defined in a comprehensive statement what these ministries at Ft.Lauderdale meant by "**A Covenant Community**". He writes:

"A Covenant Community of God's redeemed people bound together in covenant love, submitted to compassionate authority and rulership and manifesting peace, holiness and family fidelity expressed through revered fatherhood, cherished woman and motherhood with secure and obedient children. A community where loving correction and instruction produces healthy growth and maturity, where dedication to excellence produces the finest results in arts, crafts, trades and commerce, providing prosperity and abundance for all its members. A community of faith, worship, praise and a selfless ministry manifesting individually and corporately the gifts and fruit of the Holy Spirit. A community where all life is inspired and directed by the Spirit of Jesus Christ and is lived to His glory as a witness and testimony to the world." (**Restore Magazine**, 1964, Australia).

In due time, extreme teaching and practices of "covenant relationships" balanced out, although many of God's people were hurt by these extremes.

The Bible is indeed a covenant book. God is a covenant-making and covenant-keeping God. The revelation of covenant is a neglected truth, especially in the Western Christian world.

All Christians are in covenant relationship with God through Christ and are also in covenant relationship with all true believers in Christ (Matthew 26:26-28; Jeremiah 31:31-34; Hebrews 8:6-13). There is great need for understanding of covenant relationship in the Body of Christ. There is no need to make any covenant beyond the already-made **NEW Covenant**, but there is much need for teaching and understanding of relationship in that New Covenant.

Each time believers meet at the table of the Lord, it is a covenant table in which each partake together and should go and live out covenant relationship, and, not be like Judas, who partook of covenant and betrayed His Lord and his fellow apostles (Matthew 26:26-28; 1Corinthians 11:23-34).

This was another facet of truth that the Lord brought to the attention of His Church. In spite of extremes, truth is still truth and the truth of covenant remains.

5. The Kingdom of God and the Church

Another emphasis that came in the Charismatic Movement was that which pertained to "the Kingdom" and "the Church".

There is much misunderstanding and misinterpretation of the subject of the kingdom and the church. It has become one of the great areas of controversy and confusion. Many do not see the distinction and yet relationship of kingdom and church.

Dispensationalists speak of the kingdom as a Jewish thing and the church as being a parenthetical plan of God after the Jews rejected the king, Jesus Christ.

Dispensationalism teaches that the kingdom of God was postponed during the dispensation of the Holy Spirit, and that the Church is God's temporary purpose in this period of time of Jewish unbelief. However, this is far from the truth of Scripture.

It is not the purpose of this text to provide a full study on the "Kingdom and the Church", but enough outline will be given to help clarify the confusion that Dispensationalists have caused through misunderstanding and faulty hermeneutics.

(a) The word "kingdom" is made up of two words: "King's Domain", hence, King-Dom. It is the territory or area over which a king rules and reigns. God's kingdom is the reign or rule of God, whether in heaven or earth. The Greek word, "**Basileia**" speaks of the sway and administration of a king. The kingdom of God also includes, not only the territory but also the subjects in the kingdom who are ruled over by the king. The "kingdom" is used about 160 times in the New Testament.

(b) The kingdom is everlasting (Psalm 145:10,13; 103:19; Daniel 4:3). There has never been a time when the kingdom of God has not been in existence. It has neither beginning nor end. The King is eternal.

(c) The kingdom of God is sovereign, ruling over the kingdoms of this world (Psalm 103:19; Revelation 11:5).

(d) The kingdom of God is all-inclusive, including in itself, its domain, the total universe, the elect angels, heaven, the fallen angels, and all creatures and mankind on this earth. All are under His control and dominion. None could exist or act without His sustaining power (Psalm 103:19; Exodus 15:18; Psalm 145:10-13).

(e) The "kingdom of God" and the "kingdom of heaven" are one and the same thing, as a comparison of these several example Scriptures show (Matthew 23:22; Matthew 4:17 with Mark 1:4; Matthew 5:3 with Luke 6:20; Matthew 13:11,31 with Luke 8:10; 13:18,19). Other Scriptures could be given.

(f) Jesus preached the Gospel of the kingdom (Matthew 4:23; Mark 1:14).

(g) Jesus taught the kingdom was at hand and He told His disciples to preach that same Gospel (Matthew 4:17; 10:7; Luke 9:2; 10:9-11).

(h) Jesus taught His disciples to pray, "Your kingdom come" (Matthew 6:6-9).

(i) Jesus said He would build His Church and promised Peter the keys of the kingdom (Matthew 16:15-29). In these verses we see some distinction, and yet inter-relatedness between the kingdom and the Church.

The truth which came into sharper focus over the 1960's and onwards was the clear distinction and yet relationship of **The Kingdom and The Church**! The word "Church" is used some 115 times and "Kingdom" is used some 160 times in the New Testament. For some distinction and yet relatedness between kingdom and the church we note the following.

The Kingdom is eternal and unlimited. It is all encompassing. It encompasses the universe, the angelic hosts, the universe and all mankind, all creation and creatures.

The Church is a manifestation in time of an eternal purpose. The Church includes in itself all the redeemed of all ages, especially believers of the New Testament age, although Israel is spoken of as "the Church in the wilderness"(Acts 7:38). The Church includes in it all believers in both heaven and in earth. Angels are in the kingdom of God but are not in the Church. The Church is limited to the redeemed.

It is **THE CHURCH** that becomes the instrument of God to preach the Gospel of **THE KINGDOM** in all the world for a witness and then the end shall come (Matthew 24:14; 28:18-20). In the Book of Acts we see how the early Church and its leaders and people preached and taught about the kingdom of God.

* Repentance and new birth bring one into the kingdom (Matthew 4:17; John 3:1-5).

* By regeneration one is translated out of the kingdom of darkness into the kingdom of God's dear Son (Colossians 1:13-14). The kingdom is righteousness, peace and joy in the Holy Spirit (Romans 14:17).

* The Church is to preach, teach and demonstrate the Gospel of the Kingdom in all nations (Acts 1:3-6; 8:1,12; 14:22; 19:8; 20:25; 28:23,31). Apostles, evangelists and teachers and believers spoke of the kingdom in the Book of Acts.

* The Church is a kingdom of priests, of which Jesus Christ is the King-Priest after the order of Melchisedek (Revelation 1:6; 5:9-10; Hebrews 7; Psalm 110; 1Peter 2:5-9; Romans 14:17).

* The New Testament shows the "kingdom now, but not yet"(Luke 17:20-21 with Luke 19:11-27).

Therefore, even though the Kingdom and the Church are distinguishable, they are one in the purposes of God. The Church is the instrument in God's hand for the declaration and demonstration of the Kingdom Gospel! This is what the Lord was endeavouring to bring to the attention of His Church more powerfully in the 1960's and onwards. For fuller treatment on "**The Kingdom and The Church**", the reader is referred to "**The Church in the New Testament**", Chapter 6, by the author.

These are the truths God emphasized in the Charismatic Movement. These are the truths God wanted to bring to the attention of His people. In spite of the extremes and imbalance on these things, they are still Biblical truths. For the Charismatic Movement, there was much teaching on the areas of discipleship, deliverance, shepherding, covenant and the kingdom and the church! Many people received these "new wine truths". It looked as if it was possible to renew the "old denominational wineskins". But this was not to be!

C. The Parable of the Wine and Wineskins

In Luke 5:36-39 we have the twin parables of the old garment and the new patch on the old garment, and the old wineskins and the new wine. In both parables, the main lesson is seen that one cannot mix the old and the new. One cannot take new patches of a new garment and sew it on the old, tattered, torn and threadbare kind of garment. One cannot take new wine and pour it into the old, shrivelled, brittle and dry wineskin. The rent is made worse in both parables.

The parable of the new patch and old garment and the new wine and old wineskin was fulfilled once again in the Charismatic Movement. The words "**renewal**" and "**restoration**" were used a lot as synonymous words in their meanings over the 1960 years and onwards. Many believed the Holy Spirit was being poured out on them to revive the old denominational wineskins, which had become dry and brittle with no or little flexibility in it to expand.

That, however, was not the ultimate purpose of the Lord. The Lord wanted to, not only bring **renewal and revival**, but He wanted to bring **restoration of lost truth** or truths to His people. It would be a restoration of all truths which had been lost over the years of Church History.

It is here that the old denominational wineskins stayed. The result was that the old garments were torn as people tried to sew new patches of Divine visitation on them, and the old wineskins burst as they tried to pour in the new wine of God's Spirit and truth into them. Many who had received the new wine of the Holy Spirit left and moved on into some fellowship where they could move on into all the truths which God had restored to the Church. The Charismatic Movement, as a whole, has now retrenched back into their traditional expression and each denomination that once had some Charismatic or "renewal service" have virtually ceased to do so.

This is where it seems to be since the 1980's-1990's and on. Many were blessed, happy and content with the "charimata" and "glossolalia", but some of the restored truths touched too many of their traditions.

Water baptism by immersion, Church government, operation of spiritual gifts, acceptance of the fivefold ascension-gift ministries, and other restored truths - these were too traditional and denominationally shaking to be accepted! It was either to accept or retrench from them.

In Conclusion:

The Charismatic Movement, as many other movements, confirm the truth of these twin parables. It is difficult to put a new patch on the old garment, and to put new wine into the old wineskin. Many say, "the old is better" and reject the new. The old wineskin has no flexibility to expand and so schism comes and the old denominational wineskins burst. The new wine of the Spirit is lost. God has to make another new wineskin that can receive and hold the new wine truths.

History confirms the truth. Movement after movement, denomination after denomination come and go, rise and fall. They begin with that which is fresh from God and end up by becoming an old wineskin, unable to receive the new wine of restored truth. The result? Division, schisms, splits, burst wineskins, torn garments and confusion in so many places around the world are seen. Hardly a denomination in the world has not been affected by fresh awakenings, revivals or outpourings of the Spirit, as well as recovery of fresh or lost truth, that has not brought schism into their movement.

Some denominations have taken "patches" of what God is doing to sew on to their old garment and keep themselves warm. Some have taken some new wine to pour into their old wineskins. But it does not mix. The old and the new do not mix. The garment is torn. The wineskin is burst. One cannot take the portion that suits them and reject God's new garment and God's new wine. God wants to make His people new wineskins to receive the new wine truths. God wants to take away the old garment and give His people a new garment for spiritual warmth! This is the lesson of these twin parables! For fuller treatment of the parables, the reader is referred to "**Mystery Parables of the Kingdom**" by the author.

God's truth continues to march on! Those who are willing to "**buy the truth and sell it not**" realize there is a price to pay but are happy to pay the price for the truth that sets people free (Proverbs 23:23; John 8:32-34).

In the early 1990's there came a fresh moving of the Spirit in a number of places in the world. The emphasis is more distinctly on "refreshing" and revival of believers and churches, renewal in spirit, healing which touches the whole person, spirit, soul and body, and a quickened love for the Lord. This "refreshing" has accompanying manifestations similar to past revivals under John and Charles Wesley, Jonathan Edwards, Charles Finney and other revivalists of their times.

The significant thing to note, however, is that there does not seem to be further recovery of lost truth but mainly refreshing to the people of God. Many are praying that this kind of refreshing will lead to genuine revival in the Church, and that this revival will lead to a great awakening in the world. Church History has proven that **revival in the Church** always precedes **awakening in the world**.

(Refer to Bibliography: "**A History of the Worldwide Awakening of 1992-1995**", by Richard M. Riss and other books dealing with the present Refreshing).

CHAPTER THIRTY-NINE
LOST AND RESTORED

This chapter on "**Lost and Restored**" is used by kind permission of International Church of the Foursquare Gospel, 1910 West Sunset Blvd., Los Angelos, California, 90026-3282, U.S.A. The reader will see the great prophetic significance it has (and still has) on the truth of "**Restoration Theology**". It is reproduced as published by Foursquare Publications. Copyright 1990.

LOST AND RESTORED

or the

DISPENSATION OF THE HOLY SPIRIT FROM THE ASCENSION OF THE LORD JESUS TO HIS COMING DESCENSION

by AIMEE SEMPLE McPHERSON

LOST

"That which the Palmerworm hath left hath the Locust eaten; and that which the Locust hath left hath the Cankerworm eaten; and that which the Cankerworm hath left hath the Caterpillar eaten." Joel 1:4.

RESTORED

"And I will restore to you all the years that the locust hath eaten, the cankerworm, the caterpillar, and the palmerworm, My great army which I sent among you." Joel 2:25.

INTRODUCTION

On the day of Pentecost (Acts 2), Peter in explaining the working of the supernatural power of the Holy Spirit seen upon those filled with the Spirit, quotes from the prophet Joel saying: "It shall come to pass in the last days, saith God, I will pour out of My Spirit upon all flesh, and your sons and your daughters shall prophesy." It was as a direct result of this outpouring of God's spirit, that the message contained in this booklet was given in vision and prophecy under the inspiration and power of the Holy Spirit.

Ten years ago the Lord found me a thoughtless little country girl of seventeen. He not only convicted me of sin, saved and baptized me with the Holy Spirit according to Acts 2:4, but He also called me to leave Father and Mother, houses and lands, high school, and future dreams of earthly popularity, and bade me go into all the world and preach the message of salvation, the Baptism of the Holy Spirit, and the soon coming of the Lord.

Thus it was that before the age of eighteen I found myself preaching the Gospel, weak in myself, but strong in Him. Never having attended any earthly Bible school, I clung to the promise that I was to take no thought for what I should say, but that He would teach me in the needed hour, also that out of my innermost being should flow rivers of living water, knowing that "This He spake of the Spirit," who had come to dwell within me.

Time and space will not here permit me to relate the numerous times and ways the Lord took this poor, ignorant tongue of mine and spoke through me words I had never learned;

without any thought on my part they came rolling out. Vital, forceful, eloquent words poured through my lips not from my head but from my innermost being. While speaking thus with closed eyes and uplifted hands, the tears would stream down my face, and many precious souls flock to the altar seeking salvation and the baptism of the Holy Spirit, and to Jesus belongeth the Glory, for He did it all. Hallelujah!

While in London, England, waiting for the boat in which to embark for China, I was asked by a wealthy man if I would speak to a congregation of people for them that night. Inquiring of the Lord I felt it was His will and told the man that I would go. That evening a beautiful limousine with liveried attendants called for me and I entered with weak and selfconscious steps, crying: "O Lord, do help me to do Thy will tonight." On the way I wondered whether the meeting would be held in a cottage or in a mission hall, and as I gazed with wonder upon the beautiful streets and buildings, the car stopped in front of the most imposing and spacious edifice of all. Thinking that perhaps a small room in this immense building was used for a mission hall, I was hurried up the steps and into the side door of the place.

It seemed that I was led through the door and on to the platform before I had time to realize that this whole building, one big city block square, was packed with people and I was to speak to them at once. I remember vaguely my attendant whispering into my ear that we were late, and then I heard the voice of a man on the platform saying: "Now our sister will speak to us and bring the message." Before I realized it, I was standing dazed and confused before the largest audience I had ever spoken to. The gallery, the balcony, the pit and the rostrum were all filled; there was no seat for me to sit in, and to add to my confusion just then the footlights flashed into brilliancy all around me, and there I stood, a slip of a girl with my Bible in my trembling hands. I have never prepared a sermon in my life, would not know how to go about it, and not a thought came to me; I just lifted my heart to God and silently prayed:

"O God, If you ever helped me in my life help me now!"

Just then something happened: - the power of God went surging through my body, waves of glory and praise swept through my soul, until I forgot the throng of eager faces that had a moment before seemed to swim before me, forgot the footlights, and the learned men with their long tailed coats, forgot that I was only a child of eighteen, and that many there with their grey hair knew more in a moment than I in the natural could know in a lifetime, and "*I was in the Spirit.*"

All this takes a long time to write, but it happened in a moment, for those who put their trust in God shall never be put to shame. My mouth opened, the Lord took control of my tongue, my lips and vocal organs, and began to speak through me, not in tongues but in English. The Spirit spoke in Prophecy, and as He spoke through me I did not know what the next word was to be; certainly the water did flow, not from my head but from the innermost depths of my being, without my having aught to do with it.

As I spoke thus for one hour and a quarter, there did not seem to be a stir in all the vast audience, and as I spoke I saw a vision of a great circle, composed of ten smaller circles *as shown on page four. (Refer Diagram)* This big circle seemed so big that its top reached the sky: it was the dispensation of the Holy Spirit, from its opening on the day of Pentecost, to its closing at the coming of the Lord Jesus. The Vision was so indelibly stamped upon my mind that I had my husband draw it from my description that all may see it as simple and plain as the Lord showed it to me. Before starting to speak, I opened my Bible with closed eyes, trusting God for my text, and my finger was guided to a certain verse; when I opened my eyes and read it this was the verse the Lord had given me:

"That which the palmerworm hath left hath the locust eaten; and that which the locust hath left hath the cankerworm eaten; and that which the cankerworm hath left hath the caterpillar eaten." Joel 1:4.

Just so when I came to the bottom of the circle, and the dark ages were pictured in their horror, my hand automatically turned the page over to the second chapter and placed my finger upon the following verse:

"I will restore to you the years that the locust hath eaten, and the cankerworm, and the caterpillar, and the palmerworm, my great army which I sent you." Joel 2:25.

I have in these pages written the message as it was given the best I can remember it, so as you read forget the poor earthen vessel, forget the present writer, and give the glory to the Lord for it is He, and not I, who is worthy of praise forever.

I am yours, the least of all saints,

Sister Aimee Semple McPherson

THE THREE DISPENSATIONS

Just as there are three in the Godhead: Father, Son and Holy Ghost, so there have been three separate and distinct dispensations or periods of time.

First came the dispensation of the Father as recorded in God's Word throughout the Old Testament from Genesis to Malachi. Throughout the dispensation of the Father, He promised that at the close of this dispensation He would bestow a great gift, even Jesus His only begotten Son, upon the earth, as our Redeemer and the propitiation for our sins. At the close of that period of time God the Father kept His word, and true to His promise gave Jesus, as His great Love gift to the sinner.

Secondly came the dispensation of the Son, as recorded in the four Gospels, Matthew, Mark, Luke and John. Now, just as the Father had a gift to bestow upon the world, even so Jesus, who is our salvation, tells us over and over again that He longs to bestow a gift upon all those who believe on Him, even the gift of the Holy Spirit. All throughout His ministry upon this earth, with ever increasing emphasis, Jesus depicted to His followers the importance of their receiving this gift which He was to bestow upon them when He went away.

Jesus seemed to a certain degree to be limited in the scope of His ministry, was sent only to the lost sheep of the House of Israel, was able to be in only one place at a time, etc., and declared in John 16:7: *"It is expedient for you that I go away, for if I go not away the Comforter will not come unto you; but if I depart I will send Him unto you."* Plainly Jesus thought it more important for us to receive the Holy Spirit than for Himself to stay upon this earth. *Thus* just as the Father kept His promise and sent Jesus His love gift to the sinner, so now in turn Jesus kept His word and prayed the Father to send the Holy Spirit, His gift to the *believer*.

Thirdly came the dispensation of the Holy Spirit which opened on the day of Pentecost. (Acts 2.) This dispensation we are still living in and will be living in until Jesus comes for His waiting Bride.

The days of Jesus' tender ministry upon earth were over. He had eaten the last supper. He had been tried in the sinner's stead and had died in the sinner's place. He had been laid in the lonely tomb, resurrected in power and triumph, had walked forty days upon earth after His resurrection. He had promised for the last time that He would not leave His little ones comfortless, but that He would pray the Father that He would send another Comforter even the Holy Spirit who when He was come would in His office work -

take of the things of Jesus and reveal it unto them (John 16:13),

lead them into all truth (John 16:13),

not speak of Himself but of Jesus (v. 13),

show them things to come (-13),

glorify Jesus (-14),

reprove of sin, of righteousness and of judgment (-8),

teach them all things (John 14:26),

testify of Jesus (John 15:26),

endue them with power from on high (Luke 24:49),

pray through them with groanings that could not be uttered.

The last words of Jesus before His ascension, before the clouds received Him out of their sight, as recorded in Luke 24:49, and Acts 1:8, were concerning the importance of tarrying for and receiving the Comforter whom He would send.

TARRYING FOR THE COMING OF THE HOLY SPIRIT

With glowing hearts and the Master's command, *"Tarry until ye be endued with power from on high,"* still ringing in their ears, the little flock of about a hundred and twenty went their way to the "upper room" in Jerusalem, to await there the advent of the Holy Spirit, the opening of this great, new dispensation of the Spirit sent from Heaven. For ten days they waited. They *"continued with one accord in one place in prayer and supplication."* One accord, O what unbroken harmony is depicted in these simple words. Thomas was not saying to Peter: "Peter, what are you doing here? You denied the Lord thrice, you cursed and swore, the Lord will never baptize you with the Spirit." Peter was not saying to Thomas: "Well, Thomas, what are you doing here? You always were an old doubter anyway, don't think you will receive anything from the Lord." Ah no! they were with one accord in one place in prayer and supplication.

THE COMING OF THE HOLY SPIRIT

(Acts 2:4)

"And when the day of Pentecost was fully come they were all with one accord in one place. And suddenly there came a sound from Heaven." (and bless God, there has been a sound ever since when the Spirit falls and comes in). "From Heaven." (yes, thank God, in spite of what man may say, undoubtedly this sound is from Heaven). *"Like as of a rushing mighty wind, and it filled all the house where they were sitting. And there appeared unto them cloven tongues like as of fire and it sat upon each of them. And they were all filled with the Holy Ghost, and began to speak with other tongues as the Spirit gave them utterance."*

I have often tried to picture the sudden consternation and excitement which surged through the streets of Jerusalem when the hundred and twenty men and women were filled with the Holy Spirit, and burst out shouting and talking in other tongues, so filled that they acted like drunken people; (Acts 2:13). I can seem to see the crowds running up this street, and that, windows flying open, heads thrust out, doors opening, everybody running, devout men gathering up their long ministerial robes and forgetting their dignity, running with the rest to swell the one great question:

"WHAT MEANETH THIS?"

And when this was noised abroad the multitude came together." (Beloved, if the Holy Spirit is falling in your midst you will not need oyster suppers or box socials or Christmas trees to bring the multitude. Your only trouble will be to find seats for the people) *"and were confounded,"* just like you have been perhaps, *"because that every man heard them speak in his own language."* They were amazed, they marvelled, they were in doubt. Sober-minded folk asked the question: *"What meaneth this?"* Mockers declared: *"These men are full of new wine."* O what an uproar! What an excitement! You dear people who dislike confusion and demand things to be done "decently and in order" would have been scandalized.

"But Peter," a new Peter, no longer afraid of the opinions of people, *"Standing up,"* (the Holy Spirit when He endues you with power puts a real stand up for Jesus spirit within you and takes the cowardice out) *"said: these are not drunken as ye suppose . . . but this is that which was spoken by the prophet Joel. And it shall come to pass in the last days, saith God, that I will pour our of My Spirit upon all flesh."* Then as Peter preached that mighty sermon under the power of the Holy Spirit, among other things he told his vast audience to:

"Repent and be baptized every one . . . in the name of Jesus Christ for the remission of sins," and they, too, would "receive the gift of the Holy Spirit." Furthermore, just as though he looked away ahead through the coming years and saw the doubts in some of your minds, Peter declared that *the promise is* "not only *unto you*" but "*unto your children and unto them that are afar off,*" that means you, brother, sister, for he goes on to say, "*even as many as the Lord our God shall call.*" Now, if God has called you, the promise is unto you. How glad I am that the Spirit through Peter drove these nails and clinched them on the other side till there is not the shadow of a loophole for you to thrust the wedge of doubt into.

CIRCLE I.

THE USHERING IN OF THE DISPENSATION OF THE HOLY SPIRIT ACCOMPANIED BY MIGHTY SIGNS AND WONDERS

On the day of Pentecost some three thousand souls were saved. Then we see Peter and John going up to the Temple to pray, pass a lame man at the beautiful gate who asks alms of them. Peter answers: *"Silver and Gold have I none,"* (I do not think the Pentecostal people ever were or ever will be overly blessed with silver or gold) *"but such as I have I give unto thee; in the name of Jesus Christ rise up and walk."* The lame man was healed instantaneously, and whether the priests in the Temple believed in manifestations or not I know not, but at any rate the man went into that Temple walking, leaping and praising God.

In Acts 5:16 we see the multitudes out of the cities round about Jerusalem bringing sick folks and those who were vexed with unclean spirits, and they were healed *every one*. Sick were brought forth into the streets, and laid on beds and couches that at least the shadow of Peter passing by might overshadow some of them. Signs and wonders were wrought everywhere by the hands of the Apostles true to the word of Him who had said, "greater works than these shall ye do because I go to My Father."

While the tree seen in *Circle One* stood in its perfection, the Church stood blazing with the full Pentecostal Power and Glory of the Holy Spirit. Jesus' words were fulfilled, and in deed and in truth they were endued with power from on high. Timid Peter, who had feared a little girl who asked him if he knew Jesus, was timid no longer. Illiterate men and women were turned into flaming evangels.

The outpouring of the Holy Spirit was not unto the Jews alone, but also unto the Gentiles. In Acts 10 we see Peter answering the voice of the Lord who spoke to him through a vision, going down to preach Jesus unto the Gentiles. *While Peter yet spoke the Holy Ghost fell on all that heard the word;* the Jews who came with Peter were astonished that on the Gentiles also was poured out the gifts of the Holy Ghost, *for they heard them speak with tongues and magnify God.*

Again in these wonderful days of the former rain outpouring of the Holy Spirit, we see Saul, on his way to Damascus to persecute the Christians, slain and prostrated in the road by the power of the Spirit, hearing the voice of Jesus saying: "Saul, Saul, why persecutest thou Me?" Later we find Paul not only converted and baptized with the Holy Spirit with the Bible evidence of speaking with other tongues (1Cor. 14:18), but himself preaching salvation and the Baptism of the Holy Spirit. In Acts 19 Paul, finding certain disciples at Ephesus, asks them whether they have received the Holy Ghost since they believed. They tell him "No." They have not even heard whether there was any Holy Ghost. *"And when Paul had laid his hands upon them the Holy Ghost came on them and they spake in tongues and magnified God."* This marvellous manifestation of speaking in other tongues accompanied the infilling of believers with the Holy Spirit everywhere. Simon offered money for the power to bestow that which he saw and *heard*.

THE TREE WITH ITS PERFECT FRUIT

Every gift and Fruit of the Spirit was manifested in the Church till the 9 gifts and the 9 fruits of the Spirit hung as 18 perfect apples upon the perfect tree. *"For to one was given by the Spirit the Word of Wisdom, to another the Word of Knowledge by the same Spirit, to another Faith by the same Spirit, to another the gift of Healing by the same Spirit, to another the working of Miracles, to another Prophecy, to another Discerning of Spirits, to another divers kinds of Tongues, to another the Interpretation of Tongues."* The sick were healed, miracles wrought, and when messages were given in other tongues in the assembly, some one gave the interpretation. (1Cor. 14:27). Each of the nine Fruits was in the Church: Love, Joy, Peace, Gentleness, Goodness, Faith, Meekness, Temperance, Longsuffering, so we have the perfect picture visualized in "Circle 1" of the Chart on the fourth page. (Refer Diagram). Thus ends the first chapter of the early Church History, leaving the tree rooted and grounded in the faith of Jesus every limb, branch, leaf and fruit in perfect power and strength.

CIRCLE II

THE PALMERWORM AT WORK

O glorious days of harmonious love and unity, days when none called aught that he had his own, days when the children of the Lord had all things in common, days when they were beaten and imprisoned, days when prison bonds were broken, signs and wonders were wrought, how we have often wished they might have continued.

These puny minds of ours only feebly grasp events of the past, and are utterly unable to probe the depths of mystery shrouding the future. Unlike us, however, the great mind and eye of the Almighty God beholds the future as clearly as the past. Before His burning eyes of Fire, and the Glory of His presence, darkness turns to day, and the deepest mists are rolled away. Looking thus ahead with clear, unerring eye God saw, and moreover prophesied through the prophet Joel, that the Church would not always retain this glorious state of Power, saw that the palmerworm, the locust, the cankerworm and the caterpillar were going to rob and strip and mutilate and destroy this perfect tree with its gifts and fruits. He saw that the Church, or tree, was going to lose gradually more and more, till it would be left desolate, barren and despairing. The falling away and destruction of the perfect tree did not occur in one day. It was a gradual deterioration accomplished day by day and stage by stage.

One day the palmerworm appeared, eating and destroying as it went, until as the years went by the gifts and fruits of the Spirit began to disappear from view. Not so many sick were healed as of yore, not so many miracles were performed, faith was on the wane, when some one in the assembly had a message in tongues there was no one who had the gift of interpretation, messages in prophecy were not so frequent as of yore. The fruits of unselfish love and joy and peace were also attacked by the palmerworm who grew bolder and bolder day by day. Gradually the eighteen apples began to disappear from the staunch and upright tree which had stood so gloriously heavy laden for many years after the day of Pentecost.

This state of fruitlessness was indeed a condition worthy of lamentation, but the pity of it all is that the devastation did not stop with the havoc wrought by the palmerworm. Other years and other worms took up the work of destruction where the palmerworm had left off, and *"that which the palmerworm hath left hath the locust eaten."*

CIRCLE III

THE LOCUST AT WORK

The work of the locust is of course wrought upon the leaves. Sweeping over vast territories of country, he strips and lays barren all that he touches. Thus not only were the gifts and fruits of the Spirit lost sight of by the vast majority of believers, but the personal incoming and indwelling of the Holy Spirit accompanied by speaking in other tongues was also in a great measure lost sight of. The old time seekers' meetings, the earnest prayer and praise meetings were disappearing; formality and sectarianism were taking their places.

As humility, godliness, and the manifestations of the Holy Spirit vanished, persecution and reproach vanished also. As meetings of the older order were converted into dignified services of a more orthodox form, the Holy Spirit as a gentle dove was quenched and grieved and stifled till He silently withdrew His wonder working manifestations, and joy and gladness were withheld from the sons of men.

Because it meant too great a sacrifice, too much emptying out and humbling in the dust before God, too much seeking and waiting, the Baptism of the Holy Spirit was not received as of old. Then came men who professed to have the Holy Spirit in a new way, i.e., without the Bible seal or evidence of speaking with other tongues as the Spirit gives utterance. This simplified matters greatly, and the professor no longer needed to be a possessor. Thus the Baptism of the Holy Spirit was lost sight of by many, though there always was a remnant of a faithful few Spirit-filled saints through whom God manifested Himself in a real and supernatural way.

It was a sad day when the leaves were thus stripped from the tree and the locust had done its work, but days that were still more sad were to follow, for we read "that which the locust hath left hath the cankerworm eaten."

CIRCLE IV.

THE WORK OF THE CANKERWORM

After the fruit and the leaves had been destroyed, the cankerworm immediately made his appearance and began his work upon the branches and tender shoots of the tree, making cankerous and unsound that God fearing walk of Holiness above the world and sin, so long enjoyed by the children of the Lord. As the sap, the life of the tree, was consumed and the branches became more and more cankerous, and unsound things that used to seem sinful appeared sinful no longer, the world that used to be barred outside the doors of the Church now leaned back in contented languor in the cushioned pews, or sang in the choir.

Christians let down more and more in the high standard of Holiness unto the Lord which they had been holding aloft and now it trailed bedraggled and unnoticed in the dust. Quickly upon the trail of the cankerworm followed the caterpillar, and we read that *"that which the cankerworm hath left hath the caterpillar eaten."*

CIRCLE V.

THE WORK OF THE CATERPILLAR

We are now nearing the bottom of the large circle. The perfect tree is perfect no longer. Stripped of her fruits, denuded of her leaves, her branches made white, laid clean bare, it was not long till the trunk and the roots began to decay and the caterpillar made his nest in the decayed and rotted hollows of the tree.

No tree can eke out its existence without leaves through which to breathe, and its branches and limbs through which the sap of life courses through its veins. For a believer to live without the Holy Spirit, the breath of life, or the Holy life of Jesus as revealed by the Spirit, coursing through his veins, is to eke out a meagre, barren existence nowhere recorded in the Word of God. And now in circle five we see the tree in the most lamentable condition yet described, fruit gone, leaves gone, branches bare, trunk decayed and rotten, a nest for the caterpillar. In other words, the gifts and fruits of the Spirit gone, the Baptism of the Holy Spirit gone, separation and Holiness gone, Justification by Faith gone. Well might the Angels lean over the battlements of Heaven and weep, the noble Church, the perfect tree which had once stood clad with Power and Glory of the Holy Ghost, there remained now naught but a name, not even a remnant of her former splendour, as she entered into the DARK AGES.

CIRCLE VI.

THE DARK AGES

No wonder they are called the Dark Ages. Ah! Dark indeed is the night without Jesus. He is the Light of the world, and when the Church lost sight of Justification by Faith, lost sight of the atonement, the blood of Jesus, there was a total eclipse and the face of the Sun of Righteousness was obscured, and the succeeding years that followed are known as the Dark Ages.

Men and women groping in this gross darkness tried to win their way to Heaven by doing penance, by locking themselves up in dungeons, walking over red hot plowshares in their bare feet, and inflicting unnamable tortures upon themselves and upon one another, blindly trying by some work or deed to pay the debt that had already been paid on Calvary's rugged cross. They had lost sight utterly of the fact that

> "Jesus paid it all
>
> All to Him we owe,
>
> Sin had left a crimson stain,
>
> He washed it white as snow."

The great arrow you see in the chart had been steadily going down and down and down, pitilessly and relentlessly going down as I saw the vision, till it seemed as though it would never reach the bottom. And now it had struck the bottom, the church had lost all, the tree was dead.

Angels might have wept, mortals might have wrung their hands, and their souls have failed within them in utter despair, *but GOD*, Hallelujah, looking on ahead into the future still, had spoken through the prophet Joel (Joel 2:25), saying:

"I will restore to you the years that the locust hath eaten, the cankerworm, the caterpillar, and the palmerworm, my great army which I sent among you." O beloved, do you see it? Then shout aloud and praise Him! Why that was all, ALL, think of it, All that has been lost was to be restored. Hallelujah! What is impossible with man is possible with God.

Now the Church had not lost all this "all" at one time. The restoration came as "meat in due season," as line upon line, precept upon precept, here a little and there a little, till *today* we are nearing the completion of this Restoration, and Jesus is coming soon to take His perfect Church, His Bride, His fruit-laden tree unto Himself, where transplanted from earth to heaven the tree will bloom and yield her fruit by the great River of Life, forever.

No, God did not restore to the Church all at once what she had lost. He was willing to do so to be sure, but they did not have the light at that time. Therefore the last thing that had been lost was the first to be restored. They had had a name that they did live but were dead and therefore must needs repent and do their first works over again before taking any higher step.

CIRCLE VII.

THE YEARS OF THE CATERPILLAR RESTORED

Just before the arrow began to ascend, and the work of Restoration began, we see the scene of ruin depicted by Joel in all its awfulness, in the first chapter of Joel, *the meat offering and the drink offering cut off, the field wasted, the corn wasted, the new wine dried up, garner laid desolate, barns broken down, the beasts groan, the herds of cattle are perplexed, the sheep are made desolate, the rivers of water are dried up, and the fire has devoured the pastures of the wilderness.* Then one day amidst all this desolation God began to move, the treading of His footsteps was heard, and in Circle VII we see the roots of the tree again sinking deep into the earth and Justification by Faith restored. This is the way it all came about:

MARTIN LUTHER

Martin Luther one day was walking up the steps of the cathedral on his hands and knees, over broken glass, endeavouring to do penance, thereby seeking to atone for his sins. As he was toiling painfully and laboriously up the steps in this manner, blood trickling from his hands and knees, cut by the broken glass, he heard a voice from Heaven saying:

"Martin Luther, the Just shall live by Faith."

At the words, a great light fell from Heaven. It banished the darkness and doubts, it illuminated the soul of Martin Luther, and revealed the finished work of Calvary and the blood that alone can atone for sin.

> "For nothing good have I
>
> Whereby Thy grace to claim,
>
> I'll wash my garments white
>
> In the blood of Calvary's Lamb."

The days that followed were eventful days, epoch making days, fraught with self-sacrificing and suffering. The Lord had spoken, and promised that all the years that had been eaten should be restored. Out of the seas of travail and suffering that followed the preaching of Justification by Faith there was born a little body of blood-washed, fire-tried pilgrims, willing to suffer persecution for His name's sake.

You have read perhaps how Martin Luther and his followers were turned out of the churches, spoken against falsely, and accused of all manner of evil. As Martin Luther, Calvin, Knox, Fletcher and many other blessed children of the Lord stood firm for the truths of salvation and a sinless life they suffered all manner of persecution. God's Word says, "They that will live godly shall suffer persecution," (If you or your church profess to live godly and yet never suffer persecution, if you have become popular and the shame and reproach of the cross is gone, there is something radically wrong somewhere, for those who live godly still suffer persecution.)

As the noble tree again put down her roots of justification into the fertile soil-faith, as life again began to surge through the trunk and the limbs of the tree, every demon in Hell seemed to be raging and howling against those who saw and accepted the light of salvation. Martyrs were burned at the stake, stoned to death, swung from public scaffolds, suffered the tortures of the Inquisition, their eyes were put out with hot irons, they were beaten till great gashes were cut in their backs, salt was rubbed into the wounds and they were cast into the dark dungeons still true and unflinching for Jesus. They were tortured in unspeakable ways, beheaded, sent to the guillotine, the Covenanters were driven from hill to hill and often had to hide themselves in caves in order to pray or sing the praises of the Lord, hunted and harassed at every turn.

But God had said *"I will restore the years that have been eaten,"* and in spite of the burning stake, in spite of the blood and fire and the deep waters of tribulation, in spite of the raging of the demons of hell, the great arrow that had so long been going down had at last started upward and was never to stop till it reached the top and the tree was again restored to its perfection.

Persecutions cannot stop God. Floods cannot stay His step, Fire cannot delay His progress. So line upon line, precept upon precept, here a little and there a little, the work of restoration has been going on. Not only did the Lord restore the years the caterpillar had eaten but

CIRCLE VIII.

THE YEARS OF THE CANKERWORM RESTORED

An entire consecration, and holiness unto the Lord were preached; God called out a still more separated people with a deeper realization of what it meant to live a life wholly given up and consecrated to the Lord. The people a step lower always seem to fight the people a step higher. Nevertheless as the work of sifting and separation went on God led His people forth to higher heights.

As one church grew cold, lost their first love, or fought higher truths, they lost out spiritually. As soon as one creed would refuse to walk in the light as given by the Lord, or begin to organize and set up man rule, the Lord simply stepped over their walls and left them to their forms and ceremonies and took with Him the little "called out, out of a called out" flock. In many instances the recording angel had to write upon the door of the fashionable churches -

"Thou hast a name that thou livest, and art dead," or, *"You have a form of godliness, but deny the power thereof."* But the work was not stopped; somewhere people were praying, somewhere hungry hearts were meeting in little cottage prayer meetings, or on the street corners, and the tender shoots and branches were being thrust forth on the tree. Consecration and holiness were being preached and the years of the cankerworm being restored.

JOHN WESLEY

Was a man with a message. He too suffered persecution. Preaching on the street corners in those days, faithful followers were stoned, and rotten egged. They were fought, but not defeated. The power of God was manifested in the dear old Methodist Church, also in *Charles Finney's* meetings in a wonderful manner. Men and women were slain under the power of God. At times the floors were strewn with the slain of the Lord. Signs and wonders accompanied those who preached the "meat in due season."

While these churches lived godly, prayerful, mighty lives in Jesus, they suffered persecution. But when they too began to drift into the same cold, formal state as the others before them, the power and manifestation of the Spirit began to lift from their presence. When supper rooms take the place of upper rooms, and concerts the place of prayer meetings, the Spirit is grieved away. As each body began to organize and throw up walls of difference, God simply stepped over them again and called out another separated people, willing to suffer and sacrifice for Him.

Then came the day when William Booth was called upon to decide whether he would compromise or would follow the greater light God gave him. As he hesitated a moment his wife called from the balcony of that thronged church:

"Say No! William." And William Booth said "No!" and refusing to compromise went forth preaching the message that had been given him. In the early days of the Salvation Army they were unpopular, suffered persecution, were a peculiar people, just as the others before mentioned had been in the beginning. They too were stoned and imprisoned. Some were even martyred, but neither the devil nor his agents could stop God and His work of restoration. In these early days of the Army it was nothing uncommon to see men and women slain under the power of God. Some of their number received the Holy Spirit and spake with other tongues. All night prayer meetings, dancing before the Lord and mighty power were manifested in their midst. True to prophecy, while they lived their separated holy life they were persecuted and unpopular with the world. Then came the Holiness churches wonderfully blessed of God, and the Lord moved in their midst in a mighty manner.

These dear people, many of them, thought that the Lord had now restored all He was going to restore to the Church, and believed that they had all the Lord had for them. *But not so!* God had said, *"I will restore the years that the locust, the cankerworm, the caterpillar and the palmerworm hath eaten."* This necessarily meant A-L-L. Now so far only the years eaten by the caterpillar and the cankerworm had been restored. What about the years eaten by the locust and the palmerworm? When God says "ALL" does He mean *all* or only half? Why, He means all, to be sure. Therefore next

CIRCLE IX

THE YEARS OF THE LOCUST ARE RESTORED

Although in previous years many saints had received the Holy Spirit and spoken in tongues as in Bible days, yet upon the church at large the years which the locust had eaten in Circle III, the baptism of the Holy Spirit, in other words, had not been restored in any great measure. Therefore this was the next to be restored. Peter in quoting from the prophet Joel says, *"In the last days, I will pour out my Spirit upon all flesh."* Joel says that He who gave us the "former rain" moderately, will cause to come down for us the rain, both the former and the "Latter Rain" in the first month.

LATTER RAIN

It was just a few years ago that this latter rain began to fall. Perhaps you recollect the great Welsh Revival, where under the preaching of Evan Roberts, the fire fell. Many were saved, and baptized with the Holy Spirit, those who received the Comforter, the Holy Spirit, spoke with other tongues.

Over in Muki, India, a missionary, Pandita Ramabai, was praying with a band of Hindoo girls. They had spent days and nights in prayer, when suddenly the Spirit was poured out in their midst as He had been on the day of Pentecost. Visible fire is said to have been seen upon girl's bed and when the other girls went for water to extinguish the fire it was discovered that this was the fire of the Holy Spirit, such as Moses saw in the burning bush that was not consumed. These dear Hindoo girls who received the Holy Spirit, spake with other tongues as the Spirit gave them utterance when they received the Holy Spirit. One girl spake in the English language (which she had never learned) and this is the message which was spoken through her:

"Jesus is coming soon, get ready to meet Him". And the great revival spread on and on. Almost simultaneously the Spirit was pouring out in our own United States of America, in England, in Canada, in Africa, upon missionaries in China, and in the islands of the sea. Never was such worldwide revival known to spread so quickly and simultaneously. The Spirit was poured out upon praying bands in numberless places, who had never heard before of the incoming of the Holy Spirit. In every instance, without exception, those who received the Holy Spirit spake in other tongues exactly as those who had received in Bible days had done. The latter rain was falling on the earth.

In order to receive the Holy Spirit one had to be empty, and humble. Poor and rich, black or white, the mistress and the maid alike received the Holy Spirit when they humbled themselves and sought with all their hearts. Those who received, praised the Lord and magnified His name, as no one but Spirit filled saints can do. Waves of glory, floods of praise swept over assemblies who had received the Holy Spirit. There was no way of stopping this great revival, it seemed.

LATTER RAIN TRUTHS FOUGHT

Just as demons and men had fought the restoration of the years eaten by the caterpillar and cankerworm, so now they fought with renewed vigour the restoration of the years that had been eaten by the locust. Again history repeated itself and the saints a step lower, unwilling to humble themselves, fought those who had gone a step higher, and many refused to walk in the light. They failed to realize that God really meant what He had said when He promised to restore "ALL" that had been lost. They lost sight of the fact that the Lord was coming for a perfect church clad with all power and glory of the Spirit. Some even declared that the baptism of the Holy Spirit was not for these days and did not understand that we are still living in the dispensation of the Holy Spirit and will be till Jesus comes.

Preachers jumped to their pulpits and began to condemn those who had received the Holy Spirit in the Bible way; they cried "Wildfire! Excitement! Hypnotism! False Teaching!" etc. All sorts of names were flung at them, and Oh, the blindness of these dear persecutor's eyes! They who themselves had been persecuted for former light of a few years previous, were now themselves persecuting those who were moving on into greater light. Papers were printed to condemn the outpouring of the Spirit, great preachers mounted their platforms and denounced it, but they could no more stop God from restoring the Baptism of the Holy Spirit, and pouring out the latter rain than the former persecutors had been able to stop the restoration of Salvation and Holiness unto the Lord.

THOSE WHO FIGHT THE HOLY SPIRIT LOSE OUT

Those who fought the Holy Spirit, barred their doors or put up umbrellas of unbelief, began to dry up spiritually, immediately. Assemblies and churches that once were on fire for God and preaching Holiness without which no man shall see the Lord, the moment they rejected the Holy Spirit, began to lose their power. O why could they not see that this latter rain outpouring of the Spirit was just what they needed and had been pining for! Why could they not just have humbled themselves and let the Spirit who had been "with them" now come "in" them, making them the Temple of the Holy Ghost! All the fighting and persecution, however, were unable to quench the outpouring of the Spirit, upon those who sought earnestly with pure and humble hearts.

To fight the outpouring of the Holy Spirit was just like a man with a broom in his hand endeavouring to sweep back the tidal waves of the Atlantic Ocean. While he is sweeping it back in one place, it rolls in in countless others; moreover if he remains long where the full tides are rolling in, and does not withdraw, the waves will soon flow over him and he will be "one of them." Hallelujah!

A broom cannot stop the tide of the ocean, neither can fighting stay the falling of the latter rain, for God hath spoken it. "In the last days I will pour out my Spirit upon all flesh." O stop fighting God and open up your hearts to receive and welcome His gift, the Holy Spirit.

During the past twelve years, hundreds of thousands of hungry seekers have received the Holy Spirit.

Thus in Circle 9 on the chart, I saw in my vision, the leaves which had been eaten by the Locust were again restored to the tree. Just as many in Circles 7 and 8 had believed that when the Lord had restored full Salvation and Holiness they had all there was for them, so now many who had received the baptism of the Spirit believed that they had all the Lord had for them. They conscientiously believed that once they had been filled with the Spirit and had spoken with other tongues, they really had all the Lord had for them, and stopped seeking for more.

This, however, had not been all the church had lost, and was therefore not all that was to be restored.

CIRCLE X.

THE YEARS OF THE PALMERWORM RESTORED

Just as the Father bestowed the gift of His only Son Jesus to the world, and just as Jesus bestows the gift of the Holy Spirit, the promise of the Father upon the believer, so now in turn, the Holy Spirit has gifts to bestow upon those who receive Him. The nine gifts and fruits of the Spirit seen in Circle One are again being restored to the tree. Many blessed children of the Lord stop short at salvation and consecration and fail to receive the Holy Spirit, also many who have received the Holy Spirit stop short and fail to covet earnestly the best gifts.

In seeking more of God's will to be wrought in our lives after having received the Holy Spirit, do not ask for more of the Holy Spirit, because if you have received Him you have received all of Him. He is not divisible. Either you have, or have not received the Holy Spirit. Therefore if He has come in and taken up His abode and spoken through you with other tongues, as in Acts 2:4, pray that you may be more yielded to the Spirit who dwells within.

Some one says, "O do not seek the gifts, seek the Giver." But beloved, if you have received the Spirit you have received the Giver, and Paul says *"covet earnestly the best gifts. Seek that you may excel to the edifying of the church. Let him who speaketh in an unknown tongue pray that he may interpret, that the church may be edified; covet to prophesy,"* etc. There is a real, genuine gift of prophecy even though the enemy has tried to imitate it. Discerning of spirits is needed, gifts of healing, etc., should be in our midst.

THE GIFTS AND FRUITS ARE AGAIN APPEARING UPON THE TREE

In circle 10 we see the fruit not yet fully mature, perhaps, but as we pray and yield ourselves to the Spirit, He will divide to every man severally as He will, and cause the gifts and fruits of the Spirit to be visible in our midst.

JESUS IS COMING SOON

Coming for a perfect church, clad in power, in glory, for the perfect tree with every gift and fruit hanging in luscious mellow, developed perfection upon her branches. O let us wake up and press on to perfection! The winter is over and gone, the spring with its former rain has passed, the summer is passing and the latter rain has long been falling. The harvest is at hand and the Master is searching for ripened, developed fruit. Praise God for the roots and trunk of salvation! Praise God for the firm, strong limbs and branches of holiness and consecration! Praise God for the green leaves, for the Holy Spirit, but the Master demands fruit from His tree these last days before His coming. Not green, immature fruit, but perfect fruit. He is whispering just now,

I WILL RESTORE ALL THE YEARS THAT HAVE BEEN EATEN

Dear ones, there is land ahead to be possessed. Let the fruit of Love be wrought out in your life, with Joy, Peace, Long-suffering, Gentleness, Goodness, Faith, Meekness and Temperance. Let us get back to Pentecost, and on to the fullness of Pentecostal power and glory recorded in God's Word, for Jesus is coming soon, very soon, for His perfect, waiting church, His bride, unspotted with the world; His tree with its unblemished and perfect fruit. Soon He will lift us up and transplant us to the heavenly garden where our leaves shall not wither, neither shall the fruit decay.

The arrow is almost to the top now, the hour when Jesus will burst the starry floor of heaven and descend for His beloved is at hand. The great clock of time has almost reached the appointed hour. Let nothing hinder the work of preparation in your life. Let us beware that we quench not the Spirit.

Watch that we do not fall into the same snare which other people formerly used of God have fallen into snares of formality, of coldness and organization, building walls about ourselves and failing to recognize the other members of our body (for by one Spirit are we all baptized into ONE BODY). If ever we put up walls and fall into these snares of formality, God will step over our walls, and choose another people as surely as He did in days of yore. He will not give His glory to another, but will take the foolish to confound the mighty, the weak to confound the strong.

Press on therefore to perfection; do not stop short of God's best. If you lay down your crown, another will take it up, the number will be complete, none will be missing, only those who have pressed on all the way to His Standard will be caught up. If you have been doubting God, doubt no longer. He is waiting to restore all the years that have been eaten, and cause you to stand forth in that glorious perfect tree company, ready and waiting for Jesus.

AMEN.

LOST AND RESTORED

CHAPTER FORTY

RESTORATION IN THE PROPHET JOEL

In Chapter One the Scripture in Acts 3:18-26 was expounded upon. In Peter's second message in Acts he spoke of the "**times of restoration**" of all things which God had spoken by the mouth of all His holy prophets since the world began (Acts 3:21).

In this chapter we consider one of the prophets who spoke of restoration, not only for his generation but also appropriate and applicable in principle to the Church and our generation. Peter in his epistle also tells us that the prophets spoke to their generation but also to our generation as they spoke the word of the Lord (1Peter 1:10-12; 2Peter 1:20-21). The prophets were men of their time but also men for all times.

Paul tells the Corinthian believers that the things which happened to Israel happened to them for types and examples and are written for our admonition, upon whom the ends of the age are come (1Corinthians 10:6,11).

We consider the picture of restoration as set forth in the prophet Joel and as seen in the previous chapter, "**Lost and Restored**". Joel is spoken of as "the prophet of Pentecost". Joel is the prophet who is spoken of by the apostle Peter under the original outpouring of the Holy Spirit in Acts 2 on the Day of Pentecost.

The key verse in Joel is Joel 2:25. The Lord says, "I will restore to you the years ...". It speaks of lost years. Our approach will be "first the natural, then afterwards that which is spiritual" in a brief outline and overview of Joel's prophetic word (1Corinthians 15:46-47). Paul uses this principle in much of his writings.

A. First the Natural

1. Joel Chapter One

In Joel Chapter 1 we see how the Lord allowed famine and desolation to come to His people, Judah. The early and latter rains had been withheld after God's original blessing on the land. God had promised the rains of blessing upon their obedience to His laws (Leviticus 26:3-5; Psalm 65:9-13; Deuteronomy 28:38-42; 1Kings 8:27; 2Chronicles 6:18; Amos 4:9-10; Deuteronomy 8).

If Israel failed to obey the laws of the Lord, then the curse of famine, pestilence and drought and desolation would come on the land. This is the picture Joel provides us in this chapter. The plague of locusts came and destroyed the land and its produce. All the trees of the field had become denuded of beauty and fruitfulness by reason of the plague of locusts.

Joel 1:4 says: "That which the palmerworm has left, the locust has eaten; and that which the locust has left, the cankerworm has eaten, and that which the cankerworm has eaten, the caterpillar has eaten." These all belong to the locust family and represent different kinds of locusts in their various destructive stages.

* The Palmerworm - The gnawing locust.

* The Locust - The swarming locust.

* The Cankerworm - The licking locust.
* The Caterpillar - The consuming locust.

Each become more destructive in their work as it follows the previous. Locust plagues always came as a result of the curse and judgment upon the land because of Israel's sins and violations of the laws of the land (Exodus 10:4-19; Psalm 78:46; 105:34-35; Proverbs 30:27; Deuteronomy 11:1-32).

The various trees of the field and harvest of the earth are mentioned here. So serious is the drought that the priests cannot offer the daily meal and drink offering in the house of the Lord. The whole scene in Joel 1 is desolation!

2. **Joel Chapter Two**

The burden of Joel 2:1-7 is a call to repentance, weeping, fasting, mourning and calling on the Lord (Joel 1:14; 2:12,15). The trumpet sounds (Joel 2:1,15). The trumpets each had a distinct call to the nation of Israel over the years in the land (Numbers 10:1-10; Hosea 5:8; Amos 3:6; Isaiah 58:1). This trumpet call is an alarm and a call to a solemn assembly in deep and genuine repentance - not the external rending of the garments, but the internal rending of the heart (Joel 2:12-13). All are called to be in this solemn assembly regardless of position or status or age (Joel 2:16-17).

The burden of Joel 2:18-32 is restoration. After genuine repentance and turning to the Lord, the Lord visits His people. This visitation is by the rains, the former and the latter rains (Verse 23). The result is the trees blossom and bear fruit, the harvest of the earth is blessed, and God's people rejoice in all that the Lord has done (Verses 24-27).

The key note is in verse 25. "**And I will restore to you the years that the locust hath eaten, the cankerworm, and the caterpiller, and the palmerworm, my great army which I sent among you**". The years in which there were no rains and the years in which the drought and locusts cursed the land were "lost years" They were wasted years, just as the three and a half years of no rain under Elijah's ministry (1Kings 17-18).

There could be no restoration without the rains. Rain meant refreshing, revival, renewal and restoration.

The Lord in verse 25 reverses all that happened in Joel 1:4. "I will restore to you the years that the locust has eaten, the cankerworm, the caterpillar and the palmerworm, My great army which I sent among you".

The Lord promised double rains; former and latter rains. The Lord promised also double harvest; wheat and wine and oil, corn and fruit harvest. Double rains means double harvest. Double rains and harvest was double portion; twice as much as that lost through the drought. The Lord is simply fulfilling the laws of restoration He gave to Israel in the books of Moses.

So great would be the outpouring of the rains on Israel, that God promised a spiritual outpouring of Holy Spirit rains. He promised to pour out His Spirit on all flesh. All this would take place before the coming of the Lord, and whoever called on the name of the Lord would be saved. This would be fulfilled in "the last days" (Joel 2:28-32).

3. Joel Chapter Three

The end result of the restoration and outpouring of the Holy Spirit would be harvest times in the nations of the earth. This is the burden of Joel 3. Multitudes would be in the valley of decision (concision, or threshing). The Lord would put in the sickle and reap the final harvest. As it was in the natural, so it would be in the spiritual.

This is the burden of the prophet Joel for his generation, yet it reaches over to our generation and right through to the coming of the Lord. It is first (interpretation) to His people Israel. It is second (application) to His people, the Church.

B. Afterwards the Spiritual

Here we consider the spiritual lessons applicable to the New Testament Church.

1. The Church is God's field, His garden, His vineyard

God's blessing of rains was upon the early Church, as seen in the Book of Acts. The Church is God's field, His garden and vineyard, His land (1Corinthians 3:9c; Song of Solomon 4:14-16).

2. The Church failed in obedience to God's Word

Over Church History, we have seen the departure from the faith once delivered to the saints (Jude 3). The locust army of unbelief, tradition, paganism, idolatry and apostasy came in and destroyed the Church, leaving a fruitless, barren tree stump, stripped of Divine blessing. The Church declined into the "Dark Ages".

The trees, all having spiritual significance, were laid waste.

* The Vine - symbolic of unity (John 15:1-16).
* The Fig - symbolic of the gifts of the Spirit (1Corinthians 12:1-9).
* The Pomegranate - symbolic of the blood-washed seed, the cross (Ephesians2).
* The Palm - symbolic of righteousness, uprightness (Psalm 92:12; Exodus 15:27).
* The Apple - symbolic of the love and fruit of the Spirit (Song of Solomon 2:3-5).
* The Oil languishing - symbolic of the anointing failing (Luke 4:18; Psalm 133).
* The Meal and Drink Offering - symbolic of communion (1Corinthians 11:23-34).
* The Seed, Corn, Wheat, Barley - symbolic of the Word (Mark 4:28).
* The Pastures - symbolic of freshness for the sheep (Psalm 23; John 10:9).
* The Rivers - symbolic of the flow of the Holy Spirit (John 7:37-39).
* The Wine - symbolic of the joy of the Lord (Acts 2:13).
* The Rains - symbolic of the outpoured Holy Spirit (Amos 4:6-12; James 5:7).

The husbandmen, the ministers, the priests and the elders, representing the leaders of the Church, lamented the condition of God's field, the Church.

3. **The Lost Years of Church History**

   When it is remembered that, from AD400 to AD1500, the Bible as God's Book was forbidden to the people of God, these were surely "lost years". God caused a remnant to come to repentance over the condition of the Church and return to His Word.

4. **The Church in Restoration**

   The Lord had promised to restore to the Church all that had been lost. The restoration did not come all at once. It came line upon line, line upon line, precept upon precept, here a little and there a little. Truth was restored to the Church in portions at a time. The "latter rain" outpouring of the Spirit brought about restoration and recovery of lost truths. All the fruit, the gifts, the ministries and the truths were to be restored to the Church, as seen in previous chapters.

5. **The Church in Harvest Time**

   As God has been and is restoring to the Church the lost years, the lost truths, it has awakened the Church to harvest time. The rains and harvest belong together. No rain meant no restoration; no rains meant no harvests. The harvest is the end of the age, Jesus said (Matthew 13 with Revelation 14). Passover, Pentecost and the Feast of Tabernacles each had rainy seasons and their particular harvest times. So all is to be fulfilled in the Church. This is the message of the Book of Joel.

In the light of these things, it is no wonder that the Holy Spirit caused the apostle Peter to quote Joel 2:28-32 on the Day of Pentecost, the initial outpouring of the Holy Spirit and the birthday of the Church (Acts 2:14-21).

It is no wonder Peter also spoke of "the times of restoration" spoken of by the prophets in the light the prophet Joel's word (Acts 3:18-24).

The Church is living in the days of the latter rain outpouring. The Church is living in the last of the last days. The Church is living in harvest time. The Church is living in days of restoration. Believers are to ask of the Lord rain in the time of the latter rain (Leviticus 26:3-6; Deuteronomy 11:10-17; Amos 4:6-8; Jeremiah 3:1-3; Hosea 6:3; Jeremiah 5:2;4; Deuteronomy 11:4; Zechariah 10:1; Deuteronomy 32:1-2; Isaiah 55:10-11).

The apostle Peter confirms Joel's prophecy in Acts. The apostle James confirms Joel's prophecy in his epistle. He tells us that the Father, as the husbandman, is waiting for the precious fruit of the earth, until He receives the former and the latter rain. This is to be before the second coming of the Lord (James 5:7). The apostle John confirms Joel's prophecy about the sun, moon and stars being darkened before the notable day of the Lord shall come (Joel 2:30-31 with Revelation 6:12-17). Peter, James and John were the chosen three among the Twelve for special revelation in the Lord's earthly ministry. They are also chosen to write epistles to the Church and each confirm the major utterances of the prophet Joel. The Lord Jesus, as head of the Church, used Old Testament prophets with New Testament apostles to confirm the fulfilment of His Word in the Church age, in these last days (2Peter 3:1-2). These are the great lessons of restoration from the Old Testament prophet Joel.

CHAPTER FORTY-ONE

THE OLD TESTAMENT RESTORATION BOOKS

In the Old Testament there are six books that are particularly spoken of as "**Restoration Books**". These books consist of:

1. Three Historical books: Ezra, Esther and Nehemiah, and

2. Three Prophetical books: Haggai, Zechariah and Malachi.

Together they present a great picture of the message of restoration, providing many lessons for the Church on this truth.

The purpose of this chapter is not in any way to provide an exposition of these books but simply to give prominent points of the truth of restoration. We need, however, to go back to the beginning of that which was lost and eventually restored as seen in the Restoration Books!

A. The Former House of the Lord

In the Books of Kings and Chronicles we have the details of the building of God's house, spoken of as the Temple of Solomon (1Kings Chapters 3-8 with 1Chronicles 22-29; 2Chronicles 1-5). These chapters deal with the building of the Temple of the Lord.

In 2Chronicles 5 we have the account of the dedication of the Temple. There we see 120 priests making one sound in praising and thanking the Lord for His goodness and mercy. In the midst of this unity of praise, the glory of God filled the house and no one could minister by reason of the glory of the Lord. Out from the glory came the fire of the Lord and consumed the sacrifices on the altar in the outer court. The Temple of the Lord ministry began in great glory in the Feast of the seventh month, the Feast of Tabernacles. Solomon dedicated the house of the Lord in prayer as "a house of prayer for all nations".

The tragedy is that, over the years of subsequent kings and leaders in Israel, as well as the Aaronic Priesthood, the house of the Lord was neglected. Defilement came into the Temple of God.

In Ezekiel's time, in vision he saw the many abominations that were brought into the Temple. Such caused the glory of the Lord to, step by step, and reluctantly, leave the Temple because of these abominations.

A study of Ezekiel Chapters 8-10 shows the various abominations in God's house (Ezekiel 8:5-6,7-12,13-14,15-16 especially). The glory that Ezekiel had seen in Ezekiel 1 is seen to depart slowly and reluctantly. The glory which Solomon had seen come to the Lord's house, Ezekiel now sees that same glory leave the house. The steps of the departing glory are noted in these passages in Ezekiel.

1. The glory lifts from the cherubim in the Holy of Holies (Ezekiel 9:3).

2. It moves to the threshold of the house (Ezekiel 10:4).

3. The glory moves from the east gate of the Lord's house (Ezekiel 10:18-19).

4. The glory goes beyond the walls of the city and over the brook Kidron, and from the Mt of Olives departs back to heaven (Ezekiel 11:22-23).

As a result of the departing glory (The Shekinah), the Temple became desolate, "the glory has departed", or Ichabod (Read 1Samuel 4). Once this happened, it fell into the hands of the Babylonians, and under Nebuchadnezzar, King of Babylon, the Temple was destroyed. Babylon destroyed the Temple, took the vessels of the house of the Lord into Babylonian Captivity. The people of God were taken captive. Joy was gone. No one could sing the song of the Lord in a strange land, in the land of their captivity (Psalm 137; Psalm 126; Jeremiah 25:10-11).

The Lord, however, said that the Babylonian Captivity would only last for 70 years. After that, He promised that there would be a restoration of the people, the land, and the Temple (Jeremiah 25:11-14; 2Chronicles 36:21,22; Ezra 1:1; Daniel 9:2). All came to pass after the seventy years captivity.

B. The Latter House of the Lord

In the Restoration Books we see the fulfilment of God's promise. There we see the restoration of that which had been lost in the Babylonian Captivity. For the purpose of this chapter we note several major things in the restoration.

1. The Restoration Ministries

In the return from Babylonian Captivity, the Lord raised up, what may be called "restoration ministries". There was Zerubbabel, Ezra, Nehemiah, Joshua, Zechariah and Haggai, and finally Malachi. Though their ministries varied, there was but one vision, one word - that was, Restoration! These various ministries could be likened to the ministries the Lord has set in the Church.

* **Zerubbabel** - He laid the foundation of the temple, and he would finish it. This is significant of the ministry of the apostle who lays the foundation (Zechariah 4:7-10).

* **Zechariah and Haggai**, and years later, **Malachi**, were prophets and these worked with the people and the leadership in the restoration ministry. These certainly speak of the ministry of the prophets in the Church, who work along with the apostles and other leaders in their inspirational and prophetic ministry (Ezra 5:1-2),

* **Ezra** was a scribe and teacher. He was the theologian and hermeneutician of that restoration period. Ezra is spoken of as "the father of hermeneutics" and the general arranger of the Books of the Old Testament. His ministry speaks of the fivefold ascension-gift ministry of the teacher God has set in the Church. He pointed the people back to the Word of God, the law of the Lord (Ezra 9-10 chapters).

* **Nehemiah** was the governor and administrator. His ministry speaks of the necessary ministry of government and administration in the restoration period and the house of the Lord. His burden was the safety of the city, the rebuilding of the walls and gates (Book of Nehemiah). He restored the twelve gates of the city of God, dedicating it with joy and thanksgiving, with the musicians and the singers (Nehemiah 12).

* **Joshua** was the high priest and represented the Temple ministry, the ministry of sacrifice and prayer with intercession for the people. After cleansing he was given the new charge of ministering in the house of the Lord. His ministry points to the priestly ministry in the Church (Zechariah 3).

All these ministries in the restoration books point to the ministries the Lord has set in the Church for the benefit of His people in times of restoration.

2. **The Restoration Message**

   The prophet Isaiah, in his time, lamented about the fact that there was none who brought the message of restoration to the people. He says: **"But this is a people robbed and spoiled: they are all of them snared in holes, and they are shut up in prison houses: they are for a prey, and none delivereth, and none saith, Restore" (Isaiah 42:22).**

   God's people in Isaiah's times were robbed and spoiled by the religious and national leaders. They were snared, like animals, into holes. They were shut up in prison houses and became a prey to be fed upon. No one would deliver them. No one would say 'Restore!'.

   How applicable to the generation of the restoration period. The people of Judah had been snared into Babylonian Captivity, into prison houses. None were there to deliver them. No one cried for restoration. But now in the period at the close of the Babylonian Captivity, God raised up these different servants to be His ministries and bring the message of restoration. Each of the ministries, at least in principle, cried 'Restore!" This was their united message, though they varied in their distinctive ministries.

   The message of restoration went forth. All who were willing to pay the price of restoration responded and came out of Babylon. Many Jews were content to remain in Babylon. Many did not either believe or accept the message of the restoration. Those who responded came out of Babylon, paid the price to return to Jerusalem and became involved in the hard work of restoration. However, they had the restoration ministries and message to encourage them on the way.

3. **The Seven Things Restored**

   There were seven major things restored in this time of restoration, each of them having spiritual significance as well as natural significance to the people who accepted the message of restoration.

   (a) **Restoration of the Temple or the house of the Lord**

   These ministries of restoration were involved in the rebuilding of the Temple, the house of the Lord. The altar was restored first, as the foundation of blood sacrifice and acceptance to God. The Temple was restored. The worship of the Lord was restored. The prophet Haggai actually prophesied that "the glory of the latter house" would be greater than the glory of the former house (Haggai 2:1-9). In the natural and material Temple, this was not so but when Jesus Christ came to this Temple years later and ministered there, He was indeed "the greater glory" that the original house had never seen (Matthew 21:12-16). He healed the sick and the lame and ministered in His Father's name after He cleansed the material Temple. God's house was restored.

   (b) **Restoration of Davidic Worship Order**

   We see also in the restoration books that worship according to the order of David was restored. Once the foundation of the Lord's house was laid, once the altar of blood-atonement was restored, then worship could follow on that basis.

In Ezra 2:65; 3:1-13; Nehemiah 12:27-47 we see that "singing men and singing women" returned to Judah from Babylon. When the foundation of the Temple was laid, "they set the priests in their apparel with trumpets, and the Levites the sons of Asaph with cymbals, to praise the Lord, **after the ordinance of David king of Israel**. And they sang together by course in praising and giving thanks unto the Lord ..." They could take their harps off the weeping willows and now sing to the Lord in His land (Psalm 126; 137).

Later on another company of people came up out of Babylon to Judah and the Levites were set with their brethren to praise and to give thanks, according to **the commandment of David the man of God** (Nehemiah 12:24). When the walls of the city were dedicated, the Levites sought out from all places for the Levites to come to Jerusalem for the dedication. They were to do this with gladness of heart, and in companies "with **the instruments of David the man of God**" (Nehemiah 12:27,36, 44-47).

All was done according to what David had commanded in his time. The chief of the singers, the songs of praise and thanksgiving unto God, under Zerubbabel and Nehemiah came into operation again. They received their portions as this Davidic order of worship was restored (Refer to textbook by the author, "**The Tabernacle of David**", page 147).

(c) **Restoration of the City of God, Walls and Gates**

The city of God, Jerusalem, was also restored. The walls had to be built again, even in troublous times, and the twelve gates had to be restored. The city being restored speaks of safety, protection and security for the people of God. It involved much hard work to restore the walls that had been broken down and the gates that had been destroyed. The people had a mind to work in the restoration. They believed in what God was doing through them. The city restored also spoke of government and order in God's city. The Psalmist speaks of the city of God and entering in within the gates with joy and praise according to their tribes (Psalm 121-122 with the Book of Nehemiah also). Each of the gates have significant names worthy of much study. All point to the ultimate city of God in Revelation, the New and heavenly Jerusalem into which the redeemed shall enter, and from which the eternal purposes of God shall be revealed and fulfilled (Revelation 21-22 chapters).

(d) **Restoration of the People of Judah**

Restoration also involved the people of God, the house of Judah, being brought back to the Lord and the land. It involved them coming back into Divine law and order according to the Word of the Lord. Judah represented the royal house, the tribe of praise, and other tribes with them came under that canopy before the Lord. So God restored people to Himself, to relationship with Himself.

(e) **Restoration of the Early and Latter Rains**

With the restoration of the people to the land, the restoration of the house of the Lord, the restoration of the altar of God and Davidic worship came the restoration of the early and latter rains. Rains meant harvest. Rains meant the refreshing. As long as they put the Lord first (Matthew 6:33), then the Lord said He would bless their land with the rains. The prophet Haggai actually had to reprove the people because of their failure in this. The Lord withheld the rains of blessing until they came into obedience (Haggai 1 with Joel 2 also are important to read here). Restoration means rains, and rains mean restoration of lost years, lost harvests. Rains mean fruitfulness.

(f) Restoration of the Feasts of the Lord

It is significant that, under the ministries of restoration, the people of God once again entered into the Feasts of the Lord, Passover, Pentecost and the Feast of Tabernacles. Wonderful details of the joy and rejoicing of the Feast of Tabernacles are to be found in Ezra 3 and Nehemiah 8. The details are too many to record here. The reader is referred to these chapters for such. It was the feast of joy, of restoration, of the seventh month, of cleansing, of the open book of the Lord. Restoration involves these things. The people of Judah knew the joy of restoration in the Feasts of the Lord (Leviticus 23).

(g) The Restoration of Lost Years

Also in the restoration, the Lord promised through the prophet Joel that He would restore "lost years". The seventy years in Babylonian Captivity were indeed "lost years". The Babylonian Captivity was never God's will. He did permit it but it was because of the people's failure to keep the laws of the land and the laws of the Lord. They failed to keep the Temple in perspective, the sacrifices, the tithes and the Feasts of the Lord. The Babylonian Captivity was a self-inflicted judgment that the Lord permitted to come. Lost years were the result of disobedience. In the restoration, God said He would bless them and make up for those lost years.

C. The Early Church

As we compare the Old and New Testament, we see a parallel picture in the Old Testament Temple and the New Testament Temple, the Church.

The early Church was God's Temple. On the Day of Pentecost, 120 disciples (as the 120 trumpeters) were of one accord in one place. The Holy Spirit, as the Shekinah Glory, descended from heaven and filled the New Testament Temple-the Church! It was a Temple filled with the glory of God and the power of God. It was a holy Temple, a spiritual house of the Lord. All of the New Testament writers see the Church as God's house, since the cross. The Church is God's Temple in this age (1Corinthians 3:16; 6:16; Ephesians 2:19-22; 1Peter 2:5-9; 4:17; Hebrews 3:1-6).

Over the years of Church History, however, defilements and abominations came into the Temple of God by inward apostasy and pagan philosophies, as seen in previous chapters.

The Holy Spirit's power and glory lifted from the Church, slowly and reluctantly. In due time, the Church entered the "Dark Ages", and as has been seen, "the Church's Babylonian Captivity", as Martin Luther fitly described it. But this Captivity also was not to last for ever. The Scriptures promised restoration of the Church to her former - and greater - glory and power.

D. The Last Day Church

From the period of the Reformation, the period of Restoration also began. Wycliffe, Luther, Calvin, Anabaptists, the Wesleys, Holiness teachers, Baptism of the Holy Spirit outpouring, and the host of others considered in this text, all may be likened to "restoration ministries". These have been restoring to the Church the truths that have been lost over the years.

The Church was indeed "coming out of Babylon". There was much rubble and much rubbish. God's Temple - the Church - is to be restored to greater glory than the early and former Church. The restoration is not over yet. It is not complete as yet.

There were those ministries who cried "Restore!" (Isaiah 42:22). Multitudes of the people of God have been snared into holes, and prison houses of denominationalism and have been robbed of the truths of God, and spoiled by many religious leaders. Like in Messiah's times, the scribes, the Pharisees, the Sadducees, the elders and priests, robbed the people, and took away "**the key of knowledge**", so in this and past generations (Luke 11:52). They entered not into the truths of God themselves, and those that were entering in, they hindered, or forbid them to enter in. No one delivered God's people. No one brought the message of restoration.

This, however, was to change. God is shaking everything that can be shaken. He is shaking denominations, traditions, leaders and everything else that can be shaken. For God's people there is an unshakeable house (the true Church) and a kingdom that is unshakeable also (Hebrews 12:29).

In these last years, and more especially since the 1948-onwards visitation, God has been raising up ministries who believe and teach restoration truths. There are those who are praying to the Lord and crying, "Restore!" The prayers ascend that the Lord will restore to the Church the lost years, the lost truths, the lost power and the lost glory.

There are those who are proclaiming "Restore". People are responding and coming out of their "holes" and "prison houses". People are being delivered. People are receiving the truths of restoration. God is restoring to the Church all that has been lost over the years of Church History.

There are those who are - like the faithful remnant of the Babylonian Captivity - responding to the message of restoration and entering into what God is saying and doing in the Church in this generation. The spiritual lessons may be seen in the seven things restored in the Old Testament Restoration Books.

1. The **Temple** or House of the Lord is being restored.
2. The **Tabernacle of David** and Davidic Worship is being restored.
3. The **City of God**, Walls and Gates and Church Government is being restored.
4. The **People of God**, Judah, are being restored.
5. The **Rains**, Early and Latter Rains Outpouring of the Spirit are being restored.
6. The **Feasts of the Lord**, with emphasis on Tabernacles, are being restored.
7. The **Lost Years** of Church History are being restored.

This is the message of restoration! As the restoration of the material Old Covenant Temple consummated in the glory of the Messiah coming to His Temple, in the first coming, so the glory of the last day Church will consummate in the glory of the Lord in His second coming.

Both Solomon's Temple and the Restoration Temple were dedicated in the Feast of the seventh month, the Feast of Tabernacles - NOT in the Feast of Passover or the Feast of Pentecost!

In Summary:

The following diagram helps to bring into sharper focus the things dealt with in this present chapter.

Old Testament Historical Type
The Temple of Solomon
One Hundred & Twenty Priests
One Accord, One Place
Singers & Musicians
Davidic Order of Worship
Cloud of Glory & Fire
Dedication of the Temple
Feast of Tabernacles

The Prophecy and Shadow
The Restored Temple
Restoration Ministries
Restoration Message
Opposition & Pressures
Davidic Worship Restored
Glory of the Latter House
Dedication of the Temple
Feast of Tabernacles

Decline & Corruption
Glory Departs from Temple
Babylonian Captivity
Call "Come Out"
Faithful Remnant Respond

New Testament Historical
Early Church Temple
One Hundred & Twenty Disciples
New Testament Priests
One Accord, One Plac
Glory-Fire of the Holy Spirit
Dedication of the Church
Feast of Pentecost

Antitype, Susbtance, Fulfillment
Last Day Church Temple
Restoration Ministries
Restoration Message
Opposition & Pressures
Glory of the Last Day Church
Dedication of the Last Day Church
Feast of Tabernacles

Corruption & Decline
Glory Departs
"The Dark Ages"
"Babylonian Captivity"
Call - "Come Out"
Faithful Remnant Respond

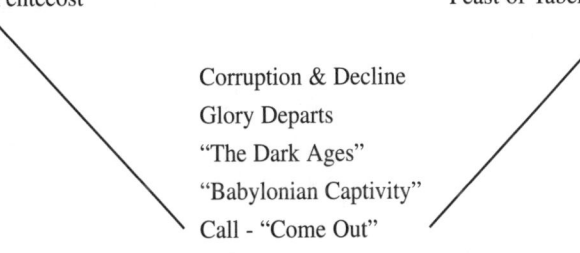

It is here that our prophetic picture ends, realizing that no one prophetic type is the full truth. This is the message of restoration as seen in the Old Testament Restoration Books!

CHAPTER FORTY-TWO

PROPHETIC TYPES OF RESTORATION

Throughout the Scriptures, there are a number of types or pictures of the message of restoration, especially seen in the Old Testament.

Paul, in writing to the Corinthians, tells them that various things which happened to Israel were for "types and examples" and that these things were written for our admonition upon whom the ends of the age are come (1Corinthians 10:1-11). In this chapter we briefly consider some of these types of restoration. The student will be able to fill in more details by further study. Also, it should be remembered, that each of these pictures have their limits and must not be pressed beyond proper hermeneutical laws of interpretation. There is no "perfect type", but each type provides some portion of truth without pressing such beyond it Scriptural boundaries.

A. The Restoration of Job

The Book of Job provides a wonderful picture of the message of restoration. The student should read the Book of Job afresh relative to the thoughts given here.

In the beginning chapters, we see here that God had blessed Job both spiritually and materially. He exercised priestly ministry in his household, offering sacrifices to the Lord on behalf of his family. His character was exemplary. God had placed a hedge around him, his house, and his possessions.

Unbeknowns to Job, there was Satan's challenge in heaven to God against Job. Job's motives for serving God were challenged. Satan charged that Job simply served God for what he could get from God.

God permitted Satan to test Job. Satan came and robbed Job of his possessions and his family and almost everything he had. Job ended up on the ash heap covered with boils, smitten of Satan.

Job's "comforters" came and all had some interesting philosophical reasons why this had happened to Job. They each thought they knew the answers, as seen in their various philosophies, reasonings and arguments of appeal against or to Job. Even Job said many things that he did not understand. But through it all, Job trusted God in the dark and at times made great confessions of faith.

In due time, God came on the scene and revealed Himself afresh to Job. After great humbling of his soul and repentance, Job prayed for his "friends", and God healed him. The closing chapters reveal how God blessed Job's latter end more than the beginning. He was blessed with a double portion - twice as much as he had lost- under Satanic attack.

For Job, the Scripture was true. "Better is the end of a thing than the beginning" (Ecclesiastes 7:8). God restored to Job all that he had lost and more, thus fulfilling His own laws of restitution. Satan came to rob, to kill and to destroy. The Lord came to bring life and that more abundantly.

Such is the picture of the Church. The Church in its beginning was separated unto the Lord, blessed of the Lord in priestly ministry. The adversary, Satan, came and attacked the Church from without and within, until the Church ended up on the ash heap of the Middle Ages, a pitiful sight.

The religious professors, like Job's "comforters", thought they knew the answers with the varying philosophies of that time. Even the Church said ignorant things. But there was a small spark of trust in God.

In due time, God came to the Church and revealed Himself. The Church came to humility and repentance and new vision. The Church now is living in the days of the double portion, the double blessing of the Lord. All that has been lost, and more, shall be restored to the Church.

The latter years will be greater than the former and the Church will know also, "Better is the end a thing than the beginning". The Lord will have fulfilled in and to His Church His own laws of restitution. The Church will see that behind it all was the adversary, Satan, who will be eternally punished and banished into the lake of fire (Revelation 20:11-15).

B. Restoration in the Life of Samson

Samson's life-story also provides another type and picture, though imperfect, of the message of restoration. The story is found in Judges Chapters 13-16 and needs to be read to refresh the mind of the details.

1. Samson's Ministry and Decline

Samson was born as a result of a miracle. The Angel of the Lord visited his father and mother and announced his miraculous birth. Samson was to be a Nazarite from his birth, separated unto the Lord. Samson was called to deliver people from the Philistines. The secret of his ministry was in "the Spirit of the Lord" coming upon him. By the power of the Spirit he did mighty exploits. He delivered God's people from the Philistines, he slew the lion, he took the gates of the city with him at the midnight hour.

The tragedy, however, was that over time Samson defiled his separation. He broke his Nazarite vow and the days of his separation were lost (Read Numbers 6:1-12). He fell into the arms of Delilah who seduced him to give away the secret of his strength. As he lay in her arms, she cut off the seven locks of his hair. The Spirit of the Lord departed from him and he did not even know it. He shook himself, as at other times, but he was weak like other men. The sign of his strength and separation to the Lord were gone.

Instead of conquering the Philistines, they conquered him. The Philistines took him captive, bound him, blinded him and made him their slave. He became the mockery of the nation. Those days were counted as "lost time", because the vow of the Nazarite had been defiled by touching forbidden things and moral defilements.

2. **The Church's Ministry and Decline**

   So it was with the Church. The New Testament Church was the result of a Divine miracle, a miracle birth. The secret of the early Church was the power of the Holy Spirit. By the power of the Holy Spirit, the early Church delivered people from the power of sin, and from Satan's kingdom. Great miracles took place by the supernatural strength of the Spirit of God.

   Over the years of Church History, however, the Church - like Samson - failed, and compromised holiness of life. Defilement and spiritual immorality took place as the Church departed from its calling. The Spirit of the Lord departed from the Church. The Church lay powerless in the arms of the "Delilah" of the Dark Ages, in the arms of the false Church.

   The Church was weak, like any other human institution. The Church became captive to the world of the Philistines. The Church was bound, blinded and mocked, losing the "seven principles" of Christ's doctrine, like Samson lost his seven locks of hair under Delilah.

   This period of time was "lost time", the "Dark Ages" of Church History, and the Church's spiritual "Philistine Captivity". Samson suffered under an evil woman and the Philistines, and the Church suffered spiritually under the same.

3. **Samson's Repentance and Restoration**

   In this state, Samson came to repentance before the Lord. He asked the Lord to restore to him what had been lost. God came to him, in mercy, and his hair (the seven locks) began to grow again. The sign of his consecration to God and the sign of his strength had not been rooted out, but shorn. Now restoration took place on the basis of repentance. Samson slew more Philistines in his death than in his whole life time before. There the picture ends.

4. **The Church's Repentance and Restoration**

   So it was with the Church! Although the picture is not perfect or complete (as all types are imperfect and incomplete by reason of human imperfections), the Church came to repentance and faith under the Reformation period. The hair began to grow again. The seven locks of Samson's hair growing into strength again could be likened to the seven principles of the doctrine of Christ being restored to the Church.

   The Church is in the end of the age and will conquer more enemies (Philistines) than in its whole history. The lost years will be restored. The Church will once again know the strength of the power of the Holy Spirit.

This is the picture and message of restoration as seen in the life of Samson. The power of the Holy Spirit, then defilement and decline into lost time, then repentance and restoration and Samson's final and greatest victory. So these steps are seen in the Church over Church History.

C. Restoration of Davidic Worship

As seen in earlier chapters, under David's reign, the Tabernacle of David had been set up. The Davidic order of worship was in due time incorporated into the Temple of Solomon. The history of the kings of Judah show the rise and fall, the recovery and decline of Davidic worship over the years. These periods of decline were indeed lost years.

Each Godly king restored the Davidic worship in the Temple, the house of the Lord. Ungodly kings departed from it and with the decline of the nation's leadership, came the decline of God's house and Davidic ministry of worship and praise. The Books of the Kings and Chronicles, along with the Restoration Books, show that there were about five major periods of recovery of Davidic worship under these Godly kings. For the purpose of this section, we note a brief outline of the history of the Tabernacle of David and the periods of restoration of worship under Godly kings. The reader is referred to "**The Tabernacle of David**" (Chapter 16), by the author. Each recovery of Davidic worship pointed to the message of restoration.

1. The Tabernacle of David Established

In 1Chronicles Chapters 15-16 we have the establishment of the Tabernacle of David. Here the order of singers and musicians and spiritual sacrifices unto the Lord was established. Mt Zion became the place of worship and praise to the Lord under king David. This was the foundation laid in Zion and these were glorious days of worship unto the Lord as the Levites ministered to the Lord continually in His Tabernacle.

2. The Temple of Solomon

In 2Chronicles Chapters 3-5 we see the Davidic order of worship and praise incorporated into the Temple order. For about thirty years, the Tabernacle of David had been in function. Now that order is taken into the Temple of the Lord. The Ark of God is placed in the Holiest of All. The priests, the singers and the musicians are all of one accord in one place. The glory-fire of the Lord fills the house and no flesh could minister (2Chronicles 5:11-14). What power and glory was seen in the dedication and early days of Solomon's Temple, the house of the Lord, built as a house of prayer for all nations.

3. The Godly King Jehoshaphat

In 2Chronicles, Godly king Jehoshaphat, after seeking the Lord in prayer and fasting, received a prophetic word concerning the battle against the Moabites and the Ammonites. The prophetic word told him to set the singers unto the Lord who would praise the Lord in the beauty of His holiness and for His mercy. The battle was won as the singers were in the front of the battle lines singing to the Lord. God used the ministry of singers, as set under David's time, to bring victory to the people of Judah.

4. The Godly King Hezekiah

In 2Chronicles Chapter 29-30 we have the great restoration of the house of the Lord and the Davidic order of worship under Godly king Hezekiah. The previous wicked king, Ahaz, had polluted the house of the Lord, and closed down the ministry of Davidic worship. Under Hezekiah, the singers and the musicians, the instruments and songs of the Lord, as commanded under David, all were restored to their rightful place in the house of the Lord. God blessed it all with His sudden presence and healing power on the people of Judah.

5. The Godly King Josiah

Once again, under Godly king Josiah, we seen a restoration of Davidic worship and this was according to the writing of David, the king of Israel, and also according to the writing of king Solomon (2Chronicles 35:4,15). The singers sang and worshipped the Lord as He had so ordained under David.

6. The Restoration of Judah from Babylon

As has been seen in previous chapters, once Judah came out of Babylonian Captivity, under Ezra and Nehemiah the Davidic order of worship, the singers and the musicians, all were restored in the rebuilding of the Temple, the house of the Lord (Read Ezra 2:65; 3:1-13; Nehemiah 12:24, 27-37, 44-47).

7. The Prophecy of Amos

In Amos 9:11-13, the prophet spoke of restoration of the Tabernacle of David. The Lord promised to build again the Tabernacle of David which had fallen down, He would raise up the ruins thereof, and rebuild it again as in the days of old, as under the time of David.

The apostle James shows how this applies to the coming in of both Jew and Gentile into the Tabernacle of David, the greater Son of David, the Lord Jesus Christ. Here in this Tabernacle, the Church, Jews and Gentiles, would praise and worship the Lord together, as one Body in Christ (Acts 15:16-18).

8. Application to Church History

All these things pointed to that which would happen in Church History. The early Church entered the truth of the Tabernacle of David, as seen in the Book of Acts and the New Testament Epistles. The early Church saw the coming in of the Gentiles. Worship in spirit and in truth was according to the Word, and singing in Psalms and Hymns and Spiritual Songs (Colossians 3:16; Ephesians 5:18-19).

However, the Church, like Judah, ended up in spiritual Babylonian Captivity. There was no song or instruments in this time of Church History, as seen in the Dark Ages. The Lord, however, promised restoration. The Church was brought out of her Babylonian Captivity. The song of the Lord, in Psalms, Hymns and Spiritual Songs came back to the Church. The harps were taken off the willow trees, mouths were filled with laughter and singing, under each recovery of truth (Psalm 126; Psalm 137).

Every revival and recovery of truth in Church History has been clothed in song. Theology of restoration has been sung into the hearts of each revival. This will continue unto the coming of the Lord. Each Godly king, like Godly leaders, will bring the people of God back to the Davidic order of worship and praise unto the Lord.

This is the picture and message of restoration seen in the stream of truth on the Tabernacle of David and the restoration of Davidic worship under Godly leadership in the nation of Judah. So it is fulfilled in the history of the Church! The Church is to be filled with music and song as the people of God have a heart like David, the example of a true worshipper in spirit and in truth (John 4:20-24). That which was lost is restored. Redemptive songs clothe the truth God recovers to His Church!

D. The Restoration of the Wells

Another great picture of the message of restoration is found in Genesis 26:12-32. The story concerns the restoration of wells of water that Abraham the father had dug in his time. Over the years the Philistines had stopped them up with dirt and the waters had ceased to flow. Isaac, Abraham's only begotten son, was born by miracle birth. He came and in time redug and restored the wells again and the waters began to flow. There was much contention by the Philistines about these wells, but Isaac recovered these wells for the people of God. Let us consider some of the spiritual lessons that may be drawn from this picture of restoration.

1. Abraham - The Father

Abraham, the father, was the owner and originator of the wells. He had these wells dug, and the waters were available for his people.

Wells in Palestine were usually excavated from the solid limestone rock, sometimes with steps to descend into them (Genesis 24:16). The brims were furnished with a curb or low wall of stone, bearing marks of high antiquity in the furrows worn by ropes used to draw water. The wells were often covered by a stone to keep filth or animals falling into the well, corrupting the waters (Read 2 Samuel 17:19). The usual methods of raising the water were by rope and a bucket or water-skin (Genesis 24:14-20; John 4:11).

So over the years, hard work had been put into the digging of the wells that Abraham along with his servants had dug. Abraham, the father, points to God the Father who has provided wells of salvation for His people also over the years.

2. The Philistines - The Enemies

The Philistines were the enemies of the people of God, from Abraham's time onwards, as Bible history shows. Over the years, the Philistines came and stopped the wells, filling them with refuse, dirt, stones and all other kinds of rubbish. The waters from the wells ceased to flow. That which father Abraham had dug was lost.

So it points to Church History. The enemies of the Father God, and of the Church, came and stopped the waters of salvation flowing over the centuries down into the Dark Ages of Church History.

3. Isaac - The Son and Restorer of Wells

Isaac, born as a result of a miracle, is known as a man of

(a) **The Altar**, Genesis 26:25 with 12:8; 13:3,18

(b) **The Name**, Genesis 26:25 with Exodus 3:1-15; 6:1-7;

(c) **The Tent**, Genesis 26:25; Hebrews 11:9-16, and

(d) **The Wells**, Genesis 26:25.

Isaac, the only begotten son of his father, Abraham, came and redug the wells that his father had dug. He restored the wells that the Philistines had stopped up. It was hard work to get out of the wells all the refuse and stones and rubbish that the Philistines had filled the wells with, causing the waters to stop flowing. The Philistines opposed Isaac and his servants as they redug the wells. There was much contention and strife. Also, it is worthy to note that Isaac gave these redug wells the same names which his father had given them.

4. The Wells Restored

At least four wells that were redug are specifically named in this chapter. It is possible that there were more wells. However, there are lessons enough in the four wells mentioned here.

The Well Esek -"Esek" means "Quarrel, Strife or Contention" (Genesis 26:20). As this well was restored, the Philistines quarrelled over this. There was strife and contention over its restoration.

The Well Sitnah - "Sitnah" means "Enmity, Strife or Hatred" (Genesis 26:21). As this well was redug and restored, there was enmity, strife and hatred by the Philistines again over its restoration.

The Well Rehoboth - "Rehoboth" means "Spaciousness, Places or Spaces" (Genesis 26:22). There was more space or room over the issue when this well was redug. Isaac moved further on and the Philistines did not strive for this well as over the previous wells.

The Well Beersheba - "Beersheba" means "Oath, or Well of the Oath, or Well of the Seven" (Genesis 21:31-33; 26:32-33). The waters of this well began to flow for Isaac and his servants. The wells were restored after much hard work!

This is the message of restoration under Isaac's ministry. Most expositors see that Abraham and Isaac are types of the Father God, and His only begotten Son, Jesus. The Father and the Son work together as one, in the same ministry, in behalf of the Church and the people of God.

Wells in Scripture are figurative of God as the source of our salvation. The prophet Isaiah speaks of drawing **"with joy out of the wells of salvation"** (Isaiah 12:3, compare with Jeremiah 2:13; John 4:10; Song of Solomon 4:15).

The early Church drew, with joy, out of the wells of salvation. Over the years, the spiritual Philistines, the enemies of God's people, stopped up the wells. They were filled with all kinds of paganism, heathenism, and religious rubbish, until the middle period, there was no flow of the waters of salvation. The Lord said He would restore.

Since the period of the Reformation, the wells of salvation have been redug and restored. Church History certainly shows the strife, the contention, enmity and hatred that arose among people over the restoration of these wells.

The well of justification by faith, the well of water baptism, of holiness, of Divine healing, of the priesthood of all believers, the baptism of the Holy Spirit, and all the other truths restored - all these are like the wells of salvation from which people can draw with joy! Restoration of these wells of salvation has been much hard work, getting rid of the rubbish and filth that has corrupted the wells flowing with pure water.

In concluding this picture of restoration, it is worthy to note several incidents in the Scripture on the significance of wells.

* As the leaders of Israel dug the well, and Israel sang to the well, the waters began to flow. The Lord gave waters to His people as they were digging and singing to the well (Numbers 21:16-18). So the Lord gives waters as we dig and sing to Him who is THE Well of living water, springing up into eternal life (John 4:1-15).

* Isaac's bride was found by a well (Genesis 24).

* Jacob's bride was found by a well (Genesis 29).

* Moses' bride was found by a well (Exodus 2:15-22).

* Jesus talked to the woman of Samaria at Jacob's well (John 4).

These provide spiritual lessons for the Church. Christ will find His bride at the wells of salvation. Like the women of old, the bride will be singing with joy as she draws waters from the wells of salvation.

E. Restoration in the Year of Jubilee

The year of Jubilee also shadows forth the message of restoration. Every fiftieth year in Israel was to be a year of Jubilee. Jubilee literally means "Shouting!". It was a time of joyous shouting, the blowing of the trumpets of Jubilee in Israel, The year of Jubilee was a year of liberty. Every slave in Israel was to be set free. Every debt was to be cancelled. Every family was to be reunited.

The year of Jubilee was also a holy year. There was to be no sowing or reaping in that year. There was to be no labour.

The year of Jubilee began on the tenth day of the seventh month, that is, on the great Day of Atonement, the most solemn day of the year for Israel. It was observed in the Feast of Tabernacles, the final feast of the year in Israel (Leviticus 25 Chapter).

When Jesus came, He read from Isaiah, speaking of "the acceptable year of the Lord", which was the year of Jubilee. Christ Jesus set the prisoners free, slaves of sin were released, the debt of sin was cancelled by His death on the cross, through Him families can be reunited. The people of God can shout unto the Lord.

Over the years from Jubilee on, people fell into debt, they became slaves, they lost inheritances, families were broken up, but in the year of Jubilee everything knew restoration!

It is significant that, from Adam to the end of this century, there is about 6000 years of human history. Every fiftieth year in Israel was a Jubilee. Dividing 6000 years by 50 years = 120 Jubilees (120 x 50 = 6000). This means that the Church is living in the 120th Jubilee of human history. Over the years of human history, from the fall of Adam to now, much has been lost. But the final Jubilee will bring everything back to God's people that had been lost in the Fall, and/or over Church History. It will indeed be a time of shouting, rejoicing, reunion, release, rest and restoration! This is the message of restoration in the Jubilee years in Israel's history.

F. Shorter Pictures of Restoration

These are several lesser pictures of restoration throughout the Scriptures, and though not as extended as the previous, they still provide thoughts worthy of study and consideration.

1. The Restored Axehead - 2Kings 6:1-7

The School of the Prophets was building a house. As the prophets were cutting down the timber for the house, one of the woodsman lost the axehead off his axe. It fell into the water. His lament to Elisha was that the axe had been borrowed. It was not his. Elisha asked him to show him the place where the axehead fell. The prophet threw in a stick and the result was the iron axehead surfaced. The axehead, representing the woodsman's power, was restored. It was no use trying to chop with a powerless handle. It would only jar the body. The secret was the power of a sharp axehead.

So it is useless and powerless for the Church to build without the Divine power of the Lord Jesus Christ, and the power of the Holy Spirit. As the axehead was restored, so the Lord wants to restore to the Church the power of the Spirit. It is necessary to go back to the place where the axehead was lost!

2. The Restored Son - 2Kings 4:8-37; 8:1-6

The Shunamite woman prepared a small room for the prophet of God. In it she placed a table, a lampstand and a bed. Her blessing was the birth of a child as she had been barren. In time the child died by a stroke in the heat of the sun in harvest time. The prophet restored the child to life, after stretching himself on the child. The child sneezed seven times as resurrection life came into him. The prophet Elisha was the prophet of the double portion. The testimony went out that this child was restored to life.

So the Church needs to know the resurrection life and power of the Lord Jesus Christ in whom is the fullness of the Spirit's life and power (John 3:33-34).

3. The Restored Inheritance - 2Kings 8:1-6

The same Shunamite woman had an inheritance. The prophet Elisha told her of the coming famine and seven years of drought. She left for the land of the Philistines over those years. In due time she returned to the land, but her inheritance had been taken. The king gave the word. All that she had lost was restored to her, and all the fruit of those lost years was given to her. She knew the truth of restoration of a lost inheritance.

So the Church has experienced famine and drought over the years. But all that was lost in the Church's inheritance, and more, shall be restored by the Lord Jesus Christ, THE Prophet of the double portion of the Spirit.

4. The Restoration to David's Army - 1Samuel 30

In this chapter there is another short picture of restoration. David was in battle against the Amalekites, the enemies of Israel. The Amalekites came to Ziklag. They destroyed the city. All were taken captive and carried away. David and his army lost their wives, their sons and daughters to the enemy. The men were so discouraged, they spoke of stoning David himself. David, however, sought the Lord and encouraged himself in the Lord. David called for Abiathar, the priest with the ephod. David asked the Lord whether he should pursue the Amalekites, and would he be able to overtake them. The Lord gave him a word through the priest. The word was threefold:

* **Pursue** (verses 8,10)

* **Overtake** (verse 8)

* **Recover all** (verses 8,18,19).

David and his army, though some were faint and could not continue, pursued the Amalekites, they overtook them and they recovered all that had been lost, and more. They took of the spoils of the enemy and David shared them with all his army, both those who had been faint and those who had conquered with him. This became a law in Israel. They understood restoration.

So the Church is in spiritual warfare with the Amalekites, the flesh-seed of Esau. The enemy has robbed the Church of so many things. Jesus is the greater Son of David. The word is to pursue, overtake and recover all that has been lost. As David recovered all, so Christ will recover all to His Church. The Church will know full restoration and victory over the enemy in these days. God's people will share alike in the spoils of the battle.

5. The Restoration under Elijah - Malachi 4:5-6

Malachi closes off the Old Testament prophetic books. He said that Elijah would come and restore all things. Elijah would turn the hearts of the fathers to the children and the hearts of the children to the fathers. The student is referred to 1 Kings Chapters 18-2 Kings Chapter 2 for the life story of Elijah. From his manifestation to his translation we have a miraculous life and ministry as well as prophetic words to the nation, the rulers and the false prophets of Baal. His ministry consummated in the fire from heaven and the judgment on the prophets of Baal worship.

His ministry was to turn the people from idolatry to the living God. His call was to turn the hearts of the fathers to the children and the hearts of the children to the wisdom and obedience of the just. This was Elijah's message of restoration.

Over the years, the Lord caused "the spirit of Elijah" to fall on various ministry which He raised up.

The spirit of Elijah came upon Elisha, in a double portion manner (2Kings 2).

The spirit of Elijah came upon John the Baptist in his message of repentance, water baptism and faith in the coming Messiah (Luke 1:17; Mark 9:12; Matthew 17:11 with Malachi 4:5-6).

The spirit of Elijah has come and will continue to come on various ministries the Lord raises up through the centuries of Church History. It is not that these ministries are Elijah personally, as some have claimed to be over the years, but it is the spirit of Elijah which comes upon them. This will continue unto His second coming. The message is to restore the hearts and lives of the people to God and restore families that have been destroyed by the modern-day prophets of Baal worship and the spiritual Jezebel's of this age. This is the message of restoration Elijah teaches.

In Conclusion:

Other Scriptures for consideration are seen in these references.

1. Christ will be the repairer of the breach and the restorer of paths to dwell in (Isaiah 58:12 with Isaiah 2:2-4). He will raise up the foundations of many generations.

2. Christ will restore the lost years to the Church (Joel 2:23).

3. Christ will restore the soul of His sheep by the still waters and green pastures (Psalm 23; John 10; Ezekiel 34; Jeremiah 23:1-6; 1Peter 5:1-3; Jeremiah 31:4). He will restore those who have been overtaken in faults and use those who are spiritual to do so (Galatians 6:1-2).

4. Christ will restore the joy of salvation to those who, like David, have fallen but have come to true repentance (Psalm 51 with 2Samuel 11-12).

5. Christ will raise up ministries who will bring the message of restoration. They will bring people out of the holes into which they have been snared and prison houses in which they have been locked, as they cry, Restore! (Isaiah 42:22; 30:20-21; 1:26).

The message of restoration is a message that gives sense and direction to those who ears to hear what the Spirit is saying to the Church in these final days. For some, these things will be a stumblingstone and rock of offence. For others, these things will become stepping stones in the ongoing purpose of God. Stumblingstone or stepping stone? The answer is determined by each individual, each leader and each congregation (Isaiah 8:13-18 with Romans 9:33; 1Peter 2:8; 1Corinthians 1:22-23).

CHAPTER FORTY-THREE

MAINTAINING BALANCE, AVOIDING EXTREMES

The Scriptures are clear when it come to the matter of balance, as the following references show. God wants His people to be balanced in the truth, and avoid extremes in doctrine. Let us consider the following Scriptures which speak of the necessity of proper balance in things pertaining to human relationships as well as things pertaining to God.

A. Maintaining Balance

"You shall do no injustice in judgment, in measurement of length, weight or volume. You shall have honest scales (balances), honest weights, and honest ephah, and an honest hin: I am the Lord your God who brought you out of the land of Egypt. Therefore you shall observe all My statutes and all My judgments and perform them: I am the Lord" (Leviticus 19:35-37. NKJV).

Again, in Deuteronomy 25:13-16, the Lord says to Israel: "You shall not have in your bag differing weights, a heavy and a light. You shall not have differing measures, a large and a small.

You shall have a perfect and just weight, a perfect and a just measure, that your days may be lengthened in the land which the Lord your God is giving you. For all who do such things, all who behave unrighteously, are an abomination to the Lord your God".

The prophets also lamented in their days how Israel had departed from just weights and just balances. They falsified the scales and were not honest in their dealings with God or the people. They said, "When will the New Moon be past, that we may sell grain? And the Sabbath that we may trade wheat? Making the ephah small and the shekel large, **falsifying the balances (the scales) by deceit**. That we may buy the poor for silver, and the needy for a pair of sandals - even sell the bad wheat" (Amos 8:5-6 with Hosea 12:7. NKJV).

The Book of Proverbs tells us what the Lord thinks about dishonest balances, dishonest scales used to deceive people.

"A false balance is an abomination unto the Lord, but a just weight is His delight" (Proverbs 11:1; 16:11). And again, "Divers weights are an abomination to the Lord, and a false balance is not good" (Proverbs 20:23).

Some of the Israelites had three sets of weights: (1) Weights according to the standard of God's sanctuary, and (2) Light weights with which they could cheat people for more when they were buying in produce, and (3) Heavy weights by which they could cheat the people when selling produce to them. Such unjust weights and tipping of the scales were an abomination to the Lord, all of which has natural and spiritual lessons for us. The heavy and light weights were weights of deception.

One of the hardest things for human nature is to keep a balanced perspective on things. The Fall threw man out of balance with God, with creation, with creatures and man himself. In Christ, God wants to bring man back to proper balance. Man's outlook on life, on Divine things and actually everything pertaining to this life, all were thrown out of balance because of sin.

The same is true of Divine truth. As seen in our brief study on Church History, every time God recovered or restored some truth to the Church, there were those who went to extremes and out of balance.

The Scriptures generally reveal that all truth must be weighed in the scales of just balances. If the scales are outweighed on either side, there is not a true balance. This may be illustrated in two of the major doctrines in the Bible.

1. The Doctrine of the Godhead

The Bible reveals that God is one. The Bible also reveals that God is three. If the Scriptures on the oneness (unity) of God are over-emphasized, the scales are tipped on one side and the false doctrine of 'Oneness' (Jesus Only) is seen. If the Scriptures on the threeness of God (tri-unity) are over-emphasized, then the heresy of tritheism arises. Balance needs to be kept on the revelation of the one true God, revealed as Father, Son and Holy Spirit (Matthew 28:19-20).

2. The Doctrine of Christ

The Bible reveals that Jesus Christ is God. The Bible also reveals that Jesus Christ is Man. If the Scriptures on the Deity of Christ are over-emphasized, it can nullify His humanity. Also, if the Scriptures on His humanity are over- emphasized, the scales are tipped and the Divinity of Christ is nullified. This is seen in the false cults in Christendom. False cults handle the Word of God in false scales, they handle the Word deceitfully, and have false balances and balances of deceit. The Bible shows that Jesus is truly God and truly man. He is the God-Man, one person having the nature of God and the nature of man.

Other doctrinal illustrations could be given.

As has been mentioned previously, heresy cannot exist apart from truth. Truth existed before heresy. Heresy arises out of truth. Heresy, as we have seen, is the taking of a portion or fragment of truth to its extreme out of proportion with the whole body of truth. This is where imbalance arises.

Over the years of restoration of truth, many genuine truths were taken to extreme, or counterfeited, or ended up in fanaticism. This caused many people to reject the truth altogether and they failed to exercise their senses to discern between good and evil (Hebrews 5:12-14; 6:1-3). The following columns focus more sharply on some of the imbalances that came on various recovery of truths.

Truth Recovered	Imbalance or Extremes
1. Justification by faith	Justification by religious works
2. Water baptism	Baptismal regeneration
3. Holiness of heart	Externalism and legalism
4. Divine healing	Rejection of Medical Fields
5. Priesthood of all believers	Priest-class of leadership
6. Holy Spirit baptism and "tongues"	Not saved unless speak in tongues
7. The Eternal Godhood	Oneness, Jesus Only
8. Triune Name of Lord Jesus Christ	"Jesus Name"
9. Laying on hands impartation	Abuse of ministry

10. Demon deliverance	Spiritfilled can be demon possessed
11. Discipleship, shepherding	Control and cultic approach
12. Kingdom now but not yet	Kingdom Jewish nationalism

The list undoubtedly could be extended. Preachers, teachers and believers must not handle the Word of God deceitfully. They must learn to rightly divide the Word of truth (2Corinthians 2:17; 4:2; 2Peter 3:16; 2Timothy 2:15).

Believers must be honest with the Word of God, using honest scales, honest weights, honest measurements. All false cults, all extremes, imbalance and fanaticism about truth arise out of falsifying the balances of Scripture by deceit. There are generally two sides to a pair of balances. There are generally two sides to every aspect of truth. The Scriptures on both sides must be evenly weighed in the scales to get the balance and present balanced doctrine.

B. Avoiding Extremes

Another illustration given in Scripture pertains to the exhortations to avoid extremes. Extreme is where a person goes too far to the left or too far to the right, instead of keeping on the pathway of life, the center of the track.

Consider these Scriptures telling us to avoid extremes by not going to either the right wing or the left, to either extreme.

The Lord commanded Israel, through Moses, to walk in His ways and "not turn aside to the right hand or the left" (Deuteronomy 5:32; 28:14; 17:11).

The Lord commanded the kings on the throne to read, write and study His laws in the book, keep humble before Him, and not to turn to the right hand or the left (Deuteronomy 17:20). Most of the kings of Israel and Judah failed to do this.

The Lord commanded Joshua not to turn to the right hand or the left and He would prosper where-ever he went (Joshua 1:7). One of the commendations of the Lord about king Josiah was, "And he did that which was right in the sight of the Lord, and walked in all the ways of David his father, and **turned not aside to the right hand or to the left**" (2Kings 22:2). Read also Numbers 20:17; 22:26; Deuteronomy 2:17; 1Samuel 6:12.

To those who desire to walk in a straight path of truth before the Lord, the Lord through the prophet Isaiah gave a wonderful promise. "And though the Lord give you the bread of adversity, and the water of affliction, yet your teachers will not be moved into a corner any more. But your eyes shall see your teachers. Your ears shall hear a word behind you, saying, **This is the way, walk in it. Whenever you turn to the right hand, or whenever you turn to the left**" (Isaiah 30:21).

A believer may not hear the voice of the Lord always, as long as he is walking in the path of truth. But, if he goes to turn to the right hand or the left hand, to either extreme, he will hear that voice. The voice will say, **THIS IS THE WAY, walk in it**. Avoid extremes!

Every truth restored to the Church must be kept in Biblical and Divine balance. The believer must seek to avoid extremes in doctrine and practice. By doing so, those who are hungry will accept the truth that sets mn free (John 8:32-34).

CHAPTER FORTY-FOUR

LEARNING LESSONS FROM HISTORY

In this chapter we consider in propositional form some of the lessons that each generation should learn from previous generations. Each of them could be elaborated on but the diligent reader will be able to do that and provide examples accordingly. A review over the contents of this text confirm most, if not all, of the propositions laid out here.

PROPOSITIONAL STATEMENTS

1. Human nature shows very often that, the only lesson we learn from history is that we never learn from history. Israel's history prefigures this as well as all nations and all generations.

2. Often the greatest "enemies" of truth are its "friends". Truth has suffered more at the hands of those who believe than those who do not believe.

3. Generally "the persecuted" of the previous visitation and restoration of truth become "the persecutors" of the next visitation and restoration of truth.

4. Controversy is never the real enemy of truth; only prejudice, bigotry and bias is. These things are often the characteristics of insecurity, fear and resistance to Divine progress.

5. Most all of God's people who receive a fresh fragment or portion of recovered truth end up forming some denomination around it and become sectarian, and sometimes even cultic, in order to "protect" that portion of truth.

6. Most denominations die by reason of separating the person of Christ from doctrine and contend for the doctrine apart from or unrelated to Him who is the truth personified.

7. The same denominational walls and structures that hope to keep truth in and error out can and often also keep further truth out. Human nature likes to feel that it has all the truth, that it has everything.

8. Those who hold tenaciously to previously recovered truth generally reject "present truth". They hold to "what God said" in the past rather than hearing what God is saying "in the present". They generally miss "the present truth" coming to their generation.

9. One of the greatest sins of the Church, both individually and corporately, is the sin of unbelief. It is possible to use the Word of God, which is meant to create faith, and use it to create unbelief, especially by ultra-dispensationalism and cessationist views of the Scripture (Romans 10:17).

10. Every work of God and recovery of truth is attacked by Satan, either by counterfeit manifestations, human carnality, or extreme, where fragments of truth are taken to their extreme thus producing heresy. As already seen, heresy is taking a portion of truth to its extreme, out of balance, with the whole body of truth.

11. Every recovery of truth has been born out of prayer, intercession, pangs and travail of soul. Such things are generally born in "a manger", a stable place and not in the high places, the temples or cathedrals. Only "the wise men" see the "guiding star" that leads them to THE TRUTH personified in the Lord Jesus Christ and His Word, while religious leaders miss it.

12. Every recovery of truth, especially among believers, still has some "leaven" in it that has to be purged out. Traditional teachings are often brought into the fresh visitation, instead of allowing the Holy Spirit to "purge out the leaven" and make a pure meal offering before the Lord. Error has to be purged from restored truth, coming from the Church's Babylonian Captivity, and spiritual "Talmudic teachings" of the "Dark Ages".

13. One of the greatest dangers of those who emphasize "present truth" is the neglect of previously recovered truth, thus creating imbalance in the Church.

14. The principal of visitation is that, the Lord always "comes to His own, and His own receive Him not, but to those who do receive, to them He gives ..." (John 1:10-12). Revival and recovery is always to the Church, not to the world. The world is "awakened" when the Church is revived!

15. God often removes the leadership of previous visitations when He is about to bring a new and fresh visitation. The "Moses" of a generation have to go before the "Joshua's" of the new generation take the people of God further on in God's purposes.

16. Human nature seeks to denominationalize anything God does. Denominations are usually formed around:

    (a) A personality God used

    (b) An experience people entered into

    (c) A doctrinal emphasis or truth God restored, or

    (d) A form of Church government.

    This is never God's will, as these things become divisive, denominational or sectarian.

17. The failure of all previous movements of God necessitates a fresh move of the Holy Spirit. This will continue to be until God gains His ultimate intention in and for the Church. Only "new wineskins" can receive the "new wine" of the Spirit's recovered truth.

18. Each generation must have its fresh visitation from God, and each generation must get to know the Lord personally, for its time (Judges 2:7-10; Psalm 24:6; 79:13).

19. Each generation must build on the Biblical foundations laid by previous generations (Isaiah 58:12; Joshua 1:1-9). Though Joshua moves the people on in the purposes of God, he must not depart from the Law of the Lord as given to Moses.

20. Each generation must pass on and explain the redemptive truths to the next generation as they ask "What meaneth this?" (Psalm 78:1-6; 48:13; Exodus 12:26-27; 13:8,14).

21. Each generation should be and set an example to the following generation (Psalm 102:18; 109:13; 145:4).

22. Each generation can break the power or curse of a past evil generation by genuine repentance and turning to the Lord from all sin (Ezekiel 18:19-32).

23. Each generation can begin a new generation whenever this is necessary. If any one be in Christ, he is a new creation, he begins a new generation (Exodus 20:1-6; 2Corinthians 5:17).

24. Each generation should learn from the experiences of previous generations, whether good or evil (Psalm 78:6-8; Hebrews 3:10).

25. Each generation must serve their generation by the will of God, even as David served his generation in the purposes and will of God, being a man after God's own heart (Acts 13:22,36; Psalm 71:18; 78:70-72)

These propositional statements provide much food for thought and amplification!

Before Christ returns again the second time, there undoubtedly will be a generation in the true Church that will enter into all that God has provided for them in Christ.

In Moses' time, ten leaders robbed a whole generation for forty years of entering into the promises of God in Canaan land. All that generation died in unbelief, except Joshua and Caleb and the younger or second generation.

Although the first generation had experienced the deliverance from Egypt through the blood of the lamb (Passover Feast), and had experienced water baptism in the Red Sea, and the Cloudy Pillar of Fire to lead them to the promised land (1Corinthians 10:1-11), and though they had experienced "Pentecost" at Mt Sinai, they failed at Kadesh-Barnea. Here was the gateway to the promised land. Here they could enter into the final Feast, the Feast of Tabernacles. Unbelief caused them to miss the covenant land promised to Abraham, Isaac and Jacob. Forty years later, Joshua and Caleb, with a new generation enter into the promised land (Numbers 13-14 with Hebrews 3-4).

About forty Jubilees (ie., 40 x 50 = 2000) years have almost gone by in Church History as the people of God have wandered in the Wilderness of Unbelief. There is a final generation that is arising, with their Joshua's and Caleb's and these together will enter into the fullness of God's promised land! **Some will not enter in because of unbelief! Some must enter in by faith!**

Religious leaders, like the Scribes and Pharisees, the Priests and the Sadducees, have taken away the "key of knowledge" from the people. They have robbed themselves and whole congregations. They would not enter in themselves, and those who wanted to enter in, they have forbidden, they have hindered (Luke 11:52).

But the Lord has decreed that there is a generation that will receive the Divine keys (Matthew 16:19-20) and enter into all that God has promised in His Word. This generation will experience all previously recovered and restored truth as well as entering into "present truth" unto the coming of the Lord Jesus Christ!

CHAPTER FORTY-FIVE

SEVENTEENTH CENTURY THEOLOGICAL GLEANINGS

In "Golden Grain" Magazine (Volume 24, Number 5, Charles Price Publishing Co. Inc., August 1949), the writer discovered this interesting article. It is entitled "**Theological Gleanings - From An Unknown Pen of The Seventeenth Century**".

Although the writer (and perhaps the reader) may not agree totally with all that is written in this article, it is well worth consideration, especially as this comes from some unknown pen of the 17th Century. Most of it will certainly be found to be prophetic in its content and much has yet to come to pass.

The arrangement into **Sixty Propositions** has been done by the writer of this text in order to help in the reading thereof.

Sixty propositions to the Philadelphia Society, whithersoever dispersed (as the Israel of God). AD1619. Written over 350 years ago.

1. There shall be a total and full redemption by Christ.

2. This is a hidden mystery not to be understood without the revelation of the Holy Spirit.

3. The Holy Spirit is at hand to reveal the same unto all holy seekers and loving enquirers.

4. The completion of such a redemption is withheld and abstracted by the Apocalyptical Seals.

5. Wherefore, as the Spirit of God shall open seal after seal, so shall this redemption come to be revealed, both particularly and universally.

6. In the gradual opening of the mystery of redemption in Christ doth consist of the unsearchable wisdom of God, which may continually reveal new and fresh things to the worthy searcher.

7. In order to which the Ark of the Testimony in heaven shall be opened before the end of this world, and the living testimony contained therein shall be unsealed.

8. The presence of the Divine Ark will constitute the life of the Philadelphian Church, and where ever that is there must the Ark of necessity be.

9. The unsealing of the living testimony within the Ark of the Lord must begin the promulgation of the everlasting Gospel of the Kingdom.

10. The proclamation of the testimony WILL BE AS BY THE SOUND OF A TRUMPET, to alarm the nations of the earth, and more especially all the professors of Christianity, because attended with the power of all acting wonders.

11. So there shall be an authoritative decision given forth immediately from Christ, to the putting to end all controversies concerning the true Church.

12. This decision will be the actual sealing of the members of this Church with the Name of God, giving them a commission to act by the same.

13. This new name will distinguish them from the seven thousand names of Babylon.

14. The election and preparation of this Church is to be after a secret and hidden manner, as David in his minority was elected and anointed by the prophet of the Lord, yet was not admitted to the outward profession of the Kingdom for a considerable time afterwards.

15. Of the stem of David, a virgin Church, which hath known nothing of man or human constitution, is yet to be born.

16. And if it is yet to be born, then it will require some considerable time before it gets out of its minority and arrives at the full and mature age.

17. The birth of the Virgin Church was typified visionally to Saint John by the great wonder in heaven bringing forth her firstborn that was caught up to the throne of God (Revelation 12).

18. For as a virgin woman brought forth Christ after the flesh, so likewise a virgin woman is designed by God to bring forth the firstborn after the spirit, who shall be filled the with Holy Ghost and power.

19. The virgin that is here designed must be as of pure spirit, so also a glorified body, and all over impregnated with the Holy Ghost.

20. This Church, so brought forth and signed with the mark of the Divine Name, shall be adorned with miraculous gifts and powers beyond what has been.

21. Hereby, all nations shall be brought into it, so that it shall be the Church, according to the genuine and utmost latitude of the word.

22. It must be an anointed Church where it may truly bear the Name of Christ or Christian, being with Him anointed to the Priestly, Prophetical and Royal dignity.

23. Hence there will be no bonds or impositions, but the holy unction among these new born spirits will be all in all.

24. This anointed Church must be perfectly holy, so that it may worthily bear the Name of the Lord our holiness.

25. Until there be made ready such a Church upon the earth, so holy, so anointed that it is without spot or wrinkle, and that is adorned as a bride to meet her husband, Christ will not personally descend to solemnize the marriage and present the same to His Father.

26. But when the Bridal Church shall be made ready, and thoroughly cleansed and sanctified from every spot of defilement through the blood of Christ, then He will no longer delay His coming in person.

27. There is not this day visible upon the earth any anointed, holy and Bridal Church, all the churches and professions being found light when weighed in the balance.

28. Therefore, they are rejected by the Supreme Judge.

29. Which rejection and condemnation will be for this end, that out of them a new and a glorious Church may rise up, in whom there shall be found no fault, like as He findeth none in the Philadelphian Church (Revelation 3:7-12).

30. Then shall the glory of God and the Lamb so rest upon the typical Tabernacle, so that it shall be called the Tabernacle of wisdom, and though this Philadelphian Church is not known in visibility, yet it may be hidden at this present time as in the womb of the morning.

31. Notwithstanding, it will be brought forth into visibility as coming forth out of the wilderness within a short period; then it will go on to multiply and propagate itself universally, not only to the number of the firstborn (144,000), but also to the remnant of the seed, against whom the Dragon shall make continual war.

32. Wherefore the spirit of David shall be most eminently be revived in this Church, and more especially in some or other select members of it, as the blossoming root, which is to precede the day of Solomon in the blessed Millennium.

33. These will have might given to them to overcome the Dragon and his angels, even as David and his army overcame Goliath and the Philistines.

34. This will be as the standing up of Michael, the great Prince of Israel, and will be as the appearance of Moses against Pharoah, in order that the chosen seed may be brought forth out from their hard servitude.

35. Egypt doth figure out this servile creation, under which each one of Abraham's seed groans.

36. But a prophet, and the most prophetical generation will the Most High raise up, who shall deliver His people by mere force of spiritual arms.

37. For which there must be raised up certain head powers to bear the first office, who are to be persons of great eminence, and in favour with the Trinity, whose dread and fear shall fall upon all nations, visible and invisible, because of the mighty acting power of the Holy Ghost which shall rest upon them.

38. For Christ, before His own distinct and personal appearance, will first appear and represent Himself in some chosen vessels, anointed to be leaders unto the rest, and to bring them into the promised land, the new creation state.

39. Thus Moses, Joshua and Aaron may be considered types as of some upon whom the same Spirit may come, yet rest in greater proportion, whereby they shall make way for the ransomed of the Lord to return to Zion; but none shall stand in any considerable office under God, but those who are tried stones after the pattern and similitude of the Chief Cornerstone, Christ.

40. This will be a fiery trial through which very few will be able to pass or bear up in, wherefore the waiters for the visible breaking out of this Church are strictly charged to hold fast that which they have, and to wait together in the unity of pure love, praying in the Holy Ghost, according to the Apostolic pattern, that they may be sent forth to multiply more universally.

41. This trial will be of absolute necessity to everyone in particular, and all in general, for the constituting and cementing of the true Philadelphian Church, by the clearing away all the remaining infirmities of nature, and burning away of all that is hay, stubble and dross, which they may have added to the work of the Lord; for nothing must remain the fire, for as a refiner will the Lord purify the sons and daughters of it, and purge them as perfect righteousness.

42. Though the operation of the Holy Spirit in these waiters may for a long time contend with many infirmities and evils, and yet if it be continually warm and watched, it cannot at the last but work out a perfect cure and bring about full and total redemption from the earth.

43. There may be some living at present who may come then to be fully and totally redeemed, having another body put on them, that is one after the Priestly Order.

44. This anointed Priestly body will render them impregnable, and qualify them for that high degree of spiritual government to which they are called.

45. Wherefore, it is required on our part to suffer the Spirit of Burning to do upon us the refining work, fanning us with the fiery breath, and searching every part within us until all be pure and clean, and thereby we arrived to a fixed body from whence these wonders are to flow out.

46. Upon this body will be the fiation of the Urim and Thummin, that are to be appropriated to the Priests of the Melchisedekian Order, whose descent is not to be counted in the genealogy of that creation which is under the Fall, but in another genealogy which is from the Restoration.

47. Hence these Priests will have a deep inward search and Divine sight into the secret things of Deity; will be able to prophesy in a clear ground, not darkly nor enigmatically, for they will know what is couched in the first originality of all beings, in the eternal anti-type of nature, and will be capacitated to bring them forth according to the Divine counsel and ordination.

48. The Lord, whose hand is lifted up, sweareth in truth and righteousness, that, from Abraham's line, according to the Spirit, there shall arise a holy Priesthood.

49. Abraham and Sarah were a type of that which should be produced and manifested in the last age of this world.

50. The mighty spirit of Cyrus is appointed to lay the foundation of the third Temple and support it in its building.

51. There are such characteristics or marks whereby the pure virgin Church so founded shall continually be known and distinguished from all others, and whereby the unction and true sound of the Holy Ghost shall be discerned from that which is false, low and counterfeit.

52. There must be a manifestation of the Spirit whereby to edify and raise up this Church suitable to the resurrection of Christ.

53. This manifestation must be in the absoluteness of power, as well as in the beauty of holiness, so bringing down heaven upon earth, and representing here the New Jerusalem State in order to which pure spirits, which are thus purely begotten and born of God, can ascend to the New Jerusalem above, where their Head in great majesty doth reign, and receive there such a mission whereby they shall be empowered to bring down to this world its transcendant glory.

54. None but those who have risen with Christ in the regeneration can thus ascend, and none but those who have so ascended and received of His glory can descend again to communicate the same, being thereby His representatives upon the new earth, and subordinate Priests and Princes under Him.

55. Now He that is ascended and glorified has made Himself, as it were, our debtor; consequently He will not be wanting in qualifying and furnishing certain high and principal instruments, who shall be most humble, and as little regarded as David was, whom He will dignify with honour and Priestly sovereignty for the drawing to them the scattered flocks, and gathering them into the one fold out of all nations and languages.

56. Therefore, there should be a holy emulation and ambition stirred up among the bands of Jesus, that they may be the firstfruits unto Him that is risen from the dead, and so be made principal agents for Him and with Him, that they may, if possible, be of the number of the firstborn of the New Jerusalem mother.

57. All true lovers of Jesus, and true waiters of His Kingdom in Spirit, under whatsoever profession or forms they are dispersed ought to be numbered among the Philadelphian spirits, to whom this message appertains.

58. The society is not the Church but preparatory to the Church of Philadelphia.

59. It consists of those who have associated themselves together in the unity of the Spirit for its glorious appearance and manifestation.

60. Wherefore, there is such a strict charge given to them throughout the message to be watchful, and quicken their pace.

Summary Comment:

This is indeed a remarkable prophetic word and the unknown writer certainly had some Divine insight into the purposes of God for the Church in the last days, in the end times. As mentioned earlier, even though the writer and reader may not totally agree with every statement, there is much truth and spiritual food for thought and prayer to all who see that the purposes of God will consummate in a victorious Church, a bride suitable to the blessed Son of God (Ephesians 5:23-32). This is what the truth of restoration is all about!

CHAPTER FORTY-SIX
THE FUTURE CHURCH

Our study has shown clearly that the Lord indeed intends to restore to His Church all that has been lost over the years - and more! He will fulfil His own laws of restitution. The Church will get back to its beginning and everything that has been taken or robbed from the Church will be given again. It will be, however, a restoration that includes in itself, not only that which was lost but far more than that which was lost. This is according to God's own laws as seen in Exodus, Leviticus and Deuteronomy.

In this concluding chapter, it may be asked: Where to now? Whither bound? What will happen in the Church before or until Jesus comes? In this chapter, we list a number of things that the writer sees, in measure, about the future Church, the last day Church, the Church that enters the 21st Century. These are things the writer believes the Church will experience through to the second advent of our Lord Jesus Christ.

1. Increased Outpouring of the Holy Spirit

There will be an increased outpouring of the Holy Spirit according to Joel 2:28-32 and Acts 2. The Holy Spirit is to be poured out on "all flesh" in the last days. The last days began with the initial outpouring and continues on to the end of the age. The Church is living in the last of the last days, and the outpouring of the Spirit will continue to increase in all nations of the earth (Revelation 4:5; 3:1 with 5:6).

John saw in his vision in Revelation the "seven Spirits of God send forth into all the earth".

The number seven speaks of perfection, and the seven Spirits of God sent forth into all the earth speak of the perfection and fullness of the Spirit's operation, powers, fruit and gifts being sent forth worldwide to finalize the purposes of God. This is to take place in the earth before Christ;'s second coming. Only time will reveal the full meaning and implications of this prophetic word.

2. Increased Illumination on the Word of Truth

There will be increased illumination on the revelation given by inspiration. That is to say, God will shine further light upon truth as He has done down through Church History in the recovery of truth (Psalm 43:1-4).

It is evident, and Church History has proven this, that there are truths in the Word of God, the Bible, that the Lord has yet to shine upon the Church. There will be a Church in the earth that comes to see, by the Spirit, accept and experience the fullness of truth as revealed in God's Word. As many of God's people have experienced, they would say when light shines on the Word, "I have never seen that before", yet it has been in the Word for thousands of years!" What happened? Light shone upon truth! So it has been with every recovery and restored truth to the Church. Each truth has been in the Book, but suddenly the spiritual eyes are opened to "see" it (Luke 24:27,31,31,44-45; Psalm 119:18).

3. The First Principles of the Doctrine of Christ

In Hebrews 6:1-3 the writer lists seven principles of the doctrine of Christ, which are as follows here:

* Repentance from Dead Works
* Faith towards God
* Baptisms (Water and Holy Spirit Baptisms)
* Laying on of Hands
* Resurrection from the Dead
* Eternal Judgment
* Perfection

These things have several designations, each having a distinct aspect of truth. They were spoken of as being:

* The First Principles of the Oracles of God. Read Psalm 28:2; Romans 3:2; with Acts 7:38; 1Kings 6:1-31. The Holiest of All was called "the oracle". It was here God spoke in audible voice to His appointed high priest. The speaking place of the voice of God was from between the cherubimed blood-sprinkled mercyseat.
* Principles of the Doctrine of Christ (Hebrews 5:12; 6:1).

    Christ taught the Father's doctrine (Hebrews 1:1-2; John 7:16-17).
* The Word of the beginning of Christ (Hebrews 6:1, Margin.KJV). All begins and ends in Christ. The first principles of Christ's doctrine are milk leading to meat.
* The Word of Righteousness (Hebrews 5:12-13). It is the Word that brings about righteous relationship and living in a believer's life as they follow the Lord.

Our study of Church History certainly points to the recovery of these First Principles of the doctrines of Christ.

Without pressing the analogy too far, or being too exact on the matter, there does seem to be a link with the history of the restoration of these truths.

The 1500's saw a recovery of "Repentance from dead works, and Faith towards God", in the period of the Reformation.

The 1600-1700's saw a recovery of the truth of Water Baptism and Sanctification, along with other truths.

The doctrine of the Baptism of the Holy Spirit and its initial sign of reception was seen in the 1900's. The doctrine of the Laying on of Hands also was recovered in the mid-1900's along with other truths.

It would seem that the Lord, by His Spirit, will shine further light on the doctrines of "Resurrection from the Dead", "Eternal Judgment" and "Perfection", in the days that are ahead. These doctrines are already in the Word of God but the Lord will shine light on truth in these areas as He has done on the three preceding principles over the years of Church History.

Hebrews 6:1-3 is not just a doctrinal statement of the early Church. These principles of Christ's doctrine have to be experienced personally and corporately in the life of a Church.

Restoration Theology

The writer says: "**let us go on unto perfection ... and this will we do if God permit**". The issue is, when a person is building a house, the first thing laid is the foundation. The building inspector comes along and inspects the foundation to see if it is properly laid. If it is, then he gives "the permit" to go and complete the house. If the foundation is not properly laid, then "the permit" is not given.

Many believers (and Churches) do not have these foundational doctrines and principles properly laid, therefore they cannot go on "unto perfection". Unless a believer or a Church has these foundational principles properly laid, they cannot continue on to full maturity.

There is an increase of understanding of the "First Principles" coming to the Church in these days as never before (Refer "**The Foundation Series**" by Derek Prince).

As the Lord used various ministries on "Repentance from Dead Works", and "Faith towards God", and "Water Baptism", "Holy Spirit Baptism", "Laying on of Hands", and other restored truths, it seems to be consistent that God will bring light and truth and a greater emphasis on these other principles spelt out here by various ministries. The Church must have an ear to hear what the Spirit would say both now and in the days that are ahead.

4. **The Gospel of the Kingdom Harvest**

Jesus gave one of the surest signs of His return in Matthew 24:14. He said that the Gospel of the Kingdom would be preached in all the world for a witness unto all nations, and then - and not until then - the end would come!

There are still several hundreds of ethnic groupings in the world that have no Scripture in their tongue, and no Gospel witness. The increase of world evangelism, home and foreign missions is evidence that the Holy Spirit is burdening the Church for the final harvest of souls in the nations of the earth.

John saw the redeemed out of every kindred, tongue, tribe and nation worshipping before the throne of God and the Lamb. The Lamb will see the fruit of His death and resurrection (John 12:24; Revelation 5:9-10).

Jesus said the harvest was the end of the age. The final harvest, in Israel's year, came in the Feast of Tabernacles. The Gospel of the Kingdom brings in the final harvest of souls (Matthew 13:36-43).

5. **The Feast of Tabernacles**

The Church has experienced the Feast of Passover and the Feast of Pentecost, both historically and personally. The third and greatest feast was the Feast of Tabernacles in the seventh month (Leviticus 23). The three important parts of this feast were:

* The Day of Blowing of Trumpets on the first day,
* The great Day of Atonement on the tenth day, and
* The Feast of Tabernacles (Booths) on the fifteenth day, after finished harvest.

    This continued for seven days, with a special crowning day afterwards.

Although these feasts have been fulfilled in and through Christ, both historically and personally, there is something in all that the Church has yet to experience. This is more especially in that which pertains to this third feast.

The Feast of Trumpets is upon the Church. Distinctive ministries are sounding out some distinctive messages to the Church. The Church must enter into experientially that which took place on the Day of Atonement. The Church will experience the Feast of Tabernacles and rejoice in the final harvest of the age before Jesus comes again. This is another important thing to find fulfilment in the future Church! Only time will tell what is the fullness of meaning in this truth and experience in the Church.

6. **The Ascension-Gift Ministries and the Body of Christ**

    According to Paul in Ephesians 4:1-16, the Body of Christ is to come to the measure of the stature of the fullness of Christ, unto a perfect and mature man.

    God has set in the Church, for this very purpose, the fivefold ascension-gift ministries of apostles, prophets, evangelists, shepherds and teachers. They are given FOR the perfecting or equipping of the saints, FOR bringing the saints into the work of their ministry, and FOR the building up of the Body of Christ.

    God has also set in the Church the gifts of the Spirit (1Corinthians 12:1-12; Romans 12:1-8). The ministries, the gifts, along with the Word of God and the work of the Holy Spirit, are all given to mature the saints into the character of Christ and fullness of the fruit of the Spirit (Galatians 5:22-23).

    Greater evidence of God's seal on apostles, prophets, evangelists, shepherds and teachers is to come. Evangelists, shepherds and teachers have generally been accepted over the years, but the foundation ministries of apostles and prophets have been rejected by most of the Church, or dispensed with as being "not for today". However, these will come more into their function to bring the Church to maturity, along with the other ministries the Lord has given. The apostles and prophets will be more evident in these last days (Read Ephesians 2:19-22; Revelation 18:20; Luke 11:49; Matthew 23:34; 1Corinthians 12:28-29).

7. **The Prayer of Jesus**

    The prayer of Jesus, our great high priest, is found in John 17. This is indeed "the Lord's prayer". In it He prayed to the Father that His people would be one, as the Father and the Son are one.

    About nineteen times Jesus mentioned "the world" in His prayer. He prayed that the unity of His people would be so great that (a) The world might know that the Father had sent His Son, and that (b) The world might believe that the Father had sent His Son.

    A serious consideration of the prayer shows that something has to happen in the true Church for the world to know and believe that the Father sent His Son. It is not that all the world will be saved, but the world will see something in the true Church that will be the most witness to it. It is too late for the world to know and believe after Jesus has come the second time.

    In the prayer of Jesus, He mentioned four things that have been given to the Church to bring about this unity.

Restoration Theology

* His Name - verses 6,11,12,26
* His Word - verses 6,8,14,17,19,20
* His Glory - verses 4,5,22,24
* His Love - verses 23,24,26 with John 3:16; 13:34-35; 15:1-13.

Jesus prayed for himself (verses 1-5), for His disciples (verses 6-19), and for the world, for all those who would believe on Him through the Church's ministry(verses 20-26).

Jesus prayed that His people would be one. Unity is one of the most powerful weapons of victory over the enemy. United we stand, divided we fall (1 Corinthians 1:10). Satan's tactics have always been "divide and conquer". A divided Church is a conquered Church. The unity preceded the glory of God at the dedication of Solomon's Temple (2Chronicles 5-6-7).

The early Church knew great power, great grace and great glory under the outpouring of the Holy Spirit because of their unity (Acts 1:14; 2:1). It is where unity is that the Lord commands the blessing, even life for ever more. The anointing on the head (Christ) flows down to the body (Church) where there is unity (Psalm 133; Psalm 102:13-22).

8. The Church Triumphant

Jesus said He would build His Church and the gates of hades would not prevail against it. This Church would have the keys of the kingdom of heaven and the power to bind and loose in heaven and earth, as the head of the Church in heaven worked with His people (Mark 16:15-20; Matthew 16:15-19).

In Acts we see Peter using the keys of the kingdom to unlock the door of faith for both Jews and Gentiles. This was under the early outpouring of the Spirit. The Church went forth spiritually militant and triumphant.

The world will yet see the Church triumphant in spiritual warfare. The wisdom of God is to be manifested in greater power to the principalities and powers and wicked spirits in heavenly places, and this by the Church (Ephesians 3:9-11).

The Church will use the spiritual weapons from the Lord's armoury and go forth conquering and to conquer (Isaiah 45:17; Song of Solomon 6:10,13; Psalm 91; Psalm 149:6-9; Revelation 2:26-27; 3:21).

9. The Double Portion of the Spirit

The Church of the last days will come to receive the double portion of the Spirit's power and grace.

When Elijah was translated to heaven without dying, Elisha, his successor, asked for a double portion of the Spirit that was upon Elijah. As Elisha kept his eyes upon Elijah, the mantle of Elijah fell from heaven. Elisha picked it up and his ministry was manifested in a double portion of miracles (Read 2Kings).

So the future Church will experience the double portion of what the early Church experienced. The mantle of the Lord Jesus Christ will fall upon this Church, and the realm of the miraculous manifestation of the gifts of the Spirit will be evidenced.

Elisha had a double portion of the Holy Spirit's power on him (2Kings 2:9-10). This was the portion for the firstborn (Deuteronomy 21:15-17). The last day Church will be "the Church of the firstborn" in strictest sense, and receive its full birthright and the double portion of the Spirit.

Israel had a double portion of manna on the sixth day as there was to be none on the seventh day (Exodus 16:4-35; notes verses 5,22). The Church is at the close of the six days of the Lord and a double portion of the manna of God's Word will be available for the Church. There is none on the seventh day (Psalm 90:4; 2Peter 3:8). The double portion of manna will be revealed. This is the "hidden manna" promised to those who are overcomers (Revelation 2:17).

10. The Manifestation of Mature Sons

Paul tells us in Romans 8:14-30 that the world is waiting for the manifestation, or the unveiling, of the sons of God.

This speaks of people coming to maturity in Christ, to full sonship ministry. The world is not waiting for this unveiling when the Church is translated to heaven. It is too late then. It points to something that will take place here on the earth.

The world waited about four thousand years for the manifestation of THE Son of God. The world has waited for about six thousand years for the unveiling of the sons of God. Many expositors put this Scripture fulfilment off to the Millennium or to the rapture of the Church, or in heaven. All power was given to Christ, both in heaven and in earth (Matthew 28:19-20).

As Christ was the express image of the Father (Hebrews 1:3), so the sons will be the express image of Christ. They will be conformed to His image and they will do "greater works" than Jesus did, according to the word He spoke to His disciples. This will be greater in quantity, not necessarily quality (John 14:12; Matthew 10:7-8; Luke 10:17-20).

11. The Order of Melchisedek

The order of Melchisedek is an order of kings and priests. Without doubt, all true believers are born to be kings and priests unto God, but how little and immature is that order. In principle, Paul writes to those who are under the law, and speaks of children being under tutors and instructors until the time appointed of the father (Galatians 4:4-7). Once the child comes of age, he receives the adoption of a son, the rights, privileges and responsibility of a son. So this is in the Church.

Many of God's people are babes in Christ, little children in the Lord. But the last day Church will come to sonship. They will exercise the ministry of kingship, ruling and reigning with Christ on the earth. They will also exercise the kingly power and authority over the power of the enemy. They will come to fuller operation of the priestly ministry also. In the world this will be seen in reconciling men to God in Christ's stead. This will be the full manifestation of the order of Melchisdek (Revelation 1:6; 5:9-10; 1Peter 2:5-9-10; 2Timothy 2:11; 20:4-6; Luke 10:17-20).

12. The Glorious Bridal Church

The climax of Pauline revelation of the Church in seen in Ephesians 5:23-32. Christ is to present to Himself a glorious Church, without spot, or wrinkle, or blemish or any such thing. This Church is to be holy, suitable to be joined to the Lord in marriage. Christ will not be unequally yoked to a bride that is not like Him. To do so would be to violate His own marriage laws.

Before the marriage of Christ to His Church can take place, the Church must be like Christ, sinless and perfect. The bride will make herself ready for the marriage by the grace of God, the cleansing of the Word, the power of the Holy Spirit. In order for the marriage to take place, the Lord will do a great work of cleansing in the Church in these last days (Ephesians 5:23-32; Revelation 19:7-8).

13. The Redemption of the Body

The apostle Paul also received a clear revelation about that Church that is to be "alive and remaining unto the coming of the Lord" (1Thessalonians 4:15-18). The Lord showed him a mystery. That is, all believers will not die. There will be a company of believers who live to the coming of Christ and will not experience death.

Speaking of the coming of the Lord, Paul saw two companies of believers:

* The dead in Christ, and,
* The alive and remaining ones in Christ.

He saw that the dead in Christ would rise first, and those that were alive would be caught up together with them to meet the Lord in the air.

In 1Corinthians 15:51-57 he says the same truth in this way. He speaks of the dead and the living in the following manner.

* This corruption shall put on incorruption (that is, the dead in Christ rise first),
* This mortal shall put on immortality (that is, the alive and remain are changed).

When this takes place, then the fullness of Christ's word to Martha will be experienced. Jesus said, "I am the resurrection and the life: he that believeth in Me though he were dead, yet shall he live, and whoever lives and believes in Me shall never die" (John 11:25-26). Jesus will be the resurrection to the dead in Christ. He will be the life to those who are alive and remain unto his coming.

This company of believers will know the redemption of their body. The grave will not have the victory over them, because the sting of death, which is sin, will be removed! There are a number of Scriptures all pointing to the truth of death being overcome in this generation of true believers who are alive to the Lord's coming. These can only be mentioned in brief for the student's consideration.

* The last enemy to be destroyed is death (1Corinthians 15:26-27). Although it is true that all are appointed to die, there will be that company who will be loosed from that appointment with death (Read Hebrews 9:27 with Psalm 102:16-21; Psalm 79:11). They will break that appointment with death, not only spiritually but also physically (Romans 8:2,11).

* This company will know and experience the redemption of the body for which all believers groan (Luke 21:25-28 with Ephesians 1:13-14; 4:30; Romans 8:23).

* This company will be like "an Enoch company" who was translated that he should not see death (Hebrews 11:5; Genesis 5:18-24; Jude 14-15).

* This company will come to know indeed that Jesus brought life and immortality to light through the Gospel (2Timothy 1:10). They will know that He has conquered him who had the power of death, that is the devil (Hebrews 2:6-15).

* This company will come to believe what Jesus said when He said, "If a man keep My saying, he will not see (or taste) of death (John 6:51-58; 8:51).

* This company will receive their house from heaven and not become unclothed by death, or become a disembodied spirit (2Corinthians 5:1-5).

* This company will come to have a body like unto Christ's glorious body (Philippians 3:21). The baptism in the Holy Spirit and the sign of speaking in tongues is the seal, the firstfruits, the earnest or down-payment of the redemption of the purchased possession, which is the body (2Corinthians 1:21-22; Ephesians 1:13-14; 4:30; Romans 8:19-25).

An important principle in Scripture is this: Before God brings His people into a new experience of something, He generally gives a revelation (light on truth!) of it in His Word, so that that Word creates faith for the experience (Hebrews 11:5 with Romans 10:17). This is where Enoch received the faith for the experience. It came from hearing a word from the Lord. "Faith comes by hearing a word (Grk."Rhema"), and this in order brought Enoch into the experience. So it was with all of the heroes of faith in Hebrews 11 as they came to know this principle.

This will be so in the generation who live to the coming of the Lord. It will not simply be because they are fortunate enough to be alive at His coming, but it will be because, as the final generation, they will receive faith by a word (The Word) for that glorious experience.

Paul, however, reminds the believers that the dead in Christ will rise first, then the alive and remaining believers will be caught up together with them to meet the Lord in the air and so for ever be with Him!

14. The Kingdom of God in the Earth

The Scriptures speak much about reigning with Christ on the earth (Revelation 5:9-10). The meek shall inherit the earth (Matthew 6:9-10; 5:5; Psalm 37:9,22,29; Isaiah 45:18). The prophets spoke about the glory of the Lord that would cover the earth (Numbers 14:21; Habakkuk 2:14,20; Isaiah 52:10; Psalm 46:8-10; 24:1; 50:6; 78:69; Isaiah 60:1-5; Haggai 2:9).

The writer speaks of this period of time being a "Christian Millennium", which precedes the great white throne judgment and the new heavens, new earth and new Jerusalem (Revelation 20-21-22 chapters). This, however, would require a textbook in itself. It is sufficient to say that the Scriptures show the triumph of the Lord and His Church and the eternal states will be one of eternal blessedness. The Church will have fulfilled God's purpose in the earth and come to full restoration of all that was lost in the Fall! This is God's ultimate intention!

In Conclusion:

The prophet Isaiah speaks assuring words to his time and also to our time. In Isaiah 43:18-21 he says:

"Remember not the former things, neither consider the things of old. Behold, I will do a new thing, now it shall spring forth; shall you not know it? This people have I formed for Myself, they shall show forth My praise".

The Lord also said that the word that had gone forth out of His mouth would not return to Him void, but it would accomplish that which He sent it to (Isaiah 55:96-12). The Lord also said that He watches over His word to perform it, to bring it to pass (Jeremiah 1:11-12). It is His Word. It has gone forth out of His mouth. He will accomplish these things.

Paul also tells us that the Lord will finish the work, and He will cut it short in righteousness, for it will be a short work that the Lord will do in the earth (Romans 9:28 with Acts 13:40-41). Though darkness will increase in the earth, the Lord will rise and shine on His people, and they will have light and glory seen upon them (Isaiah 60:1-5).

From **"This is That"** (page 668 by A.S.McPherson), we quote a portion of a prophetic word that was given in the early 1920's or thereabouts.

> "O My people, seek no longer fleshly things; seek not earthly things; but seek thou the things of the Spirit. Be not encumbered with many cares. O, for a people with one accord, in one place, with all things in common, none calling aught they possess their own! How I could show forth My glory. Yes, they would move heaven and earth with their prayers.
>
> Can you not perceive My plan? Can you not understand My workings? Behold, I show you a mystery.
>
> I have called nations from nations.
>
> I have separated people from people.
>
> I have called churches from churches.
>
> I have called out the sanctified from the lukewarm.
>
> I have called out a baptized company from the sanctified.
>
> But now, behold, I do a new work. I am seeking to call a baptized people from a baptized people, who will go all the way to the standard of My perfection.
>
> All have failed as a complete body to go all the way, and to measure up to the Word; but I will have a people who will not be satisfied with aught but My best perfection, a people who will not slumber nor sleep, but who will watch with Me this one remaining hour. Through this people will I show forth mighty signs and wonders. The people shall marvel before them, saying: What manner of people are these?
>
> They will seem but folly unto the world; but through them shall the wisdom of Jehovah be made manifest. Weak in their own words, slow to speak, few in words, but they shall speak forth My words in the power and demonstration of the Spirit" (End portion of quote).

If this prophecy was true then, surely it is more so in this generation! May the Lord find a people in whom this prophetic word shall be fulfilled! May the Lord bring to pass the complete restoration to the Church of all lost truth and that this Church will fulfill His final purpose in the earth and be a suitable bride to be joined to His blessed Son, the Lord Jesus Christ, our redeemer and bridegroom!

CHAPTER FORTY-SEVEN

THE PRESENT TRUTH

The message is complete. Creation, Man, Israel and the Church are each to be restored in the Lord and by the Lord to the early glory from which each fell. This is only "in Christ". There is no restoration apart from redemption. This is restoration theology. This is restoration truth.

The apostle Peter, when writing to the believers of his time, desired that they be "**established in the present truth**". A free paraphrase of this complete verse would read this way.

"I will not neglect to always remind you of these things, even though you know them and are established (grounded, firmly fixed) **in the present truth - the truth that is presently coming to you**, which you have received and that you now hold" (2Peter 1:12). What is meant then by "**present truth**?"

It is important for all believers to both know the truth and experience the truth. John, the beloved apostle writes to the believers that his joy is fulfilled when they "**walk in truth**". That is, they not only know the truth theologically or doctrinally, but they also know the truth experientially or practically. They walk in obedience to the truth (2John 1,2,4 with 3John 3,4). What then is meant by "present truth?"

If we were living in the period of the Reformation, then "**present truth**" would be "repentance from dead works and faith towards God". In other words, justification by faith was the truth that was presently coming to that generation.

If we were living in the period of the Anabaptists, then "**present truth**" would be water baptism by immersion, not by sprinkling of infants or the unregenerate. That was the truth that was presently coming to that generation.

If we were living in the period of the truth of sanctification, or of healing, or of the baptism in the Holy Spirit, the priesthood of all believers, or the revelation of the name of God in baptism - each of these would be "**present truth**". Each would be the truth that was presently coming to each generation.

The same holds true in the 1900's and onward to the present time. Much truth is coming to the people of God that is indeed "present truth". The truths of worship and praise, the laying on of hands, evangelism, missions, kingdom truth, and so forth as has been dealt with in this text.

The issue is: Are we walking in the truth or the truths that are presently coming to the Church? Many of God's people have not even caught up, as it were, to previously recovered truth, let alone walking in "**present truth**".

It is also important that, while believers walk in the present truth - the truth that is presently coming to them - that previously recovered truth is not neglected. The Church must maintain both doctrinally and experientially all previously recovered truth while walking in present truth!

Often times, believers walk in present truth and neglect "the ancient landmarks" of truth already recovered (Proverbs 22:28; Deuteronomy 19:14; 27:14). In gaining more of the promised land, Israel had to be careful and watchful to not lose the land already gained in warfare, as the Book of Joshua teaches.

As the Church maintains recovered and restored truth and walks in present truth, it will be contending earnestly for "the faith once and for all delivered to the saints" (Jude 3). "The Faith" will include in itself all the truths that were given by the Lord through the ministry of the Holy Spirit to the early Church and as written in the complete Word of God.

Peter's concern and desire is still the Lord's concern and desire for His Church, the people of God. "Wherefore, I will not be negligent to put you always in remembrance of these things, though you know them, and be established in the present truth" (2Peter 1:12). This is the purpose of this text! It is that all believers will be established in present truth – the truth of **Restoration Theology**!

SUPPLEMENTAL

ORDER OF WORSHIP ESTABLISHED

Tabernacle of David (New Testament Church) (Mount Zion Order)	**Tabernacle of Moses** (Old Testament Church) (Mount Sinai Order)

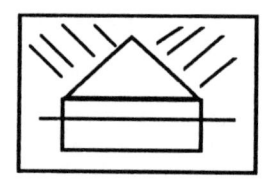

1. Singers and Singing
   (1Chronicles 15:16-27, Colossians 3:16)
2. Instruments of Music
   (1Chronicles 23:5, 25:1-7, Ephesians 5:18-19)
3. Levites Minister Before Ark
   (1Chronicles 16:37, Hebrews 6:19-20, 10:19-21)
4. Recording
   (1Chronicles 16:4, Psalms 80:1, Revelation 1:10-11)
5. Thanking
   (1Chronicles 16:4, 8, 41, 1Thessalonians 5:18)
6. Praise
   (1Chronicles 16:4, 36, Hebrews 13:15)
7. Psalm Singing
   (1Chronicles 16:7, Ephesians 5:18-19,
   1Corinthians 14:26, James 5:13)
8. Rejoicing and Joy
   (1Chronicles 16:10, 27, 31, Acts 13:52)
9. Clapping
   (Psalms 47:1)
10. Shouting
    (1Chronicles 15:28, 1Thessalonians 4:16)
11. Dancing
    (1Chronicles 15:29, Psalms 149:3, Luke 15:25)
12. Lifting Up Hands
    (Psalms 134, 1Timothy 2:8)
13. Worship - Access - Bowing
    (1Chronicles 16:29, John 4:20-24)
14. Seeking the Lord
    (1Chronicles 16:10-11, Acts 15:17)
15. Spiritual Sacrifices
    (Psalms 27:6, 116:17, 1Peter 2:3-5, Hebrews 13:15-16)
16. Standing Before The Lord
    (Psalms 134:1, 135:1-2)
17. Kneeling Before The Lord
    (2Chronicles 6:13-14, Psalms 95:6)
18. Amen (In Blessing)
    (1Chronicles 16:36, 1Corinthians 14:16)

---

1. None (Mount Gibeon – a few)
   (1Chronicles 16:37-43)
2. None
3. High Priest Only
4. None
5. None
6. None
7. None (Psalm 90 only)
8. Commanded
9. None
10. None (except Jericho, Joshua 6)
11. None (except Exodus 15)
12. None
13. Worship – Afar Off
14. Sought the Tabernacle
15. Animal Sacrifices
16. Priests Only
17. Kneel in Prayer
    (Ezra 9:5, Daniel 6:10)
18. Amen (To Curses)
    (Deuteronomy 27:15-26)

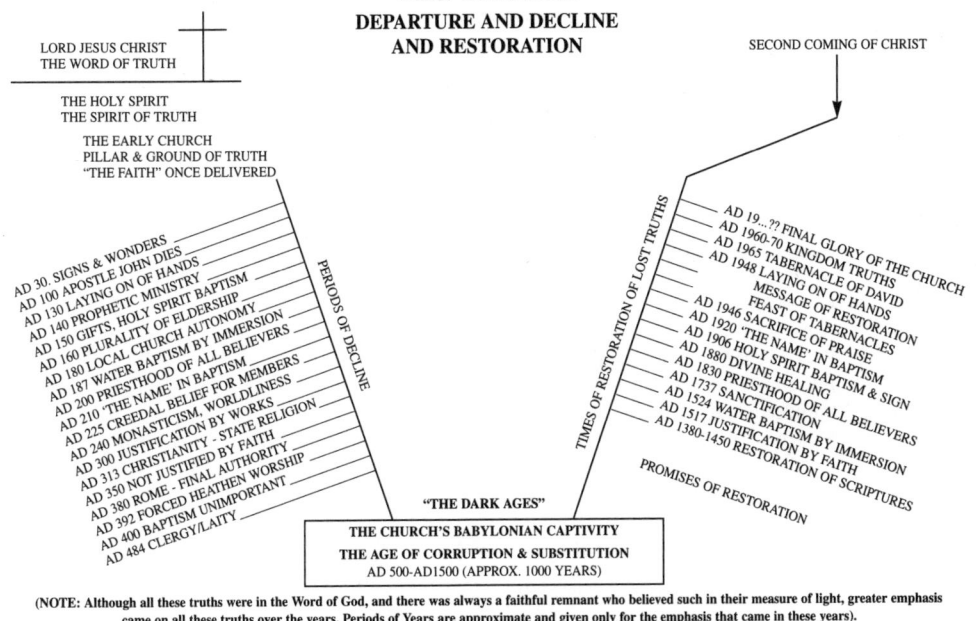

THE CHURCH
DEPARTURE AND DECLINE AND RESTORATION

LORD JESUS CHRIST
THE WORD OF TRUTH

SECOND COMING OF CHRIST

THE HOLY SPIRIT
THE SPIRIT OF TRUTH

THE EARLY CHURCH
PILLAR & GROUND OF TRUTH
"THE FAITH" ONCE DELIVERED

Periods of Decline:
- AD 30, SIGNS & WONDERS
- AD 100 APOSTLE JOHN DIES
- AD 130 LAYING ON OF HANDS
- AD 140 PROPHETIC MINISTRY
- AD 150 GIFTS, HOLY SPIRIT BAPTISM
- AD 160 PLURALITY OF ELDERSHIP
- AD 180 LOCAL CHURCH AUTONOMY
- AD 187 WATER BAPTISM BY IMMERSION
- AD 200 PRIESTHOOD OF ALL BELIEVERS
- AD 210 'THE NAME' IN BAPTISM
- AD 225 CREEDAL BELIEF FOR MEMBERS
- AD 300 MONASTICISM, WORLDLINESS
- AD 313 JUSTIFICATION BY WORKS
- AD 350 CHRISTIANITY - STATE RELIGION
- AD 380 NOT JUSTIFIED BY FAITH
- AD 392 ROME - FINAL AUTHORITY
- AD 400 FORCED HEATHEN WORSHIP
- AD 484 BAPTISM UNIMPORTANT
- CLERGY/LAITY

Times of Restoration of Lost Truths / Promises of Restoration:
- AD 19..?? FINAL GLORY OF THE CHURCH
- AD 1960-70 KINGDOM TRUTHS
- AD 1965 TABERNACLE OF DAVID
- AD 1948 LAYING ON OF HANDS
- MESSAGE OF RESTORATION
- AD 1946 FEAST OF TABERNACLES
- AD 1920 SACRIFICE OF PRAISE
- AD 1906 'THE NAME' IN BAPTISM
- AD 1880 HOLY SPIRIT BAPTISM & SIGN
- AD 1830 DIVINE HEALING
- AD 1737 PRIESTHOOD OF ALL BELIEVERS
- AD 1524 SANCTIFICATION
- AD 1517 WATER BAPTISM BY IMMERSION
- AD 1380-1450 JUSTIFICATION BY FAITH
- RESTORATION OF SCRIPTURES

"THE DARK AGES"
THE CHURCH'S BABYLONIAN CAPTIVITY
THE AGE OF CORRUPTION & SUBSTITUTION
AD 500-AD1500 (APPROX. 1000 YEARS)

(NOTE: Although all these truths were in the Word of God, and there was always a faithful remnant who believed such in their measure of light, greater emphasis came on all these truths over the years. Periods of Years are approximate and given only for the emphasis that came in these years).

THE DECLINE AS SEEN IN CHURCH HISTORY
(All Dates Given within Approximate Period of Time)

AD 67	Nero burns Rome, Great persecution of the Christians
AD 100	Last Apostle (John) died: Zenith of Roman prosperity
AD 110	Early Church Fathers persecuted
AD 130	Laying on of Hands becomes an empty form
AD 140	Ministry of Prophets disappear
AD 150	Gifts of the Spirit gone, Latin becomes language of Western Church
AD 160	Plurality of Eldership declines
AD 180	New Testament Canon of Scripture almost completed
AD 185	Christianity the most dominant religion
AD 187	Local Church autonomy threatened
AD 188	First infant baptism by Sprinkling
AD 200	Priesthood of higher order, Ministers now called 'Priest'
AD 200	Ritual Worship forms
AD 240	Rise of Monasticism - Double standards in life of Holiness
AD 250	Clergy elected by authority outside the Church
AD 284	Diocletian persecutes Christians, claimed himself to be the Sun-God
AD 300	Prayers for the Dead
AD 300	Making the Sign of the Cross
AD 300	Justification by Faith replaced by Works
AD 313	Rise of Imperial Church, Constantine ends persecution of Christians, Edict of Milan, Toleration of free worship
AD 325	"Easter Sunday" decreed by the Council of Nicea
AD 327	State Control of the Church - Church and State as one
AD 340	Mixture & Corruption of Church by Greek and oriental philosophies being mixed with Christianity plus splendour of Heathen Temple ceremonies
AD 341	Roman Empire divides, East and Western divisions
AD 350	"Christmas Day" Festivals established, from worship of "Sun-God"
AD 352	Rise of much Doctrinal confusion, heresies and error
AD 360	Scrolls replaced by books as Church draws up Canon of Scripture with agreement on twentytwo New Testament Books

Restoration Theology

AD 375	Worship of Saints and Angels
AD 380	Edict of Theodosius, abolishing crucifixion, gladiator fighting, killing of unwanted children, Heathen Temples destroyed
AD 380	Rome becomes the final Authority
AD 394	First "Mass" instituted
AD 397	New Testament Books Canonized at the Council of Carthage
AD 400	Separation of Clergy and Laity
AD 405	Latin Vulgate translated for the Catholic Church
AD 431	Worship of Mary begins
AD 438	Unlawful to disagree with beliefs of the Catholic Church of Rome
AD 440	Celibacy becomes a Law of the Roman Catholic Church for Priests
AD 450	"Mary" placed as Head of All Saints, many Festivals and worship
AD 476	Fall of the Western Roman Empire
AD 496	Prayers, Chants and instructions on "Mass"
AD 500	Priests began to dress differently from ordinary laymen
AD 517	Emperor Wunti becomes a Buddhist, introduces "new religion" to China
AD 526	Introduction of "Extreme Unction"
AD 570	Mohammed, Founder of Islam, claimed to be the last of the Prophets
AD 593	Doctrine of "Purgatory" introduced
AD 600	Worship Services conducted in Latin language, unknown tongue
AD 600	Prayers directed to Mary
AD 606	Boniface III made the First Pope
AD 709	Kissing of the Pope's foot comes in
AD 786	Worshipping of images and relics
AD 850	Holy Water introduced
AD 995	Canonization of the Dead Saints
AD 998	Fasting on Fridays and during Lent introduced
AD 1079	Celibacy of Priesthood enforced
AD 1090	Prayer Beads invented
AD 1215	Doctrine of Transubstantiation brought in
AD 1220	The Adoration of the Wafer (The Host)
AD 1229	The Scriptures (Bible) now forbidden to laymen
AD 1414	The Communion Cup now forbidden to people
AD 1439	Doctrine of Purgatory fully decreed
AD 1439	Doctrine of the "Seven Sacraments" affirmed
AD 1508	The "Ave Maria" approved
AD 1534	The Jesuit Order founded
AD 1545	Authority of Tradition becomes equal authority with the Bible
AD 1546	Apocryphal Books become part of the Catholic Bible
AD 1854	"Immaculate Conception of the Virgin Mary" brought in
AD 1864	Syllabus of Errors proclaimed
AD 1870	Infallibility of the Pope declared when he speaks "Ex Cathedra"
AD 1930	Public Schools condemned
AD 1950	Assumption of the Virgin Mary declared
AD 1965	Mary proclaimed as "The Mother of the Church"
AD 1997	Recommendations to proclaim Mary as "Co-Redemptrix of Humanity, Mediatrix of All Graces, and Advocate for the People of God". Mary then would be Co-Redeemer of Humanity with her Son, Jesus Christ.

(This has not yet been affirmed but recommended by some, resisted by others).

A consideration of this list shows the decline of the Church, the rise of ritualism and mere formalism, the exaltation of tradition with or above the Scriptures, and the rise of a priest-class above the priesthood of all believers. It shows the unScriptural additions to the Bible until the truth has been corrupted and leavened beyond imagination. The Church in general is still affected by these things and therefore, the leaven of false teachings has to be purged out from the pure meal of the Divine Word. Truly from about the fifth and sixth centuries, the Church entered the "Dark Ages" until the morning light of the Reformation began to shine forth!

BIBLIOGRAPHY

1. Bartleman, Frank., **Another Wave Rolls In** (Formerly, "What Really Happened at Azusa Street?"), Whitaker Books, Pennsylvania, USA., Voice Publications, 1925-1971.
2. Bartleman, Frank., **Azusa Street**, Logos International, Plainfield, New Jersey, USA, 1980.
3. Barclay, William., **New Testament Words**, SCM Press Ltd, London, 1964
4. Blomgren, David K., **A Biblical View of Restoration**, Bible Temple Publications, Portland, Oregon, USA, 1980.
5. Conner, Kevin J., **The Book of Acts**, Bible Temple Publications, Portland, Oregon, USA, 1973.
6. Conner, Kevin J., **The Church in the New Testament**, Acacia Press, P/L, Blackburn, Victoria, Australia, 1982
7. Conner, Kevin J/ Malmin Ken., **The Covenants**, Bible Temple Publications, Portland, Oregon, USA, 1976.
8. Conner, Kevin J., **New Covenant Realities**, Acacia Press P/L, Blackburn, Victoria, Australia, 1990.
9. Conner, Kevin J., **The Foundations of Christian Doctrine**, Acacia Press P/L, Blackburn, Victoria, Australia Edition, Copyrighted, USA, 1980.
10. Conner, Kevin J., **The Feasts of Israel**, Bible Temple Publications, Portland, Oregon, USA, 1980.
11. Conner, Kevin J., **Mystery Parables of the Kingdom**, Acacia Press P/L, Blackburn, Victoria, Australia, 1996.
12. Conner, Kevin J., **The Name of God**, Acacia Press P/L. Blackburn, Victoria, Australia Edition, Copyrighted, USA, 1975.
13. Conner, Kevin J., **Table Talks**, Excelsior Printing Works P/L, Victoria, Australia, 1996.
14. Conner, Kevin J., **The Tabernacle of David**, Bible Temple Publications, Portland, Oregon, USA, 1976.
15. Conner, Kevin J., **The Tabernacle of Moses**, Bible Temple Publications, Portland, Oregon, USA, 1976.
16. Conner, Kevin J., **The Temple of Solomon**, Acacia Press P/L, Blackburn, Victoria, Australia, 1988.
17. Conner, Kevin J/ Iverson, K.R. (Dick)., **Principles of Church Life**, Bible Temple Portland, Oregon, USA, 1972.
18. Conner, Kevin J/ Malmin, Ken., **Interpreting the Scriptures**, Bible Temple Publications, Portland, Oregon, USA.,1976.
19. Etter, M.B. Woodworth., **Signs and Wonders**, Harrison House, Tulsa, Oklohoma, 1916.
20. Gaglardi, B.Maureen., **The Pastor's Pen**, Glad Tidings Temple Publications, Vancouver, Canada, 1965.
21. Hamon, Bill., **Apostles, Prophets & The Coming Moves of God**, Destiny Image Publishers, Florida, USA, 1997.
22. Hamon, Bill., **The Eternal Church**, Christian International Publishers, Phoenix, Arizona, USA, 1981.
23. Hall, William Phillips., **A Remarkable Biblical Discovery** (or,"The Name" of God

According to the Scriptures), American Tract Society, New York, 1929.
24. Hawtin, George & Ernest., **Church Government**, North Battleford, Saskatchewan, Canada, 1949.
25. Hawtin, George R., **The Nine Gifts of the Holy Spirit**, Saskatchewan, Canada, 1949.
26. Iverson, K.R, (Dick)., **Maintaining Balance When Winds of Doctrine Blow**, Bible Temple Publications, Portland, Oregon, USA, 1989.
27. Iverson, K.R, (Dick), **Present Day Truths**, Bible Temple Publications, Portland, Oregon, USA, 1975.
28. Jacks, John A., **Exploring The Laying on of Hands & Prophecy**, Australia, 1989.
29. Kirkpatrick, M.E., **The 1948 Revival and Now**, Publishers (?), 1979 (?) Booklet.
30. Layzell, Reginald., **Unto Perfection**, Mountlake Terrace, Washington, USA, 1979.
31. McPherson, Aimee Semple., **This is That**, The Foursquare Bookshop, Los Angeles, California, USA, (1900?).
32. Offiler, W.H., **God and His Bible** (or, Harmonies of Divine Revelation), Bethel Temple Inc., Seattle, Washington, USA, 1946.
33. Offiler, W.H., **God and His Name**, Bethel Temple Inc., Seattle Washington, USA, 1932.
34. Price, G.H.S., **A Brief Synopsis of The Public History of the Church**, Cooper & Budd, London (1900?).
35. A Lion Handbook., **The History of Christianity**, Lion Publishing, England, 1977.
36. Rasmussen, A.W., **The Last Chapter**, Whitaker House, Pennsylvania, USA, 1973.
37. Riss, Richard., **A History of the Worldwide Awakening of 1992-1995**, Reproduced by Permission, MFI., Portland, Oregon, USA, 1996.
38. Riss, Richard., **Latter Rain**., Honeycomb Visual Productions Ltd, Canada, 1987.
39. Synan, Vinson., **In The Latter Days**, Servant Books, Ann Arbor, Michigan, USA, 1984.
40. Synan, Vinson., **The Holiness-Pentecostal Movements in the United States**, William B. Eerdman's Publishing Co., Grand Rapids, Michigan, USA, 1971.
41. Walker, Williston., **A History of the Christian Church**, Charles Scribner's Sons, New York, USA, 1956.
42. Warnock, George H., **The Feast of Tabernacles**, Sharon Publishers, North Battleford, Saskatchewan, Canada, 1951.

UNCOPYRIGHTED

1. Restoration-Seven Main Areas (Notes: Charlotte Baker/Ernest Gentile/Dick Iverson/ Kevin J.Conner.
2. Sharon Star Magazines (1951-1953).
3. Sharon Scripture Studies, North Battleford, Saskatchewan, Canada. A Home Study Bible Course, George R. Hawtin/Percy G.Hunt/ Ernest H. Hawtin/ George H. Warnock, 1949-1953).